KNOWLEDGE BASED PROBLEM SOLVING

Janusz S. Kowalik, Editor

AI Center
Boeing Computer Services
Bellevue, Washington
and the University of Washington

Prentice-Hall, Englewood Cliffs, New Jersey 07632

© 1986 by Prentice-Hall
A Division of Simon & Schuster, Inc.
Englewood Cliffs, New Jersey 07632

Library of Congress Catalog Card Number: 85-62829
ISBN: 0-13-516576-8

Printed in the United States of America

10 9 8 7 6 5 4 3 2 1

ISBN 0-13-516576-8 025

Prentice-Hall International (UK) Limited, *London*
Prentice-Hall of Australia Pty. Limited, *Sydney*
Editora Prentice-Hall do Brasil, Ltda., *Rio de Janeiro*
Prentice-Hall Canada Inc., *Toronto*
Prentice-Hall Hispanoamericana, S.A., *Mexico*
Prentice-Hall of India Private Limited, *New Delhi*
Prentice-Hall of Japan, Inc., *Tokyo*
Prentice-Hall of Southeast Asia Pte. Ltd., *Singapore*
Whitehall Books Limited, *Wellington, New Zealand*

CONTENTS

PREFACE

Knowledge based systems are without any doubt the most popular AI applications in science, industry, and business. They even make news in daily press and magazines. Unfortunately, there is usually a great disparity in expectations of the AI professionals and outsiders - the latter seem to be overly optimistic, to say the least. There are currently at least two kinds of barriers to commercialization of AI: (a) deficiencies in AI as a scientific methodology, and (b) pragmatic difficulties in introducing AI into the real world, such as shortages of experienced staff, reliable tools, and enlightened management.

The purpose of this book has been to collect in one volume contributions from several researchers and pioneers of AI that cover a relatively wide spectrum of issues in the knowledge based systems. We hope that the book will help the reader to assess the state-of-the-art and future prospects of the knowledge based systems.

Janusz S. Kowalik

CONTRIBUTORS

MR. JOHN H. BOOSE,   Boeing Computer Services Company, Bellevue, Washington

John Boose received a Bachelor of Architecture degree from the University of Maryland in 1977, minoring in computer science. From 1975 to 1979 he was also active in both the vision lab and the artificial intelligence group in the computer science department, and taught classes in programming and artificial intelligence. He attended graduate school at Nicholas Negroponte's Architecture Machine group at the Massachusetts Institute of Technology, and received a Master of Science degree from the University of Washington in 1985, specializing in artificial intelligence. From 1979 to 1983 John directed the in-house development of an integrated computer-aided design and drafting system for Albert C. Martin and Associates, an architectural and engineering firm based in Los Angeles. While in Los Angeles, he also helped produce computer graphics for motion pictures. In 1983, John joined the Artificial Intelligence Support Center at Boeing Computer Services in Seattle, Washington, where his major interest has been in developing knowledge acquisition techniques for knowledge-based systems.

DR. WILLIAM J. CLANCEY, Stanford University, Stanford, California

William Clancey is a member of the Stanford Knowledge Systems Laboratory. He has been active in work on explanation and tutoring systems since he joined the MYCIN project in 1975, for which he was co-developer of the antibiotic therapy and question-answering programs. He received a Ph.D in Computer Science from Stanford in 1979. Now co-director of the GUIDON/NEOMYCIN tutoring project, his interests lie in computational modeling of problem solving, particularly medical diagnosis, and the design of architectures for expert systems to facilitate construction, explanation, and multiple use. He specializes in computer-aided instruction in order to investigate, through student modeling and explanation in teaching, general principles of human learning, and knowledge representation. Clancey has published widely on tutoring and expert system methodology, and is the co-author (with E. H. Shortliffe) of "Readings in Medical Artificial Intelligence: The First Decade" published by Addison-Wesley.

DR. DOUGLAS C. DORROUGH,   Boeing Computer Services Company,
Bellevue, Washington

Douglas Dorrough is a member of the Boeing Artificial Intelligence Support Center. He developed the PACS (Probabilistic Analogical Calculus System) in collaboration with A. S. Politopoulos, while at Ford's Advanced Development Laboratory. It has been applied successfully to several high-speed target acquisition and image understanding problems. He received a Ph.D. in mathematical logic from the University of North Carolina in 1964 and subsequently acquired a Sc.D. from Cambridge in physical biochemistry. Apart from computer science, he has published widely including such fields as anesthesiology, biochemistry, formal linguistics, logic, mathematics, molecular biology, philosophy, and poetics. His current interests are focused on the applications of analogical calculi to knowledge representation and enhancement. He is also involved with the development of metrics for the evaluation of expert systems.

DR. ANTONIO L. ELIAS, Massachusetts Institute of Technology,
Cambridge, Massachusetts

Antonio Elias is an assistant professor in Aeronautics and Astronautics and a member of the Flight Transportation Laboratory of the Department of Aeronautics and Astronautics, Massachusetts Institute of Technology, where he received his S.B., M.S., E.A.A., AND Ph.D. degrees, and where he now holds the Boeing Career Development Chair. His teaching responsibilities include undergraduate courses in Linear Control Theory, Structure and Interpretation of Computer Programs, and Aircraft Design, and graduate courses in Flight Dynamics Simulation and Air Traffic Control. His research activities include Computer-Aided Engineering, Air Traffic Control automation, and low-cost radionavigation for general aviation aircraft. Before joining the M.I.T. faculty, Dr. Elias was a staff member at Draper Laboratory, where he worked on the design of the Space Shuttle Orbiter's guidance system. He is an instrument-rated pilot and a member of the AAAI, Institute of Navigation, and AIAA, where he is a member of the Technical Committee on Air Transportation Systems.

DR. JEAN-GABRIEL GANASCIA, Universite de Paris-Sud, France

Jean-Gabriel Ganascia is a member of the Laboratoire de Recherche en Informatique (LRI) at the University of Paris-Sud in Orsay (France). He developed the LITHO project in collaboration with A. Bonnet at Schlumberger, Clamart

(France). He received a Doctorat d'ingénieur in Computer Science in 1983. He is now working on rule and concept learning. He manages, with Y. Kodratoff, a learning project at the LRI. His main subjects of interest are the development, the automatic correction and the acquisition of knowledge bases for expert systems. He is now completing a Doctorat d'état in computer science, his field being rule learning applied to expert systems.

DR. PETER E. HART, Syntelligence, Sunnyvale, California

Peter Hart is President and co-founder of Syntelligence, an expert system company serving the financial services industry. Earlier, he was Director of the SRI Artificial Intelligence center, and the founder and first Director of Schlumberger's Artificial Intelligence Research Laboratory at Fairchild. He has contributed to many areas of AI research, including heuristic search, automatic planning, computer vision, and expert systems. While at SRI he initiated and led the development of PROSPECTOR, an early example of a successful expert system. Dr. Hart has served on the Executive Council of the AAAI and is a Fellow of the IEEE.

MR. THEODORE J. JARDINE, Boeing Computer Services, Bellevue, Washington

Ted Jardine is a Principal Scientist with the Boeing Artificial Intelligence Center. He has been active in AI research relating to planning systems, especially those applied to military command and control and manufacturing, since 1982. He received a Master of Science degree in Computer Science from West Coast University, Los Angeles, California in 1974. Ted's research interests include the application of planning systems to command and control, manufacturing, and robotics. He has more than twenty-three years of experience in the computer science field primarily in operating systems, telecommunications systems, and in the development of large scale software systems.

DR. S. JERROLD KAPLAN, Teknowledge, Inc., Palo Alto, California

S. Jerrold Kaplan received his Ph.D. in Computer Science from the University of Pennsylvania in 1979. He then joined the staff of the Computer Science Department of Stanford University. As a Research Associate, he served as an associate investigator on the Knowledge Base Management Systems project and the Intelligent Agents Project. His Ph.D. dissertation, "Cooperative Responses from a Portable Natural Language Data Base Query System" established him as an authority in practical natural language interfaces to data bases. As a NSF "Special Initiation" grant recipient, he has published widely in the areas of Computational Linguistics and Artificial Intelligence. He has served as a member of the Editorial Board of the American Journal of Computational Linguistics, the formal publication of the Association for Computational Linguistics.

DR. JANUSZ S. KOWALIK, Boeing Computer Services, Bellevue, Washington

Janusz Kowalik is a manager in the Boeing Artificial Support Center, responsible for the AI Technology Transfer Program and High-performance Computation and an Affiliate Professor of Computer Science at the University of Washington in Seattle. Before his current appointment he served as a scientist, a manager and a professor in industry and at universities in Norway, Australia, Canada, and the U.S.A. He received a Ph.D. in mathematics from Polish Academy of Sciences in Warsaw. He has published books and papers in various areas of computer science including parallel computation. In 1985 he was chairman of the AAAI sponsored workshop on "Coupling Symbolic and Numerical Computing in Expert Systems". His research interests include computer architectures for AI and multilevel expert systems with deep reasoning.

DR. UNMEEL MEHTA, NASA Ames Research Center, Moffett Field, California

Unmeel Mehta is a member of the Computational Fluid Dynamics Branch. He first joined this branch as a National Research Council Associate in 1973. After being a Research Associate in the Mechanical Engineering Department at Stanford University in 1975, he worked in this branch as a contractor. In 1978, he joined NASA as an Aerospace Engineer and became a member of this branch. Dr. Mehta has been active in computational aerodynamics and fluid dynamics, dealing with viscous flows. His interests lie in numerical simulation of turbulent, unsteady flows about aerospace vehicles, and in applied artificial intelligence, particularly, in automated reasoning systems. Dr. Mehta received his B.S. degree in Mechanical Engineering from University of Wisconsin in 1965; and he received his M.S. and Ph.D. degrees in Mechanical and Aerospace Engineering from Illinois Institute of Technology in 1968 and 1972, respectively. Dr. Mehta is author of numerous technical publications, some of which are published in technical books.

DR. LUC STEELS, Free University, Brussels, Belgium

Luc Steels is currently professor of computer science in the faculty of sciences at the Brussels Free University and director of the AI Laboratorium. He studied computer science at M.I.T. where he was associated with the Artificial Intelligence Laboratory. In 1980 he joined the research laboratories of Schlumberger in the U. S. where he was mostly involved in geological expert systems and knowledge-based tools for VLSI design. Steels is president of the Belgian Association for Artificial Intelligence. His public publications include a textbook on LISP and a collection of papers on AI edited with John Campbell for Ellis Horwood Publishing Company.

MR. WALTER VAN DE VELDE, Free University, Brussels, Belgium

Walter Van de Velde holds a masters degree in mathematics from the University of Antwerp. Since 1984 he has been associated with the AI Laboratorium of Brussels Free University. The focus of his doctoral research is deep reasoning and learning techniques for expert systems.

ACKNOWLEDGMENTS

This book would not have been written without the encouragement and the support of Karl Karlstrom and Pat Henry of Prentice-Hall. My secretary Joyce Hutton has contributed a great deal of effort, skill, and patience to developing the camera-ready copy of the manuscript.

PERSPECTIVE

Janusz S. Kowalik

Most of the problems that computers currently solve are amenable to conventional programs based on numerical procedures where solution steps are defined explicitly. The conventional programs are rigid structurally, their actions are predictable in advance and they cannot handle problems that their programmers did not foresee. In contrast, intelligent people can handle and frequently solve problems for which algorithms do not exist and which are characterized by ill-structure, ambiguity, incomplete problem understanding, uncertainty, and formidable complexity. Examples of such problems can be found in medical diagnosis, scientific discovery, understanding of natural languages, proving mathematical theorems, making managerial decisions, etc. The human ability to solve such problems is almost taken for granted and is not fully understood. We know, however, that our solution tools include: logic, heuristic search, extensive use of domain knowledge and uniquely human ability of common sense reasoning. One of the chief objectives of artificial intelligence is to find out if we can program computers to exhibit similar problem solving capability, or perhaps in some cases to surpass humans. Since the domain knowledge, which includes formal and empirical components, plays the key role in this experiment we call the related programs the knowledge based systems (KBS). A special case of KBS are the most popular AI programs, the expert systems.

Claims are being made that KBS can be applied virtually to every area of human cognitive activity. This may indeed happen in the future, but the current state-of-the-art indicates that some problems are more suitable for the contemporary KBS technology than others. For example, a broad range of real life problems including diagnosis and repair, catalog selection and skeletal planning are well handled in KBS by the method of heuristic classification. This method is the subject of the first chapter by Bill Clancey. The method involves three identifiable phases: data abstraction, heuristic association, and refinement. An essential property of the classification problem solving is that it involves selection of a solution from a pre-enumerated set of possible solutions. The solver has to know a priori all solutions and if it can relate them to the problem description by data abstraction, heuristic association and refinement then the problem is solved by heuristic classification. Hence, heuristic classification is a particular method for solving certain kinds of problems, not a category of problems.

Clancey makes a useful distinction between selecting and constructing solutions. In selecting a solution, the problem solver needs experiential knowledge in the form of patterns of problems and solutions, and heuristics relating them. In heuristic classification, possible object states are known to the solver and problem solving takes the form of a proof. In heuristic construction, the problem solver either generates solutions or assembles them from parts according to some constraints and requirements. Clancey proposes to regard heuristic classification as a submethod of heuristic construction where new solutions are configured. In the conclusion of his chapter Clancey suggests a scheme for matching problems with solution methods that include traditional tools such as simulation and knowledge based approaches.

Heuristic classification is one of the most useful and effective methods in KBS. It is well supported by software development tools and it represents a relatively mature methodology for building expert systems. Theoretically it rests on a classic concept in AI, the problem space model. In this general model the problem solver deals with a set of object states and a set of operators over the space. An operator takes a state as an input and generates an output state. Applied to sequences of states the operators can define paths in the problem space that link initial states with goal states, and therefore provide problem solutions. The idea of searching in problem spaces is a general problem solving paradigm in AI and it has been used successfully in many applications. However, it may be inadequate for modeling many important KBS's. One of the currently researched alternatives is the concept of open systems which resembles societal or organizational systems and management techniques (Hewitt [1985]). Open systems are characterized by: decentralized decision making, incomplete and inconsistent data bases, continuous change and evolution, and the need for negotiation among system components. From the hardware standpoint open systems can be modeled by distributed computing, i.e. networks of interconnected and interdependent computers capable of parallel asynchronous processing. In contrast to this distributed processing most of the current AI systems are implemented on stand-alone sequential computers and assume that the global knowledge they possess about the problem domain is complete and consistent. It is possible that open systems will further extend the current scope of KBS applications.

The second topic considered in the book is knowledge acquisition for expert systems. As pointed out by Kaplan in Chapter 10, the knowledge utilized in KBS does not necessarily have to come from human experts. It may come from such passive sources as books, manuals, databases, and procedures. It some cases the empirical component of knowledge can only be extracted from human experts, typically in the form of heuristic rules. The process of extracting knowledge from experts and refining it usually involves a lengthy series of interviews, engineering and test cycles before a system can achieve expert performance. It also tends to be imprecise, poorly structured, incomplete and inconsistent. In some cases human experts may feel insecure and may not wish to expose their expertise to other professionals. The purpose of the Expertise Transfer System (ETS) described in Chapter 2 by John Boose is to eliminate or to reduce some of these difficulties and streamline the knowledge engineering process. The system is easy to use and it can significantly reduce the length of time taken by the knowledge engineering. ETS interviews human experts, and they construct and analyze aspects of the knowledge that experts use to solve a particular problem. Knowledge elicited from an expert is analyzed, tested, refined, and organized into knowledge bases, which can be used directly with expert system building tools. ETS is capable of transforming the knowledge extracted from experts into production rules that can be used by such tools as S.1, M.1, OPS5, and LOOPS. It can be used for rapid prototyping and testing the knowledge scope and consistency. Its theoretical justification rests on George Kelly's Personal Construct Method. ETS is suitable for classification problems whose solutions can be pre-enumerated. Its prime strength lies in eliciting experiential knowledge which can be formulated in terms of empirical relationships and associations. Other limitations of the system are discussed by Boose in his chapter. He also outlines potential expansions of ETS such as: combining experience from multiple experts, and elicitation of procedural, strategic, and causal knowledge. ETS has proved itself as a robust and useful tool for building over two hundred prototypical industrial expert systems. The size of these rule based expert systems has ranged from thirty to two thousand rules.

In Chapter 3 Doug Dorrough takes on a formidable problem in artificial intelligence, that of analogy. The chapter contains several discussions about the setting of analogy-like statements, the distinctive verbal pattern, the context, the checkability of analogies, and a summary of the results of a set of related long-range studies. It also provides a classification of analogical statements and explains the distinction between analogical statements and similies. Analogies are crucial in our reasoning and learning, and humans feel quite comfortable with their use in science or in informal settings. Analogy helps us to connect concepts, and to develop new understandings from already comprehended ideas or objects. Dorrough exposes the subtlety of the subject of analogy and offers an approach to this elusive concept that permits an objective assessment of analogical reasoning as well as some aspects of learning by analogy. Much of the chapter's material is implemented in the PACS software, developed jointly with A. S. Politopoulos. This software has been subjected to a series of statistical tests for its validity and applicability to increasingly more complex learning situations as well as to multi-level KBS.

Despite the growing number of useful KBS based on purely heuristic experimental knowledge it becomes increasingly clear that the future KBS will be often coupled with various modes of quantitative computing such as numerical analysis, statistics, and simulations. This coupling can take several forms, including: analysis of numerical data, reduction of large sets of numerical results into symbolic information, guiding complex numerical computing processes, using knowledge for efficient exploitation of parallel supercomputers, etc. The next three chapters illustrate some of the potential advantages of coupling AI techniques with conventional computation.

Jean-Gabriel Ganascia describes in Chapter 4 the LITHO system used to interpret oil well logs which are measurements of the physical properties of the geological formations penetrated by a drill. One of the several components of LITHO is an expert system that contains five hundred production rules representing relevant geological knowledge. Information entering the expert systems consists of symbolic data and numerical data. The latter are interpreted by a conversion module before they become available to the expert system. The purpose of the conversion module is to isolate a set of characteristic features used by the expert system. The diagnostic results of the expert systems are refined by a decision module. This refinement is necessary in many cases where data are imprecise. In extreme cases data may be incomplete or erroneous to such a degree that even human experts cannot interpret them correctly. Such extreme situations are recognized and the system admits its inability to make a conclusion.

The problem of interpreting geological oil well data is difficult for humans, as well as, for computer systems. The results generated by the LITHO system suggest that except for complex cases the methodology used in LITHO is effective and can match human expertise.

In Chapter 5 Unmeel Mehta suggests that KBS will be useful in computational aerodynamics and fluid dynamics, and describes a hypothetical knowledge based system called AERODYNAMICIST. Computational aerodynamics is now applied to increasingly complex and time consuming problems, and requires the fastest available supercomputers. Knowledge based systems have potential to assist computational aero-dynamicists in their analysis and design tasks. Mehta identifies two related aspects of computational aerodynamics: reasoning and calculating. Reasoning is based on factual and experimental knowledge of both computational procedures and aerodynamics, and can be carried out by symbolic processing and inferential procedures. Calculating is guided by reasoning and based on numerical algorithms. These two modes of computation are intertwined and it is impossible to do one without the other. In the current practice the computer is used mainly to perform calculations only. Now KBS offer the opportunity to use computers as a reasoning device, and to couple both modes of computation. Symbolic processing can be applied to many elements of computational aerodynamics, such as: algebraic formula manipulation, analysis of experimental data, management of data bases, selection of problem solving methods, analysis of computational results, and facilitating man-machine interfaces. One of the currently accepted methods of aerodynamic design is the numerical optimization approach to produce designs that achieve user specified objectives. The designer specifies an initial aerodynamic body in terms of design: variables, objectives, constraints, and conditions. An optimization method is used to optimize a selected design objective while satisfying the postulated constraints. A knowledge based system can be used to guide the process of optimization. Its knowledge would utilize data bases of previous designs and experience related to speeding up the interactive optimization process. In his conclusion Mehta identifies three major stages of computational aerodynamics development cycle: research, technology transfer, and design and development. He feels that all these stages can greatly benefit from the use of knowledge based problem solving methods.

AERODYNAMICIST can be viewed as a component of a more comprehensive project currently in progress at Research Institute for Advanced Computer Science attached to NASA Ames Research Center (RIACS [1985]). The goal of the project is to integrate synergistically artificial intelligence and high speed computation into all aspects of scientific research and development, from problem formulation to dissemination of results. The proponents of the project envision two major types of computer systems used by scientists in their investigation. The SCIENIST-AIDE, an expert system, knowledgeable about a specific technical discipline, will assist the scientists in the problem solving process. The CONCURRENT-SUPPORT-SYSTEM will translate specifications of required parallel computations into executable codes for available high performance machines. The RIACS project targets primarily the aerospace applications, but in principle its objectives and concepts are relevant to many other disciplines of applied science and technology.

The problem of aircraft design process is also considered by Antonio Elias in Chapter 6. More specifically, he proposes a new method for the aircraft preliminary design that departs from the classic optimization approach identified above. In the task of aircraft design there are two types of variables: input design variables which receive values by assumption or some formal mathematical procedure, and output design variables which have their values computed by means of design functions. At the end of the preliminary design process, all design variables must have values which do not violate any of the chosen design functions. The sequence of design functions invoked to compute output variables from input variables is called the computational path which together with the input variables set and the output variables set constitutes the design path. Such a design path can be obtained by an interactive process and requires translation of declarative form of functional relationships into imperative form of functional relationships in order to execute specific computations. This problem of translating declarative knowledge into imperative knowledge is common in several areas of AI. A numerical inversion method is used to produce an imperative form of the design functions. The method is interactive and involves application of several heuristic rules. The chapter is closed with some thoughts on the future research directions.

In Chapter 7 Ted Jardine presents the results of a KBS application to a manufacturing problem in the aerospace industry. The modern process of manufacturing requires considerable effort in order to plan the operations required to create a product or a part. Numerical control planning involves many tasks which start from an engineering model and end with a manufactured part. One of these tasks is the application of machining techniques, such as: boring, cutting, drilling, grinding, milling, etc. To plan the execution of these tasks a machinability knowledge based system is used in conjunction with a knowledge base, machinability model and numerical control programs. The Metalogical Representation System (MRS) from Stanford University was used as the developmental tool.

Luc Steels and Walter Van De Velde in Chapter 8 deal with the construction of the second generation expert systems. The systems currently in use (the first generation systems) are most often rule-based. The knowledge they use is structured in the form of pattern-action rules which capture empirical associations about the systems knowledge domains. These "surface" systems can exhibit good performance as long as they operate within the scope of their heuristic knowledge. They fail dramatically beyond the boundaries of the knowledge domain. It is believed that more robust and powerful systems (the second generation systems) can be built by encoding not only empirical knowledge but also functional, causal, or other forms of "deep" knowledge (e.g. see Davis [1984] and Chapter 9 of this book). Second generation KBS requiring deep modeling can be constructed only for applications where such models are available. In general, it is felt that deep knowledge based systems will be able to solve more complex problems - after all, human experts use deep models to solve a wide range of problems. It is interesting to note that Chandrasekaran and Mittal [1984] argue that in the medical diagnosis domain there is no need for the causal models to be represented explicitly. Such models would not accomplish more than diagnostic problem-solving structures which have all the aspects of the causal knowledge compiled into them. In contrast to this position, Steels and Van De Velde offer convincing arguments in favor of deep systems for such applications as reasoning about technical systems like electronic devices, power plants, or computer programs. Two most important advantages of deep systems are: the deep model systems will be capable of graceful degradation instead of abrupt failure, and capable of acquiring new heuristic rules which amounts to learning from experience. The knowledge based systems built by Steels and Van De Velde are multilevel; they use heuristic rules, but they also have a causal model of the domain that allows deeper reasoning if the use of rules is insufficient. A learning component of the system looks at the results of deep reasoning and abstracts new rules from these results. This is certainly an important and powerful capability. Deep reasoning models can be computationally expensive and may suffer from combinatorial explosion. The ability to compile a surface model from a deep model is essential for computational efficiency of multilevel knowledge based systems.

The subject of multilevel KBS is also discussed in Chapter 9 by Peter Hart who is one of the earliest proponents of deep systems. Well codified and structured scientific and technical disciplines are the most suitable domains in which to explore multilevel systems. In many areas of engineering the objects of analysis or design can be represented by models with different levels of approximation, from very crude to extremely accurate and refined. In principle, these models of varying levels can be used jointly for reasoning in multilevel knowledge based systems. Hart identifies several research issues that arise in this connection. Among them are: communication between levels, hierarchical arrangement, use of surface models to guide the application of deep models effectively, and system's ability to recognize its own limitations and shift to an appropriate level of reasoning. Hart poses an important question: Can a surface model be "compiled" from a deep model to generate a faster system? Steels and Van De Velde attempt to address this question in the preceding chapter. The related issue of computational complexity of AI systems and required computer capability is also of principle importance. It is clear that many applications of AI will require very powerful computer systems, significantly different from the current conventional von Neumann sequential machines. In addition, the nature of symbolic processing used in AI is different from numerical computing and it is possible that the future parallel computers for AI and for numerical calculation will be architecturally distinct.

Hart also discusses some of the dimensions of the AI transition from relatively unknown academic discipline to a bona fide computer technology which has been embraced quickly by private sector and military organizations.

In the closing chapter Jerrold Kaplan continues to explore the industrialization of artificial intelligence. His initial statements put the matter right. "Artificial intelligence is not in itself a commercial field, but a science and a technology. As an academic discipline, it is a collection of concepts and ideas which are appropriate for research, but which cannot be marketed." Artificial intelligence is a scientific foundation for several applied technologies, such as vision, robotics, natural language processing, and knowledge engineering.

Kaplan contrasts data processing with knowledge engineering and concludes that in essence AI extends the current applications of computer systems from mainly clerical to intellectual tasks. We may add that this extension is not simple and constitutes a major leap in computer technology. He also discusses the development of commercial markets and the barriers to commercialization of AI. Finally, he makes some predictions on the near and the far future developments in artificial intelligence.

REFERENCES

Chandrasekaran, B. and S. Mattel, Deep Versus Compiled Knowledge Approaches to Diagnostic Problems-solving, in Developments in Expert Systems, M. J. Coombs, Editor, Academic Press, 1984.

Davis, R., Reasoning From First Principles in Electronic Trouble Shooting, in Developments in Expert Systems, M. J. Coombs, Editor, Academic Press, 1984.

Hewitt, C. The Challenge of Open Systems, BYTE, April, 1985, pages 223 - 242.

RIACS Annual Report 1984, Prepared by Peter J. Denning, January 31, 1985.

1

HEURISTIC CLASSIFICATION

WILLIAM J. CLANCEY
STANFORD KNOWLEDGE SYSTEMS LABORATORY
COMPUTER SCIENCE DEPARTMENT
STANFORD UNIVERSITY

To understand something as a specific instance of a more general case--which is what understanding a more fundamental principle or structure means--is to have learned not only a specific thing but also a model for understanding other things like it that one may encounter. (Bruner, 1960)

1. INTRODUCTION

Over the past decade, a variety of heuristic programs, commonly called "expert systems," have been written to solve problems in diverse areas of science, engineering, business, and medicine. Developing these programs involves satisfying an interacting set of requirements: Selecting the application area and specific problem to be solved, bounding the problem so that it is computationally and financially tractable, and implementing a prototype program—to name a few obvious concerns. With continued experience, a number of programming environments or "tools" have been developed and successfully used to implement prototype programs (Hayes-Roth et al., 1983). Importantly, the representational units of tools (such as "rules" and "attributes") provide an orientation for identifying manageable subproblems and organizing problem analysis. Selecting appropriate applications now often takes the form of relating candidate problems to known computational methods, our tools.

Yet, in spite of this experience, when presented with a given "knowledge engineering tool," such as EMYCIN (van Melle, 1979), we are still hard-pressed to say what kinds of problems it can be used to solve well. Various studies have demonstrated advantages of using one representation language instead of another—for ease in specifying knowledge relationships, control of reasoning, and perspicuity for maintenance and explanation (Swartout, 1981, Aiello, 1983, Aikins, 1983, Clancey, 1983a, Clancey and Letsinger, 1984). Other studies have characterized in low-level terms why a given problem might be inappropriate for a given language, for example, because data are time-varying or subproblems interact (Hayes-Roth et al., 1983). While these studies reveal the weaknesses and limitations of the rule-based formalism, in particular, they do not clarify the form of analysis and problem decomposition that has been so successfully used in these programs. In short, attempts to describe a mapping between *kinds of problems* and programming languages have not been satisfactory because they don't describe what a given program *knows*: Applications-oriented descriptions like "diagnosis" are too general (e.g., solving a diagnostic problem doesn't necessarily require a device model), and technological terms like "rule-based" don't describe what kind of problem is being solved (Hayes, 1977, Hayes, 1979). We need a better description of what heuristic programs do and know—a computational characterization of their competence—independent of task and independent of programming language implementation. Logic has been suggested as a basis for a "knowledge-level" analysis to specify what a heuristic program does and might know (Nilsson, 1981, Newell, 1982). However, we have lacked a set of terms and relations for doing this.

In an attempt to characterize the *knowledge-level competence* of a variety of expert systems, a number of programs were analyzed in detail.[1] There is a striking pattern: These programs proceed through easily identifiable phases of data abstraction, heuristic mapping onto a hierarchy of pre-enumerated solutions, and refinement within this hierarchy. In short, these programs do what is commonly called *classification*, but with the important twist of *relating concepts in different classification hierarchies by non-hierarchical, uncertain inferences*. We call this combination of reasoning *heuristic classification*.

Note carefully: The heuristic classification model characterizes *a form of knowledge and reasoning*—patterns of familiar problem situations and solutions, heuristically related. In capturing problem situations that tend to occur and solutions that tend to work, this knowledge is essentially *experiential*, with an overall form that is problem-area independent. Heuristic classification is a method of computation, not a kind of problem to be solved. Thus, we refer to "the heuristic classification method," not "classification problem."

Focusing on epistemological content rather than representational technology, this paper proposes a set of terms and relations for describing the knowledge used to solve a problem by the heuristic classification method. Subsequent sections describe and illustrate the model in the analysis of MYCIN, SACON, GRUNDY, and SOPHIE III. Significantly, a knowledge-level description of these programs corresponds very well to psychological models of expert problem solving. This suggests that the heuristic classification problem-solving model captures general principles of how experiential knowledge is organized and used, and thus generalizes some cognitive science results. A thorough discussion relates the model to schema research; and use

---

[1]Including: Ten rule-based systems [MYCIN, PUFF, CLOT, HEADMED, SACON from the EMYCIN family (Buchanan and Shortliffe, 1984), plus WINE, BANKER, The Drilling Advisor, and other proprietary systems developed at Teknowledge, Inc.], a frame-based system (GRUNDY), and a program coded directly in LISP (SOPHIE III).

of a conceptual graph notation shows how the inference-structure diagram characteristic of heuristic classification can be derived from some simple assumptions about how data and solutions are typically related (Section 4). Another detailed discussion then considers "what gets selected," possible kinds of solutions (e.g., diagnoses). A taxonomy of problem types is proposed that characterizes *solutions of problems* in terms of synthesis or analysis of some *system* in the world (Section 5). We finally turn to the issue of inference control in order to further characterize tool requirements for heuristic classification (Section 6), segueing into a brief description of constructive problem solving (Section 7).

This paper explores different perspectives for describing expert systems; it is not a conventional description of a particular program or programming methodology. The analysis does produce some specific and obviously useful results, such as a distinction between electronic and medical diagnosis programs (Section 6.2). But there are also a few essays with less immediate payoffs, such as the analysis of problem types in terms of systems (Section 5) and the discussion of the pragmatics of defining concepts (Section 4.5). Also, readers who specialize in problems of knowledge representation should keep in mind that the discussion of schemas (Section 4) is an attempt to clarify the knowledge represented in rule-based expert systems, rather than to introduce new representational ideas.

From another perspective, this paper presents a methodology for analyzing problems, preparatory to building an expert system. It introduces an abstract level of knowledge specification, above that of concepts and links, and independent of implementation language. Indeed, one aim is to afford a level of awareness for describing expert system design that enables knowledge representation languages to be chosen and used more deliberately.

We begin with the motivation of wanting to formalize what we have learned about building expert systems. How can we classify problems? How can we select problems that are appropriate for our tools? How can we improve our tools? Our study reveals patterns in knowledge bases: Inference chains are not arbitrary sequences of implications, they compose relations among concepts in a systematic way. Intuitively, we believe that understanding these high-level knowledge structures, implicitly encoded in today's expert systems, will enable us to teach people how to use representation languages more effectively, and also enable us to design better languages. Moreover, it is a well-established principle for designing these programs that the knowledge people are trying to express should be stated explicitly, so it will be accessible to auxiliary programs for explanation, teaching, and knowledge acquisition (e.g., (Davis, 1976)).

Briefly, our methodology for specifying the knowledge contained in an expert system is based on:

- a computational distinction between selection and construction of solutions;

- a relational breakdown of concepts, distinguishing between abstraction and heuristic

3

association and between subtype and cause, thus revealing the classification nature of inference chains; and

- a categorization of problems in terms of synthesis and analysis of *systems in the world*, allowing us to characterize inference in terms of a sequence of classifications involving some system.

The main result of the study is the model of heuristic classification, which turns out to be a common problem-solving method in expert systems. Identifying this computational method is not to be confused with advocating its use. Instead, by giving it a name and characterizing it, we open the way to describing when it is applicable, contrasting it with alternative methods, and deliberately using it again when appropriate.

As one demonstration of the value of the model, classification in well-known medical and electronic diagnosis programs is described in some detail, contrasting different perspectives on what constitutes a diagnostic solution and different methods for controlling inference to derive *coherent* solutions. Indeed, an early motivation for this study was to understand how NEOMYCIN, a medical diagnostic program, could be generalized. The resulting tool, called HERACLES (roughly standing for "Heuristic Classification Shell") is described briefly, with a critique of its capabilities in terms of the larger model that has emerged.

In the final sections of the paper, we reflect on the adequacy of current knowledge engineering tools, the nature of a knowledge-level analysis, and related research in psychology and artificial intelligence. There are several strong implications for the practice of building expert systems, designing new tools, and continued research in this field. Yet to be delivered, but promised by the model, are explanation and teaching programs tailored to the heuristic classification model, better knowledge acquisition programs, and demonstration that thinking in terms of heuristic classification makes it easier to choose problems and build new expert systems.

2. THE HEURISTIC CLASSIFICATION METHOD DEFINED

We develop the idea of the heuristic classification method by starting with the common sense notion of classification and relating it to the reasoning that occurs in heuristic programs.

2.1. Simple classification

As the name suggests, the simplest kind of classification is identifying some unknown object or phenomenon as a member of a known class of objects, events, or processes. Typically, these classes are stereotypes that are hierarchically organized, and the process of identification is one of matching observations of an unknown entity against features of known classes. A paradigmatic example is identification of a plant or animal, using a guidebook of features, such as coloration, structure, and size. MYCIN solves the problem of identifying an unknown organism from laboratory cultures by matching culture information against a hierarchy of bacteria (Figure 2-1).[2]

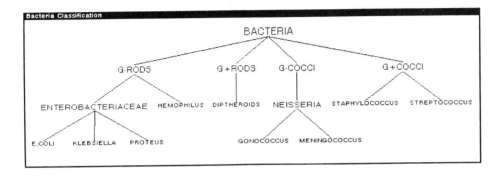

Figure 2-1: Mycin's classification of bacteria

The essential characteristic of classification is that the problem solver *selects* from a set of pre-enumerated solutions. This does not mean, of course, that the "right answer" is necessarily one of these solutions, just that the problem solver will only attempt to match the data against the known solutions, rather than construct a new one. Evidence can be uncertain and matches partial, so the output might be a ranked list of hypotheses. Besides matching, there are several *rules of inference* for making assertions about solutions. For example, evidence for a class is indirect evidence that one of its subtypes is present.

2.2. Data abstraction

In the simplest problems, data are solution features, so the matching process is direct. For example, an unknown organism in MYCIN can be classified directly given the supplied data of Gram stain and morphology. The features "Gram-stain negative" and "rod-shaped" match a class of organisms. The solution might be refined by getting information that allows subtypes to be discriminated.

For many problems, solution features are not supplied as data, but are inferred by *data abstraction*. There are three basic relations for abstracting data in heuristic programs:

---

[2]For simplicity, we will refer to classification hierarchies throughout this paper, though in practice these structures are not trees, but almost always "tangled" structures with some nodes having multiple parents.

- *definitional abstraction* based on essential, necessary features of a concept ("if the structure is a one-dimensional network, then its shape is a beam");

- *qualitative abstraction*, a form of definition involving quantitative data, usually with respect to some normal or expected value ("if the patient is an adult and white blood count is less than 2500, then the white blood count is low"); and

- *generalization* in a subtype hierarchy ("if the client is a judge, then he is an educated person").

These interpretations are usually made by the program with certainty; belief thresholds and qualifying conditions are chosen so the abstraction is categorical. It is common to refer to this knowledge as being "factual" or "definitional."

2.3. Heuristic classification

In simple classification, data may directly match solution features or may match after being abstracted. In heuristic classification, solutions and solution features may also be matched *heuristically*, by direct, non-hierarchical association with some concept in *another* classification hierarchy. For example, MYCIN does more than identify an unknown organism in terms of visible features of an organism: MYCIN heuristically relates an abstract characterization of the patient to a classification of diseases. We show this *inference structure* schematically, followed by an example (Figure 2-2).

Basic observations about the patient are abstracted to patient categories, which are heuristically linked to diseases and disease categories. While only a subtype link with E.coli infection is shown here, evidence may actually derive from a combination of inferences. Some data might directly match E.coli features (an individual organism shaped like a rod and producing a Gram-negative stain is seen growing in a culture taken from the patient). Descriptions of laboratory cultures (describing location, method of collection, and incubation) can also be related to the classification of diseases.

The important link we have added is a heuristic association between a characterization of the patient ("compromised host") and categories of diseases ("gram-negative infection"). Unlike definitional and hierarchical inferences, this inference makes a great leap. A *heuristic relation* is uncertain, based on assumptions of typicality, and is sometimes just a poorly understood correlation. A heuristic is often empirical, deriving from problem-solving experience; heuristics correspond to the "rules of thumb," often associated with expert systems (Feigenbaum, 1977).

Heuristics of this type reduce search by skipping over intermediate relations (this is why we don't call abstraction relations "heuristics"). These associations are usually uncertain because the intermediate relations may not hold in the specific case. Intermediate relations may be omitted because they are unobservable or poorly understood. In a medical diagnosis program, heuristics typically skip over the causal relations between symptoms and diseases. In Section

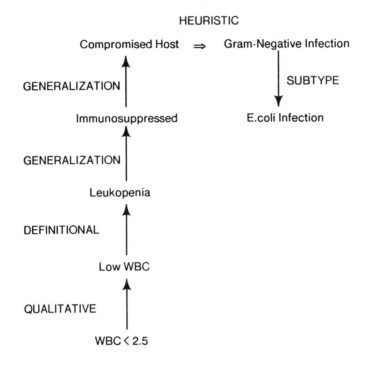

Figure 2-2: Inference structure of MYCIN

4 we will analyze the nature of these implicit relations in some detail.

To summarize, in heuristic classification abstracted data statements are associated with specific problem solutions or features that characterize a solution. This can be shown schematically in simple terms (Figure 2-3).

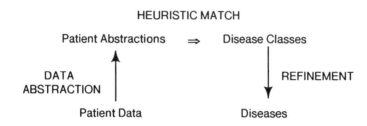

Figure 2-3:   Inference structure of heuristic classification

This diagram summarizes how a distinguished set of terms (data, data abstractions, solution abstractions, and solutions) are related systematically by *different* kinds of relations. This is the *structure of inference* in heuristic classification. The direction of inference and the relations "abstraction" and "refinement" are a simplification, indicating a common ordering (generalizing data and refining solutions), as well as a useful way of remembering the classification model. In practice, there are many operators for selecting and ordering inferences, discussed in Section 6.

3. EXAMPLES OF HEURISTIC CLASSIFICATION

Here we schematically describe the architectures of SACON, GRUNDY, and SOPHIE III in terms of heuristic classification. These are brief descriptions, but reveal the value of this kind of analysis by helping us to understand what the programs do. After a statement of the problem, the general inference structure and an example inference path are given, followed by a brief discussion. In looking at these diagrams, note sequences of classifications can be composed, perhaps involving simple classification at one stage (SACON) or omitting "abstraction" or "refinement" (GRUNDY and SACON).

In the Section 4, we will reconsider these examples, in an attempt to understand the heuristic classification pattern. Our approach will be to pick apart the "inner structure" of concepts and to characterize the kinds of relations that are typically useful for problem solving.

3.1. SACON

Problem: SACON (Bennett, et al., 1978) selects classes of behavior that should be further investigated by a structural-analysis simulation program (Figure 3-1).

Discussion: SACON solves two problems by classification—heuristically analyzing a structure and then using simple classification to select a program. It begins by heuristically selecting a simple numeric model for analyzing a structure (such as an airplane wing). The numeric model, an equation, produces stress and deflection estimates, which the program then qualitatively abstracts as behaviors to study in more detail. These behaviors, with additional information about the material, definitionally characterize different configurations of the MARC simulation program (e.g., the inelastic-fatigue program). There is no refinement because the solutions to the first problem are just a simple set of possible models, and the second problem is only solved to the point of specifying program classes. (In another software configuration system we analyzed, specific program input parameters are inferred in a refinement step.)

3.2. GRUNDY

Problem: GRUNDY (Rich, 1979) is a model of a librarian, selecting books a person might like to read.

Discussion: GRUNDY solves two classification problems heuristically, classifying a reader's personality and then selecting books appropriate to this kind of person (Figure 3-2). While some evidence for people stereotypes is by data abstraction (a JUDGE can be inferred to be an EDUCATED-PERSON), other evidence is heuristic (watching no TV is neither a necessary nor sufficient characteristic of an EDUCATED-PERSON).

Illustrating the power of a knowledge-level analysis, we discover that the people and book classifications are not distinct in the implementation. For example, "fast plots" is a book characteristic, but in the implementation "likes fast plots" is associated with a person stereotype. The relation between a person stereotype and "fast plots" is heuristic and should be distinguished from abstractions of people and books. One objective of the program is to learn better people stereotypes (user models). The classification description of the user modeling problem shows that GRUNDY should also be learning better ways to characterize books, as well as improving its heuristics. If these are not treated separately, learning may be hindered. This example illustrates why a knowledge-level analysis should precede representation.

It is interesting to note that GRUNDY does not attempt to perfect the user model before recommending a book. Rather, refinement of the person stereotype occurs when the reader rejects book suggestions. Analysis of other programs indicates that this multiple-pass process structure is common. For example, the Drilling Advisor makes two passes on the causes of drill sticking, considering general, inexpensive data first, just as medical programs commonly consider the "history and physical" before laboratory data. The high-level, abstract structure of

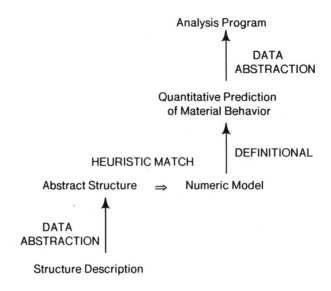

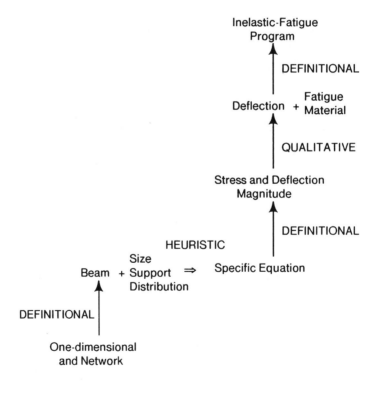

Figure 3-1: Inference structure of SACON

10

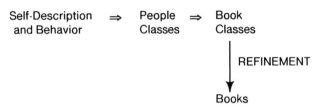

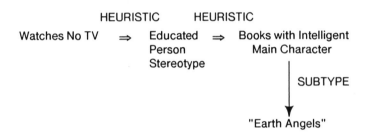

Figure 3-2: Inference structure of GRUNDY

the heuristic classification model makes possible these kinds of descriptions and comparisons.

3.3. SOPHIE III

Problem: SOPHIE III (Brown, et al., 1982) classifies an electronic circuit in terms of the component that is causing faulty behavior (Figure 3-3).

Discussion: SOPHIE's set of pre-enumerated solutions is a lattice of valid and faulty circuit behaviors. In contrast with MYCIN, SOPHIE's solutions are device states and component flaws, not stereotypes of disorders. They are related causally, not by subtype. Data are not only external device behaviors, but include internal component measurements propagated by the causal analysis of the LOCAL program. Nevertheless, the inference structure of abstractions, heuristic relations, and refinement fits the heuristic classification model, demonstrating its generality and usefulness.

4. UNDERSTANDING HEURISTIC CLASSIFICATION

The purpose of this section is to develop a principled account of why the inference structure of heuristic classification takes the characteristic form we have discovered. Our approach is to describe what we have heretofore loosely called "classes," "concepts," or "stereotypes" in a more formal way, using the conceptual graph notation of Sowa (Sowa, 1984). In this formalism, a concept is described by graphs of typed, usually binary relations among other concepts. This kind of analysis has its origins in semantic networks (Quillian, 1968), the conceptual-dependency notation of Schank, et al. (Schank, 1975), the prototype/perspective descriptions of KRL (Bobrow and Winograd, 1979), the classification hierarchies of KL-ONE (Schmolze and Lipkis, 1983), as well as the predicate calculus.

Our discussion has several objectives:

- to relate the knowledge encoded in rule-based systems to structures more commonly associated with "semantic net" and "frame" formalisms,

- to explicate what kinds of knowledge heuristic rules leave out (and thus their advantages for search efficiency and limitations for correctness), and

- to relate the kinds of conceptual relations collectively identified in knowledge representation research (e.g., the relation between an individual and a class) with the pattern of inference that typically occurs during heuristic classification problem solving (yielding the characteristic inverted horseshoe inference structure of Figure 2-3).

One important result of this analysis is a characterization of the "heuristic relation" in terms of primitive relations among concepts (such as preference, accompaniment, and causal

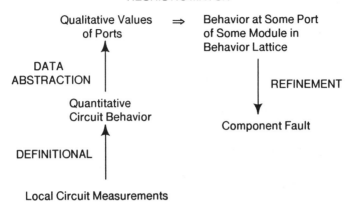

HEURISTIC MATCH

Qualitative Values   ⟹   Behavior at Some Port
    of Ports   of Some Module in
                                 Behavior Lattice

DATA
ABSTRACTION   REFINEMENT

Quantitative
Circuit Behavior   Component Fault

DEFINITIONAL

Local Circuit Measurements

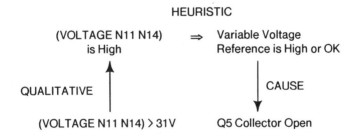

HEURISTIC

(VOLTAGE N11 N14)   ⟹   Variable Voltage
    is High   Reference is High or OK

QUALITATIVE   CAUSE

(VOLTAGE N11 N14) > 31V   Q5 Collector Open

Figure 3-3:   Inference structure of SOPHIE

enablement), and its difference from more essential, "definitional" characterizations of concepts. In short, we are trying to systematically characterize *the kind of knowledge that is useful for problem solving*, which relates to our larger aim of devising useful languages for encoding knowledge in expert systems.

4.1. Schemas vs. definitions

In the case of matching features of organisms (MYCIN) or programs (SACON), features are essential (necessary), identifying characteristics of the object, event, or process. This corresponds to the Aristotelian notion of concept definition in terms of necessary properties.[3] In contrast, features may be only "accidental," corresponding to typical manifestations or behaviors. For example, E.coli is normally found in parts of the body, an accidental property. It is common to refer to the combination of accidental and defining associations as a "schema" for the concept.[4] Inferences made using accidental associations of a schema are inherently uncertain. For example, we might infer that a particular person, because he is educated, likes to read books, but this might not be true. In contrast, an educated person must, by definition, have learned a great deal about something (though maybe not a formal academic topic).

The nature of schemas and their representation has been studied extensively in AI. As stated in the introduction (Section 1), our purpose here is to exploit this research to understand the knowledge contained in rules. We are not advocating one representation over another; rather we just want to find some way of writing down knowledge so that we can detect and express patterns. We use the conceptual graph notation of Sowa because it is simple and it makes basic distinctions that we find to be useful:

- A schema is made up of *coherent statements* mentioning a given concept, not a list of isolated, independent features. (A statement is a complete sentence.)

- A schema for a given concept contains *relations to other concepts*, not just "attributes and values" or "slots and values."

- A concept is typically described from different points of view by *a set of schemata* (called a "schematic cluster"), not a single "frame."

---

[3] (Sowa, 1984) provides a good overview of these well-known philosophical distinctions. See also (Palmer, 1978) and (Cohen and Murphy, 1984).

[4] Here we use the word "schema" as a *kind of knowledge*, not a construct of a particular programming language or notation. See (Hayes, 1979) for further discussion of this distinction.

- The totality of what people know about a concept usually extends well beyond the schemas that are pragmatically encoded in programs for solving limited problems.

Finally, we adopt Sowa's definition of a *prototype* as a "typical individual," a specialization of a concept schema to indicate typical values and characteristics, where ranges or sets are described for the class as a whole. Whether a program uses prototype or schema descriptions of its solutions is not important to our discussion, and many may combine them, including "normal" values, as well as a spectrum of expectations.

4.2. Alternative encodings of schemas

To develop the above points in some detail, we will consider a conceptual graph description and how it relates to typical rule-based encodings. Figure 4-1 shows how knowledge about the concept "cluster headache" is described using the conceptual graph notation.[5]

Concepts appear in boxes; relations are in circles. Concepts are also related by a type hierarchy, e.g., a HEADACHE is a kind of PROCESS, an OLDER-MAN is a kind of MAN. Relations are constrained to link concepts of particular types, e.g., PTIM, a point in time, links a PROCESS to a TIME. For convenience, we can also use Sowa's linear notation for conceptual graphs. Thus, OLDER-MAN can be described as a specialization of MAN, "a man with characteristic old." CLUSTERED is "an event occurring daily for a week." EARLY-SLEEP is "a few hours after the state of sleep."

We make no claim that a representation of this kind is complete, computationally tractable, or even unambiguous. For our purposes here, it is simply a *notation* with the advantage over English prose of systematically revealing how what we know about a concept can be (at least partially) described in terms of its relations to concepts of other types.

For contrast, consider how this same knowledge might be encoded in a notation based upon objects, attributes, and values, as in MYCIN. Here, the object would be the PATIENT, and typical attributes would be HEADACHE-ONSET (with possible values EARLY-MORNING, EARLY-SLEEP, LATE-AFTERNOON) and DISORDER (with possible values CLUSTER-HEADACHE, INFECTION, etc.). A typical rule might be, "If the patient has headache onset during sleep, then the disorder of the patient is cluster headache." The features of a cluster headache might be combined in a single rule. Generally, since none of the features are logically necessary, they are considered in separate rules, with certainty factors denoting how strongly the symptom (or predisposition, in the case of age) is correlated with the disease. A

---

[5]One English translation would be: "A cluster headache is a headache that occurs with a frequency in clusters, experienced by an older man, accompanied by lacrimation, with characteristic severe, of location unilateral, occurring at a point in time of early sleep."

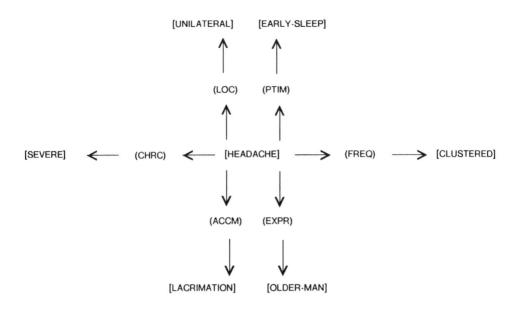

```
[EARLY-SLEEP] is
        [TIME: [STATE: [SLEEP]] -> (AFTER) -> [TIME-PERIOD: @few-hrs]]

[CLUSTERED] is
        [DAILY] <- (FREQ) <- [EVENT] -> (DURATION) -> [TIME-PERIOD: @1week]

[OLDER-MAN] is
        [MAN] -> (CHRC) -> [OLD]
```

Figure 4-1: Schema describing the concept CLUSTER-HEADACHE and some related concepts

primitive "frame" representation, as in INTERNIST, is similar, with a list of attributes for each disorder, but each attribute is an "atomic" unit that bundles together what is broken into object, attribute, and value in MYCIN, e.g., "HEADACHE-ONSET-OCCURS-EARLY-SLEEP."

The idea of relating a concept (such as CLUSTER-HEADACHE) to a set of attributes or descriptors, is common in AI programs. However, a relational analysis reveals marked differences in what an attribute might be:

- **An attribute is an atomic proposition.** In INTERNIST, an attribute is a string that is only related to diseases or other strings, e.g., HEADACHE-ONSET-EARLY-SLEEP-EXPERIENCED-BY-PATIENT.

- **An attribute is a relation characterizing some class of objects.** In MYCIN, an attribute

16

is associated with an instance of an object (a particular patient, culture, organism, or drug).

- o **An attribute is a unary relation.** A MYCIN attribute with the values "yes or no" corresponds to a unary relation, (<attribute> <object>), e.g., (HEADACHE-ONSET-EARLY-SLEEP PATIENT), "headache onset during early sleep is experienced by the patient."

- o **An attribute is a binary relation.** A MYCIN attribute with *values* corresponds to a binary relation, (<attribute> <object> <value>), e.g., (HEADACHE-ONSET PATIENT EARLY-SLEEP), "headache onset experienced by the patient is during early sleep."

- **An attribute is a relation among classes. Each class is a concept.** Taking the same example, there are two more primitive relations, ONSET and EXPERIENCER, yielding the propositions: (ONSET HEADACHE EARLY-SLEEP), "the onset of the headache is during early sleep", and (EXPERIENCER HEADACHE PATIENT), "the experiencer of the headache is the patient." More concisely, [EARLY-SLEEP] <- (ONSET) <- [HEADACHE] -> (EXPR) -> [PATIENT]. These relations and concepts can be further broken down, as shown in Figure 4-1.

The conceptual graph notation encourages clear thinking by forcing us to unbundle domain terminology into defined or schematically described terms and a constrained vocabulary of relations (restricted in the types of concepts each can link). Rather than saying that "an object has attributes," we can be more specific about the relations among entities, describing abstract concepts like "headache" and "cluster" in the same notation we use to describe concrete objects like patients and organisms. In particular, notice that headache onset is a characterization of a headache, not of a person, contrary to the MYCIN statement that "headache onset is an attribute of person." Similarly, the relation between a patient and a disorder is different from the relation between a patient and his age.[6]

Breaking apart "parameters" into concepts and relations has the additional benefit of allowing them to be easily related, through their schema descriptions. For example, it is clear that HEADACHE-ONSET and HEADACHE-SEVERITY both characterize HEADACHE, allowing us to write a simple, general inference rule for deciding about relevancy: "If a process type

---

[6]The importance of defining relations has been discovered repetitively in AI. Wood's analysis of semantic networks (Woods, 1975) is an early, well-known example. The issue of restricting and defining relations was particularly important in the development of OWL (Martin, 1979). Researchers using rule-based languages, like MYCIN's, felt curiously immune from these issues, not realizing that their "attributes" were making similar confusions.

being characterized (e.g., HEADACHE) is unavailable or not relevant, then its characterization (e.g., HEADACHE-ONSET) is not relevant." As another example, consider a discrimination inference strategy that compares disorder processes on the basis of their descriptions as *events*. Knowing what relations are comparable (e.g., location and frequency), the inference procedure can automatically gather relevant data, look up the schema descriptions, and make comparisons to establish the best match. To summarize, the rules in a program like MYCIN are implicitly making statements about schemas. This becomes clear when we separate conceptual links from rules of inference, as in NEOMYCIN.

4.3. Relating heuristics to conceptual graphs

Given all of the structural and functional statements we might make about a concept, describing processes and interactions in detail, some statements will be more useful than others for solving problems. Rather than thinking of schemas as inert, static descriptions, we are interested in how they link concepts to solve problems. The description of CLUSTERED-HEADACHE given in Figure 4-1 includes the knowledge that one typically finds in a diagnostic program. To understand heuristics in these terms, consider first that some relations appear to be less "accidental" than others. The time of occurrence of the headache, location, frequency, and characterizing features are all closely bound to what a cluster headache is. They are not necessary, but they together distinguish CLUSTER-HEADACHE from other types. That is, these relations *discriminate* this headache from other types of headache.

On the other hand, accompaniment by lacrimation (tearing of the eyes) and the tendency for such headaches to be experienced by older men are correlations with other concepts.[7] Here, in particular, we see the link between different kinds of entities: a DISORDER-PROCESS and a PERSON. This is the link we have identified as a heuristic—a direct, non-hierarchical association between concepts of different types. Observe that *why* an older man experiences cluster headaches is left out. Given a model of the world that says that all phenomena are caused, we can say that each of the links with HEADACHE could be explained causally. Whether the explanation has been left out or is not known cannot be determined by examining the conceptual graph, a critical point we will return to later.

When heuristics are stated as rules in a program like MYCIN, even known relational and definitional details are often omitted. This often means that intermediate concepts are omitted as well. We say "X suggests Y, or "X makes you think of Y." Unless the connection is an unexplained correlation, such a statement can be expanded to a full sentence that is part of the

---

[7]What discriminates is relative. If kinds of headache tended to be associated with different ages of people, then this might be a CLUSTER-ELDERLY-HEADACHE and we would consider the age of the experiencer to be a discriminating characteristic.

schema description of X and/or Y. Thus, the geologist's rule "goldfields flowers --> serpentine rock" might be restated as, "Serpentine rock has nutrients that enable goldfields to grow well." Figure 4-2 shows the conceptual graph notation of this statement (with "enable" shown by the relation "instrument" linking an entity, nutrients, to an act, growing).

```
[GOLDFIELDS] <- (OBJ) <- [GROW]
                            ↓
                (INST) -> [NUTRIENTS]
                            ↑
                (CHRC) <- [SERPENTINE]
```

Figure 4-2: A heuristic rule expanded as a conceptual graph

The concepts of nutrients and growing are omitted from the rule notation, just as the causal details that explain the growth process are skipped over in the conceptual graph notation. The rule indicates what you must observe (goldfields flowers growing) and what you can assert (serpentine rock is near the surface). It captures knowledge not as mere static descriptions, but as efficient, useful connections for problem solving. Moreover, the example makes clear the essential characteristic of a heuristic inference—a non-hierarchical and non-definitional connection between concepts of distinct classes.

Heuristics are selected statements that are useful for inference, particularly how one class choice *constrains* another. Consider the goldfields example. Is the conceptual graph shown in Figure 4-2 a schema for serpentine, goldfields, nutrient, or all three? First, knowledge is something somebody knows; whether goldfields is associated with nutrients will vary from person to person. (And for at least a short time, readers of this paper will think of goldfields when the word "nutrient" is mentioned.) Second, the real issue is how knowledge is *practically indexed*. The associations a problem solver forms and the directionality of these associations will depend on the kinds of situations he is called upon to interpret, and what is given and what is derived. Thus, it seems plausible that a geologist in the field would see goldfields (data) and think about serpentine rock (solution). Conversely, his task might commonly be to find outcroppings of serpentine rock; he would work backwards to think of observables that he might look for (data) that would indicate the presence of serpentine. Indeed, he might have many associations with flowers and rocks, and even many general rules for how to infer rocks (e.g., based on other plants, drainage properties of the land, slope). Figure 4-3 shows one possible inference path.

In summary, a heuristic association is a connection that relates data that is commonly available to the kinds of interpretations the problem solver is trying to derive. For a physician starting with characteristics of a person, the patient, connections to diseases will be

19

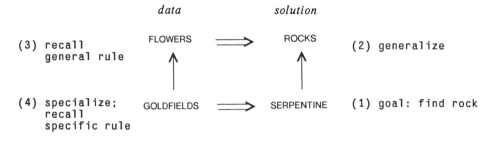

Figure 4-3: Using a general rule to work backwards from a solution

useful. It must be possible to relate new situations to previous interpretations and this is what the abstraction process in classification is all about (recall the quotation from Bruner in Section 1). The specific person becomes an "old man" and particular disorders come to mind.

Problems tend to start with objects in the real world, so it makes sense that practical problem-solving knowledge would allow problems to be restated in terms of stereotypical objects: kinds of people, kinds of patients, kinds of stressed structures, kinds of malfunctioning devices, etc. Based on our analysis of expert systems, links from these data concepts to solution concepts come in different flavors:

- agent or experiencer (e.g., people predisposed to diseases)

- cause, co-presence, or correlation (e.g., symptoms related to faults)

- preference or advantage (e.g., people related to books)

- physical model (e.g., abstract structures related to numeric models)

These relations don't characterize a solution in terms of "immediate properties"—they are not definitional or type discriminating. Rather, they capture *accidental associations between a solution and available data, usually concrete concepts.* (Other kinds of links may be possible; these are the ones we have discovered so far.)

The essential characteristic of a heuristic is that it reduces search. A heuristic rule reduces a conceptual graph to a single relation between two concepts. Through this, heuristic rules reduce search in several ways:

1. Of all possible schemas that might describe a concept, heuristic connections are those that constrain a categorization on the basis of available data (e.g., the strength of SERPENTINE rock may be irrelevant for inferring the presence of hidden deposits).

2. A heuristic eliminates consideration of intermediate (and often invariant) relations between the concepts it mentions, associating salient classes directly (e.g., the goldfields rule omits the concept NUTRIENT).

While not having to think about intermediate connections is advantageous, this sets up a basic conflict for the problem solver—his inferential leaps may be wrong. Another way of saying that the problem solver skips over things is that there are *unarticulated assumptions* on which the interpretation rests. We will consider this further in the section on inference strategies (Section 6).

4.4. Relating inference structure to conceptual graphs

In the inference-structure diagrams (such as Figure 3-2) nodes stand for propositions (e.g., "the reader is an educated person"). The diagrams relate propositions on the basis of how they can be inferred from one another: type, definition, and heuristic. So far in this section we have broken apart these atomic propositions to distinguish a heuristic link from essential and direct characterizing relations in a schema; and we have argued how direct, accidental connections between concepts, which leave out intermediate relations, are valuable for reducing search.

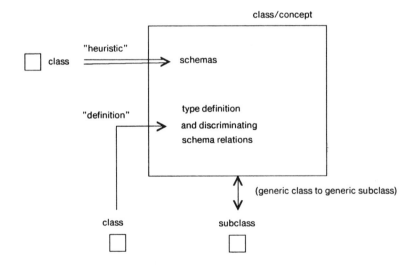

Figure 4-4: Conceptual relations used in heuristic classification

Here we return to the higher-level, inference-structure diagrams and include the details of the kinds of links that are possible. In Figure 4-4 each kind of inference relation between

21

concepts is shown as a line. Classes can be connected to one another by any of these three kinds of inference relations. We make a distinction between heuristics (direct, non-hierarchical, class-class relations, such as the link between goldfields and serpentine rock) and definitions (including necessary and discriminating relations, plus qualitative abstraction (see Section 2.2)). Definitional and subtype links are shown vertically, to conform to our intuitive idea of generalization of data to higher categories, what we have called *data abstraction.*

It is important to remember that the "definitional" links are often non-essential, "soft" descriptions. The "definition" of leukopenia as white blood count less than normal is a good example. "Normal" depends on everything else happening to the patient, so inferring this condition always involves making some assumptions.

Note also that this is a diagram of static, structural relations. In actual problem solving other links will be required to form a *case-specific model,* indicating propositions the problem solver believes to be true and support for them. In particular, *surrogates* (Sowa, 1984) (also called *individuals* (Brachman, 1977), such the MYCIN "context" ORGANISM-1) will stand for unknown objects or processes in the world that are identified by associating them with a class in a type hierarchy.[8]

Now we are ready to put this together to understand the pattern behind the inference structure of heuristic classification. Given that a sequence of heuristic classifications, as in GRUNDY, is possible, indeed common, we start with the simplest case by assuming that data classes are not inferred heuristically. Instead, data are supplied directly or inferred by definition. When solution classes are inferred by definition, we have a case of *simple classification* (Section 2.1), for example, when an organism is actually seen growing in a laboratory culture (like a smoking gun). In order to describe an idealized form of heuristic

---

[8]It is not often realized that each MYCIN "context" has a *distinguished attribute* called its "name" that corresponds to the link between the surrogate (entity to be classified) and a classification hierarchy. The pattern was only evident to system designers to the extent that they realized that each "context" type has some identifying attribute that allows it to be translated. For example, after identifying an organism, the program says "the E.coli" rather than ORGANISM-1 (or whatever its number was), referring to the object/context hierarchy if there are more than one, "the E.coli from the blood culture of 3/14/77." Thus, we have the identity of the organism, name of the infection, site of the culture, etc. Corresponding to each of these identifying attributes is a hierarchy of "values" with static properties. Thus, there are tables of organisms, infections, culture sites, etc. It is in such a table that MYCIN stores the information that E.coli is a gram-negative rod. A single, general rule uses the table to identify the unknown organism. These tables are also called "grids"; we were unaware at the time (1974-1977) that we were recording the same kind of information other AI programmers were storing in "frame hierarchies." The pattern was partially obscured by our use of special-case rules, for example, to allow for incorrect data, making the grids appear to be a convenient computational short-hand for collapsing similar rules, rather than a notation for describing classes.

classification, we leave out definitional inference of solutions. Finally, inference has the general form that problem descriptions must be abstracted (proceeding from subclass to class) and partial solutions must be refined (proceeding from class to subclass).

If we thus specialize the right side of the inference diagram in Figure 4-4 to a data class and a solution class and glue them together, we get a refined version of the original inverted horseshoe (Figure 2-3). Figure 4-5 shows how data and solution classes are typically inferred from one another in the simplest case of heuristic classification.

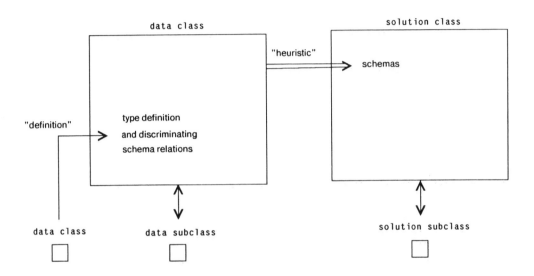

Figure 4-5: Typical conceptual relations in simplest form of heuristic classification

In summary, the original heuristic classification inference diagram, which we found to be a good description of reasoning in several heuristic programs, can be derived from a basic model of how data and solution concepts can be and typically are related.

4.5. Pragmatics of defining concepts

In the course of writing and analyzing heuristic programs, we have been struck by the difficulty of defining terms. What is a "compromised host?" How is it different from "immunosuppression"? Is an alcoholic immunosuppressed? We do not simply write down descriptions of what we know. The very process of formalizing terms and relations changes what we know, and itself brings about concept formation.

In many respects, the apparent unprincipled nature of MYCIN is a good reflection of the raw state of how experts talk. Two problems we encountered illustrate the difficulty of proceeding without a formal conceptual structure, and thus, reflect the unprincipled state of what experts know about their own reasoning:

- Twice we completely reworked the hierarchical relations among immunosuppression and compromised host conditions. There clearly is no agreed-upon network that we can simply write down. People do not know schema hierarchies in the same sense that they know phone numbers. A given version is believed to be better because it makes finer distinctions, so it leads to better problem solving.

- The concepts of "significant organism" and "contaminant" were sometimes confused in MYCIN. An organism is significant if there is evidence that it is associated with a disease. A contaminant is an organism growing on a culture that was introduced because of dirty instruments or was picked up from some body site where it normally grows (e.g., a blood culture may be contaminated by skin organisms). Thus, evidence against contamination supports the belief that the discovered organism is significant. However, a rule writer would tend to write "significant" rather than "not contaminant," even though this was the intended, intermediate interpretation. There may be a tendency to directly form a general, positive categorization, rather than to make an association to an intermediate, ruled-out category.

To a first approximation, it appears that what we "really" know is what we can conclude given other information. That is, we start with just implication (P -> Q), then go back to abstract concepts into types and understand relations among them. For example, we start by knowing that "WBC < 2500 -> LEUKOPENIA." To make this principled, we break it into the following pieces:

1. "Leukopenia" means that the count of leukocytes is impoverished:
   [LEUKOPENIA] = [LEUKOCYTES] -> (CHRC) -> [CURRENT-COUNT] -> (CHRC) -> [IMPOVERISHED]

2. "Impoverished" means that the current measure is much less than normal:
   [IMPOVERISHED: x] =
   [CURRENT-MEASURE: x] -> (<<) -> [NORMAL-MEASURE: x]

3. The (normal/current) count is a kind of measure:
   [COUNT] < [MEASURE]

4. A fact, the normal leukocyte count in an adult is 7000:
   [LEUKOCYTES] -> (CHRC) ->
   [NORMAL-COUNT] -> (MEAS) ->

[MEASURE: 7000 /mm3].

With the proper interpreter (and perhaps some additional definitions and relations), we could instantiate and compose these expressions to get the effect of the original rule. This is the pattern we follow in knowledge engineering, constantly decomposing terms into general types and relations to make explicit the rationale behind implications.

Perhaps one of the most perplexing difficulties we encounter is distinguishing between subtype and cause, and between state and process. Part of the problem is that cause and effect are not always distinguished by our experts. For example, a physician might speak of a brain-tumor as a kind of brain-mass-lesion. It is certainly a kind of brain mass, but it causes a lesion (cut); it is not a kind of lesion. Thus, the concept bundles cause with effect and location: a *lesion* in the *brain* caused by a *mass* of some kind is a brain-mass-lesion (Figure 4-6).

```
[MASS]  -> (CAUS) -> [LESION]  -> (LOC)  -> [BRAIN]
```

Figure 4-6:   Conceptual graph of the term "brain-mass-lesion"

Similarly, we draw causal nets linking abnormal states, saying that brain-hematoma (mass of blood in the brain) is caused by brain-hemorrhage (bleeding). To understand what is happening, we profit by labeling brain-hematoma as a *substance* (a kind of brain-mass) and brain-hemorrhage as a *process* that affects or produces the substance. Yet when we began, we thought of brain-hemorrhage as if it were equivalent to the escaping blood.

It is striking that we can learn concepts and how to relate them to solve problems, without understanding the links in a principled way. If you know that WBC < 2500 is leukopenia, a form of immunosuppression, which is a form of compromised host, causing E.coli infection, you are on your way to being a clinician. As novices, we push tokens around in the same non-comprehending way as MYCIN.

Once we start asking questions, we have difficulty figuring out how concepts are related. If immunosuppression is the state of being unable to fight infection by mechanisms, then does impoverished white cells *cause* this state? Or is it *caused by* this state (something else affected the immunosystem, reducing the WBC as a side-effect)? (Worse yet, we may say it is an "indicator," completing missing the fact that we are talking about causality.) Perhaps it is one way in which the immunosystem can be diminished, so it is *a kind of* immunosuppression. It is difficult to write down a principled network because we don't know the relations, and we don't know them because we don't know what the concepts mean—we don't understand the processes involved. Yet, we might know enough to relate data classes to therapy classes and save the patient's life!

25

A conceptual graph or logic analysis suggests that the relations among concepts are *relatively* few in number and fixed in meaning, compared to the number and complexity of concepts. The meaning of concepts depends on what we ascribe to the links that join them. Thus, in practice we jockey around concepts to get a well-formed network. Complicating this is our tendency to use terms that bundle cause with effect and to relate substances directly, leaving out intermediate processes. At first, novices might be like today's expert programs. A concept is just a token or label, associated with knowledge of how to infer truth and how to use information (what to do if it is true and how to infer other truths from it). Unless the token is defined by something akin to a conceptual graph, it is difficult to say that the novice or program understands what it means. But in the world of action, what matters more than the functional, pragmatic knowledge of knowing what to do?

Where does this leave us? One conclusion is that "principled networks" are impossible. Except for mathematics, science, economics, and similar domains, concepts do not have formal definitions. While heuristic programs sometimes reason with concrete, well-defined classifications such as the programs in SACON and the fault network in SOPHIE, they more often use experiential schemas, the knowledge we say distinguishes the expert from the novice. In the worst case, these experiential concepts are vague and incompletely understood, such as the diseases in MYCIN. In general, there are underlying (unarticulated or unexamined) assumptions in every schema description. Thus, the first conclusion is that for concepts in nonformal domains this background and context cannot in principle be made explicit (Flores and Winograd, 1984). That is, our conceptual knowledge is inseparable from our as yet ungeneralized memory of experiences.

An alternative point of view is that, regardless of ultimate limitations, it is obvious that expert systems will be valuable for replacing the expert on routine tasks, aiding him on difficult tasks, and generally transforming how we write down and teach knowledge. Much more can be done in terms of memory representation, learning from experience, and combination of principled models with situation/action, pragmatic rules. Specifically, the problem of *knowledge transformation* could become a focus for expert systems research, including compilation for efficiency, derivation of procedures for enhancing explanation (Swartout, 1981), and re-representation for detecting and explaining patterns, thus aiding scientific theory formation. Studying and refining actual knowledge bases as exemplified by this section, is our chief methodology for improving our representations and inference procedures. Indeed, from the perspective of knowledge transformation, it is ironic to surmise that we might one day decide that the "superficial" representation of EMYCIN rules is a fine executable language, and something like it will become the target for our knowledge compilers.

5. ANALYSIS OF PROBLEM TYPES IN TERMS OF SYSTEMS

The heuristic classification model gives us two new angles for comparing problem-solving methods and kinds of problems. First, it suggests that we characterize programs by whether solutions are selected or constructed. This leads us to the second perspective, that different "kinds of things" might be selected or constructed (diagnoses, user models, etc.). In this section we will adopt a single point of view, namely that a solution is most generally a set of beliefs describing what is true about a system or a set of actions (operations) that will physically transform a system to a desired description. We will study variations of system description and transformation problems, leading to a hierarchy of *kinds of problems* that an expert might solve.

5.1. What gets selected?

This foray into systems analysis begins very simply with the observation that all classification problem solving involves *selection* of a solution. We can characterize kinds of problems by *what is being selected*:

- *diagnosis*: solutions are faulty components (SOPHIE) or processes affecting the device (MYCIN);

- *user model*: solutions are people stereotypes in terms of their goals and beliefs (first phase of GRUNDY);

- *catalog selection*: solutions are products, services, or activities, e.g., books, personal computers, careers, travel tours, wines, investments (second phase of GRUNDY);

- *model-based analysis*: solutions are numeric models (first phase of SACON);

- *skeletal planning*: solutions are plans, such as packaged sequences of programs and parameters for running them (second phase of SACON, also first phase of experiment planning in MOLGEN (Friedland, 1979)).

Attempts to make knowledge engineering a systematic discipline often begin with a listing of kinds of problems. This kind of analysis is always prone to category errors. For example, a naive list of "problems" might list "design," "constraint satisfaction," and "model-based reasoning," combining a kind of problem, an inference method, and a kind of knowledge. For example, one might solve a VLSI chip design problem using constraint satisfaction to reason about models of circuit components. It is important to adopt a single perspective when making a list of this kind.

In particular, we must not confuse what gets selected—what constitutes a solution—with the method for computing the solution. A common misconception is that there is a kind of problem called a "classification problem," opposing, for example, classification problems with design problems (for example, see (Sowa, 1984)). Indeed, some tasks, such as identifying bacteria from culture information, are inherently solved by *simple classification*. However, heuristic classification as defined here is *a description of how a particular problem is solved by a particular problem solver.* If the problem solver has a priori knowledge of solutions and can relate them to the problem description by data abstraction, heuristic association, and refinement, then the problem can be solved by classification. For example, if it were practical to enumerate all of the computer configurations R1 might select, or if the solutions were restricted to a predetermined, explicit set of designs, the program could be reconfigured to solve its problem by classification. The method of solving a configuration problem is not inherent in the task itself.

With this distinction between problem and computational method in mind, we turn our attention to a systematic study of problem types. Can we form an explicit taxonomy that includes the kinds of application we might typically encounter?

5.2. Background: Problem categories

One approach might be to focus on objects and what can be done to them. We can design them, diagnose them, use them in a plan to accomplish some function, etc. This seems like one way to consistently describe kinds of problems. Surely everything in the world involves objects.

However, in attempting to derive such a uniform framework, the concept of "object" becomes a bit elusive. For example, the analysis of problem types in Building Expert Systems (hereafter BES, (Hayes-Roth et al., 1983), see Table 5-1) indirectly refers to a program as an object. Isn't it really a process? Are procedures objects or processes? It's a matter of perspective. Projects and audit plans can be thought of as both objects and processes. Is a manufacturing assembly line an object or a process? The idea of a "system" appears to work better than the more common focus on objects and processes.

```
INTERPRETATION   Inferring situation descriptions from sensor data
PREDICTION       Inferring likely consequences of given situation
DIAGNOSIS        Inferring system malfunctions from observables
DESIGN           Configuring objects under constraints
PLANNING         Designing actions
MONITORING       Comparing observations to plan vulnerabilities
DEBUGGING        Prescribing remedies for malfunctions
REPAIR           Executing a plan to administer a prescribed remedy
INSTRUCTION      Diagnosis, debugging, and repairing student behavior
CONTROL          Interpreting, predicting, repairing, and monitoring system
                 behaviors.
```

Table 5-1: Generic categories of knowledge engineering applications.
From
(Hayes-Roth et al., 1983) Table 1.1, page 14

By organizing descriptions of problems around the concept of a system, we can improve upon the distinctions made in BES. As an example of the difficulties, consider that a situation description is a description of a system. Sensor data are observables. But what is the difference between INTERPRETATION (inferring system behavior from observables) and DIAGNOSIS (inferring system malfunctions from observables)? Diagnosis, so defined, includes interpretation. The list appears to deliberately have this progressive design behind it, as is particularly clear from the last two entries, which are composites of earlier "applications." In fact, this idea of multiple "applications" to something (student behavior, system behavior) suggests that a simplification might be found by adopting more uniform terminology. As a second example, consider that the text of BES says that automatic programming is an example of a problem involving planning. How is that different from configuration under constraints (i.e., design)? Is automatic programming a planning problem or a design problem? We also talk about experiment design and experiment planning. Are the two words interchangeable?

We can get clarity by turning things around, thinking about systems and what can be done to and with them.

5.3. A system-oriented approach

We start by informally defining a *system* to be a complex of interacting objects that have some process (I/O) behavior. The following are examples of systems:

a stereo system
a VLSI chip
an organ system in the human body
a computer program
a molecule
a university
an experimental procedure

Webster's defines a system to be "a set or arrangement of things so related or connected as to form a unity or organic whole." The parts taken together have some structure. It is useful to think of the unity of the system in terms of how it behaves. Behavior might be characterized simply in terms of inputs and outputs.

Figures 5-1 and 5-2 summarize hierarchically what we can do to or with a system, revising the BES table. We group operations in terms of those that *construct* a system and those that *interpret* a system, corresponding to what is generally called *synthesis* and *analysis*. Common synonyms appear in parentheses below the generic operations. In what follows, our new terms appear in upper case.

INTERPRET operations concern a working system in some environment. In particular, IDENTIFY is different from DESIGN in that it requires taking I/O behavior and mapping it onto a system. If the system has not been described before, then this is equivalent to (perhaps only partial) design from I/O pairs. PREDICT is the inverse, taking a known system and describing output behavior for given inputs. ("Simulate" is a specific method for making

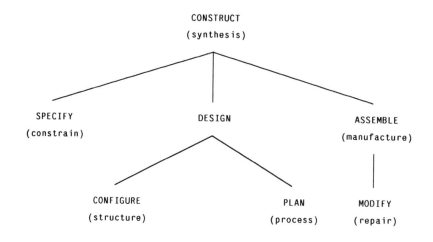

Figure 5-1: Generic operations for synthesizing a system

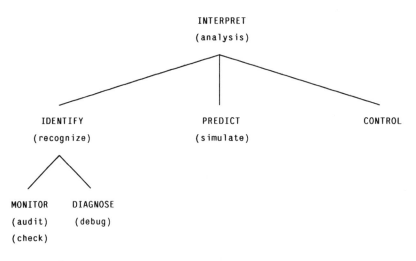

Figure 5-2: Generic operations for analyzing a system

predictions, suggesting that there is a computational model of the system, complete at some level of detail.) CONTROL, not often associated with heuristic programs, takes a known system and determines inputs to generate prescribed outputs (Vemuri, 1978). Thus, these three operations, IDENTIFY, PREDICT, and CONTROL, logically cover the possibilities of problems in which one factor of the set {input, output, system} is unknown.

Both MONITOR and DIAGNOSE presuppose a pre-existing system design against which the behavior of an actual, "running" system is compared. Thus, one identifies the system with respect to its deviation from a standard. In the case of MONITOR, one *detects* discrepancies in behavior (or simply characterizes the current state of the system). In the case of DIAGNOSE, one *explains* monitored behavior in terms of discrepancies between the actual (inferred) design and the standard system.

To carry the analysis further, we compare our proposed terms to those used in Building Expert Systems:

- "Interpretation" is adopted as a generic category that broadly means to describe a working system. The most rudimentary form is simply identifying some unknown system from its behavior. Note that an identification strictly speaking involves a specification of constraints under which the system operates and a design (structure/process model). In practice, our understanding may not include a full design, let alone the constraints it must satisfy (consider the metarules of HERACLES versus our vague understanding of why they are reasonable). Examples of programs that identify systems are:

  o DENDRAL: system = molecular (structure) configuration (Buchanan, et al., 1969) (given spectrum behavior of the molecule).

  o PROSPECTOR: system = geological (formation) configuration (Hart, 1977) (given samples and geophysics behavior).

  o DEBUGGY: system = knowledge (program) configuration of student's subtraction facts and procedure (Burton, 1982) (given behavior on a set of subtraction problems).

- "Prediction" is adopted directly. Note that prediction, specifically simulation, may be an important technique underlying *all* of the other operations (e.g., using simulation to generate and test possible diagnoses).

- "Diagnosis" is adopted directly as a kind of IDENTIFICATION, with some part of the design characterized as faulty with respect to a preferred model.

- "Design" is taken to be the general operation that embraces both a characterization of structure (CONFIGURATION) and process (PLANNING).

- "Monitoring" is adopted directly as a kind of IDENTIFICATION, with system behavior checked against a preferred, expected model.

31

- "Debugging" is dropped, deemed to be equivalent to DIAGNOSIS plus MODIFY.

- "Repair" is more broadly termed MODIFY; it could be characterized as transforming a system to effect a redesign, usually prompted by a diagnostic description. MODIFY operations are those that change the *structure* of the system, for example, editing a program or using drugs (or surgery) to change a living organism. Thus, MODIFY is a form of "reassembly" given a required design modification.

- The idea of "executing a plan" is moved to the more general term ASSEMBLE, meaning the physical construction of a system. DESIGN is conceptual; it describes a system in terms of spatial and temporal interactions of components. Assembly is the problem of actually putting the system together in the real world. For example, contrast R1's problem with the problem of having a robot assemble the configuration that R1 designed. ASSEMBLY is equivalent to planning at a different level, that of a system that builds a designed subsystem.

- "Instruction" is dropped because it is a composite operation that doesn't apply to every system. In a strict sense, it is equivalent to MODIFY.

In addition to the operations already mentioned, we add SPECIFY—referring to the separable operation of constraining a system description, generally in terms of interactions with other systems and actual realization in the world (resources affecting components). Of course, in practice design difficulties may require modifying the specification, just as assembly may constrain design (commonly called "design for manufacturing").

5.4. Configuration and planning

The distinction between configuration and planning requires some discussion. We will argue that they are two points of view for the single problem of designing a system. For example, consider how the the problem of devising a vacation travel plan is equivalent to configuring a complex system consisting of travel, lodging, restaurant, and entertainment businesses and specifying how that system will service a particular person or group of people. "Configure" views the task as that of organizing objects into some system that as a functioning whole will process/transform another (internal) system (its input). "Plan," as used here, turns this around, viewing the problem in terms of how an entity is transformed by its interactions with another (surrounding) system. Figure 5-3 illustrates these two points of view.

VLSI design is a paradigmatic example of the "configuration" point of view. The problem is to piece together physical objects so that their behaviors interact to produce the desired system behavior.

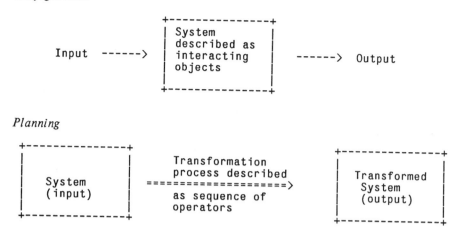

Configuration

Planning

Figure 5-3:   The design problem seen from two perspectives

The "planning" point of view itself can be seen from two perspectives depending on whether a subsystem or a surrounding global system is being serviced:

1. *We service some system by moving it around for processing by subsystems of a surrounding world.* Paradigmatic examples are experiment planning (e.g., MOLGEN (Stefik, 1980, Friedland, 1979)) and shop scheduling (e.g., ISIS (Fox and Smith, 1984)). ASSEMBLY always involves planning of this form, and strictly speaking Stefik's MOLGEN solves an assembly problem, designing a system that physically constructs a DNA/cell configuration (a pre-designed subsystem).   Equivalent examples are errand planning (Hayes-Roth and Hayes-Roth, 1979), vacation, and education plans. Here there is a well-defined object that is transformed by a well-defined sequence of interactions.   In general, we do not care how the surrounding system is modified by these interactions, except that there are resource constraints effecting planning when many systems are being serviced.

2. *We specify how a well-defined object system will service a larger system in which it is contained.* Servicing is done by "moving the object system around."   The paradigmatic example is the traveling salesman problem.   Most realistic problems are hybrid because the "service subsystem" is resource limited and must be "restocked" and "refueled" by the surrounding system. *Truckin'*, the game used for teaching LOOPS (Stefik, et al., 1983), makes this clear.   The traditional traveling salesman problem takes this form when allowance is made for food or fuel stops, etc.

While we appear to have laid out three perspectives on design, they are all computationally equivalent. It's our point of view about *purpose* and structuredness of interactions that makes it easier to understand a system in one way rather than another. In particular, in the first form of planning, the serviced subsystem is getting more organized as a result of its interactions. The surrounding world is modified in generally entropy-increasing ways as its resources are depleted. In the second form of planning the serviced world is getting more organized, while the servicing subsystem depletes its resources. Without considering the entropy change, *there is just a single point of view of a surrounding system interacting with a contained subsystem.*

"Configuration" is concerned with the construction of well-structured systems. In particular, if subsystems correspond to physically-independent components, design is equivalent to literally assembling pieces so they spatially fit together with flow from input to output ports producing the desired result. (Note that R1 is given some of the pieces, not the functional properties of the computer system it is configuring. The functional design is implicit in the roster of pieces it is asked to configure—the customer's order.) It is a property of any system that can be described in this way that it is hierarchically decomposable into modular, locally interacting subsystems—the definition of a well-structured system. As Simon (Simon, 1969) points out, it is sufficient for design tractability for systems to be "nearly decomposable," with weak, but non-negligible interactions among modules.

Now, to merge this with the conception of "planning," consider how an abstract process can be visualized graphically in terms of a diagram of connected operations. The recent widespread availability of computer graphics has revolutionized how we visualize systems (processes and computations). Examples of traditional and more recent attempts to visualize the structure of processes are:

- *Flowcharts.* A program is a system. It is defined in terms of a sequence of operations for transforming a subsystem, the data structures of the program. Subprocedures and sequences of statements are subsystems that are structurally blocked and connected.

- *Automata theory.* Transition diagrams are one way of describing finite state machines. Petri nets and dataflow graphs are other, related, notations for describing computational processes (see (Sowa, 1984) for discussion).

- *Actors.* A system can be viewed in terms of interacting, independent agents that pass messages to one another. Emphasis is placed on rigorous, local specification of behaviors (Hewitt, 1979). Object-oriented programming (Goldberg and Robson, 1983) is in general an attempt to characterize systems in terms of a configuration, centering descriptions on objects that are pieced together, as opposed to centering on data transformations.

- *Thinglab.* (Borning, 1979) emphasized the use of multiple, graphic views for depicting a dynamic simulation of mutually constrained components of a system. Borning mentions the advantages of visual experimentation for understanding complex system interactions.

- *Rocky's Boots.* In this personal computer game[9], icons are configured to define a program, such as a sorting routine that operates on a conveyor belt. Movement icons permit automata to move around and interact with each other, thus describing "planning" (how systems will interact) from a "configuration" (combination of primitive structures) point of view.

- *FLIPP Displays.* Decision rules can be displayed in analog form as connected boxes that are interpreted by top-down traversal (see Figure 5-4). Subproblems can be visually "chunked"; logical reasoning can be visualized in terms of adjacency, blocking, alternative routes, etc. Characteristic of analog representations, such displays are economical, facilitating encoding and perception of interactions (Mackinlay and Genesereth, 1984).

- *Streams.* The structure of procedures can be made clearer by describing them in terms of the *signals* that flow from one stage in a process to another (Abelson, et al., 1985). Instead of modeling procedures in terms of time-varying objects (variables, see "planning" in Figure 5-3), we can describe procedures in terms of time-invariant streams. For example, a program might be characterized as ENUMERATE + FILTER + MAP + ACCUMULATE, a configuration of connected subprocesses. Stream descriptions, inspired by signal processing diagrams, allow a programmer to visualize processes in a succinct way that reveals the structural similarity of programs.

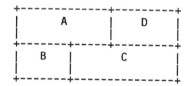

Figure 5-4: Simple FLIPP display, encoding rules A->B, A->C, and D->C. (From (Cox, 1984).)

These examples suggest that we have not routinely viewed "planning" problems in terms of

---

[9]The Learning Company, Menlo Park, CA.

35

system "configuration" because we have not had adequate notations for visualizing interactions. In particular, we have lacked tools for graphically displaying hierarchical interactions and movement of subsystems through a containing system. Certainly a large part of the problem is that interactions can be *opportunistic*, so the control strategy that affects servicing (in either form of planning) is not specifiable as a fixed sequence of interactions. The inability to graphically illustrate flexible strategies was one limitation of the original Actors formalism (Hewitt, 1979). On the other hand, control strategies themselves may be specifiable as a hierarchy of processes, even though they are complex and allow for opportunism. The representation of procedures in HERACLES as layered rule sets (corresponding to tasks) (with both data-directed reasoning encoded as a separate set of tasks and inherited "interrupt" conditions) is an example of a well-structured encoding of an opportunistic strategy. More generally, strategy might be graphically visualized as layers of object-level operations and agenda-processing operations.

In general, a configuration point of view is impossible when physical or planning structures are unstable, with many global interactions (Hewitt, 1979). It is difficult or impossible to plan in such a world; this suggests that most practical planning problems can be characterized in terms of configuration. It is interesting to note that replacing state descriptions (configurations) with process descriptions has played an important role in scientific understanding of the origins of systems (Simon, 1969). As illustrated by the examples of this section, to understand these processes, we return to a configuration description, but now at the level of the structure of the process instead of the system it constructs or interprets.

5.5. Combinations of system problems

Given the above categorization of construction and interpretation problems, it is striking that expert systems tend to solve a sequence of problems pertaining to a given system in the world. Two sequences that commonly occur are:

- **The Construction Cycle:** SPECIFY + DESIGN {+ ASSEMBLE}
  An example is R1 with its order processing front-end, XSEL. Broadly speaking, selecting a book for someone in GRUNDY is *single-step planning*; the person is "serviced" by the book. Other examples are selecting a wine or a class to attend. The common sequence of terms in business, "plan and schedule," are here named SPECIFY (objectives) and PLAN (activities).

- **The Maintenance Cycle:** {MONITOR + PREDICT +} DIAGNOSE + MODIFY
  This is the familiar pattern of medical programs, such as MYCIN. The sequence of MONITOR and PREDICT is commonly called *test* (repeatedly observing system behavior on input selected to verify output predictions). MODIFY is also called *therapy.*

This brings us back to the BES table (Figure 5-1), which characterizes INSTRUCTION and CONTROL as a sequence of primitive system operations. We can characterize the expert systems we have studied as such sequences of operations:

- MYCIN = MONITOR (patient state) + DIAGNOSE (disease category) + IDENTIFY (bacteria) + MODIFY (body system or organism)

- GRUNDY = IDENTIFY (person type) + PLAN (reading plan)

- SACON = IDENTIFY (structure type) + PREDICT (approximate numeric model) + IDENTIFY (classes of analysis for refined prediction)

- SOPHIE = MONITOR (circuit state) + DIAGNOSE (faulty module/component)

When a problem solver uses heuristic classification for multiple steps, as in GRUNDY, we say that the problem-solving method is *sequential heuristic classification.* Solutions for a given classification (e.g., stereotypes of people) become data for the next classification step. Note that Mycin does not strictly do sequential classification because it does not have a well-developed classification of patient types, though this is a reasonable model of how human physicians reason. However, it seems fair to say that MYCIN does perform a monitoring operation in that it requests specific information about a patient to characterize his state; this is clearer in NEOMYCIN and CASNET where there are many explicit, intermediate patient state descriptions. On the other hand, SOPHIE provides a better example of monitoring because it interprets global behavior, attempting to detect faulty components by comparison with a standard, correct model (discrepancies are violated assumptions).

It should be noted that how a problem is characterized in system terms may depend on our purpose, what "problem" we are attempting to solve in doing the system analysis or in building an expert system. For example, the OCEAN program (a product of Teknowledge, Inc.) checks configurations of computer systems. From a broad perspective, it is performing a MONITOR operation of the system that includes the human designer. Thus, OCEAN's inputs are the constraints that a designer should satisfy, plus the output of his designing process. However, unlike DEBUGGY, we are not interested in understanding and correcting the designer's reasoning. Our purpose is to determine whether the computer system design meets certain specification constraints (e.g., power and space limitations) and to make minor corrections to the design. Thus, it seems more straightforward to say that OCEAN is doing a CONFIGURATION task, and we have given it a possible solution to greatly constrain its search.

Finally, for completeness, we note that robotics research is concerned chiefly with ASSEMBLY. Robotics is also converting CONTROL of systems from a purely numeric to a symbolic processing task. PREDICT in systems analysis has also traditionally involved numeric models. However, progress in the area of qualitative reasoning (also called mental models)

(Bobrow, 1984) has made this another application for heuristic programming. Speech understanding is a strange case of identifying a system interaction between two speakers, attempting to characterize its output given a partial description (at the level of sounds) and environmental input (contextual) information.

Heuristic classification is particularly well-suited for problems of interpretation involving a system that is known to the problem solver. In this case, the problem solver can select from a set of systems he knows about (IDENTIFY), known system states (MONITOR), known system faults (DIAGNOSE), or known system behaviors (PREDICT/CONTROL). The heuristic classification method relies on experiential knowledge of systems and their behaviors. In contrast, constructing a new system requires construction of new structures (new materials or new organizations of materials). Nevertheless, we intuitively believe that experienced problem solvers construct new systems by modifying known systems. This confluence of classification and constructive problem solving is another important area for research.

Another connection the reader may have noticed: We made progress in understanding what expert systems do by describing them in terms of inference-structure diagrams. This vividly demonstrates the point made about streams, that it is highly advantageous to describe systems in terms of their configuration, *structurally*, providing dimensions for comparison. Gentner points out (Gentner and Stevens, 1983), that structural descriptions lie at the heart of analogy formation. A structural map of systems reveals similar relations among components, even though the components and/or their attributes may differ. This idea has been so important in research in the humanities during this century that it has been characterized as a movement with a distinct methodology, termed *structuralism* (De George and De George, 1972). The quotation by Bruner at the front of this paper describing the advantage of classification for a problem solver, applies equally well to the knowledge engineer.

6. INFERENCE STRATEGIES FOR HEURISTIC CLASSIFICATION

The arrows in inference-structure diagrams indicate the flow of inference, from data to conclusions. However, the actual order in which assertions are made is often not strictly left to right, from data to conclusions. This process, most generally called *search* or *inference control* has several aspects in heuristic classification:

- How does the problem solver get data? Is it supplied or must it be requested?

- If data is requested, how does the problem solver order his requests? (Called a *question-asking strategy*.)

- Does the problem solver *focus* on alternative solutions, requesting data on this basis?

38

- When new data is received, how is it used to make inferences?

- If there are choices to be made, alternative inference paths, how does the problem solver select which to attempt or which to believe?

In this section we first survey some well-known issues of focusing including data gathering, hypothesis testing, and data-directed inference. In this context, we introduce the HERACLES program, which is designed to solve problems by heuristic classification, and discuss its inference strategies. After this, we consider a kind of heuristic classification, termed *causal-process classification*, in order to understand the problem of choosing among inference paths. This discussion finally serves as a bridge to a consideration of non-classification or what we call *constructive* problem solving.

6.1. Focusing in heuristic classification

Focusing concerns what inferences the problem solver makes given new information or what inferences he attempts to make towards finding a solution.

The idea of a "triggering" relation between data and solutions is pivotal in almost all descriptions of heuristic classification inference (see (Rubin, 1975), (Szolovits and Pauker, 1978), (Aikins, 1983)). It is called a *constrictor* by Pople in recognition of how it sharply narrows the set of possible solutions (Pople, 1982). We say that "a datum triggers a solution" if the problem solver immediately thinks about that solution upon finding out about the datum. However, the assertion may be conditional (leading to an immediate request for more data) and is always context-dependent (though the context is rarely specified in our restricted-domain programs) (Clancey, 1984a). A typical trigger relation (from NEOMYCIN) is "Headache and red painful eye suggests glaucoma"—red, painful eye will trigger consideration of headache and thus glaucoma, but headache alone will not trigger this association. In PIP (Pauker et al., 1976), there is a two-stage process in which possible triggers are first brought into working memory by association with solutions already under consideration. In general, *specificity*—the fact that a datum is frequently associated with just a few solutions—determines if a datum suggests a solution concept ("brings it to mind") in the course of solving a problem.

Triggers allow search to non-exhaustively combine reasoning forwards from data or backwards from solutions. Simple classification is constrained to be hierarchically top-down or directly bottom up from known data, but heuristic triggers make search opportunistic. Briefly, a given heuristic classification network of data and solution hierarchies might be interpreted in three ways:

1. *Data-directed search*: The program works forwards from data to abstractions, matching solutions until all possible (or non-redundant) inferences have been made.

2. *Solution- or Hypothesis-directed search*: The program works backwards from solutions, collecting evidence to support them, working backwards through the

39

heuristic relations to the data abstractions and required data to solve the problem. If solutions are hierarchically organized, then categories are considered before direct features of more specific solutions.

3. *Opportunistic search*: The program combines data and hypothesis-directed reasoning (Hayes-Roth and Hayes-Roth, 1979). Data abstraction rules tend to be applied immediately as data become available. Heuristic rules trigger hypotheses, followed by a focused, hypothesis-directed search. New data may cause refocusing. By reasoning about solution classes, search need not be exhaustive.

Data- and hypothesis-directed search are not to be confused with the implementation terms "forward" or "backward chaining." R1 provides a superb example of how different the implementation and knowledge-level descriptions can be. Its rules are *interpreted* by forward-chaining, but it does a form of hypothesis-directed search, systematically setting up subproblems by a fixed procedure that focuses reasoning on spatial subcomponents of a solution (McDermott, 1982).

The degree to which search is focused depends on the level of indexing in the implementation and how it is exploited. For example, MYCIN's "goals" are solution classes (e.g., types of bacterial meningitis), but selection of rules for specific solutions (e.g., E.coli meningitis) is unordered. Thus, MYCIN's search within each class is unfocused (Clancey, 1983b). Generalized heuristics, of the form "data class implies solution class" (e.g., "compromised host implies gram-negative rods" or "flowers imply underlying rocks") make it possible to focus search on useful heuristics in both directions (e.g., if looking for serpentine rock, recall that flowers identify rocks; if describing area and see flowers, recall that flowers identify rocks).[10]

Opportunistic reasoning requires that at least some heuristics be indexed so that they can be applied in either direction, particularly so new data and hypothesized solutions can be related to previously considered data and solutions. The HERACLES program (Heuristic Classification Shell, the generalization of NEOMYCIN) cross-indexes data and solutions in several ways that were not available in EMYCIN. HERACLES' inference procedure consists of 75 metarules comprising 40 reasoning tasks (Clancey, 1984a). Focusing strategies include:

- working upwards in type hierarchies before gathering evidence for subtypes;

- discriminating hypotheses on the basis of their descriptions as processes;

---

[10]How human knowledge is indexed plays a major role in knowledge acquisition dialogues. The heuristic-classification model suggests that it may be efficient to proceed from data classes, asking the expert for associated solution classes. But it may be difficult to enumerate data classes. Instead, the expert might find it easier to work backwards from solutions (e.g., book categories) and then use a generate and test method to scan data prototypes (e.g., people stereotypes) for a match. Knowledge acquisition for heuristic classification is briefly considered in (Clancey, 1984b). See also the discussion of ETS in Section 10.

- making inferences that relate a new hypothesis to previously received data;

- seeking general classes of data before subclasses; and

- testing hypotheses by first seeking triggering data and necessary causes.

In HERACLES, the operators for making deductions are abstract, each represented by a set of metarules, corresponding to a procedure or alternative methods for accomplishing a task. Such a representation makes the explicit the inference control that is implicit in MYCIN's rules (Clancey, 1983b). As an example, Figure 6-1 illustrates how NEOMYCIN's abstract operators use backward deduction to confirm a hypothesized solution. (The program attempts to test the hypothesis TB by applying a domain rule mentioning ocular nerve dysfunction; to find this out, the program attempts to rule it out categorically, discovering that there is a CNS problem, but there are no focalsigns; consequently, the domain rule fails.)

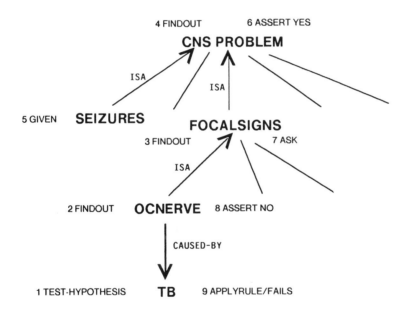

Figure 6-1: Backward deduction in NEOMYCIN to confirm a solution

As a second example, the following are some of the forward-deductive data-interpretation operators that HERACLES uses to relate a new datum to known solutions.

- Finding out more specific information so that a datum can be usefully related to hypotheses (e.g., given that the patient has a headache, finding out the duration and location of the headache).

- Making deductions that use the new datum to confirm "active" solutions (those previously considered, their taxonomic ancestors, and immediate siblings), sometimes called "focused forward-reasoning."

- Triggering possible solutions (restricted to abnormal findings that must be explained or "non-specific" findings not already explained by active solutions).

In general, the rationale for an inference procedure might be very complex. A study of HERACLES' inference procedure reveals four broad categories of constraints:

- mathematical (e.g., efficiency advantages of hierarchical search)

- sociological (e.g., cost for acquiring data),

- cognitive (e.g., computational resources), and

- problem expectations (e.g, characteristics of typical problems).

These are discussed in some detail in (Clancey, 1984a). Representing inference procedures so they can be explained and easily modified is currently an important research topic (e.g., see (Clancey, 1983a, Genesereth, 1983, Neches, et al., 1985). Making the *assumptions* behind these procedures explicit so they can be reasoned about and dynamically modified is a challenging issue that AI is just beginning to consider.

In its inference procedure representation, HERACLES brings together the advantages of rule and frame representations. The "frame" paradigm advocates the point of view that domain concepts can be represented as hierarchies, separated from the inference procedure—an essential point on which the generality of the heuristic classification model depends. On the other hand, the "rule" paradigm demonstrates that much of the useful problem-solving knowledge is in non-hierarchical associations, and that there are clear engineering benefits for procedures to be encoded explicitly, as well-indexed conditional actions. In HERACLES domain concepts are hierarchically related; domain rules represent heuristic, non-hierarchical associations; and metarules represent an inference procedure that interprets the domain knowledge, solving problems by heuristic classification. The architecture of HERACLES, with details about the encoding of metarules in MRS (Genesereth et al., 1981), a metarule compiler, and explanation program, is described in (Clancey, 1985).

6.2. Causal-process classification

A generic form of heuristic classification, commonly used for solving diagnostic problems, is *causal-process classification*. Data are generally observed malfunctions of some device, and solutions are abnormal processes causing the observed symptoms. We say that the inferred model of the device, the diagnosis, *explains* the symptoms. In general, there may be multiple causal explanations for a given set of symptoms, requiring an inference strategy that does not realize every possible association, but must reason about *alternative chains of inference.* In the worst case, even though diagnostic solutions are pre-enumerated (by definition), assertions might be taken back, so reasoning is non-monotonic. However, the most well-known programs that solve diagnostic problems by causal-process classification are monotonic, dealing with alternative lines of reasoning by assigning weights to the paths. Indeed, many programs do not even compare alternative explanations, but simply list all solutions, rank-ordered.

In this section, we will study SOPHIE in more detail (which reasons non-monotonically, using assumption-based belief maintenance), and compare it to CASNET (Weiss, et al., 1978) (which compares alternative chains of inference without explaining contradictions), and NEOMYCIN (Clancey and Letsinger, 1984) (which reasons exhaustively, using certainty factors to rank alternative inference chains). In these programs, solutions are pre-enumerated, but paths to them must be constructed. Our study serves several purposes: 1) to use the heuristic classification model to relate electronic and medical diagnosis, revealing that medical programs are generally trying to solve a broader problem; 2) To describe alternative heuristic classification inference strategies; and 3) To distinguish between classification and constructive problem solving.

6.2.1. Electronic and medical diagnosis compared

In SOPHIE, valid and abnormal device states are exhaustively enumerated, can be directly confirmed, and are causally related to component failures. None of this is generally possible in medical diagnosis, nor is diagnosis in terms of component failures alone sufficient for selecting therapy. Medical programs that deal with multiple disease processes (unlike MYCIN) do reason about abnormal states (called *pathophysiologic states,* e.g., "increased pressure in the brain"), directly analogous to the abnormal states in SOPHIE. But curing an illness generally involves determining the cause of the component failure. These "final causes" (called diseases, syndromes, etiologies) are processes that affect the normal functioning of the body (e.g., trauma, infection, toxic exposure, psychological disorder). Thus, medical diagnosis more closely resembles the task of computer system diagnosis in considering how the body relates to its environment (Lane, 1980). In short, there are two problems: First to explain symptoms in terms of abnormal internal states, and second to explain this behavior in terms of external influences (as well as congenital and degenerative component flaws). This is the inference structure of programs like CASNET and NEOMYCIN (Figure 6-2).

A network of pathophysiologic states causally relates data to diseases. States are linked to states, which are then linked to diseases in a classification hierarchy. Diseases may also be non-hierarchically linked by heuristics ("X is a complication of Y" (Szolovits and Pauker, 1978)). The causal relations in these programs are heuristic because they assume certain

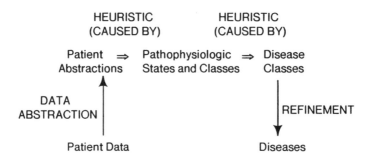

Figure 6-2: Inference structure of causal process classification

physiologic structure and behavior, which is often poorly understood and not represented. In contrast with pathophysiologic states, diseases are abstractions of *processes*—causal stories with agents, locations, and sequences of events. Disease networks are organized by these process features (e.g., an organ system taxonomy organizes diseases by location). A more general term for disease is *disorder stereotype*. In *process control* problems, such as chemical manufacturing, the most general disorder stereotypes correspond to stages in a process (e.g., mixing, chemical reaction, filtering, packaging). Subtypes correspond to what can go wrong at each stage (Clancey, 1984a).

Structure/function models are often touted as being more general by doing away with "ad hoc symptom-fault rules" (Genesereth, 1984). But programs that make a single fault assumption, such as DART, select a diagnosis from a pre-enumerated list, in this case negations of device descriptions, e.g., (NOT (XORG X1)), "X1 is not an exclusive-or gate." However, a structure/function model makes it possible to *construct tests* (see Section 7). Note that it is not generally possible to construct structure/function models for the human body, and is currently even impractical for the circuit SOPHIE diagnoses (IP-28 power supply).

To summarize, a knowledge-level analysis reveals that medical and electronic diagnosis programs are not all trying to solve the same kind of problem. Examining the nature of solutions, we see that in an electronic circuit diagnosis program like SOPHIE solutions are component flaws. Medical diagnosis programs like CASNET attempt a second step, *causal process classification*, which is to explain abnormal states and flaws in terms of processes external to the device or developmental processes affecting its structure. It is this experiential knowledge—what can affect the device in the world—that is captured in disease stereotypes. This knowledge can't simply be replaced by a model of device structure and function, which is concerned with a different level of analysis.

The heuristic classification model and our specific study of causal process classification programs significantly clarifies what NEOMYCIN knows and does, and how it might be improved:

1. Diseases are processes affecting device structure and function;

2. Disease knowledge takes the form of schemas;

3. Device history schemas (classes of patients) are distinct from diseases;

4. Pathophysiologic states are malfunctioning module behaviors.

Furthermore, it is now clear that the original (bacteremia) MYCIN system does a combination of heuristic classification (using patient information to classify cultures as contaminated or significant) and simple classification (matching features of organisms, such as Gram stain and morphology). The meningitis knowledge base is more complex because it can infer the organism class heuristically, from patient abstractions, without having a culture result. NEOMYCIN goes a step further by dealing with *different processes* (infectious, trauma, psychogenic, etc.) and reasoning backwards from internal descriptions of current system states (e.g., brain mass lesion) to determine original causes (etiologies).

An important idea here is that medical diagnostic programs should separate descriptions of people from descriptions of diseases heuristically associated with them. Triggers should suggest patient types, just as they select diseases. Thus, medical diagnostic reasoning, when it takes the form of heuristic classification, is analogous to the problem-solving stages of GRUNDY, the expert librarian.

6.2.2. Inference control for coherency

As mentioned above, programs differ in whether they treat pathophysiologic states as independent solutions (NEOMYCIN) or find the causal path that best accounts for the data (CASNET). If problem features interact, so that one datum causes another (D1 -> D2 in Figure 6-3), then paths of inference cannot be correctly considered independently. The second feature explains the first, so classifications (alternative explanations) of the former can be omitted; there is a "deeper cause" (C2 dominates C1). This presumes a single fault, an assumption common to programs that solve problems by heuristic classification. CASNET uses a more comprehensive approach of finding the path with the greatest number of confirmed states and no denied states. The path describes a causal process, with an etiology or ultimate cause at the head and the path of states linking the etiology to the findings serving as a causal explanation of the findings.

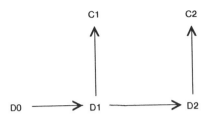

Figure 6-3: Interacting data in classification

In the simplest rule-based systems, such as MYCIN, search is exhaustive and alternative reasoning paths are compared by numerical belief propagation (e.g., certainty factors). For example, Figure 6-4 shows that a datum, D1, is explained by two processes, C1 and C2. MYCIN and NEOMYCIN would make all three inferences, using certainty factor combination to determine which of C1 and C2 is more likely.

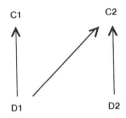

Figure 6-4: Multiple explanations for a datum

A more complicated approach involves detecting that one reasoning path is subsumed by another, such as the conflict-resolution strategy of ordering production rules according to specificity. HERACLES/NEOMYCIN's treatment of non-specific and "red flag" triggers is similar. In this case, assuming that D1 is a non-specific finding (associated with many disorders and may not need to be explained) and D2 is a red-flag finding (serious symptom that must be explained) that triggered C2, NEOMYCIN will not make the inference relating D1 to C1 because D1 is already explained by C2. Therefore, C1 will not be added to the list of possible solutions.

After finding some single classification that accounts for the most data, a residue of unexplained findings may remain. The approach used in CASNET and INTERNIST is to remove the explained data and simply begin another cycle of classification to explain what remains. In our example, both D1 and D2 would be explained by C2, so nothing would remain.

To summarize, when there are multiple causal links for classifying data—multiple explanations—inference must be controlled to avoid redundancy, namely multiple explanations were one would have been sufficient. The aim is to produce a *coherent* model that is *complete* (accounting for the most data) and *simple* (involving one fault process, if possible). In contrast with the idea of focussing discussed earlier, coherency places constraints on the sum total of inferences that have been made, not just the order in which they are made.

Of course, for an explanation based on a pathophysiological network to be coherent, it is necessary that inferences be consistent. For example, if D1 and D2 are contradictory, the network shown in Figure 6-4 will not produce consistent explanations. (C2 would depend on contradictory facts.) Presumably the knowledge engineer has ensured that all paths are consistent and that contradictory alternatives are explicit (e.g., by introducing (NOT D1) to the path including D2).

An ideal way to avoid these problems is to perform the diagnosis using a model of a correctly working device, in contrast with a network of pathophysiological states. This is the method used by SOPHIE. A consistent interpretation includes the observed data and assumptions about the operation of circuit components. A fault is detected by making inferences about circuit behavior in the case at hand until a contradiction is found. Specifically, SOPHIE uses assumption-based belief maintenance to detect faults. It propagates constraints (describing device behavior), records assumptions (about correct behavior of components and modules) upon which inferences are based, explains contradictory inferences in terms of violated assumptions, and makes measurements to narrow down the set of possibly violated assumptions to a single fault. Making assumptions explicit and reasoning about them ensures coherency, rather than relying on its implicit and ad hoc encoding in the design of a state network.

6.2.3. Multiple solutions and levels of detail

The first step beyond selecting single pre-enumerated faults is to dynamically construct *sets of alternative faults*, as proposed for CADUCEUS (Pople, 1982). Each set of faults constitutes a *differential diagnosis* or set of alternative diagnoses. Each diagnosis consists of one or more faults. A diagnosis of multiple faults is constructed by operators that combine disorders in terms of subtype and cause. For example, referring to Figure 6-4, one differential diagnosis would include C1 & C2; another would include C2, but not C1.

The next more complicated approach allows for interactions among disorders, as in ABEL (Patil, 1981a). Interaction can take the form of masking or subtracting (quantitative) effects, summation of effects, or superimposition with neither subtraction or summation. These interactions are predicted and explained in ABEL by finding a state network, including normal states, that is *consistent on multiple levels of detail*. Combinatorial problems, as well as elegance, argue against pre-enumerating such networks, so solutions must be constructed. Each diagnostic hypothesis is a separately constructed *case-specific model*—the links describing the individual case do not all pre-exist in the knowledge base.

A simple way of comparing this kind of reasoning to what occurs in classification is to consider how concepts are instantiated and related in the two approaches. In a program like

MYCIN, there are case-specific instances, but they are only the most general concepts in the knowledge base—the the patient, laboratory cultures, organisms, and drugs. Links among these instances (or individuals), constituting the "context tree," are dynamically created (albeit given as data) to form a case-specific model. In contrast, in ABEL case-specific, constructed descriptions are also at the level of individual disorders and their causes—disease components are instantiated and linked together in novel ways (thus allowing for interaction among diseases).

6.2.4. Constructing implication paths vs. constructing solutions

If all programs construct inference paths, aren't they all solving problems by construction of solutions? At issue is a point of view about what is a solution.

In NEOMYCIN, CASNET, and SOPHIE, the solutions are single faults, pre-enumerated. Reasoning about inference paths is a mechanism for selecting these solutions. While an inference path through the causal network of CASNET or NEOMYCIN is a disease process description, it is only a linear path, no different from a chain of implication in MYCIN. While links represent subtype and cause, they are interpreted in a uniform way for propagating weights. We conclude that if there is only one operator for building inference paths, the program is not constructing a solution, but is only selecting the nodes at the end points of its reasoning chains. All of the programs we characterize as doing constructive problem solving either have a generator for solutions or must choose among multiple operators for constructing a solution. The solutions aren't explicitly enumerated, so there can be *no pre-existing links for mapping problem descriptions to solutions directly.* In ABEL and CADUCEUS, solutions are descriptions of disease processes, constructed by operators for incrementally elaborating and aggregating solution components, which is more than just propagating belief (what we commonly call "implication"). The constructed solution is not simply an inference path from data to solution, but a *configuration* of primitive solution components; these programs *configure disease descriptions*, they do not select them directly.

It should now be abundantly clear that it is incorrect to say that diagnosis is a "classification problem." As Pople concluded in analyzing the inadequacies of INTERNIST, only *routine* medical diagnosis problems can be solved by classification (Pople, 1982). When there are multiple diseases, there are too many possible combinations for the problem solver to have considered them all before. The problem solver must construct a consistent network of interacting diseases to explain the symptoms. The problem solver *formulates a solution*; he doesn't just make yes-no decisions from a set of fixed alternatives. For this reason, Pople calls non-routine medical diagnosis an ill-structured problem (Simon, 1973), though it may be more appropriate to reserve this term for the theory formation task of the physician-scientist who is defining new diseases. To make the point most boldly: GRUNDY, the librarian, could satisfy a reader by constructing a solution, that is, writing a new book.

7. CONSTRUCTIVE PROBLEM SOLVING, AN INTRODUCTION

In a study of problem solving, Greeno and Simon characterize kinds of problems in terms of the constraints imposed on the problem solver.

> In a transformation problem such as the Tower of Hanoi, or finding a proof for a theorem, the goal is a specific [given] arrangement of the problem objects, such as a specific location for all of the disks in the Tower of Hanoi, or a specific expression to be proved in logic. Thus, the question is not what to construct, as it is in a problem of design, but how the goal can be constructed with the limited set of operators available.... (Greeno and Simon, 1984)

While different tasks do impose different constraints on the problem solver, we have argued that experiential knowledge allows a "design" problem to be solved as if it were a "transformation" problem. For while design problems may not generally provide the problem solver with a specific solution to attain, he may from experience know of a solution that will work. In heuristic classification the solution space is known to the problem solver as a *set* of explicit alternatives, and problem solving takes the form of "proving" that one of them is best or acceptable.[11]

For example, in diagnostic programs that assume a single fault, such as NEOMYCIN, CASNET, SOPHIE, and DART, the inference process is equivalent to finding the most specific and most likely theorem (solution) that can be proved correct. Thus, the spectrum of problem solving effort and methodology is aligned at least as much with experience as with the nature of the task. Amarel makes this point in distinguishing between "derivation" and "formation" problems (Amarel, 1978), emphasizing that experience provides knowledge for mapping problem conditions to solutions. Thus, experience moves tasks for a given problem solver to the "derivation" end of the spectrum—heuristic classification.

Often problems of DESIGN and DIAGNOSIS are not amenable to solution by heuristic classification because possible final "states" cannot be practically enumerated, exhaustively learned (from experience or direct teaching), or for some reason a previously used solution is just not acceptable; solutions must be constructed rather than selected. However, even when solutions are constructed, classification might play a role, for example, in planning the problem-solving process or in selecting the pieces to be configured. The essential differences between heuristic construction and classification are the need for some "data structure" to post the assembled solution and operators for proposing and reasoning about solution fragments (Erman, et al., 1981). In classification, triggers focus the search, but may not be necessary; controlled forward-deduction from given data and hierarchical search in the set of fixed

---

[11]In adopting the heuristic classification model as a psychological theory, we must be more careful about this issue of explicitness. Human memory has properties different from knowledge base representations, so there is a difference between "explicitly known now" and "previously known." In practice, remembering a previous solution may require reconstruction, and hence some elements of constructive problem-solving.

solutions may be sufficient. In construction, triggers may be essential, as well as knowledge about how parts of a solution fit together.

The following are some examples of heuristic construction operators:

- In HASP, the ocean surveillance signal interpretation system (Nii, et al., 1982), one operator attaches a new line segment (from the input sensor) to a previous line that was last heard less than thirty minutes ago (with a certainty of .5), thus extending the model of the location of a particular vessel.

- ABEL has six "structure building" operators, including *projection* (to hypothesize associated findings and diseases suggested by states in the case-specific model) and *causal elaboration* (to determine causal relations between states at a detailed level, based on causal relations between states at the next aggregate level) (Patil, 1981b).

- AM has operators for proposing (syntactic) structural modifications to concepts. For example, a concept is generalized by deleting a conjunction in its characteristic function definition in Lisp (Lenat and Brown, 1984). One lesson of Eurisko is that complex concept formation requires a more extensive set of operators (defined in terms of conceptual relations, or as Lenat puts it, "slots for describing heuristics").

- MOLGEN (Stefik, 1980) has both assembly-design operators and laboratory-domain operators. PROPOSE-OPERATOR is a design operator that proposes a laboratory operator that will reduce differences between the goal and current state, extending the plan forward in time. It is "responsible for linking new laboratory steps correctly to the neighboring laboratory steps and goals." There are four kinds of physical, structure-modifying laboratory operators: merge, amplify, react, and sort.

- In DART, diagnosis is done by classification (and the use of the proof method is made explicit in the program description), but testing the circuit to gather more information (MONITOR) is done by construction. The abstract operator (IF (AND a1 ... am Ob) THEN (OR (NOT P1) ... (NOT Pn))) serves as a template for generating tests, where the ai's are achievable settings or structure changes, Ob is one or more observations to be made, and the Pi's are assumptions about correct device structure or function. Thus, a particular device setting and observations will confirm that one or more assumptions are violated, narrowing down the set of possible faults (similar to SOPHIE). Note that the heuristics used in DART are general search strategies used to control the deductive process, not domain-specific links. DART has heuristics and uses classification (for diagnosis), but it does not do heuristic classification, in the form we have described it. Specifically, it lacks experiential, schema knowledge for classifying device states and describing typical disorders.

- MYCIN's antibiotic therapy program (Clancey, 1984c) generates combinations of drugs from "instructions" that abstractly describe how the number of drugs and their preference are related. These generator instructions can be viewed as operators (or a grammar) for constructing syntactically correct solutions.

To summarize the alternative means of computing solutions we have seen:

1. Solutions might be *selected* from a pre-enumerated set, by classification.

2. Solutions may be *generated* whole, as in DENDRAL and MYCIN's therapy program.

3. Solutions may be *assembled* from primitives, incrementally, as in HASP.

As Simon indicates (Simon, 1969), these methods can be combined, sequentially or hierarchically (as in hierarchical planning), with perhaps alternative decompositions for a single system.

8. RELATING TOOLS, METHODS, AND TASKS

In our discussion we have emphasized the question, "What is the method for computing a solution?" We have made a distinction between data and solution in order to clarify the large-scale computational issues of constructing a solution versus selecting it from a known set. The logical next step is to relate what we have learned about conceptual structures, systems problems, and the classification/construction distinction to the tools available for building expert systems. Conventionally, the thing to do at this point would be to provide a big table relating tools and features. These can be found in many books (e.g., (Harmon and King, 1985)). The new analysis we can provide here is to ask which tool features are useful for heuristic classification and which are useful for constructive problem solving.

While simple rule-based languages like EMYCIN omit knowledge-level distinctions we have found to be important, particularly schema hierarchies, they have nevertheless provided an extremely successful programming framework for solving problems by classification. Working backwards (backchaining) from a pre-enumerated set of solutions guarantees that only the relevant rules are tried and useful data considered. Moreover, the program designer is encouraged to use means-ends analysis, a clear framework for organizing rule writing. EMYCIN and other simple rule-based systems are appropriate for solving problems by heuristic classification because inference chains are short (commonly five or fewer steps between raw data and solution), and each new rule can be easily viewed as adding a link in the mapping between data (or some intermediate abstraction) and solutions.

With the advent of more complex knowledge representations, such as KL-ONE, it is unclear whether advantages for explicit representation will be outweighed by the difficulty of learning to use these languages correctly. The analysis needed for identification of classes and relations and proper adherence to representational conventions might require considerable experience, or even unusual analytical abilities (recall the analysis of concepts in Section 4.5). Recent research indicates that it might be difficult or practically impossible to design a language for conceptual structures that can be unambiguously and consistently used by knowledge engineers (Brachman, et al., 1983). Just as the rule notation was "abused" in MYCIN by ordering rule clauses to encode hierarchical and procedural knowledge, users of KL-ONE implicitly encode knowledge in structural properties of concept hierarchies, relying on the effect of the interpreter to make correct inferences. Brachman, et al. propose a model of *knowledge representation competence*, in which a program is told what is true and what it should do, and left to encode the knowledge according to its own conventions to bring about the correct reasoning performance.[12]

While many of the conceptual structures and inference mechanisms required to encode a heuristic classification problem solver have now been identified, no knowledge engineering tool today combines these capabilities in a complete package. Perhaps the best system for classification we could imagine might be a combination of KL-ONE (so that conceptual relations are explicit and to provide automatic categorization of concepts (Schmolze and Lipkis, 1983)), HERACLES (so that the inference procedure is explicit, well-structured, and independent of domain knowledge representation), and SHRINK (Kolodner, 1982) (to provide automatic refinement of classifications through problem-solving experience). In this respect, it should be noted there is some confusion about the nature of heuristic classification in some recent commercial tools on the market. Close inspection reveals that they are capable of only simple classification, lacking structures for data abstraction, as well as a means to separate definitional features from heuristic associations between concepts (Harmon and King, 1985).

Regarding constructive problem solving, the major distinction among tools appears to be the method for coping with alternative choices in configuring a solution. Tools for constructive

---

[12]See (Levesque, 1984) for details. In apparent conflict with our use of inference diagrams to describe what a heuristic-classification problem solver knows, Levesque says, "There is nothing to say about the *structure* of these abstract bodies of knowledge called knowledge bases." One way of resolving this is to say that knowledge *content* has structure, but knowledge-level specification is not *about* structures in the agent (problem solver). This is supported by Newell's remark, "Relationships exist between goals, of course, but these are not realized in the structure of the system, but in knowledge." (Newell, 1982) This is our intent in separating the abstract characterization of what a problem solver knows (heuristic classification model) from its encoding in the agent's symbol system (expert system representation).

problem solving necessarily include methods for controlling search that go beyond the focusing operations found in tools that solve problems by classification. For example, well-known search control methods used in construction include: Least-commitment (Stefik, 1980) (avoiding decisions that constrain future choices), representing explicitly multiple "hypothetical" worlds (branching on choices to construct alternative solutions), variable propagation or relaxation (systematic refinement of solutions), backtracking (retracting constructions), version space search (Mitchell, 1982) (bounding a solution using variables and constraints), and debugging (Sussman, 1975) (modifying an unsatisfactory solution).

What have we learned that enables us to match problems to tools? Given a task, such as troubleshooting, we might have previously asked, "Is this tool good for diagnosis?" Now, we insert an intermediate question about *computational requirements*: Is it possible or acceptable to pre-enumerate solutions? Is it possible or acceptable to rank order solutions? Rather than matching tasks to tools directly, we interpose some questions about the method for computing solutions. The basic choice of classification versus construction is the missing link for relating implementation terminology ("rules," "blackboard," "units") to high-level conceptual structures and inference requirements.

In summary, we suggest the following sequence of questions for matching problems to tools:

1. Describe the problem in terms of a sequence of operations relating to systems. If the problem concerns ASSEMBLY or construction of a perceptual system, seek a specialist in another area of AI. If the problem concerns numerical SIMULATION or CONTROL, it might be solved by traditional systems analysis techniques.

2. Do constraints on customization or naturally occurring variety allow the solution space to be practically pre-enumerated? If so, use heuristic classification. If not, is there a hierarchical or grammatical description that can be used to generate possible solutions? Are there well-defined solution-construction operators that are constrained enough to allow an incremental (state-space) search?

3. Are there many uncertain choices that need to be made? If a few, exhaustive generation with a simple certainty-weighing model may be sufficient; if many, some form of lookahead or assumption/justification-based inference mechanism will be necessary.

The notation of inference structures diagrams used in this paper can also be used to form a knowledge specification that can then be mapped onto the constructs of a particular knowledge representation language. First, identify and list possible solutions, data, and intermediate (more general) categories. Examining inference chains, classify links between concepts as definitional, type categorization, and heuristic. Draw an inference structure diagram to arrange relations within a type hierarchy vertically and show heuristics as horizontal lines. Finally, map this diagram into a given representation language. For example, subtype links are represented as ordered clauses in an EMYCIN rule: "If the patient has an infection, and the kind of infection is meningitis, and ...."

Our study suggests two additional perspectives for critiquing constructive tools. Viewing *solutions* as models of systems in the world, we require means for detecting and controlling the coherency (completeness and consistency) of inferences. In describing *computational methods* in terms of operators, we need means to construct, record, and relate inference graphs. We conclude that the method by which inference is controlled—how an inference graph representing a system model is computed—is a crucial distinction for comparing alternative knowledge engineering tools for constructive problem solving. Relating the above methods for constructing solutions (e.g., version space, least commitment, blackboard architecture) to problem tasks is beyond the scope of this paper. It is possible that the problem categories of Section 5 will be useful. Though they may prove to be an orthogonal consideration, as we discovered in distinguishing between classification and construction.

9. KNOWLEDGE-LEVEL ANALYSIS

As a set of terms and relations for describing knowledge (e.g, data, solutions, kinds of abstraction, refinement operators, the meaning of "heuristic"), the heuristic classification model provides a *knowledge-level analysis* of programs (Newell, 1982). As defined by Newell, a knowledge-level analysis "serves as a specification of what a reasoning system should be able to do." Like a specification of a conventional program, this description is distinct from the representational technology used to implement the reasoning system. Newell cites Schank's conceptual dependency structure as an example of a knowledge level analysis. It indicates "what knowledge is required to solve a problem... how to encode knowledge of the world in a representation." It should be noted that Newell intends for the knowledge-level specification to include the closure of what the reasoning system *might* know. Our approach to this problem is to characterize the problem solver's computational method and the structure of his knowledge. What a heuristic classification problem solver "is able to do" is specified in terms of the patterns of problem situations and solutions he knows and the space of (coherent) mappings from raw data to solutions.

After a decade of "explicitly" representing knowledge in AI languages, it is ironic that the pattern of heuristic classification should have been so difficult to see. In retrospect, certain views were emphasized at the expense of others:

- *Procedureless languages.* In an attempt to distinguish heuristic programming from traditional programming, procedural constructs are left out of representation languages (such as EMYCIN, OPS, KRL (Lehnert and Wilks, 1979)). Thus, inference relations cannot be stated separately from how they are to be used (Hayes, 1977, Hayes, 1979).

- *Heuristic nature of problem solving.* Heuristic association has been emphasized at the expense of the relations used in data abstraction and refinement. In fact, some expert systems do only simple classification; they have no heuristics or "rules of thumb," the key idea that is supposed to distinguish this class of computer programs.

- *Implementation terminology.* In emphasizing new implementation technology, terms such as "modular" and "goal directed" were more important to highlight than the content of the programs. In fact, "goal directed" characterizes any rational system and says very little about how knowledge is used to solve a problem. "Modularity" is a representational issue of indexing, how the knowledge objects can be independently accessed.

Nilsson has proposed that logic should be the *lingua franca* for knowledge-level analysis (Nilsson, 1981). Our experience suggests that the value of using logic is in adopting a set of terms and relations for describing knowledge (e.g., kinds of abstraction). Logic is especially valuable as a tool for knowledge-level analysis because it emphasizes *relations*, not just implication.

10. RELATED ANALYSES IN PSYCHOLOGY AND ARTIFICIAL INTELLIGENCE

Only a monograph-length review could do justice to the vast amount of research that relates to heuristic classification. Every discipline from ancient philosophy through modern psychology seems to have considered some part of the story.

Several AI researchers have described heuristic classification in part, influencing this analysis. For example, in CRYSALIS (Engelmore and Terry, 1979) data and solution abstraction are clearly separated. The EXPERT rule language (Weiss, 1979) similarly distinguishes between "findings" and a taxonomy of hypotheses. In PROSPECTOR (Hart, 1977), rules are expressed in terms of relations in a semantic network. In CENTAUR (Aikins, 1983), a variant of MYCIN, solutions are explicitly *prototypes* of diseases. Chandrasekaran and his associates have been strong proponents of the classification model: "The normal problem-solving activity of the physician... (is) a process of classifying the case as an element of a disease taxonomy" (Chandrasekaran and Mittal, 1983, Gomez and Chandrasekaran, 1984). Recently, Chandrasekaran, Weiss, and Kulikowski have generalized the classification schemes used by their programs [MDX (Chandrasekaran, 1984) and EXPERT (Weiss and Kulikowski, 1984)] to characterize problems solved by other expert systems.

In general, rule-based research in AI emphasizes the importance of heuristic association; frame systems emphasize the centrality of concepts, schema, and hierarchical inference. A series of knowledge representation languages beginning with KRL have identified structured abstraction and matching as a central part of problem solving (Bobrow and Winograd, 1979). These ideas are well-developed in KL-ONE, whose structures are explicitly designed for classification (Schmolze and Lipkis, 1983).

Building on the idea that "frames" are not just a computational construct, but a theory about a kind of knowledge (Hayes, 1979), cognitive science studies have described problem solving in terms of classification. For example, routine physics problem solving is described by Chi (Chi, et al., 1981) as a process of data abstraction and heuristic mapping onto solution schemas ("experts cite the abstracted features as the relevant cues (of physics principles)"). The inference structure of SACON, heuristically relating structural abstractions to numeric models, is the same. In NEWTON, De Kleer referred to packages of equations, associated with problem features, as RALCMs (Restricted Access Local Consequent Methods) ("with this representation, only a few decisions are required to determine which equations are relevant") (de Kleer, 1979).

Related to the physics problem solving analysis is a very large body of research on the nature of schemas and their role in understanding (Schank, 1975, Rumelhart and Norman, 1983). More generally, the study of classification, particularly of objects, also called *categorization*, has been a basic topic in psychology for several decades (e.g., see the chapter on "conceptual thinking" in (Johnson-Laird and Wason, 1977) and (Rosch and Lloyd, 1978)). However, in psychology the emphasis has been on the nature of categories and how they are formed (an issue of learning). The programs we have considered make an identification or selection from a pre-existing classification (an issue of memory retrieval). In recent work, Kolodner combines the retrieval and learning process in an expert system that learns from experience (Kolodner, 1982). Her program uses the MOPS representation, a classification model of memory that interleaves generalizations with specific facts (Kolodner, 1983).

Probably the most significant work on classification was done by Bruner and his colleagues in the 1950's (Bruner, et al., 1956). Bruner was concerned with the nature of concepts (or categories), how they were attained (learned), and how they were useful for problem solving. A few quotes illustrate the clarity and relevance of his work:

> To categorize is to render discriminably different things equivalent, to group objects and events and people around us into classes, and to respond to them in terms of their class membership rather than their uniqueness. (Bruner, et al., 1956) (page 1)

> ...the task of isolating and using a concept is deeply imbedded in the fabric of cognitive life; that indeed it represents one of the most basic forms of inferential activity in all cognitive life. (page 79)

> ...[what] we have called "concept attainment" in contrast to "concept formation" is the search for and testing of attributes that can be used to distinguish exemplars from nonexemplars of various categories, the search for good and valid anticipatory cues. (page 233)

Bruner described some of the heuristic aspects of classification:

> ... regard a concept as a network of sign-significate inferences by which one goes beyond a set of observed criterial properties exhibited by an object or event in question, and then to additional inferences about other *unobserved* properties of the object or event. (page 244)

> What does categorizing accomplish for the organism? ... it makes possible the sorting of functionally significant groupings in the world. (page 245)

We map and give meaning to our world by relating classes of events rather than by relating individual events. The moment an object is placed in a category, we have opened up a whole vista for "going beyond" the category by virtue of the superordinate and causal relationships linking this category to others. (page 13)

Bruner was well ahead of AI in realizing the centrality of categorization in problem solving. Particularly striking is his emphasis on strategies for selecting cues and examples, by which the problem solver directs his learning of new categories ("information gathering strategies"). Bruner's study of hypothesis formation and strategies for avoiding errors in learning is particularly well-developed, "For concern about error, we contend, is a necessary condition for evoking problem-solving behavior" (page 210) [compare to "failure-driven memory" (Schank, 1981) and "impasses" (VanLehn, 1983)].

On the other hand, Bruner's description of a concept is impoverished from today's point of view. The use of toy problems (colored cards or blocks, of course) suggested that categorization was based on "direct significants"—a logical combination of observable, discriminating (perhaps probabilistic) features. This Aristotelian view persisted in psychology and psychometrics well into the 1970's, until the work of Rosch, who argues that concepts are prototypical, not sets of definitional features (Rosch, 1978, Mervis and Rosch, 1981, Cohen and Murphy, 1984, Greeno and Simon, 1984). Rosch's work was influenced by AI research, but it also had its own effect, particularly in the design of KRL (Bobrow and Winograd, 1979).

The heuristic classification model presented in this paper builds on the idea that categorization is not based on purely essential features, but rather is primarily based on *heuristic*, non-hierarchical, *but direct* associations between concepts. Bruner, influenced by game theory, characterizes problem solving (once a categorization was achieved) in terms of a payoff matrix; *cues are categorized to make single decisions of actions to take.* Influenced by the psychology of the day, he views problem solving in the framework of a stimulus and a response, where the stimulus is the "significant" (cues) and the response is the action that the categorization dictates. He gives examples of medical diagnosis in this form.

We have had the advantage of having a number of working models of reasoning to study—expert systems—whose complexity go well-beyond what Bruner was able to formally describe. We have observed that problem solving typically involves a sequence of categorizations. Each categorization can be characterized generically as an operation upon a system—specify, design, monitor, etc. Most importantly, we have seen that each classification is not a final consequence or objective in "a payoff matrix governing a situation" (page 239). Rather it is often a plateau chaining to another categorization. Bruner's payoff matrix encodes heuristic associations.

Building upon Rosch's analysis and developments in knowledge representation, recent research in cognitive science has significantly clarified the nature of concepts (Cohen and Murphy, 1984, Rosch, 1978). In particular, attention has turned to why concepts take the form they do.

While many concepts are based on *natural kinds* (e.g., MYCIN's organisms and GRUNDY's books), others are *experiential* (e.g., reader and patient stereotypes of people), or *analytic* (e.g., SOPHIE's module behavior lattice and SACON's programs). Miller (Miller, 1978) suggests that formation of a category is partly constrained by its heuristic implication. Thus, therapeutic implication in medicine might serve to define diagnostic and person categories, working backwards from pragmatic actions to observables. This functional, even behavioral, view of knowledge is somewhat disturbing to those schooled in the definition of concepts in terms of essential features, but it is consistent with our analysis of expert systems. Future studies of what people know, and the nature of meaning, will no doubt depart even more from essential features to consider heuristic "accidental" associations in more detail.

Finally, learning of classifications has been a topic in AI for some time. Indeed, interest goes back to early work in pattern recognition. As Chandrasekaran points out (Chandrasekaran, 1984), it is interesting to conceive of Samuels' hierarchical evaluation functions for checker playing as an implicit conceptual hierarchy. Recent work in classification, perhaps best typified by Michalski's research (Michalski and Stepp, 1983), continues to focus on learning essential or definitional features of a concept hierarchy, rather than heuristic associations between concepts. However, this form of learning, emphasizing the role of object attributes in classification, is an advance over earlier approaches that used numeric measures of similarity and lacked a conceptual interpretation. Also, working from the traditional research of psychometrics, Boose's ETS knowledge acquisition program (Boose, 1984) makes good use of a psychological theory of concept associations, called *personal construct theory*. However, ETS elicits only simple classifications from the expert, does not exploit distinctions between hierarchical, definition, and heuristic relations, and has no provision for data abstraction.

Perhaps the greatest value of the heuristic classification model is that it provides an overarching point of view for relating pattern recognition, machine learning, psychometrics, and knowledge representation research.

11. SUMMARY OF KEY OBSERVATIONS

The heuristic classification model may seem obvious or trivial after it is presented, but the actual confusion about knowledge engineering tools, problem-solving methods, and kinds of problems has been quite real in AI for the past decade. Some might say, "What else could it be? It had to be classification"—as if a magic trick has been revealed. But the point of this paper is not to show a new kind of trick, or a new way of doing magic tricks, but to demystify traditional practice.

Sowa's reference to Levi-Strauss' anthropological "systems analysis" is apt:

The sets of features ... seem almost obvious once they are presented, but finding the right features and categories may take months or years of analysis. The proper set of categories provides a structural framework that helps to organize the detailed facts and general principles of a system. Without them, nothing seems to fit, and the resulting system is far too complex and unwieldy.

Expert systems are in fact *systems*. To understand them better, we have given high-level descriptions of how solutions are computed. We have also related the tasks of these programs to the kinds of things one can do to or with a concrete system in the world. Below is a summary of the main arguments:

- A broad view of how a solution is *computed* suggests that there are two basic problem-solving methods used by expert systems: heuristic classification and construction.

- Kinds of inference in different stages of routine problem solving vary systematically, so data are often generalized or redefined, while solutions are more often matched schematically and refined. A domain-specific heuristic is a direct, non-hierarchical association between different classes. It is not a categorization of a "stimulus" or "cue" that directly matches a concept's definition. Rather, there may be a chain of abstraction inferences before reaching categories that usefully characterize problem features. This pattern is shown two ways in Figures 2-3 and 4-5. The inference structure of heuristic classification is common in expert systems, independent of the implementation representation in rules, frames, ordinary code, or some combination.

- Selecting solutions involves a form of proof that is often characterized as derivation or planning; constructing solutions involves piecing together solutions in a manner characterized as configuration. To *select* a solution, the problem solver needs experiential ("expert") knowledge in the form of *patterns of problems and solutions* and heuristics relating them. To *construct* a solution, the problem solver applies models of structure and behavior, in the form of constraints and inference operators, by which objects can be designed, assembled, diagnosed, employed in some plan, etc.

- A broad view of kinds of problems, described in terms of synthesis and analysis of *systems*, suggests two points of view for describing a system's design: a configuration in terms of structural relations of functional components, versus a plan for the processes that characterize the system's behavior. From the point of view of a *system*, reasoning may involve a limited set of generic operations, e.g., MONITOR, DIAGNOSE, REPAIR. In heuristic classification, this takes the form of a sequence of mapping between classifications corresponding to each generic operation.

- In a manner analogous to *stream* descriptions of computer programs, the inference structure diagrams used in this paper reveal the patterns of reasoning in expert systems.

12. IMPLICATIONS

A wide variety of problems can be solved by heuristic mapping of data abstractions onto a fixed, hierarchical network of solutions. This problem-solving model is supported by psychological studies of human memory and categorization. There are significant implications for expert systems research. The model provides:

- *A high-level structure for decomposing problems*, making it easier to recognize and represent similar problems. For example, problems can be characterized in terms of sequences of system classifications. Catalog selection (single step planning) programs might be improved by incorporating a more distinct phase of user modelling, in which needs or requirements are classified first. Diagnosis programs might profitably make a stronger separation between device-history stereotypes and disorder knowledge. "Blackboard" systems might re-represent "knowledge sources" to distinguish between classification and construction inference operators.

- *A specification for a generic knowledge engineering tool* designed specifically for heuristic classification. The advantages for knowledge acquisition carry over into explanation and teaching.

- *A basis for choosing application problems.* For example, problems can be selected using the systems taxonomy (Figures 5-1 and 5-2), allowing knowledge engineers to systematically gain experience in different kinds of problems. Problems might be chosen specifically because they can be solved by heuristic classification.

- *A foundation for characterizing epistemologic adequacy of representation languages* (McCarthy and Hayes, 1969), so that the leverage they provide can be better understood. For example, for classification it is advantageous for a language to provide constructs for representing problem solutions as a network of schemas.

- *A focus for cognitive studies* of human categorization of knowledge and search strategies for retrieval and matching, suggesting principles that might be used in expert programs. Human learning research might similarly focus on the inference structure of heuristic classification.

Finally, it is important to remember that expert systems are programs. Basic computational ideas such as input, output, and sequence, are essential for describing what they do. The methodology of our study has been to ask, "What does the program conclude about? How does it get there from its input?" We characterize the flow of inference, identifying data abstractions, heuristics, implicit models and assumptions, and solution categories along the way. If heuristic programming is to be different from traditional programming, a knowledge-level analysis should always be pursued at least one level deeper than our representations, even if practical constraints prevent making explicit in the implemented program everything that we know. In this way, knowledge *engineering* can be based on sound principles that unite it with studies of cognition and representation.

Acknowledgments

These ideas were originally stimulated by discussions with Denny Brown in our attempt to develop a framework for teaching knowledge engineering. I am grateful to Teknowledge for providing an environment that allowed me to study and analyze a variety of expert systems.

I would also like to thank Tom Dietterich, Steve Hardy, and Peter Szolovits for their suggestions and early encouragement. Discussions with Jim Bennett, John Boose, Keith Butler, Lee Erman, Rick Hayes-Roth, Ramesh Patil, Paul Rosenbloom, Kurt Van Lehn, and Beverly Woolf have also been helpful.

This research has been supported in part by ONR and ARI Contract N00014-79C-0302 and the Josiah Macy, Jr. Foundation. Computational resources have been provided by the SUMEX-AIM facility (NIH grant RR00785).

References

Abelson, H., Sussman, G. J. and Sussman, J. *Structure and Interpretation of Computer Programs.* Cambridge: The MIT Press 1985.

Aiello, N. *A comparative study of control strategies for expert systems: AGE implementation of three variations of PUFF,* in *Proceedings of the National Conference on AI,* pages 1-4, Washington, D.C., August, 1983.

Aikins J. S. Prototypical knowledge for expert systems. *Artificial Intelligence,* 1983, *20(2),* 163-210.

Amarel, S. *Basic themes and problems in current AI research,* in *Proceedings of the Fourth Annual AIM Workshop,* pages 28-46, June, 1978.

Bennett, J., Creary, L., Englemore, R., and Melosh, R. *SACON: A knowledge-based consultant for structural analysis.* STAN-CS-78-699 and HPP Memo 78-23, Stanford University, Sept 1978.

Bobrow, D. G. Qualitative reasoning about physical systems: An introduction. *Artificial Intelligence,* 1984, *24(1-3),* 1-5.

Bobrow, D. and Winograd, T. KRL: Another perspective. *Cognitive Science,* 1979, *3,* 29-42.

Boose, J. *Personal construct theory and the transfer of human expertise,* in *Proceedings of the National Conference on AI,* pages 27-33, Austin, TX, August, 1984.

Borning, A. *Thinglab: A constraint-oriented simulation laboratory.* STAN-CS 79-746, Stanford University, July 1979.

Brachman, R. J. What's in a concept: Structural foundations for semantic networks. *International Journal of Man-Machine Studies,* 1977, *9,* 127-152.

Brachman, R. J., Fikes, R. E., and Levesque, H. J. KRYPTON: A functional approach to knowledge representation. *IEEE Computers,* 1983, *16(10),* 67-73.

Brown, J. S., Burton, R. R., and de Kleer, J. Pedagogical, natural language, and knowledge engineering techniques in SOPHIE I, II, and III. In D. Sleeman and J. S. Brown (editors), *Intelligent Tutoring Systems,* pages 227-282. Academic Press, London, 1982.

Bruner, J. S. *The Process of Education.* Cambridge: Harvard University Press 1960.

Bruner, J. S., Goodnow, J. J., and Austin, G. A. *A Study of Thinking.* New York: John Wiley & Sons, Inc. 1956.

Buchanan, B. G. and Shortliffe, E. H. *Rule-based Expert Systems: The MYCIN Experiments of the Stanford Heuristic Programming Project.* Reading: Addison-Wesley Publishing Company 1984.

Buchanan, B. G., Sutherland, G., and Feigenbaum, E. A. Heuristic dendral: A program for generating explanatory hypotheses in organic chemistry. In B. Meltzer and D. Michie (editors), *Machine Intelligence,* pages 209-254. Edinburgh University Press, Edinburgh, 1969.

Burton, R. R. Diagnosing bugs in a simple procedural skill. In D. Sleeman and J. S. Brown (editors), *Intelligent Tutoring Systems,* pages 157-183. Academic Press, New York, 1982.

Chandrasekaran, B. Expert systems: Matching techniques to tasks. In W. Reitman (editor), *AI Applications for Business*, pages 116-132. Ablex Publishing Corp., 1984.

Chandrasekaran, B. and Mittal, S. Conceptual representation of medical knowledge. In M. Yovits (editor), *Advances in Computers*, pages 217-293. Academic Press, New York, 1983.

Chi, M. T. H., Feltovich, P. J., Glaser, R. Categorization and representation of physics problems by experts and novices. *Cognitive Science*, 1981, *5*, 121-152.

Clancey, W. J. *The advantages of abstract control knowledge in expert system design*, in *Proceedings of the National Conference on AI*, pages 74-78, Washington, D.C., August, 1983.

Clancey, W. J. The epistemology of a rule-based expert system: A framework for explanation. *Artificial Intelligence*, 1983, *20(3)*, 215-251.

Clancey, W. J. *Acquiring, representing, and evaluating a competence model of diagnosis*. HPP Memo 84-2, Stanford University, February 1984. (To appear in Chi, Glaser, and Farr (Eds.), *Contributions to the Nature of Expertise*, in preparation.).

Clancey, W. J. *Knowledge acquisition for classification expert systems*, in *Proceedings of ACM Annual Conference*, pages 11-14, October, 1984.

Clancey, W. J. Details of the revised therapy algorithm. In B. G. Buchanan and E. H. Shortliffe (editors), *Rule-based Expert Systems: The MYCIN Experiments of the Stanford Heuristic Programming Project*, pages 133-146". Addison-Wesley, 1984.

Clancey, W. J. Representing control knowledge as abstract tasks and metarules. (To appear in *Computer Expert Systems*, eds. M. J. Coombs and L. Bolc, Springer-Verlag, in preparation).

Clancey, W. J. and Letsinger, R. NEOMYCIN: Reconfiguring a rule-based expert system for application to teaching. In Clancey, W. J. and Shortliffe, E. H. (editors), *Readings in Medical Artificial Intelligence: The First Decade*, pages 361-381. Addison-Wesley, Reading, 1984.

Cohen, B. and Murphy, G. L. Models of concepts. *Cognitive Science*, 1984, *8*, 27-58.

Cox, D. J. FLIPP: A method for acquiring and displaying Domain Knowledge for Expert Systems. (Center for Creativity, Inc.).

Davis R. *Applications of meta-level knowledge to the construction, maintenance, and use of large knowledge bases*. HPP Memo 76-7 and AI Memo 283, Stanford University, July 1976.

De George, R. T. and De George, F. M. (editors). *The Structuralists: From Marx to Levi-Strauss*. Garden City: Doubleday & Company, Inc., Anchor Books 1972.

de Kleer, J. Qualitative and quantitative reasoning in classical mechanics. In P. H. Winston and R. H. Brown (editors), *Artificial Intelligence: An MIT Perspective*, pages 9-30. The MIT Press, Cambridge, 1979.

Engelmore, R. and Terry, A. *Structure and function of the CRYSALIS system*, in *Proceedings of the Sixth International Joint Conference on Artificial Intelligence*, pages 250-256, August, 1979.

Erman, L. D., London, P. E., and Fickas, S. F. *The design and example use of Hearsay-III*, in *Proceedings Seventh International Joint Conference on Artificial Intelligence*, pages 409-415, August, 1981.

Feigenbaum, E. A. *The art of artificial intelligence: I. Themes and case studies of knowledge engineering*, in *Proceedings of the Fifth International Joint Conference on Artificial Intelligence*, pages 1014-1029, August, 1977.

Flores, C. F. and Winograd, T. Understanding computers and cognition: A new foundation for design. Unpublished manuscript.

Fox, M. S. and Smith, S. F. ISIS-A knowledge-based system for factory scheduling. *Expert Systems*, 1984, *1(1)*, 25-49.

Friedland, P. E. *Knowledge-based experiment design in molecular genetics.* Technical Report STAN-CS-79-771, Stanford University, October 1979.

Genesereth, M. R. *An overview of meta-level architecture*, in *Proceedings of The National Conference on Artificial Intelligence*, pages 119-124, August, 1983.

Genesereth, M. R. The use of design descriptions in automated diagnosis. *Artificial Intelligence*, 1984, *24(1-3)*, 411-436.

Genesereth, M.R., Greiner, R., Smith, D.E. *MRS Manual.* Heuristic Programming Project Memo HPP-80-24, Stanford University, December 1981.

Gentner, D. and Stevens, A. (editors). *Mental models.* Hillsdale, NJ: Erlbaum 1983.

Goldberg, A. and Robson, D. *Smalltalk-80: The Language and its Implementation.* Menlo Park: Addison-Wesley Publishing Company 1983.

Gomez, F. and Chandrasekaran, B. KNowledge organization and distribution for medical diagnosis. In W. J. Clancey and E. H. Shortliffe (editors), *Readings in Medical Artificial Intelligence: The First Decade*, pages 320-338. Addison-Wesley Publishing Company, Reading, 1984.

Greeno, J. G. and Simon, H. A. *Problem solving and reasoning.* UPITT/LRDC/ONR/APS 14, University of Pittsburgh, February 1984. To appear in Stevens' Handbook of Experimental Psychology, (Revised Edition). New York: John Wiley & Sons.

Harmon, P. and King D. *Expert Systems: Artificial Intelligence in Business.* New York: John Wiley & Sons 1985.

Hart, P. E. *Observations on the development of expert knowledge-based systems*, in *Proceedings of the Fifth International Joint Conference on Artificial Intelligence*, pages 1001-1003, August, 1977.

Hayes, P.J. *In defence of logic*, in *Proceedings of the Fifth International Joint Conference on Artificial Intelligence*, pages 559-565, August, 1977.

Hayes, P. The logic of frames. In D. Metzing (editor), *Frame Conceptions and Text Understanding*, pages 45-61. de Gruyter, 1979.

Hayes-Roth, B. and Hayes-Roth, F. A cognitive model of planning. *Cognitive Science*, 1979, *3*, 275-310.

Hayes-Roth, F., Waterman, D., and Lenat, D. (eds.). *Building expert systems.* New York:

Addison-Wesley 1983.

Hewitt, C. Control structure as patterns of passing messages. In P. H. Winston and R. H. Brown (editors), *Artificial Intelligence: An MIT Perspective (Volume 2)*, pages 433-465. The MIT Press, Cambridge, 1979.

Johnson-Laird, P. N. and Wason, P. C. *Thinking: Readings in Cognitive Science*. Cambridge: Cambridge University Press 1977.

Kolodner, J. L. *The role of experience in development of expertise*, in *Proceedings of the National Conference on AI*, pages 273-277, Pittsburgh, PA, August, 1982.

Kolodner, J. Maintaining organization in a dynamic long-term memory. *Cognitive Science*, 1983, *7*, 243-280.

Lane, W. G. Input/output processing. In Stone, H. S. (editor), *Introduction to Computer Architecture, 2nd Edition*, chapter 6. Science Research Associates, Inc., Chicago, 1980.

Lehnert, W., and Wilks, Y. A critical perspective on KRL. *Cognitive Science*, 1979, *3*, 1-28.

Lenat, D. B. and Brown, J. S. Why AM and EURISKO appear to work. *Artificial Intelligence*, 1984, *23(3)*, 269-294.

Levesque, H.J. Foundations to a functional approach to knowledge representation. *Artificial Intelligence*, 1984, *23(2)*, 155-212.

Mackinlay, J. and Genesereth, M. R. *Expressiveness of languages*, in *Proceedings of the National Conference on ARticial Intelligence*, pages 226-232, August, 1984.

Martin, W. A. Descriptions and the specialization of concepts. In Winston, P. H. and Brown, R. H. (editor), *Artificial Intelligence: An MIT Perspective*, pages 375-419. The MIT Press, Cambridge, 1979.

McCarthy, J. and Hayes, P. Some philosophical problems from the standpoint of Artificial Intelligence. In B. Meltzer and D. Michie (editors), *Machine Intelligence 4*, pages 463-502. Edinburgh University Press, 1969.

McDermott, J. R1: A rule-based configurer of computer systems. *Artificial Intelligence*, 1982, *19(1)*, 39-88.

Mervis, C. B. and Rosch, E. Categorization of natural objects. *Annual Review of Psychology*, 1981, *32*, 89-115.

Michalski, R. S. and Stepp, R. E. Learning from observation: conceptual clustering. In R. S. Michalski, R. E. Stepp, and T. M. Mitchell (editors), *Machine Learning*, pages 331-363. Tioga Publishing Company, Palo Alto, 1983.

Miller, G. A. Practical and lexical knowledge. In E. Rosch and B. B. Lloyd (editors), *Cognition and Categorization*, pages 305-319. Lawrence Erlbaum Associates, Hillsdale, 1978.

Mitchell, T. M. *Toward combining empirical and analytical methods for inferring heuristics*. LCSR-TR 27, Laboratory for Computer Science Research, March 1982.

Neches, R., Swartout, W. R., and Moore, J. Explainable (and maintainable) expert systems.

Newell, A. The knowledge level. *Artificial Intelligence*, 1982, *18(1)*, 87-127.

Nii, H. P., Feigenbaum, E. A., Anton, J. J., and Rockmore, A. J. Signal-to-symbol transformation: HASP/SIAP case study. *The AI Magazine*, 1982, *3(2)*, 23-35.

Nilsson, N. J. The interplay between theoretical and experimental methods in Artificial Intelligence. *Cognition and Brain Theory*, 1981, *4(1)*, 69-74.

Palmer, S. E. Fundamental aspects of cognitive representation. In E. Rosch and B. B. Lloyd (editors), *Cognition and Categorization*, pages 259-303. Lawrence Erlbaum Associates, Hillsdale, 1978.

Patil, R. S., Szolovits, P., and Schwartz, W. B. *Causal understanding of patient illness in medical diagnosis*, in *Proceedings of the Seventh International Joint Conference on Artificial Intelligence*, pages 893-899, August, 1981.

Patil, R. S. *Causal representation of patient illness for electrolyte and acid-base diagnosis.* MIT/LCR/TR 267, Massachusetts Institute of Technology, October 1981.

Pauker, S. G., Gorry, G. A., Kassirer, J. P., and Schwartz, W. B. Toward the simulation of clinical cognition: taking a present illness by computer. *AJM*, 1976, *60*, 981-995.

Pople, H. Heuristic methods for imposing structure on ill-structured problems: the structuring of medical diagnostics. In P. Szolovits (editor), *Artificial Intelligence in Medicine*, pages 119-190. Westview Press, 1982.

Quillian, M. R. Semantic memory. In M. Minsky (editor), *Semantic Information Processing*, . MIT Press, Cambridge, MA, 1968.

Rich, E. User modeling via stereotypes. *Cognitive Science*, 1979, *3*, 355-366.

Rosch, E. Principles of categorization. In E. Rosch and B. B. Lloyd (editors), *Cognition and Categorization*, pages 27-48. Lawrence Erlbaum Associates, Hillsdale, 1978.

Rosch E. and Lloyd B. B. (editors). *Cognition and Categorization*. Hillsdale: Lawrence Erlbaum Associates, Inc. 1978.

Rubin, A. D. *Hypothesis formation and evaluation in medical diagnosis.* Technical Report AI-TR-316, Artificial Intelligence Laboratory, Massachusetts Institute of Technology, January 1975.

Rumelhart, D. E. and Norman, D. A. *Representation in memory.* Technical Report CHIP-116, Center for Human Information Processing, University of California, June 1983.

Schank, R. C., and Abelson, R. P. *Scripts, Plans, Goals, and Understanding.* Hillsdale, NJ: Lawrence Erlbaum Associates 1975.

Schank, R. C. Failure-driven memory. *Cognition and Brain Theory*, 1981, *4(1)*, 41-60.

Schmolze, J. G. and Lipkis, T. A. *Classification in the KL-ONE knowledge representation system*, in *Proceedings of the Eighth International Joint Conference on Artificial Intelligence*, pages 330-332, August, 1983.

Simon, H. A. *The Sciences of the Artificial.* Cambridge: The MIT Press 1969.

Simon, H. A. The structure of ill structured problems. *Artificial Intelligence*, 1973, *4*, 181-201.

Sowa, J. F. *Conceptual Structures.* Reading, MA: Addison-Wesley 1984.

Stefik, M. *Planning with constraints.* STAN-CS-80-784 and HPP Memo 80-2, Stanford University, January 1980.

Stefik, M., Bobrow, D. G, Mittal, S., and Conway, L. Knowledge programming in loops: Report on an experimental course. *The AI Magazine,* 1983, *4(3),* 3-13.

Sussman, G. J. *A Computer Model of Skill Acquisition.* New York: American Elsevier 1975.

Swartout W. R. *Explaining and justifying in expert consulting programs,* in *Proceedings of the Seventh International Joint Conference on Artificial Intelligence,* pages 815-823, August, 1981.

Szolovits, P. and Pauker, S. G. Categorical and probabilistic reasoning in medical diagnosis. *Artificial Intelligence,* 1978, *11,* 115-144.

van Melle, W. *A domain-independent production rule system for consultation programs,* in *Proceedings of the Sixth International Joint Conference on Artificial Intelligence,* pages 923-925, August, 1979.

VanLehn, K. *Human procedural skill acquisition: Theory, model, and psychological validation,* in *Proceedings of the National Conference on AI,* pages 420-423, Washington, D.C., August, 1983.

Vemuri, V. *Modeling of Complex Systems: An Introduction.* New York: Academic Press 1978.

Weiss, S. M. and Kulikowski, C. A. *EXPERT: A system for developing consultation models,* in *Proceedings of the Sixth International Joint Conference on Artificial Intelligence,* pages 942-947, August, 1979.

Weiss, S. M. and Kulikowski, C. A. *A Practical Guide to Designing Expert Systems.* Totowa, NJ: Rowman and Allanheld 1984.

Weiss, S. M., Kulikowski, C. A., Amarel, S., and Safir, A. A model-based method for computer-aided medical decision making. *Artificial Intelligence,* 1978, *11,* 145-172.

Woods, W. A. What's in a link: Foundations for semantic networks. In D. G. Bobrow and A. Collins (editors), *Representation and Understanding,* pages 35-82. Academic Press, New York, 1975.

2

ETS: A SYSTEM FOR THE TRANSFER OF HUMAN EXPERTISE

JOHN H. BOOSE
ARTIFICIAL INTELLIGENCE CENTER
BOEING COMPUTER SERVICES
SEATTLE, WASHINGTON

1 INTRODUCTION

The bottleneck in the process of building expert systems is usually the retrieving of appropriate problem-solving knowledge from information sources, especially a human expert. Methods from psychotherapy based on George Kelly's Personal Construct Theory are applied to this process, and a framework for knowledge elicitation, analysis, and testing is shown. The Expertise Transfer System (ETS) is described, which interviews a human expert and then constructs and analyzes aspects of the knowledge that the expert uses to solve a particular problem. The system elicits the initial knowledge needed to solve *analysis* problems without the intervention of a knowledge engineering team. Fast (two hour) initial prototyping of expert systems that run on KS-300™ (an extended version of EMYCIN), S.1™, M.1™*, OPS5, LOOPS, and other systems is also performed. Conflicts in the problem-solving methods of the expert may be enumerated and explored. Techniques are also being tried for combining expertise from multiple experts.

Expert Systems and Knowledge Acquisition

An *expert system* is a computer system that uses the experience of one or more experts in some problem domain, and applies their problem-solving expertise to make useful inferences for the user of the system. This knowledge is typically gathered in the form of rules of thumb, or *heuristics*. Heuristics enable a human expert to make educated guesses when necessary, to recognize promising approaches to problems, and to deal effectively with incomplete or inconsistent

---

* KS-300, S.1, and M.1 are products of Teknowledge, Inc., of Palo Alto, California.

data. Acquiring such knowledge from the expert is the central task in building expert systems and is referred to as *knowledge engineering.*

Getting an expert to articulate problem solving knowledge is one of the main problems in building expert systems. A long series of incremental interview, build, and test cycles are necessary before a system achieves expert performance. The time typically required to build an expert-level prototype is from six to twenty-four months [Buchanan et al., 1983; McDermott, 1982, 1984].

Figure 1 shows our methodology for knowledge elicitation, testing, combination, and expert system delivery. Knowledge is elicited from information sources, and placed into an information base. From there, it is analyzed and organized into knowledge bases, which are directly used with expert system tools such as KS-300/EMYCIN and OPS5. These tools are used for rapid prototyping and to extensively test the knowledge for necessity and sufficiency. Test case histories are built up as the knowledge base is incrementally refined. Individual knowledge bases are then combined into knowledge networks, where further testing occurs. Finally, delivery systems are tailored for efficiency, and on-the-job case records are kept in order to further improve the system.

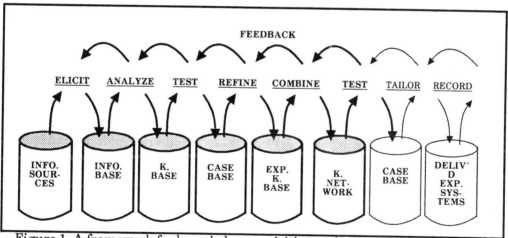

Figure 1. A framework for knowledge acquisition and expert systems delivery.

The Expertise Transfer System (ETS) is an Interlisp-D-based tool which interviews an expert, analyzes the information gathered, and produces production rule knowledge bases for several expert system tools [Boose, 1984]. It also contains several tools for refining and testing the resulting knowledge.

Several experiments have been performed using ETS to combine expertise from different experts. The shaded, bold areas in Figure 1 represent the current capabilities of ETS.

ETS offers assistance in the knowledge engineering process. It can significantly shorten this process and help improve the quality of the elicited problem-solving knowledge. To do this, ETS helps the expert construct and analyze an initial set of heuristics and parameters for the problem. Experts need no special training to use ETS; an initial fifteen minute explanation is usually all that is needed.

The quality of the problem-solving information elicited from the expert in the early stages of the knowledge acquisition process is improved over manual methods because ETS provides the expert with knowledge analysis tools and mechanisms for exploring internal conflicts in the way that different problem cases are handled. *Consistency* is used conceptually to elaborate important problem aspects.

In addition to eliciting the initial knowledge and producing knowledge base reports and listings, ETS is capable of testing the problem-solving ability of the knowledge. ETS contains an inference engine which supports end-user consultations by transforming the knowledge from the expert into production rules.

George Kelly's Personal Construct Theory

ETS employs clinical psychotherapeutic interviewing methods originally developed by George Kelly. He was interested in how a person categorizes experiences and classifies the environment. When a person realizes how this organization is being achieved, he can use that awareness to predict events more accurately and act more effectively, and also to change the organization to specific perceived needs [Shaw, 1981]. George Kelly's theory of a "personal scientist" was that each individual seeks to predict and control events by forming theories, testing hypotheses, and weighing experimental evidence [Kelly, 1955].

Certain techniques for use in psychotherapy were developed by Kelly, based on his philosophy. In one form of a Repertory Grid Test for eliciting role models, Kelly asked his clients to list, compare, and rate role models to derive and analyze character traits. Role models were listed along the top of a grid; Kelly referred to these items as *elements*. Then, clients were asked to compare successive sets of three elements, listing distinguishing characteristics and their opposites down the right hand side of the grid: "What trait distinguishes any two of the elements from the other one?" A trait and its opposite represented an internal bipolar scaled *construct*, and were called the left and right hand poles of the construct, respectively. This information was placed on a grid, and the subject was asked to mark the two similar elements with an "X," and to also place an "X" near every other element to which the left hand pole applied. A collection of elements, traits, and ratings was referred to as a *rating grid*. Kelly used manual analysis techniques to analyze these grids. The results helped him understand the degree of similarity or difference between uses of the constructs.

Following construction and analysis of the grid, the clinician entered a manual interviewing phase. Typically, in this phase, the interviewer would attempt to help the subject expand upon and verify the relationships between constructs pointed out by the grid analysis.

One technique is known as *laddering*. This interview method is used to help connect the constructs in their *superordinate* and *subordinate* relationships. For instance, the clinician might start with the construct "warm-cold" (as applied to people), and ask the patient, "Why is someone warm?" The patient might respond, "Because they're loving." Next, he might ask, "Why is someone loving?" and obtain the response, "Because they're good," and so on. Each "Why" answer develops another *super*ordinate connection in the network hierarchy of constructs, in which "loving" is superordinate to "warm," and "good" is superordinate to "loving." To move in the *sub*ordinate direction in the grid, "How" questions are asked, such as "How do you know that?," "What is your evidence for that?," or "What do you mean by that?" Moving in the superordinate direction uncovers constructs that are more general, while moving in the subordinate direction uncovers those that are more specific.

Another technique is useful in verifying relationships pointed out indirectly by the grid analysis. In this analysis, the examiner assumes that a statistical relationship between constructs reflects a conceptual relationship that may or may not be true. For example, if a "loving-harsh" construct is highly matched with the "answers questions-won't answer questions" construct, the examiner might attempt to verify this relationship by asking such questions as, "If you mean someone is loving, do you also mean that they are almost always willing to answer your questions?" and "If someone is always willing to answer your questions, are they almost always loving?" and so on.

Hinkle [1965] further developed the idea that constructs have locations and logical relationships in a hierarchy of implications. He describes some of the possible implications between two constructs A-B and X-Y as follows (see Figure 2):

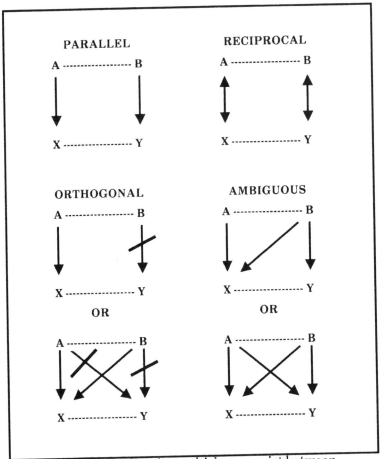

Figure 2. Implications which may exist between
two constructs A - B and X - Y.

- Parallel. A implies X, and B implies Y (e.g., love-hate; pleasantness-unpleasantness).
- Orthogonal. A implies X, but B does not imply Y; also A implies X, and B implies X, but neither A nor B imply Y (e.g., employed-unemployed; has income-has no income).

- <u>Reciprocal.</u> A implies X, and B implies Y, and X implies A, and Y implies B (e.g., nervous-calm; tense-relaxed). Hinkle notes that a reciprocal relationship suggests a functional equivalence between the two label pairs.
- <u>Ambiguous.</u> A and B imply X, and B implies Y; also A implies X and Y, and B implies X and Y (realism-idealism; desirable-undesirable, in which the subject says that realism and idealism both implied desirable and undesirable aspects for him). Hinkle suggests that this situation may arise when: (1) a subject has an incomplete abstraction of the differences between the contexts in which the construct is used, or (2) a subject uses one construct label for two or more independent constructs. He also felt that the processes of psychological movement, conflict resolution, and insight depend on locating such points of ambiguous implication, and then resolving them into parallel or orthogonal forms. As will be seen later, this can be a useful approach for resolving conflicts and inconsistencies during knowledge engineering.

Hinkle was interested in psychological change, and developed a *resistance to change grid*, as well as an *implication grid*, that were based on a subject's willingness to change relationships in the construct hierarchy. Such information can be used to elicit the relative importance and stability of constructs.

Researchers have extended Kelly's original binary rating method ("X" or blank) to include rating scales. Thus, instead of simply deciding whether or not some left hand part of a construct pair applies to an element, the subject rates the construct's applicability on a scale from one to five, which allows expression of finer shades of distinction. Another rating technique goes beyond this, and allows subjects to use "N" (for "neither pole applies"), and "B" (for "both poles apply"), in addition to a one-to-five rating scale.

More recently, elicitation and analysis of repertory grids have been made available through interactive computer programs. A variety of grid analysis techniques using distance-based measures between vectors (either rows or columns of the grid) have been used, where both elements and constructs may be graphically compared by the subject to find similarities and differences. Some of these techniques include a form of principal components analysis [Slater, 1977], a Q-Analysis of the grid in a cluster-analyzed hierarchical format [QARMS, Atkin, 1974], and a linear cluster analysis [FOCUS, Shaw, 1980].

A more formal description of implication relationships than that used by Hinkle, based on logic, is presented by Gaines and Shaw [1981]. Instead of looking at grid rows and columns as vectors in space, they are viewed as assignments of truth-values to logical predicates. In binary rating systems, such as that used in Kelly's original grid methodology, an "X" simply means true and a blank means false. A grid, then, can be seen as a matrix of truth values. The right hand side of a construct can be looked at as the logical negation of the left hand side. Further, a left hand side of a construct C1 can logically imply the right hand side of a different construct C2 if, when an element is assigned to the left hand side of C1, it is always (necessarily) assigned to the right hand side of C2. Gaines and Shaw go on to show how to derive implications from grids which use rating scales rather than binary scales based on multi-valued logics using fuzzy set theory. The implication relation can be extended to include *implication strength*. ENTAIL [Gaines and Shaw, 1981] produces graphs showing these relations among constructs and elements.

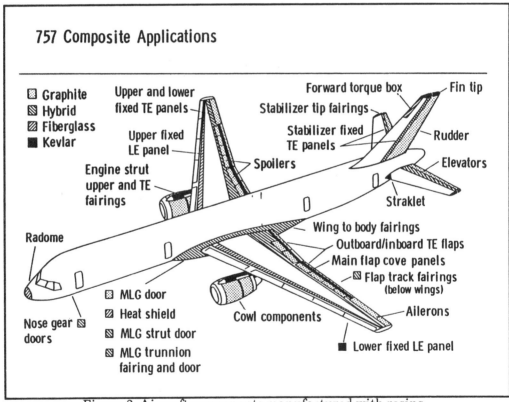

Figure 3. Aircraft components manufactured with resins.

Many of these techniques have been incorporated into ETS.

2 ETS - SYSTEM DESCRIPTION

The following section shows excerpts from a session with ETS. ETS runs in the Interlisp-D environment on the Xerox 1100 and 1108 Lisp Machines, using the high-resolution bitmap windows, pop-up menus, and mouse interaction capabilities provided. An expert is attempting to build a knowledge base for a Fiber Advisor. Fibers are being used by Boeing as the basic material for many *composite fiber* aircraft parts, such as rudders, spoilers, elevators, cowl components, and so on (see Figure 3). Different types of fibers are selected by making tradeoffs between design performance and cost of manufacture. Access to fiber experts by design engineers is limited, and the current knowledge concerning fibers is always changing. These problem traits make the Fiber Advisor a possible candidate for a consultant expert system. Assistance during this session was provided by Frank Jackson, a knowledge engineer at Boeing.

Initial Knowledge Elicitation

Initially, the Expertise Transfer System elicits conclusion items (elements) from the expert. These elements represent conclusions that should be made by the proposed expert system: specific diseases, management decisions, diagnostic recommendations, and so on. In the following example case, the elements are the specific fibers which the expert recommends to design engineers (see Figures 4 and 5). The expert starts by listing four such fibers. The workstation screen is divided into several windows. Information is entered by the expert in the "ETS Transcript Window." Eventually, a rating grid and analysis results will be shown in other windows.

If the expert cannot verbalize the conclusion elements initially, ETS enters an incremental interview mode of operation based on DYAD [Keen and Bell, 1981], in which elements are elicited one at a time, based on differences between and similarities to three initial "seed" elements.

After the expert has listed the fibers he wishes to consider, ETS asks the expert to compare successive groups of three fibers, and name an important attribute or trait that distinguishes any two members of this triad from the third one (see Figure 6).

By comparing *three* elements at a time, Kelly argues, the subject is asked to think about both similarities and differences in a manageable manner. The use of

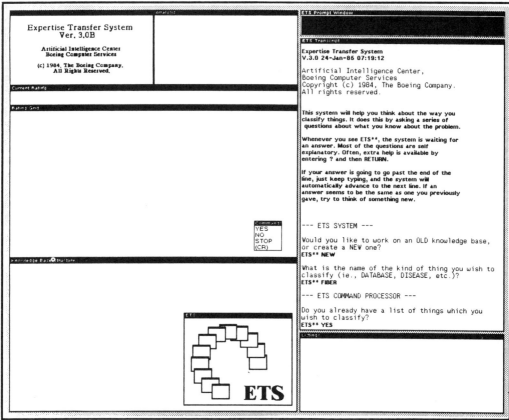

Figure 4. ETS system startup.

only two elements, rather than three, would elicit traits based solely on either elements' differences or similarities. With three elements, the expert is asked to think about similarities *and* differences. With more than three elements, the task is made more complex for the expert without much more potential for eliciting different types of traits [Kelly, 1955)].

It can be seen that the particular traits which are elicited depend on which elements are combined into triads. ETS builds these triads in the order in which the elements are given by the expert. This initial set of constructs will probably not be a sufficient window into the expert's problem-solving construct system. However, the constructs elicited will tend to be significant since they are based on discriminations among important conclusions. Later in the interviewing process, ETS uses other methods to help expand and refine the knowledge base. So far,

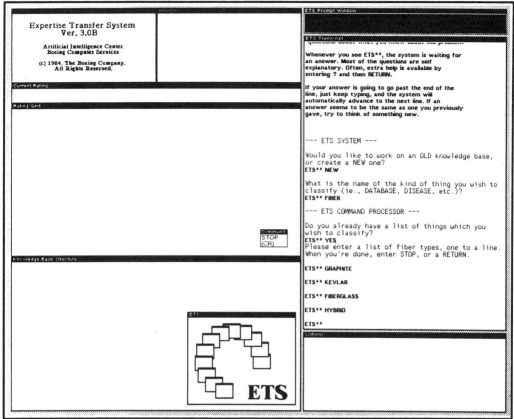

Figure 5. Element enumeration.

these techniques have been sufficient for building rapid prototype systems which exhibit reasonable behavior.

The result of this first phase of the interview process is a list of elements to be classified, and a list of classification parameters, all of which were derived from the expert, using his own language and terms.

Constructing a Rating Grid

Next, the system asks the expert to rate each element against each pair of traits. A rating grid of values is formed (see Figure 7). In addition to numerically scaled ratings, ETS accepts the ratings "N" ("neither side of construct seems to apply to the element") and "B" ("both sides of the construct seem to apply to the element"). The expert may review the grid information and change any ratings by pointing at the rating, clicking a mouse button, and entering the new rating.

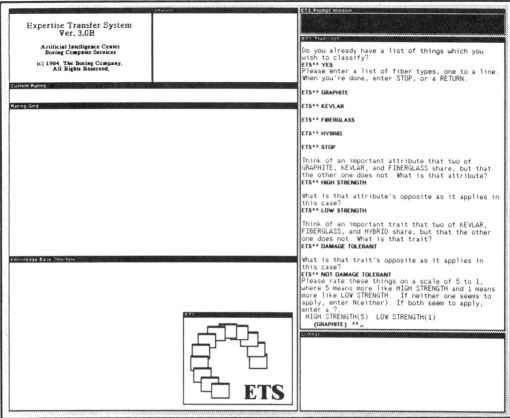

Figure 6. Triad comparison.

Grid Analysis Methods

Once a rating grid is established, ETS invokes several analysis methods to structure the knowledge. First, the system builds an entailment graph of implication relationships using the method of ENTAIL [Gaines and Shaw, 1981]. The expert may begin to see some structure and organization in the information. The entailment graph (in the "Knowledge Base Structure" window, Figure 8) shows implication relationships between various poles of the constructs. Initially, there are no implications between the traits - all the traits are independent. Later on, when more traits have been added, implication relations will be created.

Next, the expert asks ETS to combine more elements together to form new triads. A new trait is elicited, rated against all the fibers, and added to the rating grid (see Figure 8). The rating grid is again analyzed for implications; this time,

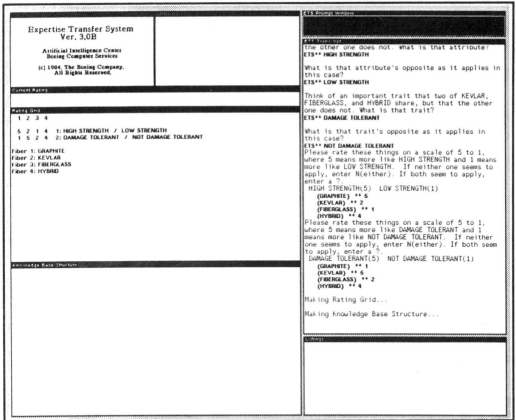

Figure 7. Building a rating grid.

several are found (see Figure 9). For instance, "high strength" implies "primary structure." This means that, given the examples in the rating grid, every fiber that has "high strength" is also useful for "primary structures." The information in the graph corresponds roughly to a semantic network representation of "IS-A" hierarchies. The thickness of the arrows representing the implication arcs shows the relative strength of each inductive generalization. The strengths are also listed numerically in the transcript window. These arcs should correspond with paths in the expert's superordinate and subordinate construct system. However, as was pointed out in the discussion above, verbal representations do not necessarily correspond with a person's internal construct hierarchy. The "training examples" represented by the rating grid may contain errors and be inconsistent or incomplete. Typically, the expert is surprised at many of the

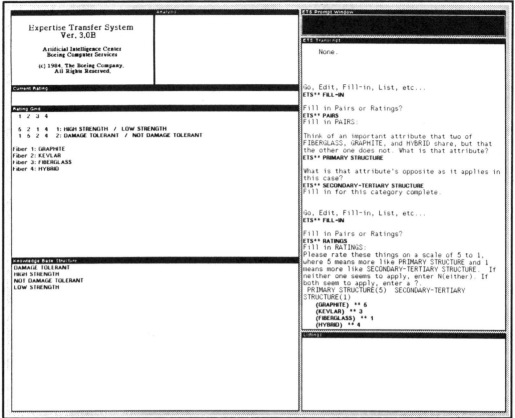

Figure 8. Creation of additional triads for comparison.

relationships that are revealed by the graph. The expert uses ETS to review these implications later on in the session.

Next, ETS computes matching scores between traits and elements (see Figure 10 and 11). The expert is asked questions to help separate traits or elements which are closely matched. For instance, ETS points out that the two pairs "primary structure / secondary-tertiary structure" and "high strength / low strength" are closely matched (at the 88% level). The expert is then asked to *separate* the meaning between these two trait pairs by supplying a new fiber which is either "primary structure and low strength" or "secondary-tertiary structure and high strength." If the expert can do this, then the new element is entered, rated against all the existing traits, and the implication graph is regenerated. If the expert cannot do this, then ETS asks the expert if the two trait pairs should be subsumed into one pair. If the expert can do neither, ETS notes

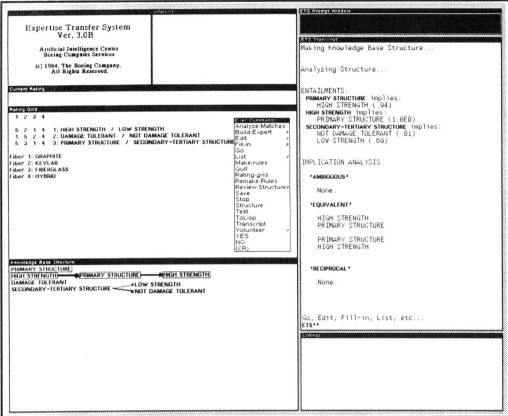

Figure 9. Expanded rating grid and entailment graph showing implications between traits.

this fact and asks the expert to examine the next set of closely matched traits or elements. This technique is based on a method shown in PEGASUS [Shaw, 1980].

Production Rule Generation

After the implication graph has been constructed, ETS can generate two types of production rules: *conclusion* rules and *intermediate* rules. Each production rule is generated with a *belief strength*, or "certainty factor." Certainty factors can represent slightly different concepts in different expert system building tools. In KS-300/EMYCIN, for example, certainty factors represent a "strength of belief" that the expert associates with the conclusion of the rule. This is the definition used by ETS. It could be changed to fit other definitions. ETS employs empirical algorithms to generate certainty factors for each rule type. The general features of these algorithms will be discussed in the following paragraphs.

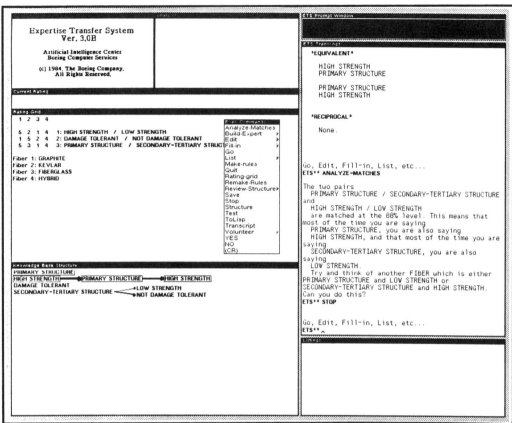

Figure 10. Interviewing to discriminate between similar traits and similar elements.

Conclusion rules are created from individual ratings in the grid. Each rating may be used to generate a rule. To do this, ETS firsts asks the expert to assign concept names to each pair of traits (see Figure 12). Then the expert rates the relative importance of each of the concepts in his problem-solving behavior (see Figures 12 and 13). For instance, the expert feels that STRENGTH is more important than DAMAGE-TOLERANCE.

Based on the given information, rules may now be generated for each grid location (see Figures 13 and 14). For instance, the fiber *graphite* is rated five against the pair "high strength / low strength." This means that the expert rated graphite strongly toward the "high strength" end of the pair. ETS generates rules of the form:

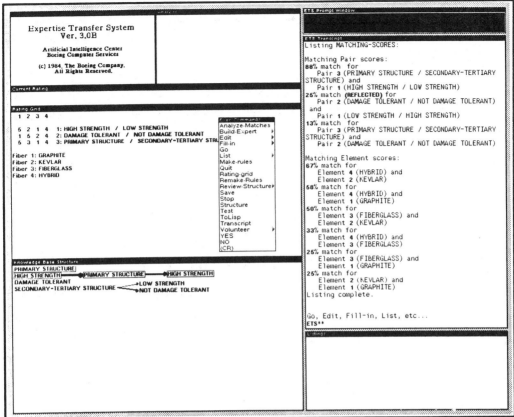

Figure 11. Listing of matching score similarities for traits and fibers.

IF: desired STRENGTH is HIGH-STRENGTH
THEN: The fiber to use may be GRAPHITE (.75)

and

IF: desired STRENGTH is LOW-STRENGTH
THEN: The fiber to use may be GRAPHITE (−.75)

The certainty factors (.75, −.75) are generated in a range from −1.0 (certainly false) to 1.0 (certainly true). A grid rating of four, rather than five, would have caused the certainty factors to be somewhat lower (in this case, .375 and −.375). When rules are generated, the relative importance of the trait pair, as assigned by the expert, contributes to the relative weights of the certainty factors. Conclusions from constructs that the expert feels are more important will be more heavily weighted. When employed, conclusion rules generate evidence that may be gathered by an expert system for its conclusions.

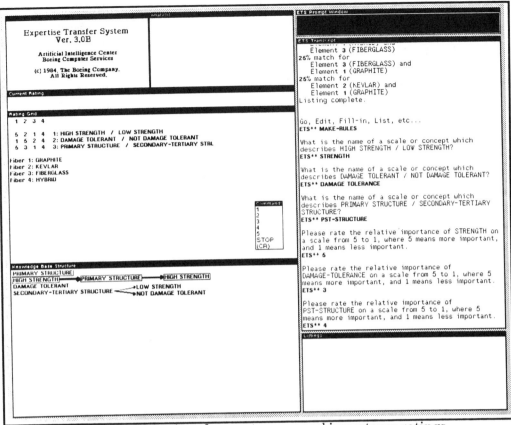

Figure 12. Elicitation of concept names and importance ratings.

The expert is interested mainly in the *relative values* of certainty factors. Exact numbers are only important when generating a particular knowledge base for an expert system tool. In general, the empirical algorithm that ETS uses to generate strength of belief factors will be different for any given expert system building tool.

In summary, conclusion rule certainty factors are generated by applying the relative strength of the rating in the grid and the relative importance rating assigned to the construct by the expert to a particular certainty scale - in this case, from −1.0 to 1.0.

Intermediate rules are based on relations in the implication graph. For each implication, one rule is generated. The strength of the rule's certainty factor is based on the relative strength of the implication. These rules generate

84

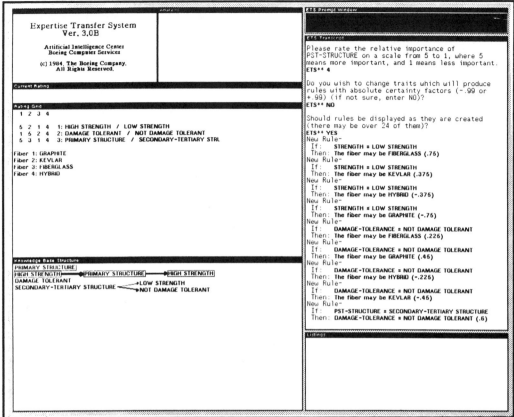

Figure 13. Generation of rules from implications and the rating grid.

intermediate pieces of evidence at a higher conceptual level than those of conclusion rules. For instance, ETS generates this intermediate rule:

IF: The PST-STRUCTURE is PRIMARY-STRUCTURE
THEN: The STRENGTH should be HIGH-STRENGTH (.87)

After ETS generates conclusion rules and intermediate rules based on the current knowledge base, the expert may review the rules. Each rule represents a chunk of knowledge, with which the expert may agree or disagree. Although this knowledge is still logically equivalent to the knowledge in the rating grid and implication graph, seeing it in a new representation tends to help the expert consider the problem in another way. If the expert disagrees with particular rules, a rating examination and laddering process may be used to identify sources

85

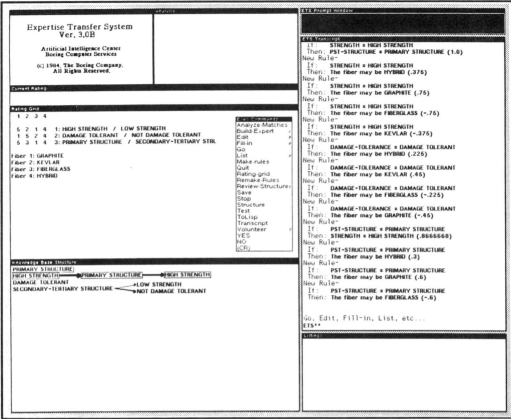

Figure 14. Production rule generation (continued).

of potential conflict either in ETS's knowledge base or between the knowledge base and the expert's internal constructs.

Allowing the expert to work with multiple forms of his stated problem-solving knowledge is an important aspect of ETS. Lenat [1982] argues that knowledge representations should shift as different needs arise. Each different representation method in ETS potentially helps the expert think about the problem in a new way and tends to point out conflicts and inconsistencies over time. Rather than trying to force the expert to eradicate inconsistencies, or simply not allowing them to exist, ETS takes advantage of the important psychological and problem-solving aspects of such inconsistencies by helping the expert explore them. It was this same process that Kelly felt was important in the clinical setting for bringing about critical psychological change [Kelly, 1955].

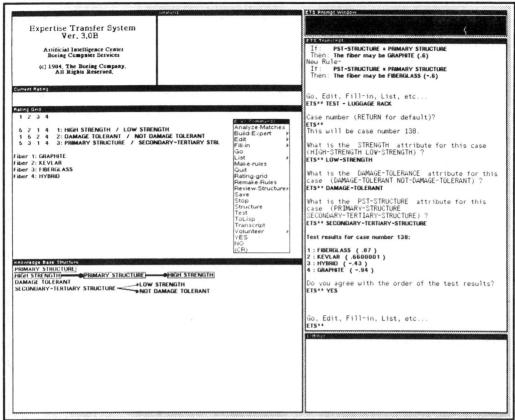

Figure 15. Immediate testing of the prototype expert system with ETS's inference engine.

Testing the Knowledge Base - Consultation Cases

Once production rules have been generated, the expert can test the knowledge base. This may done by generating a knowledge base for an expert system shell or by using ETS's internal inference engine. In this session, the expert first used ETS's internal test facility and then generated an OPS5 knowledge base.

A test case is run by asking the end user (in this case, the expert) to specify an application problem in terms of the traits in the rating grid (see Figure 15). For instance, the first consultation question asked is, "What is the STRENGTH attribute for this case (HIGH-STRENGTH LOW-STRENGTH)?" The expert selects the appropriate response from a pop-up menu. In this test case, the expert is considering a luggage rack. Luggage racks don't need to be strong, but they do need to be damage tolerant. The expert specifies the traits, the rules are "fired," and ETS gives the consultation results. In this case, the expert agreed with the order of the fiber recommendations. If enough such test cases are eventually successful, this would give the expert and knowledge engineers an indication that the knowledge involved was useful and approaching sufficiency.

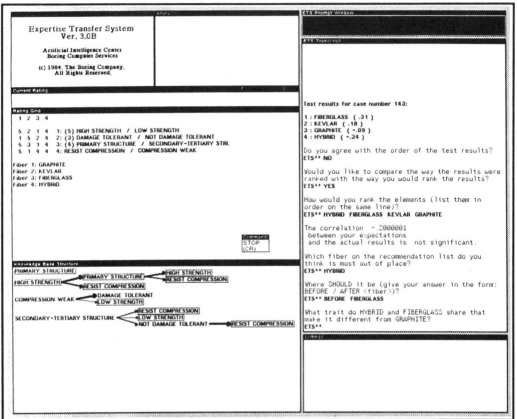

Figure 16. Test case review facility to measure performance and refine knowledge.

If the expert does not agree with the test results, ETS attempts to help the expert refine the knowledge base (see Figure 16, which was generated later in the session). First, the expert may compare his own rank ordering to that produced by ETS. Spearman's coefficient of rank correlation is used to measure the difference between the two ordered lists. A correlation of 1.0 means that the lists are identical; a correlation of -1.0 means the lists are exactly reversed; a correlation of 0.0 means that the lists are "randomly" ordered with respect to each other. ETS also notes whether or not a high positive correlation is statistically significant at the 5% or 1% levels. The expert may use the rank correlation scores to measure progress while refining the knowledge base.

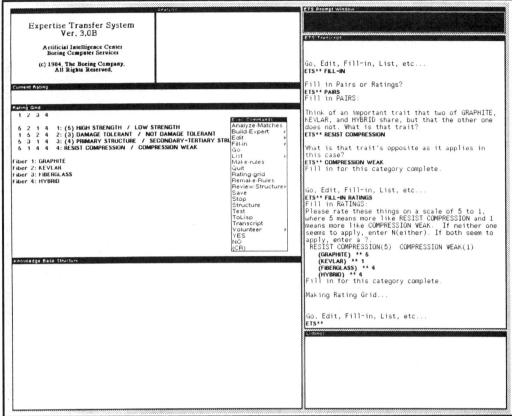

Figure 17. Additional triads to elicit new traits.

The expert then named the fiber which he felt was most out of order, and told ETS where it *should* have fallen in the list. ETS uses this information to try to elicit a new trait. Theoretically, including this new trait during another consultation will make the named fiber closer to where the expert thought it should have been in the recommendation list. After adding the trait, the expert can regenerate the rules, and retest the knowledge.

Further Knowledge Base Refinement

Next, the expert again asks ETS to form new triads. Another trait is elicited and added to the grid (see Figure 17). The structure is re-analyzed, and the new implication graph is displayed (see Figure 18). Notice that the complexity of the graph is increasing.

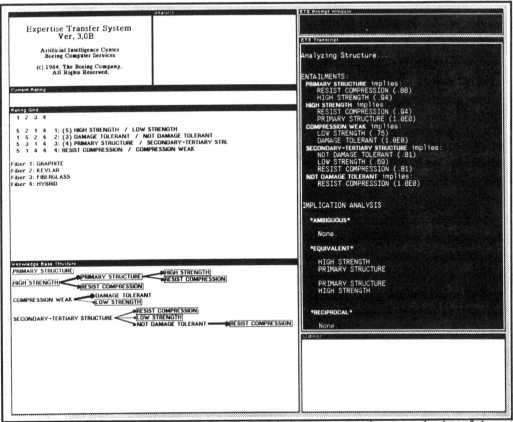

Figure 18. Analysis of expanded rating grid showing growing complexity of the implication graph.

If the expert *disagrees* with a relationship in the implication graph, ETS can help the expert explore the implication. Since the implications are all "logically true" given the information on the rating grid, one of several things could be possible: (1) one or more ratings are wrong; (2) there are important elements that the expert omitted that would have generated exceptions to the implication, thereby creating a different graph if they had been included; (3) the expert is inconsistent in the way the trait is applied to each different element; or (4) the implication really *was* sound, and the expert just never considered the information in that way before.

ETS helps the expert track down suspicious implications by allowing him to review each one in a structured manner (see Figure 19). The expert may edit the

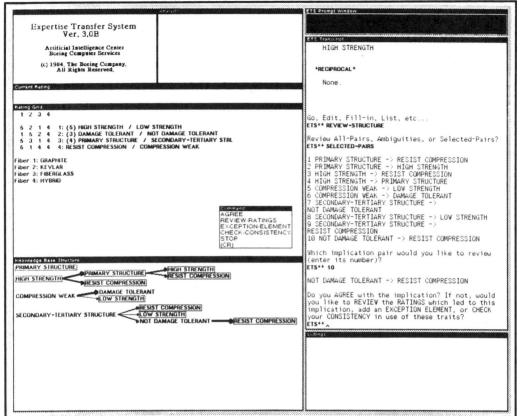

Figure 19. ETS helps the expert explore the relationships revealed by the implication graph.

ratings which led to the implication. If this does not correct the perceived problem shown by the graph, the expert can specify a new element which would be an exception to the implication. If the expert can think of an exception, then that element is added to the knowledge base, rated against all the constructs, and the implication graph is regenerated. If this still does not correct the problem, ETS asks the expert if he would like to "refine" the constructs involved in the implication relation by checking their consistency. This involves breaking up a suspect trait pair into two or more new trait pairs. To do this, a simple laddering method is used that asks "Why?" and "How?" questions concerning the constructs. Any new constructs are added to the knowledge base, and the rating grid and implication graph are then regenerated.

If the implication still exists on the graph after this exploration process, the expert may indeed agree that the implication relationship is sound, and that he

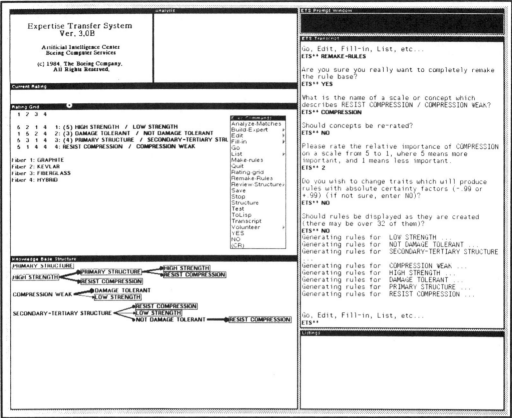

Figure 20. Regeneration of production rules after knowledge base expansion.

just never thought about the problem in that way before. In this way, ETS helps the expert structure the problem solving knowledge based on his own operative internal construct network. On the other hand, if the implication relationship still exists, and the expert still disagrees with it, then this represents an important inconsistency in the way the expert thinks about the problem. What has happened, in effect, is that ETS has captured an important internal conflict in the expert's construct hierarchy.

Ambiguous construct relations also point out internal conflicts. When the expert is finished correcting implication arcs, ETS searches for and lists ambiguous relations. Laddering may again be used to try and refine these points of conflict into parallel or orthogonal forms.

Both types of conflict points (ambiguous relations and relations with which the expert disagrees) are important points in the expert's problem-solving methods.

The process of resolving these conflicts (either with ETS or in later discussions between the knowledge engineer and the expert) involves "psychological movement, conflict resolution, and insight" [Hinkle, 1965]. These are precisely the points of interest where further exploration is necessary, both in producing the expert system and in refining the expert's own problem-solving processes. Transcripts are kept of all the interactions with ETS, and a set of conflict points is generated as part of the knowledge base report listings.

At this point in the ETS session, the expert regenerated rules based on the new information in the rating grid (see Figure 20). Then, the expert re-tested the luggage rack example and still agreed with the order of the test results (see Figure 21). The expert also tried a different test case - a foil (see Figure 22). Notice that the expert can also apply a certainty factor to the consultation responses. This allows the specification of values between the two "opposite poles" of the construct.

In addition to the methods already mentioned, the knowledge base in ETS may be expanded in several other ways:

- Information (elements and traits) may be volunteered by the expert.
- Elements and traits may be directly edited.
- The expert can ask ETS to start or continue an interview dialog to continue to expand the knowledge base incrementally.
- Laddering can be invoked on any portion of the implication graph in order to expand the hierarchy of constructs.

Generating Knowledge Bases for Expert System Shells

Currently, ETS can generate knowledge bases for KS-300/EMYCIN, M.1, S.1 (expert system tools from Teknowledge, Inc., of Palo Alto, California); OPS5 [Forgy, 1981]; LOOPS (Xerox, Inc.); MRS (Stanford University); and Prolog (the POP11 system). In this session, the expert generated a knowledge base for OPS5 (see Figure 23). A portion of the OPS5 knowledge base is shown in Figure 24. Each rule contains a *screening clause* which names the expert responsible for the rule. Rule bases produced by ETS can thus be combined. The end user can select from among a set of given experts to help solve the problem, and these clauses will act as filters.

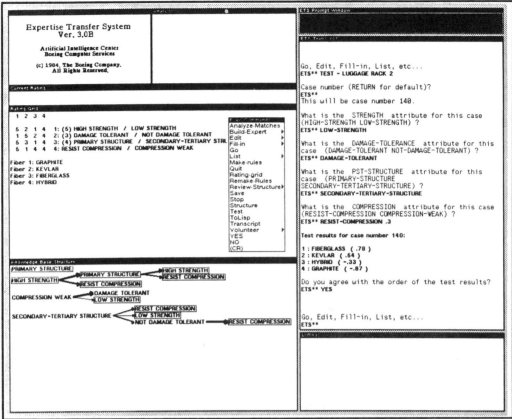

Figure 21. Testing the new knowledge base on the original test case.

Reports and Listings

ETS generates reports and listings of the knowledge from each session. When reviewing these reports later, the expert tends to think of new traits and elements and finds more inconsistencies and other points for further exploration. The expert may then re-run ETS with his existing knowledge base and revise it.

Occasionally, the expert may wish to start over again with a different set of conclusion elements, or with a different level of abstraction in mind for producing construct pairs. Using current manual interviewing techniques, this may mean a major revision to the knowledge base. For instance, a new abstraction of knowledge may be needed to overcome some perceived limitations in the current abstraction. With ETS, however, new abstractions may be tentatively explored

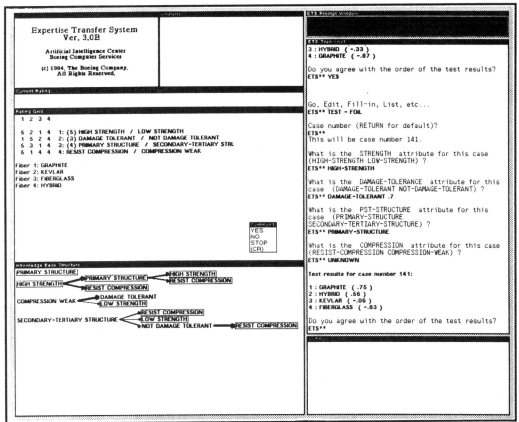

Figure 22. Testing the knowledge base on a foil test case.

without major resource expenditures. By modifying the knowledge base in these ways, the expert starts his own knowledge refinement cycles.

The listings and reports are also helpful in later manual interviewing phases of the knowledge engineering process. The knowledge engineering team does not need to begin from scratch when starting discussions with the expert. They have in hand basic vocabulary, important problem traits, implication hierarchies of these traits, vocabulary, areas of conflict where discussions may begin, a prototype expert system, and test case histories. This has been an invaluable aid in streamlining the knowledge acquisition process in building several expert systems at Boeing Computer Services. Knowledge engineers may also use associated interviewing techniques from personal construct methodology, such as laddering and the resolution of ambiguous construct relationships.

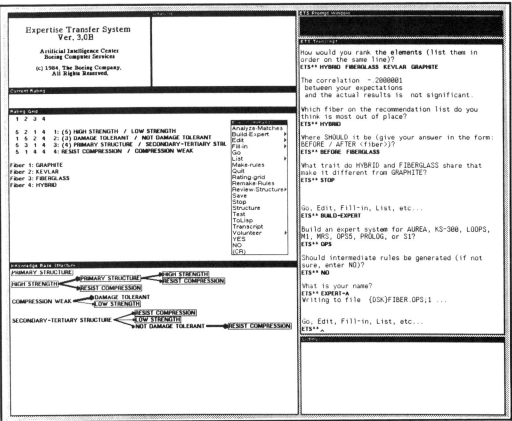

Figure 23. Automatic generation of a knowledge base for OPS5 from the ETS knowledge base.

Expert Level Performance

An expert system that performs at an expert level will still need to evolve through the human interview-test-modify process with the expert, at least at this time. It is not suggested that the initially generated knowledge base will necessarily be similar in structure to the "final" one. However, fast prototyping is a very helpful feedback mechanism, can help demonstrate project feasibility in a matter of hours, and establishes a basis for communication between the knowledge engineering team and the expert.

A few experiments have been performed to attempt to validate knowledge bases produced by ETS (Boose, 1985). The methodology involved systematically comparing the results of the ETS test case consultations with the expectations of the experts. For the most part, ETS performed reasonably.

```
; (FILECREATED by ETS "24-Jan-85 19:10:41" {DSK}FIBER.OPS;1)
;
(strategy mea)
;    Set up trait prompts:                           :
(p ccpaira0001
 ( fiber ↑ property strength ↑ is unknown)
 -->
 (write (crlf) What is the strength  characteristic of this fiber  " ( high-strength or
 low-strength ) " ? (crlf))
 (make input ↑ property strength ↑ text (acceptline))
 (remove 1) )
;    Sample rules:                           :
(p kfiberrulea0139
 ( fiber ↑ property expert ↑ is expert.a ↑ cert <cf0>)
 ( fiber ↑ property compression ↑ is resist-compression ↑ cert <cf>)
 -->
 (bind <cfn> (minn <cf0> <cf>))
 (make fiber ↑ property value ↑ is graphite ↑ cert (compute <cfn> * .252 ) ↑ tag (genatom)) )

(p kfiberrulea0138
 ( fiber ↑ property expert ↑ is expert.a ↑ cert <cf0>)
 ( fiber ↑ property compression ↑ is resist-compression ↑ cert <cf>)
 -->
 (bind <cfn> (minn <cf0> <cf>))
 (make fiber ↑ property value ↑ is fiberglass ↑ cert (compute <cfn> * .126 ) ↑ tag (genatom)) )
                                                                    :
(p kfiberrulea0127
 ( fiber ↑ property expert ↑ is expert.a ↑ cert <cf0>)
 ( fiber ↑ property strength ↑ is high-strength ↑ cert <cf>)
 -->
 (bind <cfn> (minn <cf0> <cf>))
 (make fiber ↑ property value ↑ is kevlar ↑ cert (compute <cfn> * -.315 ) ↑ tag (genatom)) )

(p kfiberrulea0126
 ( fiber ↑ property expert ↑ is expert.a ↑ cert <cf0>)
 ( fiber ↑ property strength ↑ is high-strength ↑ cert <cf>)
 -->
 (bind <cfn> (minn <cf0> <cf>))
 (make fiber ↑ property value ↑ is fiberglass ↑ cert (compute <cfn> * -.63 ) ↑ tag (genatom)) )

(p kfiberrulea0125
 ( fiber ↑ property expert ↑ is expert.a ↑ cert <cf0>)
 ( fiber ↑ property strength ↑ is high-strength ↑ cert <cf>)
 -->
 (bind <cfn> (minn <cf0> <cf>))
 (make fiber ↑ property value ↑ is graphite ↑ cert (compute <cfn> * .63 ) ↑ tag (genatom)) )
;    KB consultation setup:                           :
(defun memset ()(remove *)
 (make fiber ↑ property compression ↑ is unknown)
 (make fiber ↑ property pst-structure ↑ is unknown)
 (make fiber ↑ property damage-tolerance ↑ is unknown)
 (make fiber ↑ property strength ↑ is unknown)
 (make fiber ↑ property expert ↑ is unknown) )
                                    :
```

Figure 24. A portion of the OPS5 Resin Advisor knowledge base created by ETS.

The expert system tool itself can also be used to refine the knowledge base. However, this means that the expert needs to be trained in the use of the tool, sometimes extensively. KS-300/EMYCIN contains knowledge base editors, for example, that check for syntactic and semantic consistency in the rule base. It also incorporates TEIRESIAS, a tool for incrementally adding to and debugging an existing knowledge base [Davis and Lenat, 1982].

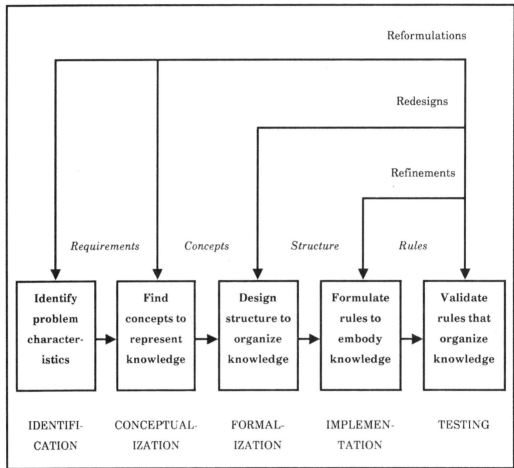

Figure 25. Expert system life cycle [Buchanan et al., 1983].

ETS and Traditional Knowledge Engineering

It is almost always difficult for the expert to articulate problem-solving knowledge in terms that are ready for expert system use. Human interviewing processes elicit knowledge that is imprecise, incomplete, and inconsistent. The knowledge is often subconscious, and the expert usually has not needed to be precisely introspective about his work. In addition, the expert must come to trust the interviewer enough to overcome any fears or insecurities felt about the expert system building process, especially at the outset of the project. The expert may feel insecure about losing his job, or feel threatened by the encroachment of computers into his private domain, or not want to expose his problem-solving methods to the scrutiny of other experts or the general public. These problems inevitably lead to difficulties in all phases of knowledge acquisition. It is difficult to isolate an appropriate set of concepts during conceptualization, which eventually leads to incorrectly and incompletely stated knowledge in the program. With the use of ETS, the expert usually becomes interested and enthusiastic about the project and understands the nature of the knowledge that is expected of him. The expert tends to look on the knowledge engineer as an assistant rather than as an encroacher in his private domain.

Eventually, the expert will feel that he needs help beyond ETS in order to further expand and refine the knowledge base. At this point the manual knowledge engineering process starts, and the knowledge engineering team uses the results of the ETS sessions as a starting point. Knowledge engineers feel that the use of ETS saves at least two months of calendar time.

The use of ETS has been of key importance in streamlining and assisting manual interviewing methods during the *expert system life cycle* (see Figure 25):

1. Identification - Initially, ETS helps the expert organize his thoughts. This can be useful before describing and defining the formal problem scope, since many tentative ideas can be quickly tested. ETS helps identify what class of problem can be solved and how these problems are characterized. The system helps partition the problem by helping to structure the problem-solving knowledge into a construct hierarchy. Much of the data, important terms, and their interrelations are identified. Problem solution sets are described. Some essential aspects of the necessary human expertise are identified.

2. Conceptualization - This stage is initially minimized, since ETS helps the expert explore key concepts and relations needed to describe the problem-solving process.

3. Formalization - ETS automatically maps the key concepts into several representations, which can immediately be used for automatic rapid prototyping.

4. Implementation - ETS automatically "implements" an initial expert system, by building a knowledge base for a target production rule expert system building tool.

5. Testing - Several tools and techniques are provided for incrementally improving ETS's knowledge base, using knowledge expansion methods and feedback from the prototype expert system.

ETS and Knowledge Representation

ETS elicits and presents knowledge in several different forms. Each form is useful in different situations, and the diversity of methods provides a framework for synergistic interaction during the knowledge elicitation and refinement process.

Predicate calculus / logic. As mentioned above in the discussion of implications, the rating grid can be viewed as a matrix of predicates and truth values. The truth values, however, are not simply true and false. The expert can assign a range of truth values to any particular predicate-attribute-value three-tuple, for example, "(HIGH-STRENGTH GRAPHITE 5)". In addition, truth values are extended to include both ("B") and neither ("N"). In this way, predicate calculus is extended to include the four concepts Told-True, Told-False, Told-Neither, and Told-True-and-Told-False, where true and false can take on a range of values using the methods of multi-valued logic [Rescher, 1969].

Given these extensions, logical entailments are derived from the grid based on multi-valued logics using fuzzy set theory [Zadeh, 1965]. The implications link together to form a number of disjoint, possibly inconsistent relationship hierarchy graphs. The expert may use ETS to compare these logically derived relationships to his own internal construct hierarchy and explore points of conflict.

Production rules. The rating grid and implication relations are used to create production rules. Rules are useful descriptions of expert knowledge that may be directly used in conjunction with expert system building tools.

Semantic networks. The relations in the implication graphs correspond roughly to the arcs in semantic network "IS-A" hierarchies.

<u>Frames.</u> The grid itself can be looked on as a frame whose slots are multiplied and filled in during an ETS session. Although frame system ideas do not as yet appear to be useful in ETS, one could imagine that the system could be driven by fill-in rules for empty slots (elements and constructs), that would present the expert with a variety of strategies for knowledge extraction.

<u>Decision tables.</u> The information in the rating grid can be viewed as a type of decision table. In fact, the internal inference engine in ETS uses the rating grid information directly during a consultation rather than the production rules because it is more efficient.

The use of these multiple representation methods helps the expert look at the problem-solving knowledge in different ways, thereby leading to a deeper understanding of the problem-solving process.

3 DISCUSSION

ETS has significantly reduced the knowledge acquisition time for a database management system advisor, an airplane engine fault diagnostic system, and several other projects. Knowledge engineers feel that ETS can save at least two months of project calendar time. This estimate is made by comparing the time taken for knowledge acquisition for similar projects. The reduction in time results in savings of both the expert's time and the knowledge engineers' time. Some of the prototype knowledge-based systems that have been built with ETS are shown in Figure 26. So far over two hundred such systems have been built, ranging in size from thirty rules to over two thousand rules.

It took the expert less than one hour to complete the example Fiber Advisor ETS session.

Due to ETS's rapid prototyping capability, project feasibility is being demonstrated in several areas that otherwise might not have received consideration. Consequently, a large number of these small prototypes are being accrued, giving resource managers a concrete basis to compare potential applications and sets of applications. For instance, consideration is being given to supplying a software engineering workstation with several small, communicating expert systems. These would then help the software engineering team with resource allocation decisions, personnel management, requirements and specifications production, testing, debugging, documentation production, and

Age Guesser (by facial features)
AI Library Advisor
AI Tools Advisor
Aircraft Identifier
Aircraft Fault Isolator
Airplane Configuration Mass Property Estimation Risk
    Analyzer
Airplane Design Flutter Analyzer
Alphanumeric Character Recognizer (by feature)
Animal Identification Advisor
Artificial Intelligence Citation Tutor
Automated Numerical Control - Cutter Consultant
Automatic Flight Controls Diagnostic Aid
ATLAS Structural Analysis Advisor
AXOTL Software Advisor
Bank Examiner
Bar-Tender's Assistant
Bicycle Selector
Bond Durability Consultant
Business Computing Needs Advisor
Business Graphics Package Consultant
Car Engine Diagnostic Aid
Character Recognizer
Car Horn Diagnostic Aid
Climbing Gear Advisor
Composite Materials - Design Optimization
Composite Materials - Design Retrieval
Composite Materials - Materials Retrieval
Composite Materials - Process Planning
Computer Communications System Bug Advisor
Computer Languages Consultant
Conflict of Interest Advisor
Curriculum Advisor
Database Management System Consultant
Documentation Update Consultant
Energy Control System Model Evaluator
Expert System Application Advisor
Expert System Tools Advisor
Failure Modes and Effects Analyzer
Fast Food Advisor
Finish Advisor for Design Engineers
Finish and Corrosion Control Consultant
Flight Controls Human Factors Assistant
Flight Mode Manager
Geology Analyzer
Graphics Package Advisor
GT-STRUDL Structural Analysis Advisor
Houseplant Disease Identifier
Ice Cream Flavor Selector
Japanese Restaurant Advisor (for Seattle)
Jet Engine Diagnostic Aid

Jet Engine Fault Isolator
Jet Engine Manual Advisor
Materials Technology Advisor / Database Pilot
Meal Advisor
Mental Health Diagnostic Aid
Micro Computer - Needs Analysis
Micro Computer - System Recommendations Consultant
Micro Computer - Workstation Configuration Advisor
Molded Rubber Seal Advisor
Motorcycle Selector
MugWump Political Advisor
Newspaper Selection Consultant
Office Automation System Advisor
Office Automation Workstation Advisor
Organization Development Intervention Consultant
Personality Factor Advisor
Personnel Resource Management Decision Aid
Pet Locator
Palo Alto Restaurant Advisor
PAN AIR Aerodynamic Analysis Software - Geometry
    Advisor
PAN AIR Aerodynamic Analysis Software - Front End
    Advisor
PAN AIR Aerodynamic Analysis Software - Back End
    Analyzer
Portfolio Management Aid
Program Bug Advisor (FORTRAN)
Programming Language Advisor
Programming Language Applications Advisor
Programming Language Evaluator and Selector
Propulsion System Advisor
Radio Diagnostician
Rapid Software Prototyping Aid
Relational Database Construction Advisor
Resin Advisor for Composite Parts
Reporting Assignment Advisor
Rivet Selector
Robotic System Application Advisor
Software Bug Diagnosis and Prescription Consultant
Software Management Consultant
Software Release Advisor
Software Services Advisor
Statistics Package Use Advisor
Structural Analysis Software Selector
Tax Regulation Consultant
Technical Sales and Services Consultant
Telephone Feature Selection Consultant
Transport Airplane Configuration Initial Selection
    Advisor
Travel Agent for Domestic Cities
Travel Agent for Foreign Cities
Velocity Analysis Advisor
Visual Target Identifier
Wine Advisor
Wood Identifier
Word Processing System Consultant

Figure 26. Some of the rapid prototype knowledge bases built using ETS.

configuration management. Rapid simulation of the components of such an environment is greatly facilitated by using ETS.

The quality of the problem-solving information elicited from the expert in the early stages is improved over manual methods because ETS provides the expert with knowledge analysis methods and a mechanism for exploring internal conflicts in the way that he handles different problem cases. Consistency is used conceptually to elaborate important problem aspects and not as a set of criteria for rejecting "bad" heuristics.

Experts and their managers have been enthusiastic about ETS's knowledge elicitation process. Gaining the confidence of the expert early in the knowledge acquisition phase is important, as discussed above.

Multiple representation strategies and analysis methods are available to the expert that enable the knowledge to be viewed and modified in a number of interrelated ways.

Much attention has been paid to the development of a friendly and robust user interface. As in all computer systems, interfaces must be engineered with end-user acceptance in mind. Commands may be entered from pop-up menus with the system mouse or simply keyed in. Interlisp's spelling completion and correction facilities are used to manage user interaction when appropriate. This interface has been critical in gaining the acceptance of experts who use ETS.

Combining Expertise from Multiple Experts

As mentioned in Slater [1981] and Gaines and Shaw [1981], methods are being developed to combine psychological information from several subjects in the form of rating grids. These techniques may help to overcome a serious practical problem with building consultation expert systems - combining knowledge from many experts. Two experts, for example, may attempt to solve a problem, using similar or dissimilar methods, and may or may not achieve the same results. Trying to capture this type of information in one coherent expert system has proved to be very difficult.

By letting several experts build grids independently and then combining them together into one consultation system, the refine-and-test cycles can be shortened, since more specialized and diverse special case knowledge will be uncovered earlier in the knowledge acquisition process. Promising experiments have been performed in our research center using ETS to combine expertise from several experts. For instance, ETS produced knowledge bases from four experts for an Artificial Intelligence Tool Advisor which were combined to produce one large consultation system (over 2200 rules). The end user could then select the expertise of any subset of experts during the consultation and receive "consensus" and "dissenting" recommendations [Boose, 1985]. The "dissenting opinion" mechanism tends to preserve expertise concerning special cases and exceptions. Negotiating techniques based on grid analyses presented by Slater [1977] and Gaines and Shaw [1981] have also been used successfully.

Other Efforts in Building Knowledge Acquisition Systems

Each of the current tools described below helps solve some aspect of the knowledge acquisition process. ETS could be used in combination with each as a front-end processor to elicit initial problem traits and heuristics.

TEIRESIAS is a subsystem of KS-300/EMYCIN which aids the expert and knowledge engineers in their attempt to refine an existing knowledge base [Davis and Lenat, 1982]. The system develops a model of the knowledge forms based on the current knowledge base and tests new knowledge to see if it "fits." TEIRESIAS also contains explanation and debugging methods to help the expert track down specific problems related to test cases. This system stresses an incremental approach to building a knowledge base. Davis calls this process the transfer of expertise. TEIRESIAS is the most advanced example of this class of knowledge acquisition aids.

ETS can be used to supply the initial knowledge base to TEIRESIAS, since TEIRESIAS is not capable of eliciting such information on its own. This is what happens when ETS produces a rapid prototype expert system for KS-300/EMYCIN; TEIRESIAS in KS-300/EMYCIN can then be used to aid the incremental debugging process.

META-DENDRAL and AQ11 both do classification analyses of training examples to produce generalized rules using inductive inference strategies. META-DENDRAL learns rules that predict how classes of compounds fragment in a mass spectrometer [Buchanan and Feigenbaum, 1978], and AQ11 formulates rules from traits and test cases [Michalski, 1980].

Both of these systems still need an initial set of problem traits before classification can begin. Therefore, it is up to the expert and knowledge engineers to make the initial list of applicable traits and relevant training examples.

Again, ETS could be used as a front-end for these systems, to elicit the problem characteristics.

NANOKLAUS attempts to elicit a classification hierarchy from an expert through a natural language dialog [Hass and Hendrix, 1983]. The information is then used for certain classes of deductive data retrieval.

The emphasis in the NANOKLAUS system is on the natural language interface. "Is-a" (class hierarchy and instance) information is entered by the expert. Currently, the system is not capable of eliciting or producing heuristics. The system works best with concrete physical objects, starting with special "seed" concepts (physical objects, people, men, women, measures, and things), and the expert describes new concepts in terms of these old ones. The expert needs to already have such a hierarchy developed in his mind before using the system. Again, ETS could be combined with such a system not only to help elicit relevant concepts and "IS-A" implications in terms of constructs derived from objects, but also to produce heuristic information.

System Limitations

There are some fundamental limitations to the use of ETS for knowledge acquisition:

- Kelly's grid methodology is best suited for *analysis* class problems (debugging, diagnosis, interpretation, classification) whose solutions may be enumerated ahead of time. The system cannot readily handle *synthesis* class problems where unique solutions are built up from components (design and planning), or problems that require a combination of analysis and synthesis (control, monitoring, prediction, repair). However, ETS can handle the analytic portions of these problems, and it should be noted that many planning and design problems involve synthesizing the results of several analytic components (for instance, R1 [McDermott, 1980a and 1980b]). These components may be investigated with ETS.

- It is difficult to apply grid methodology to elicit "deep" *causal* knowledge, *procedural* knowledge, or *strategic* knowledge. ETS elicits traits and builds relationships, but does not find out much about *how* or *when* this information is used in the problem-solving process. Some of this information could be gathered by modifying ETS to ask for more specific constructs during the interview process.

For instance, to elicit procedural knowledge, ETS could ask, "Think of a procedure, or part of a procedure, that would be useful for concluding about two of "a," "b," and "c," but not the other. What is that procedure?" This has been tried in manual interviewing following the initial use of ETS, but the results have been mixed. The process depends on the ability of the expert to think about the problem at a useful level of abstraction. Similarly, ETS could ask about strategic knowledge. Causal knowledge could only be elicited by breaking down analysis problems into smaller subproblems, and breaking these down into smaller problems, and so on, asking questions about how the problem components work together as a system. This is much more difficult for the expert, since he needs to keep global relationships in mind continuously, as well as the specific aspect of the problem he is focusing on. The interview process would also be much more difficult to control. Another interviewing technique is being applied to this problem in MDIS, a maintenance and diagnostic and information elicitation system [Antonelli, 1983]. It may be possible to tie these two techniques together in one knowledge acquisition system.

- It is sometimes difficult for the expert to identify conclusion sets that are at similar, useful levels of granularity. For instance, in a maintenance system, the expert may include the elements "engine" and "ignition coil." This can lead to problems when constructs are elicited since those applied to the engine will be at a different level of abstraction (more general) than those applied to the ignition coil. However, once the expert understands how the elements and constructs work together to build rules, consistent levels of abstraction can usually be identified at the next ETS session, starting over from scratch. At most the expert will have "wasted" a few hours in coming to grips with a more consistent abstraction of his knowledge.

- Methods are also being examined to allow the expert to combine several ETS knowledge bases at varying levels of abstraction. This paradigm is based on Clancey's description of generic structured selection (analytic) problem-solving [Clancey, 1984]. When an inference engine is built which can handle multiple ETS rating grids, other types of problems may be experimented with. For instance, time and context could be associated with specific grids; this could allow some forms of planning problem-solving knowledge to be captured.

- All constructs are bipolar; they may only take on two values. It may be more convenient to describe a single trait that could take on any number of discrete values rather than just two values. This becomes particularly awkward when the construct is numerical, and there are many critical points on the scale. Currently, all such points (and their "negations") must be represented as individual pairs of traits.

These are some of the limitations of grid methodology reviewed by Kelly [1955]:

- Representative elements - The assumption is that the elicited set of elements will be a sufficient representation of the problem conclusion set. It must be assumed that the expert knows what these conclusions are, or that the relevant set will be built with ETS knowledge expansion methods or subsequent manual interviewing.

- Representative constructs - It is more difficult to verify that a sufficient set of constructs has been elicited. Inappropriate constructs are relatively easy to weed out of the system (see the discussion of construct types above), but errors of omission are harder to detect. Some important constructs that are missing may be elicited using ETS's knowledge expansion techniques, but there is no guarantee that a sufficient set will be found. This is a problem with knowledge acquisition in general. Expert-level performance of the final expert system is critically dependent on obtaining and effectively using a sufficient set of problem-solving knowledge.

- Stability of conception - It is assumed that the expert will use the internal constructs described by his construct pair labels in a consistent manner when making ratings. Some inconsistencies are captured when ETS reformulates knowledge representations, but all of them may not be captured. It is also assumed that the use of constructs will not change significantly over time. Actually, grid methodology has been used to track psychological change over time by having subjects periodically redo grids on the same topic. This method could eventually help keep the expert system updated as the expertise changes.

- Word labels - It is assumed that the expert can communicate the meanings behind the construct labels to the knowledge engineers, and, ultimately, to the end user. "Fuzzy" definitions need to be refined during the manual knowledge acquisition process. At least ETS gives a working definition of these constructs by showing them in use.

Several limitations exist in the prototype expert systems that are built by ETS:

- It is difficult to make minor corrections directly based on the final recommendation set, since the constructs and elements that produced the rules are so interrelated. The methodologies mentioned above that compare the expert's expectations with consultation results can be used to circumvent this problem to some extent.

- Individual certainty factors associated with rules may have little meaning when examined by the expert. Each factor only has significance when compared with all the other factors in the system. Thus, some loss of system transparency is incurred.

Future Work

ETS is being expanded in a number of different areas to improve its utility:

- Implement some of the manual methods described above to try to elicit procedural, strategic, and causal knowledge.

- Add principal components analysis to detect interdependent parameters and compute the strength of the interdependence [Slater, 1977].

- Implement a form of cluster anaiysis [ADDTREE or EXTREE, Sattath and Tversky, 1977].

- Implement an element preference analysis to assist in certainty factor generation and relative element importance analysis. Produce resistance to change grids that would provide other measures of the relative importance of constructs in the expert's hierarchy. Create implication grids that provide an additional method of analyzing the relationships in the expert's construct hierarchy [Hinkle, 1965].

- Continue to experiment with methods for combining expertise from many experts.

- User models could be based on a representation of that portion of the user's construct hierarchy that deals with the given problem. For instance, a user construct hierarchy could be modeled based on manual drafting techniques and then used as the basis for an intelligent user interface for a computer-aided design system. The user interface could use the knowledge in the construct hierarchies to hypothesize about what specific task the user was trying to perform, offer suggestions, automatically correct errors, complete routine sequences of commands, and so on. System actions could be based on the results a user would predict. The user interface could also be smart enough to derive that portion of the problem-solving hierarchy that is peculiar to an individual and evolve an idiosyncratic interface.

- Elicit constructs from the expert in terms of the way that constructs are internally managed for problem solving. Such "meta-constructs" as impulsivity, rigidity, and propositionality are thought to control learning and change [Hinkle, 1965]. Learning occurs in terms of changes in the construct hierarchy and the anticipated results of that change. These principles of personal construct system management could be used to explore the expert's problem-solving methods, especially when the expert is solving problems on the edge of his understanding. For instance, Hinkle suggested that it is easier to change one's subordinate constructs if their superordinate constructs are temporarily stabilized, and vice-versa. A teacher might tell a pupil, "You're doing very well generally in arithmetic, but you need to exert more effort in learning long division." Hinkle's hypothesis is that constructive change may only take place from a position of relative stability. This implies that a *construct management system* would avoid massive, traumatic changes in the construct hierarchy. Some questions to explore for problem-solving might be: 1) Are there specific construct relationships (parallel, orthogonal, reciprocal, ambiguous) or patterns of network relationships that are more readily changed than others? 2) What is the value of resistance to change in a working system? 3) How does the construct management system control the stabilization and destabilization processes? 4) What are the criteria for allowing change? and 5) On a meta-level, how is stability vs. growth (learning) managed?

In spite of the limitations of ETS, it has been an invaluable aid to the knowledge engineering process. Especially in situations where analysis problems can be solved using the production system paradigm, ETS dramatically streamlines the knowledge acquisition process.

ACKNOWLEDGEMENTS

Thanks to Ray Allis, Roger Beeman, Alistair Holden, Earl Hunt, Frank Jackson, Ted Jardine, Janusz Kowalik, Art Nagai, Steve Tanimoto, Lisle Tinglof, Steve White, and Bruce Wilson for their contributions and support.

REFERENCES

Antonelli, D., "The Application of Artificial Intelligence to a Maintenance and Diagnostic Information System (MDIS)," in *The Proceedings of the Joint Services Workshop on Artificial Intelligence in Maintenance*, Boulder, Col., 1983.

Atkin, R. H., *Mathematical Structure in Human Affairs*, London: Heinemann, 1974.

Bannister, D., and Mair, J. M. M., *The Evaluation of Personal Constructs*, New York: Academic Press, 1968.

Boose, J. H., "Personal Construct Theory and the Transfer of Human Expertise," the *Proceedings of the National Conference on Artificial Intelligence* (AAAI-84), Austin, 1984.

Boose, J. H., "Combining Expertise from Multiple Experts," forthcoming paper, 1985.

Buchanan, B. G., and Feigenbaum, E. A., "DENDRAL and META-DENDRAL: Their Applications Dimension," *Artificial Intelligence*, 11, 1978.

Buchanan, B. G., Barstow, D., Bechtel, R., Bennett, J., Clancey, W., Kulikowski, C., Mitchell, T., and Waterman, D., "Constructing an Expert System," in Hayes-Roth, F., Waterman, D. A., and Lenat, D. B. (eds.), *Building Expert Systems*, Addison-Wesley, 1983.

Clancey, W. J., "Classification Problem Solving," the *Proceedings of the National Conference on Artificial Intelligence* (AAAI- 84), Austin, 1984 (also, see this book, Chapter 1).

Davis, R., and Lenat, D. B., *Knowledge-Based Systems in Artificial Intelligence*, New York: McGraw-Hill, 1982.

Forgy, C. L., *OPS5 User's Manual*, Department of Computer Science, Pittsburgh: Carnegie-Mellon University, 1981.

Gaines, B. R., and Shaw, M. L. G., "New Directions in the Analysis and Interactive Elicitation of Personal Construct Systems," in M. Shaw (ed.), *Recent Advances in Personal Construct Technology*, New York: Academic Press, 1981.

Hass, N., and Hendrix, G., "Learning by Being Told: Acquiring Knowledge for Information Management," in R. S. Michalski, J. Carbonell, and T. M. Mitchell (eds.), *Machine Learning: An Artificial Intelligence Approach*, Palo Alto, Calif: Tioga Press, 1983.

Hayes-Roth, F., Waterman, D. A., and Lenat, D. B., *Building Expert Systems*, Addison-Wesley, 1983.

Hinkle, D. N., "The Change of Personal Constructs from the Viewpoint of a Theory of Implications," Ph.D. Dissertation, Ohio: Ohio State University, 1965.

Keen, T. R., and Bell, R. C., "One Thing Leads to Another: A New Approach to Elicitation in the Repertory Grid Technique," in M. Shaw (ed.), *Recent Advances in Personal Construct Technology*, New York: Academic Press, 1981.

Kelly, G. A., *The Psychology of Personal Constructs*, New York: Norton, 1955.

Kelly, G. A., in B. Maher (ed.), *Clinical Psychology and Personality: The Selected Papers of George Kelly*, New York: Wiley, 1968.

Lenat, D. B., "The Nature of Heuristics," *Artificial Intelligence* 19, 1982.

McDermott, J., "R1: An Expert in the Computer Systems Domain," in *AAAI 1*, 1980a.

McDermott, J., "R1: An Expert Configurer," Report no. CMU-CS-80-119, Computer Science Department, Pittsburgh: Carnegie-Mellon University, 1980b.

McDermott, J., "R1: A Rule-Based Configurer of Computer Systems," *Artificial Intelligence* 19(1), 1982.

McDermott, J., "R1 Revisited: Four Years in the Trenches," *The AI Magazine*, Vol. 5, No. 3, 1984.

Michalski, R. S., "Pattern Recognition as Rule-guided Inductive Inference," *IEEE Transactions of Pattern Analysis and Machine Intelligence* 2, no. 4, 1980.

Michalski, R. S., Carbonell, J., and Mitchell, T. M. (eds.), *Machine Learning: An Artificial Intelligence Approach*, Palo Alto, Calif: Tioga Press, 1983.

Rescher, N., *Many-Valued Logic*, New York: McGraw-Hill, 1969.

Sattath, S., and Tversky, A., "Additive Similarity Trees," *Psychometrika*, Vol. 42, No. 3, 1977.

Shaw, M. L. G., and Gaines, B. R., "Fuzzy Semantics for Personal Construing," in *Systems Science and Science*, Kentucky: Society for General Systems Research, 1980.

Shaw, M. L. G., and McKnight, C., "ARGUS: A Program to Explore Intra-Personal Personalities," in Shaw, M., *Recent Advances in Personal Construct Technology*, New York: Academic Press, 1981.

Slater, P. (ed.), *Dimensions of Intrapersonal Space*, Vol. 2, London: Wiley, 1977.

Slater, P., "Construct Systems in Conflict," in Shaw, M., *Recent Advances in Personal Construct Technology*, New York: Academic Press, 1981.

Zadeh, L. A., "Fuzzy Sets," *Information and Control*, 8, 1965.

3

ANALOGY: A PRIORI REQUIREMENTS
FOR DEEP EXPERT SYSTEM APPLICATIONS

DOUGLAS C. DORROUGH
BOEING ARTIFICIAL INTELLIGENCE CENTER
BELLEVUE, WASHINGTON

1.0 INTRODUCTION

Earlier we reported [1, 2, 3] the results of investigations of the distinct, but closely related, notions of "similarity," "analogy," and "metaphor."

These results were primarily directed to investigators in the fields of formal linguistics, logic, and mathematics. However, evaluations [4, 5] of recent attempts [6, 7, 8, 9, 10] to utilize one or more of the indicated notions within the software of intelligent automatons reveal the need for some focused assessments about a priori parameters of analogy. These in turn could then be applied to analogical statements and their relationships to knowledge bases, inference engines, and learning systems.

In this chapter, we shall limit the discussion to the notion of "analogy." Although the related notions of "similarity" and "metaphor" are very important for the development of machine-intelligent software, analogy is more fundamental [11]. Accordingly, the body of the paper is subdivided into discussions about the typical settings (pragmatics), the distinctive verbal pattern, the context, and the checkability of analogies, with some final remarks concerning future directions.

Our point of departure will be a list of analogy-like statements the members of which will subsequently function as subject matter for our analyses. We shall refer to the members of this list as "analogy-like" or "analogical" simply because the list is, in certain respects, dichotomous. As we hope to demonstrate, on the list are to be found examples of at least two distinct types and several subtypes of statements. We have included among the members of the list examples of those types of statements to which the term "analogy" has, at one time or another, been attached:

a-1)   Life is to two eternities as an isthmus is to two continents.

a-2)   Zeno was to Parmenides as Aristotle was to Plato.

a-3)   Nine is to twenty-seven as one is to three.

a-4)   Saint Cyr is to the Army of France as West Point is to the Army of the United States.

a-5)   It is as sport to a fool to do wickedness; and *so is* wisdom to a man of understanding.

a-6)   Physical objects are to Prime Matter as garments are to cloth.

a-7)   Two is to four as one is to two.

a-8)   The geographical location of Switzerland is to that of Italy as the geographical location of Canada is to that of the United States.

a-9)   Twenty-five is to one hundred as one is to four.

a-10) The primary meaning of the expression "male sibling" is to the primary meaning of the term "brother" as the primary meaning of the expression "male parent" is to the primary meaning of the term "father."

a-11) Italy's representation of a map is to that of Switzerland as Italy is to Switzerland.

a-12) Substance is to different properties at different times as a piece of gold is to different shapes at different times.

a-13) Electrons are to the nucleus of an atom as planets are to the sun.

a-14) Albert's first-order statements are to first-order falsity as his second-order statements are to second-order falsity.

113

a-15)　　Buddhism was to the development of Asiatic civilization as Christianity was to the development of Western civilization.

a-16)　　. . . as sight is to the eye, so intellect is to the mind.

a-17)　　As vinegar to the teeth, and as smoke to the eyes, so is the sluggard to them that sent him.

a-18)　　The connective " . " is to the statements which it connects as a circuit alpha is to the voltage levels which it relates.

2.0　　DO ANALOGICAL STATEMENTS HAVE A TYPICAL SETTING?

An adequate account of analogy cannot be given unless one delineates the normal, i.e., constant, conceptual situation (as opposed to behavioral or purely physical situations) in which analogy-like statements occur. Thus, as a part of our investigation of analogy, we shall consider such a delineation. If established, the situation in question will be referred to as the setting of analogy-like statements.

2.1　　Method

We shall first consider examples of a promising candidate for such a setting. Next, we shall look for legitimate counterexamples (examples of analogy-like statements whose setting varies significantly from that indicated by our original candidate) in terms of which we shall have to either modify or abandon completely our original candidate. Finally, we shall determine a general setting which can be found in all of the varied specific examples of the use of analogy-like statements.

2.2　　A Promising Candidate

If some intelligent person, let us call him "Inquirer," with a cursory knowledge of Greek history were to ask, "What was Zeno's relation to Parmenides?" one could reply in one of two modes: Mode I, "Zeno was (among other things) the most prominent pupil of Parmenides," or Mode II, "Zeno was to Parmenides as Aristotle was to Plato." Both Mode I and Mode II reply to Inquirer's question (I. Q.). Moreover, other examples would suggest that all such questions can be given at least two different modes of reply: Mode I is usually composed of a single statement which not only replies to the I. Q. but also explicitly answers it, and Mode II is composed of an analogy-like statement and several other statements which reply to the I. Q. but do not explicitly answer it. ("Reply" means the statements which (a) are uttered by the respondent, (b) occur after the I. Q., and (c) explicitly or implicitly answer the I. Q.) ("Answer" means that reply which explicitly satisfies the I. Q.) In other words, Mode II implies an answer but invites Inquirer himself to formulate it explicitly.

But let us unpack a little more our previous example of a Mode II reply. In the face of the I. Q. concerning the relation of one classical personality to another, we should pose our Mode II reply as follows: We would first ask whether or not he knows the relationship of Aristotle to Plato. If his reply is affirmative, we would then explain that the relation of Zeno to Parmenides is the same as the relation of Aristotle to Plato. If Inquirer's reply is negative, we would describe the relation of Aristotle to Plato in another analogy-like statement which involves a pupil-teacher relation and which is better known to him.

Spelled out, our dialogue (E-1) would appear as follows:

1-1)	Inquirer:	"What was the relation of Zeno to Parmenides?"
1-2)	Respondent:	"Do you know what the relation of Aristotle to Plato was?"
1-3)	Inquirer:	"Yes."
1-4)	Respondent:	"Well then, Zeno was to Parmenides as Aristotle was to Plato."
1-5)	Inquirer:	"I see. Then, Zeno was the most prominent pupil of Parmenides."
1-6)	Respondent:	"Correct."

If our Inquirer's response at 1-3 had been negative, the rest of the dialogue (E-2) might have proceeded in the following way:

| 2-4) | Respondent: | "Well then, perhaps you remember Miss W." |

2-5)	Inquirer:	"Do I! She was your most prominent student."
2-6)	Respondent:	"Exactly. And just as Miss W. was to me so Aristotle was to Plato. Moreover, this is the same relation which Zeno had to Parmenides."
2-7)	Inquirer:	"Then, Zeno was the most prominent student of Parmenides."
2-8)	Respondent:	"Correct."

Another way in which the dialogue (E-2) could have proceeded after a negative responese at 1-3 is the following:

3-4)	Respondent:	"Then, I shall simply tell you that Aristotle was the most prominent pupil of Plato."
3-5)	Inquirer:	"I see."
3-6)	Respondent:	"And further, that as Aristotle was to Plato so Zeno was to Parmenides."
3-7)	Inquirer:	"All right, I understand."

Let us consider a question from Inquirer about an entirely different subject. Let us suppose that he is learning very elementary arithmetic and he asks the following question: "What is the relation of nine to twenty-seven?" (We assume interest is in a relation between these two numbers, not between the corresponding numerals.)

Again, the Respondent (perhaps this time he is Inquirer's teacher) has at least two possible modes of reply. In Mode I fashion, he can simply say: "Nine is one-third of twenty-seven." However, in an effort toward something more pedagogical, our Respondent more likely will proceed in Mode II fashion with the following dialogue (E-4):

4-2)	Respondent:	"Do you know the relation of the number one to the number three?"
4-3)	Inquirer:	"Yes."
4-4)	Respondent:	"What is the relation?"
4-5)	Inquirer:	"One is a third of three."
4-6)	Respondent:	"Well then, nine is to twenty-seven as one is to three."

4-7)	Inquirer:	"Oh! Then, nine is one-third of twenty-seven."
4-8)	Respondent:	"Correct."

As in E-1, if Inquirer's response at 4-3 had been negative, the rest of the dialogue would have followed closely the lines of E-2 or E-3.

Finally, let us pose a third question from Inquirer. Imagine that he is a poet, a budding philosopher, or the like. As a member of one of these groups, he will probably, at some time or other, ask the question: "What is life?" Although he may address such a question solely to himself, it is equally possible that he will put the question to another.

Assuming that a Mode I reply is eschewed by Inquirer's Respondent, a dialogue similar to E-1 through E-4 would eventuate. Let us further assume that the Respondent in such a dialogue possesses some literary ability and that he is not mistaking the question for a purely biological one. Our hypothetical dialogue (E-5) would then proceed somewhat as follows:

5-2)	Respondent:	"I am certain that you know what an isthmus is."
5-3)	Inquirer:	"Yes, I do."
5-4)	Respondent:	"Fine, because it seems to me that life is to two eternities as an isthmus is to two continents."
5-5)	Inquirer:	"I take it that by such a statement you wish to imply that life is a narrow connection."
5-6)	Respondent:	"Yes, but I wish to imply a great deal more."
5-7)	Inquirer:	"Well then, let's pursue these implications."

Etc.

So far, we have considered examples in which a single question from Inquirer prompts the Respondent to construct an analogy-like statement in reply. But what about the situation in which Inquirer, after a few appropriate questions put to the Respondent, constructs his own analogy-like statement? Spelled out, such a dialogue (E-6) might take the following form:

6-1)	Inquirer:	"Wasn't Zeno the most prominent student of Parmenides?"

6-2)	Respondent:	"Yes."
6-3)	Inquirer:	"And wasn't Aristotle the most prominent student of Plato?"
6-4)	Respondent:	"Yes."
6-5)	Inquirer:	"Then, in this respect, Zeno was to Parmenides as Aristotle was to Plato (or: Aristotle was to Plato as Zeno was to Parmenides)."
6-6)	Respondent:	"Correct."

From dialogues E-1 through E-6, it is possible to state some generalizations that characterize the behavioral process in which analogy-like statements occur. However, the process takes two forms, corresponding to the two types of dialogues, E-1 through E-5 on the one hand and E-6 on the other. We shall generalize for each but shall refer to both as the AIP (Analogy Involving Process). The generalizations can be represented verbally or by flow charts as in Figures 2.2-1 and 2.2-2.

In Form I of the AIP, Inquirer asks Respondent a question concerning a particular relation. The Respondent replies with a question of his or her own in the form: "Do you know X?" where X stands for some other particular relation. To this question Inquirer replies either positively or negatively. If his answer is positive, the Respondent constructs an analogy-like statement which essentially replies to Inquirer's original question. If his reply is negative then Respondent must ask questions of lesser difficulty (as in E-2) until he receives a positive reply or he must answer his own question (as in E-3), which elicited the negative reply from Inquirer in the first place. In any case, an analogy-like statement is eventually constructed, and with its construction, the reply to the I.Q. is virtually complete. The only thing required further is a statement from Inquirer indicating that he apprehends, in whole or in part, what is implied by Respondent's analogy-like statement. With this last step, any particular AIP of this type is complete.

In Form II of the AIP, Inquirer usually poses two questions serially. To each question the Respondent answers either positively or negatively. If Inquirer receives positive answers to both questions, he constructs an analogy-like statement and thereby completes the AIP.

We have extensively examined the behavioral situations in which many analogy-like statements are located because such situations contain (some of

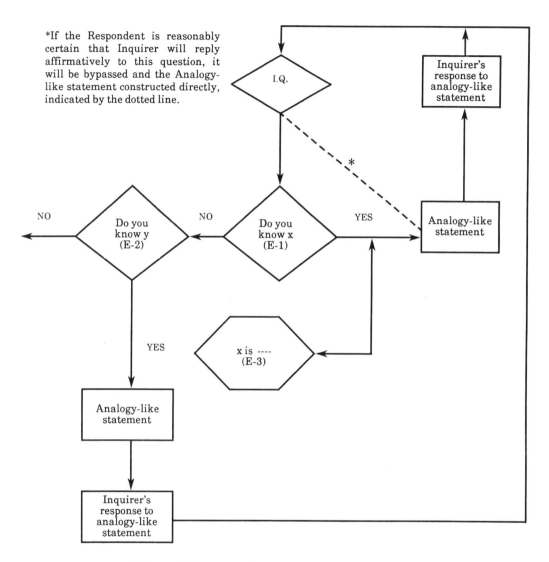

*If the Respondent is reasonably certain that Inquirer will reply affirmatively to this question, it will be bypassed and the Analogy-like statement constructed directly, indicated by the dotted line.

I.Q.

Inquirer's response to analogy-like statement

*

NO

Do you know y (E-2)

NO

Do you know x (E-1)

YES

Analogy-like statement

YES

x is ---- (E-3)

Analogy-like statement

Inquirer's response to analogy-like statement

Flow Diagram for Form I of AIP Model
Figure 2.2-1

119

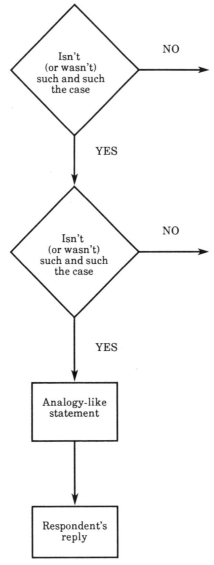

Flow Diagram for Form II of AIP
Figure 2.2-2

them quite explicitly) that conceptual situation we desire to identify with the setting for all analogy-like statements. Careful analysis of some of the dialogues will better elucidate our target.

Perhaps the best dialogue with which to begin is E-2, in which our sought-for situation is clearly exhibited. When this dialogue has been completely unpacked, the following inference emerges:

2-5)   She (i.e., Miss W.) was your most prominent student.

2-6)   As Miss W. was to me (Respondent) so Aristotle was to Plato and so also Zeno was to Parmenides.

2-7)   Then, Zeno was the most prominent student of Parmenides.

We can say that 2-7 is inferred from 2-5 and 2-6 jointly. We apply the word "inference" solely to argumentative discourse in which the author is trying to make a point. In a way, 2-5 and 2-6 furnish "logical" support for 2-7. This becomes more evident when we abstract completely from the particular dialogue. The inference then stands out as the following: From the ostensibly true statements that (1) "Miss W. was the Respondent's most prominent student," (2) "Aristotle was to Plato as Miss W. was to the Respondent," and (3) "Zeno was to Parmenides as Aristotle was to Plato," it follows that (4) "Zeno was the most prominent student of Parmenides" is also true.

In dialogue E-6 we have an inference involving an analogy-like statement where the latter is the conclusion of the inference, i.e., the statement inferred, rather than one of the premises. Transforming each question and its positive answer into a statement, we arrive at the following:

6-1) and 6-2)   Zeno was the most prominent student of Parmenides.

6-3) and 6-4)   Aristotle was the most prominent student of Plato.

6-5)   Zeno was to Parmenides as Aristotle was to Plato.

Here, the inference would be articulated in this way: From the ostensibly true statements that (1) "Zeno was the most prominent student of Parmenides" and (2) "Aristotle was the most prominent student of Plato," it follows that (3) "In this respect, Zeno was to Parmenides as Aristotle was to Plato" is true.

Finally, in its abbreviated form, dialogue E-4 presents us with the same type of inference as E-2:

4-5)   One is a third of three.

4-6)   Nine is to twenty-seven as one is to three.

4-7)   Then, nine is one-third of twenty-seven.

So far we have presented evidence that a typical setting for analogy-like statements is that of an inference. But we now wish to consider some apparent uses of analogy-like statements which do not seem to fit our hypothesis about such a setting. Specifically, we wish to consider examples of analogy-like statements employed as other than components of an inference. One such employement is exemplified by a mathematical problem of a type which can be found repeatedly in textbooks on elementary arithmetic:

If 20 men assemble 8 machines in a day, how many men are needed to assemble 12 machines in a day?

Solution: 8 machines need 20 men
             12 machines need ? men
             $8 : 12 : : 20 : x$
             $8 x = 240$
             $x = 30$, Answer

But this is really a bogus example. Like many problems of this kind, this is not an analogy-like statement but an incomplete expression that resembles one. It is true that aside form differences in notation, the expression "$8 : 12 : : 20 : x$" resembles the analogy-like statements on our original list. But it lacks an essential ingredient of such statements, namely, a complete set of analogates (where the latter donotes constants on either side of " : "; see Section 3.2.) In fact, the point of the exercise is to find an analogate to replace x which will transform the expression into an analogy-like statement that is true. Most mathematical exercises involving the partial skeletons of analogy-like statements are of this sort. We may therefore discount such exercises as legitimate claimants to a noninferential setting for analogy-like statements.

Another employment of analogy-like statements for which frequently an inferential setting seems to be lacking is the literary employment. The following biblical ones are as typical as any:

> I) It is as sport to a fool to do wickedness; and *so is* wisdom to a man of understanding.

Like many statements of this sort, this one must be recast and unpacked before its analogical form is evident. Transformed and properly dissected, it appears as:

> II) Wisdom is to a man of understanding as the doing of wickedness is to a fool,

and

> III) The doing of wickedness is as sport to a fool.

Now, II and its contextual statement, III, together seem to invite us to conclude that:

> IV) Wisdom (i.e., the doing of wise deeds and the saying of wise statements) is as sport to a man of understanding.

But if the preceding paraphrase is correct, I definitely has an inferential setting, which needed only the proper orchestration to be appreciated. We were greatly aided in this orchestration by the presence of the auxiliary statement, III.

In the next example we have no such aid:

> V) As vinegar to the teeth, and as smoke to the eyes, So is the sluggard to them that sent him.

When properly analyzed, this statement, like I, becomes the fraternal twins:

> VI) The sluggard is to them that send him
> As vinegar is to the teeth.
> VII) The suggard is to them that send him

As smoke is to the eyes.

The statements surrounding V in Proverbs are not immediately relevant so that we are presented with an analogy-like statement which is not overtly a component of an inference. In showing that this negative overt character is misleading, we shall concentrate upon VII, assuming that what can be demonstrated for VII also can be demonstrated for VI.

Under the penalty of otherwise writing nonsense, the author of V had to assume that (1) one or more statements of the relation of sluggards to people who send sluggards to do a job are true and are known by his readers to be true; (2) one or more statements of the relation of smoke to eyes are true and known as such by his readers; or (3) both 1 and 2. This, of course, assumes that the proverb purports to be true. Thus, in line with 1, he could have assumed that "the sluggard is an irritation to them that send him," "the sluggard is a hindrance to them that send him," or any other plausible substitute. In line with 2, our proverb maker could have presumed that "smoke is an irritant to the eyes" or that "smoke is a hindrance to the eyes," etc. Now, the tenor of the context of V strongly suggests that our writer had presumed one or more statements that further explicate 2. And if this is so, the *outline* of an inference can be composed:

VIII) Smoke is a hindrance to the eyes

or

Smoke is an irritant to the eyes

or etc.

IX)   The sluggard is to them that
      send him. As smoke is to the eyes.

X)   Therefore, the sluggard is a hindrance or an irritant or .... to
      those that send him.

We cannot specify the inference more precisely because we do not know which of the statements in VIII was actually presumed. It is possible that the author of the proverb presumed more than one statement. Be that as it may,

124

we have demonstrated that in some cases where the immediate context of a particular analogy-like statement is irrelevant, one can be sketched. Moreover, from this sketched context and its relevant analogy-like statement, an inference can be outlined. Although we have not proved and shall not prove it in this paper [12], we submit that the foregoing reconstruction can be implemented for all contextually isolated analogy-like statements, except for those few whose authors are deliberately and systematically obscure.

3.0 DO ANALOGICAL STATEMENTS HAVE A DISTINCTIVE VERBAL PATTERN?

In the next several paragraphs we shall (1) give a generic difinition of "verbal pattern"; (2) specify what we mean by "representative verbal pattern"; (3) indicate, in terms of 1 and 2, what we mean by "*the* representative verbal pattern," i.e., what we mean by a representative verbal pattern with priviliged status; and (4) relate the items of 1 to 3 to the possibility of *the* representative verbal pattern of analogical statements.

3.1 What Do We Mean By "Distinctive Verbal Pattern"?

By "verbal pattern" we mean the regulated combinations and permutations of expressions (symbols and their collocations), on both the intra- and the intersentential level, related to making statements, posing questions, giving commands, etc. Although this definition is broad enough to include verbal patterns of sentences other than statements, we will be concerned only with the latter.

By the expression "representative verbal pattern" we mean a verbal pattern exemplified by sentences used to make different types of statements. Another way of putting this is to say that we are interested in a verbal pattern common to statements of this or that type. Thus, the sentence used to make statement (A) "John is a human being," has as the representative verbal pattern (B) "x is a member of y" or more symbolically, "x ε y." We say that B is a representative verbal pattern of A because A shares that pattern with a large number of otherwise different sentences. A different verbal pattern is exemplified by the sentence used to make assertion (C), "The evening star is the morning star." C has the representative verbal pattern (D), "x is identical with y," or more symbolically, "x = y." Finally, (E), "If John is a man then John is rational, and John is a man; therefore, John is rational," exemplifies the representative verbal pattern (F), "If P then Q and P, therefore Q."

At this point, our position on the nature of representative verbal pattern encounters difficulties, which are, however, surmountable. First, a sentence may exemplify more than one representative pattern. Thus, the sentence (G), "John is wise," can be interpreted as exemplifying verbal pattern B, "John is a member of the class of wise people." However, G can also be considered to have representative verbal pattern (H), "x is θ," or more symbolically, "θx" where 'θ' stands in place of the predicate "wise" and x for the subject "John."

Naturally, we are not interested in every representative verbal pattern exemplified by a given sentence. In most cases and contexts, one pattern is selected as *the* intended representative pattern. Moreover, the way in which a pattern is given such special status depends upon the type of statements of which it is representative. Thus, to say that F is *the* representative verbal pattern for E is to say that F is the pattern from which E results by replacing each distinct statement variable of F by a different simple statement from E. However, to say in the case of C that D is *the* representative verbal pattern is to say that D is the pattern from which C results by replacing each distinct term variable in D with a different term from C. We mean by "term" any and only such expressions as proper nouns, common nouns or definite descriptions, where the latter is any locution of the pattern, "the so and so .... ." We will delineate in a similar way *the* representative verbal pattern for analogical statements. If we are successful, we shall call such a pattern a "distinctive" verbal pattern of analogical statements.

The second difficulty can be divided into two subdifficulties. First, different linguistic expressions may have the same use. Thus, in some contexts the role played by the word "if" may be played by the word "assuming," or, depending upon context, by "on the condition that," "given that," etc. Secondly, the same expression may in different contexts play different roles. Hence, the word "is" plays a role in A that is entirely different from its role in C. But these two difficulties are overcome by observing two regulative principles:

(1) A representative verbal pattern selected for each type of statement should indeed be representative; i.e., it should be very frequently exemplified by the type of statements we have in mind.

(2) The expressions occurring in such a verbal pattern should have the use they usually have in statements which exemplify that pattern.

3.2 Mathematical Analogy-Like Statements

Let us first scrutinize the following analogical statements:

AA)   Two is to four as one is to two.

BB)   Twenty-five is to one hundred as one is to four.

CC)   Nine is to twenty-seven as one is to three.

A verbal pattern common to AA - CC can be indicated by the following:

DD)   One number is to a second as a third number is to a fourth.

Another way of indicating such a pattern is:

EE)   ----is to ---- as ---- is to ----,

where the blanks would normally be occupied by numerals.

The expression EE or any of its synonyms represents, in a sense, a constant. The occurrence twice in EE of " - - - is to - - -," with each occurrence separated by " as," might lead one to suppose that any analogical statement contains two distinct constants, " is to " and " as ," which must be separately accounted for. However expressions such as "two is to four," "one is to three," etc., in AA - CC do not make sense by themselves. This indicates that EE is a verbal pattern for a four-term relation in which "is to" and "as" are merely typographical parts that have no independently defined significance.

As long as EE is not changed, the other expressions of AA - CC can be varied within limits. So long as the variants are numbers, the pattern expressed by DD or EE can be maintained. Thus, the nouns "two," "four," "twenty-five," "three," etc., can be replaced by nouns denoting other numbers without changing the verbal pattern of DD or EE. In fact, where "a," "b," "c," and "d" indifferently represent whole numbers, i.e., can be considered variables, DD or EE may be rewritten as:

FF)   a is to b as c is to d.

Moreover, provided that use of the expression:

GG)   ---- : ---- : : ---- : ----

is stipulated to correspond to a particular use of the constant EE, FF can in turn be translated into the following familiar mathematical pattern:

HH) $a : b : : c : d.$

But what is the particular meaning of EE to which GG must correspond? Part of this question can be answered by noting that each statement in AA - CC can be expanded to read:

AAA)   Two is related to four as one is related to two.
BBB)   Twenty-five is related to one hundred as one is related to four.
CCC)   Nine is related to twenty-seven as one is related to three.

Moreover, statements AAA - CCC are in turn translatable, *salva veritate et salva significatione*, into:

A'A'A')   Two is related to four in the same way as one is related to two.
B'B'B')   Twenty-five is related to one hundred in the same way as one is related to four.
C'C'C')   Nine is related to twenty-seven in the same way as one is related to three.

A'A'A' - C'C'C' in turn translate, with the same preservation of meaning and truth-value, into:

A̲ A̲ A̲)   There is at least one relation such that two has that relation to four and one has it to two.
B̲ B̲ B̲)   There is at least one relation such that twenty-five has that relation to one hundred and one has it to four.
C̲ C̲ C̲)   There is at least one relation such that nine has that relation to twenty-seven and one has it to three.

The prolixity of these translations may seem needless. However, what appears to be a cumbersome way of translating is actually a deliberate effort to render diaphanous the extended parallelism on which the major argument of this section turns.

Thus, the use of "---- : --- : : ---- : ----" corresponds to the use of "---- is to ---- as --- is to ---" when the latter is translatable into the expression "--- is related to --- in the same way as ---- is related to ----," which in turn is taken to mean identity between relations. Moreover, two relations R_1 and R_2 are extensionally identical if and only if, for any two things x and y, x has R_1 to y if and only if x has R_2 to y.

At this point, we say that if any mathematical statement exemplifies the verbal pattern indicated by HH, it is a substitution instance of HH. Further, any mathematical statement is a substitution instance of a verbal pattern such as HH if the former can be directly derived from the latter by making appropriate substitutions for its variables. However, there are cases of statements which are disguised substitution instances, i.e., statements which must be recast before they are directly derivable from a verbal pattern such as HH by appropriate substitutions for its variables. Examples can be found at A A A - C C C, which must be translated into, respectively, A'A'A' - C'C'C' before they can be considered a legitimate substitution instance of HH. We refer to that statement into which another statement must be translated before it can become a substitution instance of HH as a standard form of expression or a statement in standard form. Thus, A'A'A' - C'C'C' are standard forms of expression for, respectively, A A A - C C C.

If one attends to the components of the substitution instances of HH, one can make some fruitful distinctions. Thus, we shall speak of the "analogues" of mathematical analogy-like statements, where the term "analogue" refers to that part of a statement in standard form occurring on either side of the locution "in the same way as." Usually, though not necessarily, a mathematical analogy-like statement will be composed of two analogues. Thus, "two is related to four" and "one is related to two" are the analogues of A'A'A'. Likewise, "nine is related to twenty-seven" and "one is related to three" are analogues of C'C'C'. We shall also use the term "analogate," which we define as that part of an analogue of a statement in standard form occurring on either side of the expression "is related to." Ordinarily an analogical statement of the mathematical variety will contain four analogates. In the case A'A'A', these are "two," four," "one," and "two." For C'C'C', they are "nine," "twenty-seven," "one," and "three."

Now we are in a position to state what we mean by "*the* representative verbal pattern for mathematical analogy-like statements." First, we say that HH is *the* representative pattern for such statements, i.e., HH is their distinctive verbal pattern. Secondly, we indicate that to say that HH is the representative verbal pattern for analogical statements of the mathematical variety is to say that statements such as A'A'A' (the standard form of expression for AA) are substitution instances of HH, i.e., that A'A'A' is directly derivable from HH by replacing each distinct analogate variable in the latter by a different analogate and by replacing " : " in HH in each case by "is related to" and " : : " by "in the same way as."

3.3   Nonmathematical Analogy-Like Statements

We turn now to a description of the distinctive verbal pattern for analogical statements of the nonmathematical variety. First, let us consider the following nonmathematical analogy-like statements:

II)   Zeno was to Parmenides as Aristotle was to Plato.

JJ)   Saint Cyr is to the Army of France as West Point is to the Army of the United States.

KK)   The geographical location of Switzerland is to that of Italy as the geographical location of Canada is to that of the United States.

Similarly to the treatment given AA - CC, the verbal pattern common to II - KK can be indicated by:

LL)   One person (place or thing) is to a second as a third person (place or thing) is to a fourth,

or by:

MM)   ---- is to ---- as ---- is to ----,

where MM, like its twin EE, is regarded as a constant with the blanks occupied by non-numerical expressions that have been used denotatively. Hence, "Zeno," "Parmenides," "Aristotle," "Plato," "Saint Cyr," etc., can be

130

replaced by expression denoting other persons, places, or things without changing the verbal pattern expressed by LL and MM.

Like EE, MM can be rewritten as:

NN)   a is to b as c is to d,

where "a," "b," "c," and "d" can be regarded as variables. Finally, NN can be translated into:

OO)   a : b : : c : d.

OO has the same significance as HH because a complete parallelism between the two can be demonstrated. Thus, the following considerations indicate that the constant "---- : ---- : : ---- : ----" is used identically in both places. Hence, like AA - CC, I I - KK can be unpacked to read:

I I I)   Zeno was related to Parmenides as Aristotle was related to Plato.

JJJ)   Saint Cyr is related to the Army of France as West Point is related to the Army of the United States.

KKK)   The geographical location of Switzerland is related to that of Italy as the geographical location of Canada is related to that of the United States.

And like AAA - CCC, I I I - KKK are translatable, without loss of truth-value or original meaning, into the following statements:

I'I'I')   Zeno was related to Parmenides in the same way as Aristotle was related to Plato.

J'J'J')   Saint Cyr is related to the Army of France in the same way as West Point is related to the Army of the United States.

K'K'K')   The geographical location of Switzerland is related to that of Italy as the geographical location of Canada is related to that of the United States.

These in turn can be recast, again with conservation of meaning and truth-value, in the following way:

131

<u>I I</u> I)   There is at least one relation such that Zeno had that relation to Parmenides and Aristotle had it to Plato.

<u>J J</u> J)   There is at least one relation such that Saint Cyr has that relation to the Army of France and West Point has it to the Army of the United States.

<u>K K</u> K)   There is at least one relation such that the geographical location of Switzerland has that relation to the geographical location of Italy and the geographical location of Canada has it to the geographical location of the United States.

Thus, up to this point there seems to be an exact parallelism between analogy-like statements such as AA - CC on the one hand and I I - KK on the other. Both permit the extraction of a representative verbal pattern in which the constant "---- : ---- : : ---- : ----" is used identically. Hence, what is a representative verbal pattern for one is also a representative verbal pattern for the other. It remains to be determined whether *the* representative verbal pattern for one is also *the* representative verbal pattern for the other.

As with AA - CC, if each of I I - KK exemplifies the verbal pattern OO, then each is a substitution instance of OO. Such a direct derivation is possible only if, like AA - CC, I I - KK are statements in standard form, i.e., in this case, are the statements I'I'I' - K'K'K'. This means, that because I'I'I' - K'K'K' parallel A'A'A' - C'C'C', they are each analyzable into analogues and their respective analogates.

Thus, to complete the parallel between HH and OO, we say that the latter is *the* representative verbal pattern for statements I I - KK, i.e., I'I'I', for example, is directly derivable from OO by replacing each distinct analogate variable in the latter by a different analogate and by replacing " : " in OO by "is related to" and ": :" by "in the same way as." That is, for I I - KK, OO is a distinctive verbal pattern which is identical in this respect to HH. Hence, for statements like AA - CC and I I - KK there is only one distinctive verbal pattern, that which occurs at both HH and OO.

However, on our original list of analogical statements can be found certain ones for which HH is definitely not a distinctive verbal pattern. Thus, if we give the same sort of consideration about verbal pattern to such statements as:

QQ)   Life is to two eternities as an isthmus is to two continents.

and

RR)   . . . as sight is to eye so intellect is to the mind,

as we gave to AA - CC and I I - KK, we arrive at the expression:

SS)   a is to b as c is to d

and thence at:

TT)   a : b : : c : d .

Again, the use of the symbol " : " precisely equates to the expression "is related to" in:

QQQ)   Life is related to two eternities as an isthmus is related to two continents.

RRR)   . . . as sight is related to the eye, so intellect is related to the mind.

However, here the parallel with AA - CC and I I - KK terminates. For it is not possible, *salva veritate et significatione*, to translate QQQ and RRR into, respectively:

Q/Q/Q/)   Life is related to two eternities in the same way as an isthmus is related to two continents.

and

R/R/R/)   Intellect is related to the mind in the same way as sight is related to the eye,

and still mean by "-----is to ---- in the same way as ---- is to ----" what we meant by it in previous translations.

It has been suggested that sufficient with latitude in interpretation, one could always produce a sufficiently general relation between each pair of analogates to permit statements like QQQ and RRR to be translated into statements like Q/Q/Q/ and R/R/R/. Thus if the context of QQ permitted the

133

relation of, respectively, life to two eternities and an isthmus to two continents to be specified as "an interval between," Q/Q/Q/ would be an accurate translation of QQQ. However, such a suggestion involves several difficulties only one of which will be discussed here: The context of a particular analogical statement may preclude interpreting its relations in a sufficiently general fashion to allow for identity between them. For example, in type theory the analogical statement, "all of Albert's first-order statements are to first-order falsity as all of his second-order statements are to second-order falsity" could never be interpreted as asserting an identity of relations without risking the generation of paradox. Thus, unlike their use in the verbal pattern in HH or OO, the use of "--- : --- : : --- : ---" and its English counterpart in SS and TT necessitates translations different from those of Q/Q/Q/ and R/R/R/. The following translations preserve the intended meaning of QQ and RR:

Q'Q'Q')   Life is related to two eternites somewhat as an isthmus is related to two continents.

R'R'R')   Intellect is related to the mind somewhat as sight is related to the eye.

Paralleling A A A - K K K, Q'Q'Q' and R'R'R' can be translated, preserving the original meanings and truth-values of QQ and RR, into:

QQQ)   There are at least two relations, R_1 and R_2, such that life has R_1 to two eternities and an isthmus has R_2 to two continents and R_1 and R_2 are ordinally similar.

RRR)   There are at least two relations, R_1 and R_2, such that sight has R_1 to the eye and the intellect has R_2 to the mind, and R_1 and R_2 are ordinally similar.

Faced with this obvious ambiguity of the expression " - - - is to - - - as - - - is to - - -" in analogical statements and with the fact that " - - - : - - - : : - - - : - - - " has already been assigned a precise meaning, we introduce the constant " - - - : - - - ≈ - - - : - - - " and substitute it for the former in TT so as to obtain:

UU)   "a : b ≈ c : d."

Further, let it be stipulated that " - - - : - - - ≈ - - - : - - - " be interpreted by the expression " - - - is to - - - as - - - is to - - -" only if the latter comes to be synonymous with the expression " - - - is to - - - somewhat as - - - is to - - -" where the latter is defined in terms of ordinal similarity or isomorphism.

In order to define adequately "ordinal similarity" we shall have to discuss certain relevant paraphernalia of relational logic. Thus, we begin with some definitions of notions which are auxiliary to defining those concepts that are directly relevant to the definition of ordinal similarity.

We shall first consider the expression, "converse of a relation." The converse of a given relation is that relation between y and x which holds whenever the given relation holds between x and y. Thus, the relation "less than" is the converse of the relation "greater than" and "earlier" is the converse of "later." The set of individuals that have a given relation to something is the "domain" of that relation. Hence, the set of all fathers is the domain of the relation of father to offspring. The "converse domain" is the domain of that relation's converse. Hence, the set of wives is the converse domain of the relation of husband to wife. The "field of a relation" is that class which is the logical sum of a relation's domain and converse domain. Finally, the "relative product" of any two relations P and Q is that relation which obtains between x and z when and only when, for some y, x has P to y and y has Q to z.

Now, let us assume the terms w, x, y, and z and the relations P, S, and Q such that the situation is an illustrated by the following diagram:

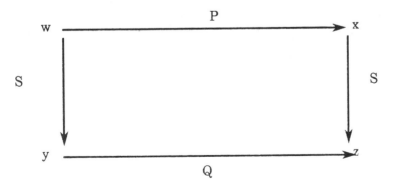

In the diagram, w has the relation P to x, y has the relation Q to z, and w has the relation S to y, while x has the same relation to z. Now, if this happens with every pair of terms such as x and y, and if the converse happens with every pair of terms such as z and w, it is clear that for every instance in which the relation P holds there is a corresponding instance in which the relation Q holds, and vice versa. More concisely, we can say that under the conditions illustrated by our diagram, the relation P is the same as the relative products of S and Q and the converse of S. This becomes evident when one realizes that one may proceed from w to x via two routes: (1) from w via P to x or (2) from w via S to y, from y via Q to z, and finally from z via the converse of S to x.

Relations such as S are often referred to in logic and mathematics as correlations and may be defined in the following way: Given any two relations P and Q, a third relation S is said to be their correlator if S is one-one, if its converse domain is the field of Q, and if P is the same as the relative product of S, Q, and the converse of S. One can go on to say that the relations P and Q are ordinally similar or isomorphic if and only if P and Q have at least one correlator. By this definition, we have arrived at the position that if one of two relations holds between two terms, the other relation holds between the correlates of these two terms.

Because up to the point where the expression " - - - is to - - - as - - - is to - - -" in QQ and RR had to be interpreted, an exact parallelism of translation with AA - CC and I I - KK could be found, and because after this point, a parallelism of translation exists, except for the interpretation of that expression "- - - is related to - - - somewhat as - - - is related to - - -," we talk of UU as a representative verbal pattern for such statements as QQ and RR. However, it remains for us to specify in what way UU is *the* representative verbal pattern for such statements.

If QQ and RR each exemplify the verbal pattern UU, then each can be derived directly from UU by appropriate substitutions for its variables. However, such a direct derivation is possible only if QQ and RR, like their predecesors AA - CC and I I - KK, are statements in standard form. In this instance, such statements would be Q'Q'Q' and R'R'R'. If QQ and RR are in standard form, then we can define the term "analogue" for them as that part of a statement in standard form occurring on either side of the locution "somewhat as," with the term "analogate" defined as it was before.

We say, then, that *the* representative verbal pattern for QQ - RR is UU, meaning that Q'Q'Q' or R'R'R' is directly derivable from UU by replacing in the latter each different analogate variable by a different analogate and by replacing " : " in each case by the expression "is related to" and "≈" by the

136

expression "somewhat as." This is another way of specifying UU as a distinctive verbal pattern for statements like QQ and RR.

Now, because it can be demonstrated that identity of relations is a proper subcase of isomorphism (i.e., identical relations are always isomorphic but the converse of this is not true), we can say that one distinctive verbal pattern, HH, is a subcase of the other, UU. Hence, if an analogical statement has the verbal pattern HH, it also has the verbal pattern UU; but if an analogical statement has the verbal pattern UU, it does not necessarily have the verbal pattern HH. In this sense, UU is *the* representative verbal pattern for all analogy-like statements.

4.0 DO ANALOGICAL STATEMENTS HAVE A CONTEXT?

In Section 3.0, we demonstrated the need for some sort of relevant context to facilitate the exposition of an inferential setting for certain analogy-like statements. In this section, we shall continue by defining context and then identifying the notions of proper and nonproper contexts for analogy.

4.1 What Do We Mean By Context?

We adduced evidence that the constant or normal conceptual setting for an analogy like statement is that of an inference. A closer examination of this inferential setting reveals, besides the analogy-like statement itself, other statements which contribute to the composition of the inference. It is to these latter statements, taken collectively, that we attach the predicate "context." Each individual statement of a context will be referred to as a contextual factor. Consider the following inference:

I.   α) Zeno was the most prominent student of Parmenides.

        β) Aristotle was the most prominent student of Plato.

        ∂) Hence, in this respect, Zeno was to Parmenides as Aristotle was to Plato.

Here, the statements α and β are together the context of ∂. But consider the inference:

II.   α) One is a third of three.

       β) Nine is to twenty-seven as one is to three.

       ∂) Thus, nine is one-third of twenty-seven.

In this case, the contextual factors of α and ∂ form the context of β'.

It is evident that not just any context for an analogy-like statement is permissible. There are proper and improper contexts for analogy-like statements. A review of the latter should furnish us with the basis for a definition of the former.

Previous analysis (Section 3.0) permits ∂ in I to be expanded to ∂', "In this respect, Zeno was related to Parmenides as Aristotle was related to Plato." Let us replace the relational expression "most prominent student of" in α of I by the relational expression "a close friend of," which changes the meaning of the statement without changing its truth-value. This produces the new statement, α', "Zeno was a close friend of Parmenides" and the illicit inference:

α') Zeno was a close friend of Parmenides.

β) Aristotle was the most prominent student of Plato.

∂') Hence, in this respect, Zeno was related to Parmenides as Aristotle was related to Plato.

But because ∂' cannot be legitimately inferred from them, α' and β together cannot be considered a proper, i.e., relevant, context for ∂'. Nor taken together can they be considered a proper context for any analogy-like statement. And the reason for this is easy to see. As evidenced by ∂', an analogy-like statement requires that the two statements composing its proper context (contextual factors) assert the same relation. Linguistically this means that the relational predicate of one contextual statement must also be the relational predicate of the other. It is of course possible that α' and β could each be a contextual factor in the context of an analogy-like statement different from that of the other.

In view of our restriction, it could be asked whether the statements "two is two-fourths of (bears the ratio two-fourths to) four" and "one is one-half of (bears the ratio one-half to) two" could be considered the legitimate proper context of an analogy-like statement such as, "two is to four as one is to two." The answer is affirmative, and we shall ground that answer in the following way.

In logic and mathematics, a relation which is reflexive, symmetric, and transitive is called an equivalence relation. Now, the equivalence relation that holds between the two ordered pairs of positive integers $< x, y >$ and $< u, v >$ when $xv = yu$ is:

$$R = \overset{\wedge}{\alpha} \; \overset{\wedge}{\beta} \, (\, \exists x, y, u, v) \, [\alpha = <x, y> \bullet \beta = <u, v> \bullet xv = uy]$$

Thus, R specifies the equality of any two ratios without using the notion of "ratio." The corresponding equivalence classes can be used to define "ratio." Thus, the definition of R allows us to say that $<x, y> \, R \, <u, v>$ if and only if the ratio x/y is equal to the ratio u/v. So the equivalence class R" $\{ <x, y> \}$ of $<x, y>$ will be the class of all ordered pairs $<u, v>$ with the ratio u/v equal to the ratio x/y. We can use this equivalence class to define the ratio x/y:

$$x/y = {}_{Df} \; R" \, \{ <x, y> \} \bullet$$

We shall then have

$$R" \, \{ <3, 4> \} = R" \{ <9, 12> \}.$$

This illuminates the distinction between a certain ratio R" $\{ <3, 4> \}$ and various "names" of it, such as 3/4, 9/12, 12/16, etc.

Suppose now that instead of changing the relational expression in α of I, we substitute the names "Aquinas" and "Albertus Magnus" for the names "Zeno" and "Parmenides," respectively. The eventuating statement would be α', "Aquinas was the most prominent student of Albertus Magnus." The inference is as follows:

α')   Aquinas was the most prominent student of Albertus Magnus.

β)   Aristotle was the most prominent student of Plato.

∂)   Hence, in this respect, Zeno was to Parmenides as Aristotle was to Plato.

Again α' and β could not be a proper context of ∂ or of its expansion ∂'; i.e., it would be impossible to infer ∂ from α' and β. Statement β could be a contextual factor in the proper context of an analogy-like statement, S, which differed from ∂ by having as one of its pair of analogates the names "Aquinas" and "Albertus Magnus," which are not found in ∂.

So far, we have considered examples of improper contexts for an analogy-like statement. There is the case in which the relations expressed in the two contextual factors are not identical. Then there is the case in which the terms of a relation asserted by one of the contextual factors do not match, respectively, the pair of analogates of one or another analogue of the analogy-like statement. The following definition of proper context eventuates: For any two statements to be the proper context of an analogy-like statement, (1) they must assert identical relations, and (2) each relation must possess as terms, respectively, the analogates of one of the analogues of the analogy-like statement.

In formulating our definition we have relied heavily upon the possibility of inferring the analogy-like statement in question from the pair of statements purported to be its context. Thus, if an analogy-like statement can be inferred from two statements taken together, the two statements obey criteria 1 and 2 of our definition. But there *seem* to be contexts which do not obey either 1 or 2 or both, but from which analogy-like statements can be inferred. Thus, from the pair (α) "Switzerland is north of Italy" and (β) "Canada is north of the United States," (∂) "the geographical location of Switzerland is to that of Italy as the geographical location of Canada is to that of the United States" can be inferred. Now, α and β ostensibly violate criterion 2 of our definition. But closer inspection reveals that this violation is only apparent. For α and β can be restated as, respectively, the statements (α) "the geographical location of Switzerland is immediately north of that of Italy" and (β) "the geographical location of Canada is immediately north of that of the United States," which together do obey both 1 and 2. The statements α "Zeno was younger than Parmenides" and β "Aristotle was younger than Plato" can be similarly reformulated to permit the inference α "the chronological age of Zeno was to that of Parmenides as the chronological age of Aristotle was to that of Plato."

But there are even more recalcitrant examples of contexts which do not obey our definition of proper context; yet analogy-like statements can be inferred from them. One example is the following: From the pair (α) "Italy's representation on the map is below that of Switzerland" and (β) "Italy is south of Switzerland," (∂) "Italy's representation on the map is related to that of Switzerland somewhat as Italy is related to Switzerland" can be inferred. In this case α and β violate criterion 1 of our definition of proper context, and there seems to be no possibility of reformulation without, of course, changing the meaning. But there is really no need for reformulation. For here we are dealing with a different kind of context which we shall call "nonproper" and define in the following way: For any two statements to be the nonproper context of an analogy-like statement, (1) they must assert ordinally similar relations and (2) each relation must possess as terms, respectively, the analogates of one of the analogues of the analogy-like statement. Criterion 2 is identical with criterion 2 of the definition of "proper context."

If we assume the setting of a type-grammar, another example of a nonproper context can be located in the inference from the statements:

III)   Albert's first-order statements are first-order false,
         Albert's second-order statements are second-order false,

to the analogical statement,

(IV)   Albert's first-order statements are to first-order falsity as his second-order statements are to second-order falsity,

where the latter would be translatable into,

(V)   Albert's first-order statements are related to first-order falsity somewhat as Albert's second-order statements are related to second-order falsity.

The definitions of proper and nonproper context to which we have committed ourselves do not completely exhaust the set of possible contexts. As indicated in our discussion of proper context there are examples of improper context which do not obey criterion 2 of either definition. Hence, we say that an improper context is one which is neither proper nor nonproper. Because criterion 2 of both definitions is the same, it is evident that an improper context destroys the inferential nature of an analogical statement's conceptual setting. By our general definition of "context," this means that an improper context is no context at all.

4.2   The Relationship Between An Analogy-Like Statement And Its Proper Context

It is clear from our definition that a specific analogy-like statement for which a proper context is possible may have almost any number of proper contexts. However, our definition in no way guarantees that all of these proper contexts will be true. A context is true if and only if both its contextual factors are true. Many will fulfill the requirements of our definition and still be false. One could, therefore, ask whether a true analogy-like statement has more than one true proper context. The answer to such a question depends upon consideration of two important subquestions. The first is: Can more than one relational predicate be truthfully attached to any two analogates of any particular analogue of an analogy-like statement? The answer is yes. But such an answer is another way of saying that between any two individuals, more than one relation always holds. Thus, in the analogical statement (a) "two is to four as one is to two," some of the relational predicates that can be truthfully attached to "two" and "four" are "less than" and "factor of." These give rise to such statements as:

b) Two is less than four.
c) Two is a factor of four.

Moreover, the same relational predicates can be truthfully attached to the analogates "one" and "two" of the other analogue, giving rise to such statements as:

d) One is less than two.
e) One is a factor of two.

We see immediately that in b - e we have two proper contexts: b, d and c, e. But this leads to a second subquestion: Are there always two or more relational predicates truthfully attachable to both pairs of analogates of any analogy-like statement? The answer to this subquestion is also yes, as indicated by consideration of b - e, as well as examples like the following:

f) Zeno was to Parmenides as Aristotle was to Plato.

By appropriately attaching the relational predicates "the most prominent student of," "friend of," and "younger than" to the analogates "Zeno" and "Parmenides" in the left-hand analogue (i.e., the analogue to the left of "as") of f, we generate the true statements:

g) Zeno was the most prominent student of Parmenides.
h) Zeno was a friend of Parmenides.
i) Zeno was younger than Parmenides.

The same predicates can be attached to the analogates in the right-hand analogue of f, giving rise to the true statements:

j) Aristotle was the most prominent student of Plato.

k) Aristotle was a friend of Plato.

l) Aristotle was younger than Plato.

The pairs g and j, h and k, and i and l each form a proper context for f. Moreover, consideration of an analogy-like statement such as:

m) Buddhism was to the development of Asiatic civilization as Christianity was to the development of Western civilization,

indicates that it has an indeterminate number of true proper contexts. Finally, if we considered other analogical statements, two or more true proper contexts could be uncovered for each. Proof of this is given elsewhere [12].

From examples a - e, we observe that if the pair b and d are both true, a is also true. But if a is true, it does not follow that b and d are true; the denial of b and d together does not entail the denial of a. The same observation holds for the relation between a and the pair c and e. We can state, then, that each and every proper context of a is only a sufficient condition of a's truth. Further, such a statement can also be made about the proper contexts of f and m. Finally, on the basis of the statements already considered, we state the conjecture that any analogical statement that can have a proper context can exhibit several such contexts which are true, with the truth of each being only a sufficient condition for the truth of the particular analogical statement. The question of whether or not an analogy-like statement is a necessary condition for the truth of its proper contexts is discussed elsewhere [13].

4.3 Relationship Between An Analogy-Like Statement And Its Nonproper Context

It might appear from Section 4.2 that a context of an analogical statement is a sufficient condition for that statement only if the context is proper. However, such is not the case. Some nonproper contexts are also sufficient conditions for their respective analogical statements.

Consider the analogical statement:

n) Italy's representation on the map is to that of Switzerland as Italy is to Switzerland.

According to our analysis in Section 3.3, n can be translated into:

n') Italy's representation on the map is related to that of Switzerland somewhat as Italy is related to Switzerland.

As with examples a and e, we can attach relational predicates to the analogates of both analogues. Thus, the predicates "below" and "adjacent to" are attached to "Italy's representation on the map" and "that of Switzerland," giving rise to the true statements:

o) Italy's representation on the map is below that of Switzerland.
p) Italy's representation on the map is adjacent to that of Switzerland.

Further, the relational predicates "south of" and "borders upon" are attached to the analogates "Italy" and "Switzerland," giving rise to the true statements:

q) Italy is south of Switzerland.
r) Italy borders upon Switzerland.

Together, o and q form the nonproper context of n', i.e., o and q assert ordinally similar relations between, respectively, the individuals designated by the analogates of the right-hand analogue and those designated by the analogates of the left-hand analogue. The evidence for this is that whenever the relation "south of" holds on the Earth, the relation "below" holds on the map, and the converse is also the case. Moreover, the same thing can be said for the pair p and r.

Thus, n' has at least two nonproper contexts, the pair o, q and the pair p, r, such that n' must be true if o and q are true. But if n' is true, it is not necessary that o and q be true. The same can be said for the truth-value relations between n' and p, r. We say, therefore, that each and every nonproper context of n' is a sufficient condition for n'. Finally, we state the conjecture that, as for analogical statements with proper contexts, for any analogical statement that can have a nonproper context, two or more such contexts which are true can be exhibited, with the truth of each being only a sufficient condition for the truth of the analogical statement in question. Proof of this conjecture is given elsewhere [13].

All analogy-like statements which are true possess a context, a set of statements which, together with the analogical statement in question, contribute to the composition of an inference. On the basis of context we have distinguished two fundamental types of analogical statements: those which possess a proper context and those which possess a nonproper context. In both cases, we have been able to make out at least one extensional relation between an analogical statement and each of its contexts; i.e., each context of an analogical statement, proper or nonproper, is a sufficient condition for that statement. Hence, we say that the inference in which an analogy-like statement has its setting is actually deductive in nature; i.e., the inference is a deductive argument, for which it is logically impossible for the conclusion to be false if the premises are true.

5.0   ARE ANALOGY-LIKE STATEMENTS CHECKABLE?

In Section 4.3, we considered some of the truth relations between an analogy-like statement and its context. Such considerations assumed that the analogy-like statement under discussion was true. We wish now to concern ourselves with the general way in which the truth-values of analogy-like statements are established. To do this we shall first define the term "checkable." We shall then determine how checkable analogy-like statements are checked. Next, we shall determine whether there are analogy-like statements which are uncheckable, and if so, why. Finally we shall answer the question: "Are analogy-like statements amenable to some sense test?"

5.1   What Do We Mean By The Term Checkable?

The term "checkable" is essentially an epistemic metapredicate (one which designates a property that accrues to propositions in relation to the state of our knowledge about them) not necessarily dependent upon some empirical considerations for its application to statements, i.e., its application or nonapplication is not decidable in all instances by observation. The predicate's application to an analogy-like statement merely indicates that some effective method for determining the truth or falsity of that statement can be specified.

By "effective method," we mean a procedure consisting of a finite number of clearly specifiable steps that terminate in a decision about the truth-value of a particular statement. Thus, if the truth-value of the statement (1) "The grass in front of the White House is green" had to be decided, inspection of the White Hourse front lawn would be the effective method for making the decision. In the case of the statement (2) "7 x (14 + 8) = 85 + 69," carrying out the indicated arithmetic operations, reducing each side of the equation to a single number, and comparing the number with the single number on the opposite side of the equation would constitute an effective method for deciding the statement's truth-value. By calling these methods "effective," we mean that a person would be regarded as irrational if, after employing them to establish the truth-values of 1 and 2, he inquired whether 1 and 2 were true or false.

Statements for which no effective method of deciding truth-value can be specified are referred to as "uncheckable." For example, the statement (3) "Gabrilla caborni in the grass" would, in the absence of clarification of the terms "Gabrilla" and "caborni," be an example of a "statement" lacking an effective method for deciding its truth-value. That is, it lacks such a method in principle: Short of supplying meanings to some of its terms, no effective method for deciding its truth-value is possible. However, the statement (4) "There are two craters on the far side of the moon," does not lack checkability in principle but only practically; i.e., one could reply "wait and see" to 4 but not to 3.

Finally, many meaningful sentences that purport to make statements turn out to be uncheckable after examination. Upon further analysis, many such sentences can be demonstrated to be making a linguistic recommendation rather than a statement. Thus, our criterion of checkability implies that essentially uncheckable "statements" are not statements at all but something quite different, perhaps "dressed" in the grammatical garb of statements.

5.2   Are Analogy-Like Statements Checkable By A Uniform Method?

A significant question is whether there is a uniform method for checking all checkable analogy-like statements. Before answering such a question, we must consider briefly the conditions under which an analogical statement's meaning is sufficiently clear to permit the statement to be checked.

Provided that (A) the analogates of a particular analogical statement have meaning and (B) the same statement exemplifies one of the two verbal patterns described in Section 3.0 (ensuring that an analogical statement is syntactically correct), then we say that the analogical statement in question has meaning. Thus, the statement:

5) Nine is to twenty-seven as one is to three,

which can be translated into:

6) Nine is related to twenty-seven in the same way as one is related to three,

possesses meaning in the sense of A and B. It is in this respect that an analogical statement differs from one such as 3, which does not satisfy proviso A. As it stands, 6 can be translated into a molecular statement composed of the logical sum of the members of the set of proper contexts of 6. Hence, in this respect, 6 is ambiguous, though not meaningless; its meaning is completed (i.e., completely specified) by each of the meanings of its various contexts. Thus, one of its contexts:

7) Nine is less than twenty-seven and one is less than three,

specifies a meaning for 5 different from the meaning specified by another context:

8) Nine is a factor of twenty-seven and one is a factor of three.

As conjectured in Section 4.3 and proven elsewhere [12, 13], an analogical statement always posseses a set of possible contexts composed of two or more members. But the person employing a particular analogy-like statement frequently intends only the members of a subset of the statement's set of possible contexts as its permissible interpretations. Thus, for the analogical statement:

147

9)   Zeno was to Parmenides as Aristotle was to Plato,

let us assume that the following contexts completely exhaust its set of possible contexts:

10)   Zeno was a student of Parmenides and Aristotle was a student of Plato.

11)   Zeno was younger than Parmenides and Aristotle was younger than Plato.

12)   Zeno was a friend of Parmenides and Aristotle was a friend of Plato.

Now suppose that there are three historians, X, Y, and Z, engaged in a discussion, such that at each employment of 9 by X, he indicates that 10 is to be the only interpretation of 9. At each employment of 9 by Y, he indicates that 10 or 11 is an allowable interpretation of 9. At each employment of 9 by Z, he indicates 10 or 11 or 12 is an allowable interpretation. Under such circumstances, we would say: For X, if 10 is true, then 9 is true and if 10 is false, then 9 is false; for Y, if 10 or 11 is true, then 9 is true and only if both 10 and 11 are false is 9 false; and for Z, if 10, 11, or 12 is true, then 9 is true and only if all three are false is 9 false.

In any given instance of employment of a particular analogy-like statement A, the following things are involved: (I) The number of contexts permitted in the set of contexts of A is in part a function of the intent of the person employing A and in many cases is a circumscribed subset of the set of possible contexts of A. (II) In some employments of A, its set of contexts may have a single member while in other instances its set of contexts may include two or more members. (III) Where A's set of contexts includes more than one member, each by itself will be only a sufficient condition for A, but the logical sum of all members will be both a necessary and a sufficient condition for A. (This does not conflict with what we have said in Section 4.0 about the relation between an analogy-like statement and its context, because in Section 4.0 we are talking, *in abstracto*, about each member of an analogical statement's set of possible contexts, in which the latter is not arbitrarily limited.) Using I - III, we can say that the truth-value of A is determined by establishing the truth-value of A's admissible contexts. If there is more than one admissible context, A's truth-value is determined by establishing the truth-value of a molecular statement composed of the logical sum of A's admissible contexts. The problem of determining whether there is a uniform method for checking analogy-like statements therefore becomes a problem of determining whether there is a uniform method for checking the admissible contexts of such statements.

As indicated in Section 4.0, the context of any analogy-like statement is true if, and only if, both of its factors are true. Thus, checking an analogical statement reduces to checking each factor of the statement's context. In this respect, an analogical statement's context is materially or factually true if and only if it is not the case that either one or both of its factors are false. A statement's context is logically true if and only if both of its factors are logically, i.e., analytically, true. This last distinction indicates that some analogical statements are empirically true while others are analytically true.

Let us illustrate all of this by an example.

Suppose that a mathematics teacher indicates that for analogical statement 5, above, he intends the set composed only of 7 and 8 to be the set of admissible contexts. He then asks the class to effectively determine the truth-value of 5. Our previous considerations show 5 to be true if and only if the logical sum of statements 7 and 8 is true. The logical sum of 7 and 8 is true if and only if at least one of them is true. One of them is true if and only if both of its contextual factors are true. Thus, the class could effectively decide the truth-value of 5 by the following method: (A) Decide the truth-value of each contextual factor of, say, context 7. (B) From the results of A, decide the truth-value of 7. (C) Decide directly the truth-value of 5 if the results of B found 7 to be true or (D) Check the truth-values of the contextual factors of 8. If step D is taken, then (E) Decide the truth-value of 8, and from the results, (F) Determine the truth-value of 5.

In this case, step D is unnecessary. We generalize the method of A - F for most analogical statements by the flow diagram of Figure 5.2-1. There, steps III and V distinguish two types of analogical statements which may be checked with different submethods. If the factors being checked for each admissible context at III and V are analytic, then the context of which they are factors is also analytic and hence that this particular analogical statement is ultimately checked analytically. If the factors being checked for each admissible context at III and V are statements about matters of fact, then this

149

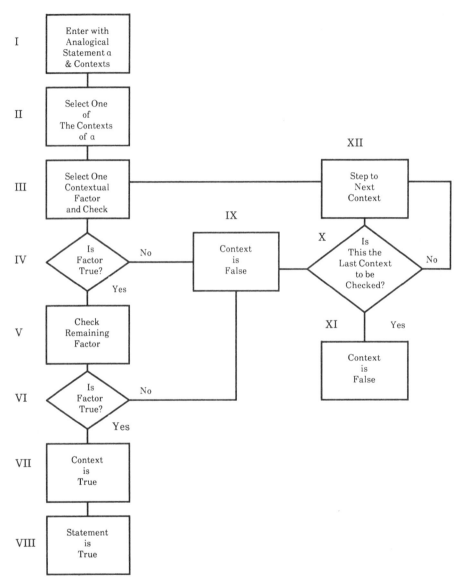

General Method for Checking Analogical Statements
Figure 5.2-1

particular analogical statement is ultimately checked empirically by observation or experiment. An example of each type of statement has already be given: 5 represents an analogical statement which is checked analytically and 9 is one which is checked empirically.

Other examples could be cited. Suppose that while instructing students in the primary use of certain terms in English, the instructor proffers the statement:

13)   The primary meaning of the expression "male sibling" is to the primary meaning of the term "brother" as the primary meaning of the expression "male parent" is to the primary meaning of the term "father."

The instructor stipulates that the only admissible context is the one composed of the following factors:

14)   The primary meaning of the expression "male sibling" is the primary meaning of the term "brother."

and:

15)   The primary meaning of the expression "male parent" is the primary meaning of the term "father."

Steps III and V of our general methof for checking analogical statements would render 14 and 15, respectively, analytically true.

Another example might arise in a geography lesson, where the instructor is interested in having the class understand the relationship between maps and the things that they map. He might say:

16)   Italy's representation on a map is to that of Switzerland as Italy is to Switzerland.

He then might indicate that he intends as contexts of 16 the two statements with the following contextual factors:

17) Italy's representation on a map is immediately below that of Switzerland.

and:

18) Italy is immediately south of Switzerland.

or:

19) Italy's representation on a map is immediately adjacent to that of Switzerland.

and:

20) Italy borders upon Switzerland.

Either 17 and 18 or 19 and 20 are empirically checkable; that is, they are in each case checkable by some finite set of observations which could be easily specified by the teacher or his class. For example, direct inspection of a map would check 19, while aerial surveys, inspection of "trig" stations, etc., could effectively check 20.

5.3 Are There Analogy-Like Statements To Which Our General Method Does Not Apply?

As significant as developing a uniform method for effectively checking analogical statements is determining whether or not there are analogical statements to which this general method does not apply, and if so, determining in what way it does not apply. There do seem to be analogical statements to which our general method for checking does not apply. Thus, the statement:

21) Life is to two eternities as an isthmus is to two continents,

is difficult or impossible to check by the general method. It does not fulfill condition A in 5.2-1 above, with respect to meaning: one of its analogates, the expression "two eternities," is meaningless. However, it is possible that someone could, at the time of employing 21, give this expression a carefully defined meaning which would permit the application of our general method for checking the statement.

An analogical statement which satisfies both conditions A and B and yet presents difficulties in checking is the following:

22)   Physical objects are to Prime Matter as garments are to cloth.

The author clearly indicates as its context,

23)   Physical objects are produced (*efficiuntur*) from Prime Matter,

and

24)   Garments are produced from cloth.

Clearly it would be easy to determine the truth-value of 24 at either step III or step V of our general method. Going to a garment factory and observing the steps from a "raw" piece of cloth to a completed garment would be sufficient. But it is impossible to see how 23 can be either verified or disverified. Prime Matter (defined as "that which is pure potentiality, lacking all positive characteristics") is a notion arrived at by a conceptual analysis of what constitutes a thing. And although the notion is assigned a meaning, that meaning neither permits the term "Prime Matter" to be ostensive nor involves physical objects being produced from Prime Matter. Hence it is not possible to determine the truth-value of 23 either empirically or analytically. (This does not suggest, of course, that no philosophical statements are checkable.)

Another example, ultimately from Aquinas [14] is:

25)   Substance is to different properties at different times as a piece of gold is to different shapes at different times.

For the Thomist, the term "substance" does not simply mean that which is named by the subject term of a sentence and can be named only by the subject term of a sentence. Thus, " 'substance' is not only the subject of predication, it is also the subject of information: it really bears accidents. Therefore, the concept of 'standing under' cannot be explained only by a second intention (i.e., only by a definition), viz, the relation of subject to predicate; it has to be explained also in terms of the real property of 'standing under' what really informs." [14] Hence, the truth-values of the contextual factors of the context usually indicated for 25 are not to be determined analytically.

Of the two factors:

26) A piece of gold takes on different shapes at different times,

27) Substance takes on different properties at different times,

the truth-value of 26 could be decided empirically at either step III or step V of our general method. However, the truth-value of 27 seems far from decidable empirically. Given the above meaning of "substance," it is impossible to state a finite set of observations from which the truth-value of 27 could be determined at either step III or step V. Therefore, 25 is not checkable within the framework of our general method.

But this is exactly the way we regard 21 and 22. Ultimately, our reason for considering them not checkable by our general method is that none of them could be checked either empirically or analytically. However, we are not suggesting that such statements are absolutely uncheckable; only failure to fulfill conditions A or B above would render analogical statements absolutely uncheckable. For the statement,

(28) The set of all possible checkable statements is entirely composed of two discrete subsets (i.e., subsets whose intersection is null): a subset of statements checked analytically and a subset of statements checked empirically,

is itself checkable neither analytically nor empirically. Moreover, there appears to be a small number of checkable statements which are not checked by either submethod in our general method of checking analogical statements: that class of statements whose members are often called "synthetic a priori" [15].

Although it is possible that our general method for checking analogical statements is not of sufficient scope to apply to all such statements, certain properties of statements not checkable by our method indicate a different possibility. The lack of checkability of analogy-like statements such as 21, 22, and 25 is due to the presence of members of a certain class of expressions as analogates within those statements. "Prime Matter," "substance," and "two eternities" are technical vocabulary which have no clearly established usage apart from a particular metaphysical system. Moreover, within the metaphysical system in which each expression is employed, it does not refer to anything that can be observed or physically exemplified. These expressions purport to indicate certain "features of the world" [16] but do not refer to specific relations or qualities. Another way of putting this is to say that employing such expressions is an invitation by their employer to view a dimension of the world in a certain way.

What then are we to make of analogical statements in which such vocabulary occurs? We certainly do not want to call them nonsense. Wherever they are explicitly formulated, it would be almost monstrous to say that their authors are deliberately uttering gibberish, and it would beg the question to maintain that the authors are being systematically misled by their own analogical statements. Thus, in subscribing to and proposing the comparison suggested by the analogical statement,

29) Electrons are to the nucleus of the atom as the planets are to the sun,

Bohr and his followers were neither nonsensical nor misled. Yet 29 is not empirically checkable in our sense of the term (although such theoretical statements have a "pragmatic" checkability which is a function of their fruitfulness in bringing order to scientific data), and it is questionable whether any context of 29 would be analytic. It is true that the terms "electron," "proton," "neutron," etc., cannot be completely understood without reference to the deductive system of physics in which the propositions expressed by means of them occur. However, such a contention in no way implies that every true statement in which such terms appear is analytic.

Thus, although 29 is a theoretical statement associated with physics, not philosophy like 21, 22, or 25, all four statements have this in common: As employed, they are not checkable by our general method. And this is because all four are not statements at all, except grammatically, but rather they are linguistic recommendations.

But what do we mean by this? At least three kinds of linguistic recommendations can be distinguished: (1) The nominal kind, in which someone proposes a particular name for some object, situation, or event; (2) the substitutive kind, in which someone proposes that a term or expression be used in the place of or as an equivalent to another term or expression; and, (3) the structural or relational kind in which someone proposes that terms or expressions be related in a certain way to call attention to a specific way of describing a particular dimension of reality. This third kind of linguistic recommendation is exemplified by those analogical "statements" which are not checkable by our general method. Such statements introduce technical terms (analogates) and give some rule for their correct employment by relating that employment to two or more other terms for which an established and interrelated employment already obtains. Some evidence for this view can be found in the fact that all the analogy-like statements so far found to be uncheckable by our general method possess contexts in which one contextual factor is checkable by that method while the other one is not. Moreover, in all cases the technical vocabulary occurs in the latter. For example, 29 is properly translatable into a sentence such as the following:

30)   In dealing with the subatomic world, let us introduce the terms "electron" and "nucleus" and employ them interrelatedly in a way very similar to the way in which, respectively, the terms "planet" and "sun" are employed interrelatedly in celestial mechanics.

Or 22 is properly translatable into a recommendation worded in the following way:

31)   In effecting a partial conceptual analysis of what it is that constitutes a thing, let us introduce the term "Prime Matter" and employ it in relation to our employment of the term "physical objects" in a way which is similar to the way in which we employ the term "garment" in relation to the employment of the term "cloth."

The exact wording of 30 and 31 depends in part upon the precise situations in which 29 and 22 are used.

5.4   Are Analogy-Like Statements Amenable To Some Sense-Test?

Before determining whether analogical statements are amenable to some sense-test, we must clearly define the term "sense-test." By "sense-test," we mean the submission of a statement to being verified or disverified by either a direct (spatio-temporally immediate) or an indirect (causal, translational, or inferential) confrontation of one or more of the internal or external senses (touch, taste, smell, sight, hearing, and the somaesthetic and kinaesthetic senses) within the objects or states of affairs about which the statement is made. Statements to which the definition applies will be referred to as sense-testable. The definition shows us that any set of sense-testable statements is a proper subset of the set of checkable statements.

Our prior analyses and our general method for checking analogical statements indicate that some but not all analogical statements are sense-testable. Thus those analogical statements whose set of admissible contexts include only members with empirically checkable contextual factors would be sense-testable. In addition, all of the analogates of this type of analogical statement are expressions which are ostensive or observational and in general empirical.

6.0   WHAT ARE ANALOGICAL STATEMENTS?

The title of this section may appear somewhat curious. For there is a sense of the word "know" in which all of us already know what an analogical statement is. At least we have sufficient skill with such statements to formulate and employ them in our daily lives with a reasonable degree of correctness. It seems, however, that such skill is of little help in answering certain probing questions about analogical statements generated by the investigations and constructions of investigators in machine intelligence. Rather, what seems to be required by such questions is a careful analysis of analogy-like statements with the view toward exhibiting, if possible, their defining features and subtypes.

Accordingly, we began in Section 2 to consider the question of whether or not analogies have a particular kind of conceptual setting. Here, our investigations of a spectrum of fairly representative analogy-involving processes (AIP) required us to conclude that within any behavioral setting for analogical statements could be found a conceptual setting which is that of

157

a purported inference, i.e., a piece of purportedly argumentative discourse. Although no conclusions were drawn in Section 2 about whether such purported inferences are inductive or deductive, later in Section 5 a decision about this matter is made. Consideration of the question of whether or not analogies have a distinctive verbal pattern produced the conclusion that every analogical statement has one of two distinctive but similar verbal patterns, i.e., either the pattern "a : b :: c : d " or the pattern " a : b $\approx$ c : d," where the differences between the two are locatable in the two constants " - - - : - - - :: - - - : - - - " and " - - - : - - - $\approx$ - - - : - - - " which were defined in terms of, respectively, the notion of the identity of relations and the notion of ordinal similarity of relations. Examples of the first kind of verbal pattern were found to be such statements as "Nine is to twenty-seven as one is to three" or "Zeno was to Parmenides as Aristotle was to Plato." Statements exemplifying the second kind of verbal pattern were found to be such as "Italy's representation on the map is to that of Switzerland as Italy is to Switzerland" or " . . . as sight is related to the eye, so intellect is related to the mind." Section 4 was concerned with questions of analogical context and continued, in a sense, the inquiry of Section 3 by further dissecting the purported inferential setting of an analogy-like statement into the statement itself and its context, where the latter was defined as the set of statements which together with a particular analogical statement purport to compose an inference. At this point, it was determined, after defining the notions of "proper context" and "nonproper context," that some analogy-like statements have the former while other such statements have the latter. In both cases, however, it was determined that a context of an analogical statement is at least a sufficient condition for that statement. In this respect, then the inferential relationship discussed in Section 3 and mentioned above comes to be regarded as deductive in nature. Finally, in Section 5, we addressed ourselves to the problem of whether or not analogical statements are checkable. Actually, our problem in this section was to determine whether or not there is a uniform method for checking checkable analogy-like statements and, if so, what the details of that method would be. Before doing this a definition of a notion of checkability was given, i.e., a statement is checkable if it is amenable, at least in principle, to some finite, clearly defined procedure for effectively deciding its truth-value. The details of a method which conformed to this definition and which seemed to applicable to most analogical statements were spelled out. In terms of this method, it was found: (1) those statements to which the method is applicable subdivide into (a) those which are checkable analytically and (b) those which are checkable empirically; (2) a small number of analogical "statements" are not checkable at all. Further consideration of (2) resulted in taking one of two positions: Either the range of applicability of our method in inadequate or the analogical statements to which it does not apply are really not statements at all but only have the grammatical form of a statement and are really some other kind of linguistic entity. Based upon certain evidence, we chose the latter alternative and attempted to make a case for the proposal that those analogical statements which are not checkable by our method are actually a certain type of linguistic recommendation.

6.1   First Conclusion: Kinds Of Analogical Statements

Involved in the results of our investigation of analogical statements is the bifurcation of such statements into two basic classes, one of which is a subclass of the other. Thus, we have noted analogical statements with a verbal pattern " a : b :: c : d " and those with a verbal pattern " a : b $\approx$ c : d ." But is is clear that where the constant " - - - : - - - :: - - - : - - - " is defined in terms of identity and the constant " --- : --- $\approx$ --- : ---" is defined in terms of isomorphism, any statement bearing the former must be a member of the class of statements each bearing the latter, since it can be demonstrated that identical relations are always isomorphic. However, since the converse of this is not the case and since, as indicated above, there are analogical statements which do bear the verbal pattern " a : b $\approx$ c : d " but not the verbal pattern " a : b :: c : d ," we say that with respect to verbal pattern there are two distinguishable types of analogical statement.

Correlated with each verbal pattern is a particular kind of context. Thus, such statements from our original list as:

a-3)   Nine is to twenty-seven as one is to three,

or

a-2)   Zeno was to Parmenides as Aristotle was to Plato,

bear the verbal pattern " a : b :: c : d " and also possess a context (called proper) which is different from that (called nonproper) of such statements as:

159

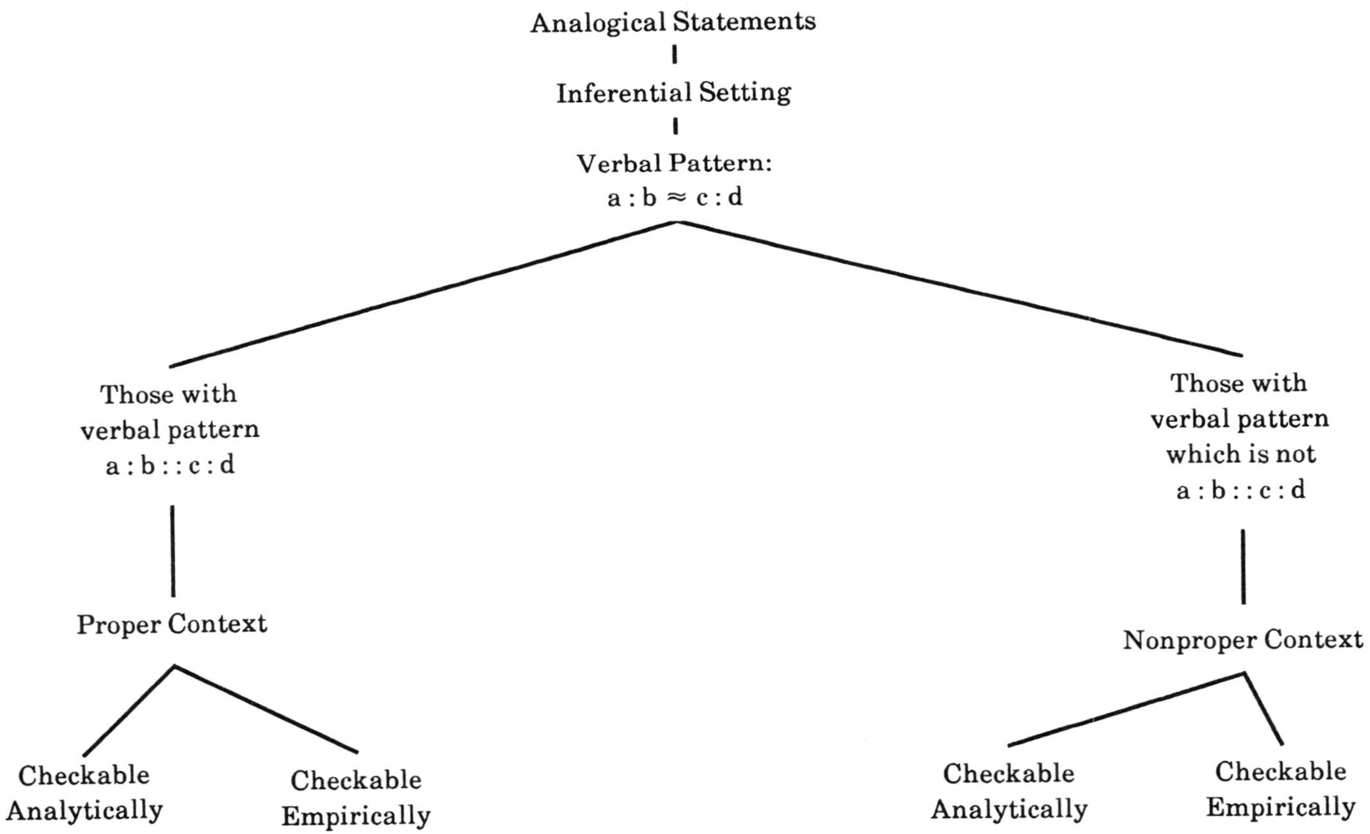

Analogical Statements
|
Inferential Setting
|
Verbal Pattern:
a : b ≈ c : d

Those with verbal pattern a : b :: c : d

Proper Context

Checkable Analytically

Checkable Empirically

Those with verbal pattern which is not a : b :: c : d

Nonproper Context

Checkable Analytically

Checkable Empirically

Figure 6.1-1

a-15)   Albert's first-order statements are to first-order falsity as his second-order statements are to second-order falsity,

or

a-12)   Italy's representation on a map is to that of Switzerland as Italy is to Switzerland,

which bear solely the more general verbal pattern " $a : b \approx c : d$." The difference between the two types of context is specified in terms of a difference in kind of relation between the two relations asserted by the contextual factors of each context. Thus, the contextual factors of the various possible contexts of a a-3 and a-2 assert identical relations, whereas the factors of the various possible contexts of a-15 and a-12 assert only similar relations. At this point, we have, therefore, two basic types of analogical statements: those bearing the verbal pattern "$a : b :: c : d$" and possessing a proper context and those bearing only the verbal pattern " $a : b \approx c : d$ " and possessing a nonproper context.

Although an analogical statement's context (whether proper or nonproper) is, *in abstracto*, only a sufficient condition for that statement, actual employment of such a statement usually limits the number of its contexts in such a way as to permit their logical sum to be both a necessary and a sufficient condition for the statement in question. Moreover, since an analogical statement's meaning is completely specified only in terms of its context, it follows that the technique for checking that statement is basically the technique for checking its context. Thus, each analogical statement, no matter of what basic type, is either checkable analytically or checkable empirically.

To sum up, then, we have two basic types of analogical statements with properties and distinctions which are perhaps best indicated by the illustration in Figure 6.1-1 on the following page.

6.2   Second Conclusion: Definition Of "Analogical"

Besides distinguishing the various types of analogical statements, we wish to distinguish carefully such statements as a class from that class of statements which is nonanalogical in character. In short, we wish to determine a meaning for the predicate "analogical," as applied to statements, such that it can be correctly, i.e., unambiguously, applied and that with its correct application to a particular statement, that statement can be clearly distinguished as an example of a kind different from other kinds of statements.

Definition: We say that a statement is analogical if and only if (a) it has a purportedly inferential setting, (b) it possesses a context which is either proper or nonproper, (c) it is checkable either analytically or empirically, and (d) it exemplifies either the verbal pattern " a : b : : c : d " or at least the more general verbal pattern, " a : b ≈ c : d ."

Now, it is clear that parts a to c of the defining portion of our definition are generic in nature, i.e., in terms of a to c, analogical statements would still have properties in common with statements that appear as elements of argumentative discourse. But since all well formulated statements are potentially components of such discourse, a to c would, as a definition, be inadequate. It is d which completely discriminates statements of the analogical variety from those which are not.

6.3 Third Conclusion: Distinction Between Analogical Statements And Similes

Since the previous discussion evidences that of all of the different kinds of figurative language, simile is closest to and most often confused with analogical statement, i.e., both are a kind of comparison made explicit by the employment within both of the expression "as," it seems imperative explicitly to distinguish the two. Moreover, with the formulation of our definition of the term "analogical" as used in the expression "analogical statement" complete, we are in a position to make this distinction.

Now, it is clear that parts a to d of our definition are together a necessary and sufficient condition for an analogical statement. Hence, if a to d can be asserted of a particular statement, then that statement is analogical, and if a statement is analogical, then a to d are assertable of it. But such is not the case of similes. Thus, with the simile, "My love is like a red red rose," parts a, b, and d of our definition do not apply. And with the simile, "Life is to two eternities as an isthmus is to two continents," without further clarification of the expressions "two eternities" and "life," c of our definition clearly does not apply and a and b are questionably applicable, even though d does apply. We are therefore, constrained to regard similes as not only quite different from analogical statements but also as easily distinguishable from them.

6.4   Exempli Gratia

In order briefly to relate some of the material discussed in this paper to non-rule-based expert system utilization and improvement of domain knowledge, we shall summarize the results of *one* of a set of relevant long-range studies that actually involved a sophisticated series of screenings and tests [17]. These were carefully structured to produce statistically valid results with respect to the ways in which both "experts" and their counterparts acquire and/or utilize "new" knowledge. This series demonstrated some very clear uses of analogy that follow the rubrics described earlier in this chapter.

For example, the now extensively familiar problem of transferring knowledge of how to (1) prove that the product of two even numbers is itself even to (2) proving that the product of any two odd numbers is itself also an odd number was effectively demonstrated by 78% of the 286 individuals involved in one of the tests in the series. This is to say that after having been exposed briefly, and for the first time, to the proof of 1, these individuals successfully proved 2. In their anecdotal meta-records, as well as in the structured interrogations about those records that immediately followed the test, the successful group clearly evidenced uses of analogy that employed the conditions produced by the analyses of this paper. Of equal (if not greater) importance is the fact that the unsuccessful 22% clearly violated two or more of the conditions developed in this paper. One of the most permeating and frequently violated meta-conditions was the analogy: "The representation of an even number is to the proof that the product of two even numbers is even as the representation of an odd number is to the proof that the product of two odd numbers is odd."

Ex vitio alterius sapiens emendat suum!

REFERENCES AND NOTES

1. Dorrough, D. C., *A Prolegomenon to Some Future Considerations of the Notion of Analogy*, University Microfilms 65-9004, 1964, (Doctoral dissertation, U.N.C., 1963).

2. Dorrough, D.C., "A Logical Calculus of Analogy Involving Functions of Order 2," *Notre Dame Journal of Formal Logic*, Vol. XI, No. 3, 1970.

3. Dorrough, D. C., "Distance Matrices and Their Relation to Similarity Functors in the Ramified Theory of Types", *TOHOKU*, Vol. C-1, pp. 204 - 218, 1972.

4. Dorrough, D. C., A. S. Politopoulos, and B. Parvin, *Application Potential of the Theories of Analogy of Winston and Carbonell*. Internal Report, Advanced Development Laboratory, (ADL), Ford Aerospace and Communications Corporation, 1983.

5. Dorrough, D. C., and A. S. Politopoulos, *Evaluation of the Behaviour of Carbonell's Difference Metric with Respect to Its Application to Three Types of Expert Systems*. Internal Report, Advanced Development Laboratory, Ford Aerospace and Communications Corporation, 1984.

6. Evans, T.G., "A Program for the Solution of a Class of Geometric-Analogy Intelligence-Test Questions," *Semantic Information Processing* (M. Minsky, editor), The MIT Press, 1968. (Originally a doctoral dissertation under the title "A Heuristic Program to Solve Geometric Analogy Problems," 1963.)

7. Moore, J. A., and A. Newell, "How can Merlin Understand," *Knowledge and Cognition* (L. Gregg, editor), Lawrence Erlbaum Associates, 1974.

8. Ꮐ Winston, P. H., "Learning and Reasoning by Analogy," *CACM, Vol. 23, No. 12, 1979.* Cf. Memo 520, M. I. T. AI Laboratory, 1979.

9. Carbonell, J. G., "Metaphor: An Inescapable Phenomenon in Natural Language Comprehension," *Knowledge Representation for Language Systems* (Lehnart and Ringle, editors), 1982. Cf. "Invariance Hierarchies in Metaphor Interpretation," *Proceedings of the Third Meeting of the Cognitive Science Society*, 1981.

10. Ꮐ Carbonell, J. G., "Learning by Analogy: Formulating and Generalizing Plans from Past Experience," *Machine Learning: An Artificial Intelligence Approach*, (R. S. Michalski, J. G. Carbonell, and T. M. Mitchell, editors), Tioga Publishing Company, 1983. Cf. "A Computation Model of Analogical Problem Solving," *Proceedings of the Seventh International Joint Conference on Artificial Intelligence*, 1981.

11. Ꮐ The contention that "analogy" is more fundamental than "similarity" or "metaphor" refers to the conceptual representation of knowledge and not to its inductive (learning) derivation. Examination of this priority occurs in Dorrough, D. C., "Conceptual and Causal Presuppositions of the Notions of 'similarity' and 'metaphor'," *The Journal of Computing Research* (in press).

12. Proof of this conjecture can be found in Dorrough, D. C., "All Semantically Proper Analogical Statements have Constructable Contexts: An Inductive Existence Proof," *Zeitschrift für Mathematische Logik und Grundlagen der Mathematik* (in press).

13. Dorrough, D. C., "Some Results on the Necessity and Sufficiency of Analogies and their Contexts," *Logique et Analyse* (in press).

14. My own translation of the Vatican edition of *Aquinas' Questiones Disputate De Ente et Essentia* (R. Spiazzi, editor), Taurini, 1949.

15. Pap, A. "Are There Synthetic A Priori Truths?", *Proceedings of the Aristotelian Society*, Vol. S-15, 1958.

16. The meaning of "feature of the world" is perhaps nowhere better stated than in Hall, E. W., "The Metaphysics of Logic," *The Philosophical Review*, Vol. LVIII, No. 1, 1949.

17. The results of the studies alluded to in this section are contained in a group of internal Ford ADL reports and will be forthcoming in a special series of monographs from North Holland Publishing Company.

4

USING AN EXPERT SYSTEM IN MERGING
QUALITATIVE AND QUANTITATIVE DATA ANALYSIS

JEAN-GABRIEL GANASCIA
LABORATOIRE DE RECHERCHE EN INFORMATIQUE
UNIVERSITE PARIS-SUD

1. INTRODUCTION

Simulation of reasoning and efficient numerical computation seem *a priori* incompatible. On one hand, expert systems are usually designed to deal with symbolic data. They solve problems in domains where computers failed before, but they are not able to perform efficiently sophisticated computation or complex numerical data analysis. On the other hand, in many disciplines we require analyses of large volumes of numerical data, and efficient algorithms have been developed for this purpose. Yet, use of experience and specialized knowledge are required in numerical processing, either to understand output or to adjust input parameters. Our aim is to use expert systems to achieve these tasks, i.e. both to interpret symbolic features extracted from numerical data by classical techniques and to adjust input parameters according to automatic expert diagnosis. This way expert systems will be used to merge symbolic data with numerical data. In this chapter we present an overview of the LITHO system which is an expert system handling numerical processing.

2. NUMERICAL DATA PROCESSING AND ARTIFICIAL INTELLIGENCE

Many professional disciplines, especially those in experimental fields such as geology, chemistry, medicine, etc., regularly face the need to analyze large volumes of numerical data. The data are usually generated by physical sensors and large volumes of these data make analysis difficult. In the past, before the "computer age," some graphic displays, such as curves or diagrams, were used in order to facilitate interpretation. Currently, traditional data analysis tools, including various statistical techniques, clustering or pattern recognition, are used to refine the data and to make the presentation of these data more understandable. Typically such data have to be interpreted by a human expert, the role of data analysis being only to facilitate this interpretation.

Recently the development of computer science has provided us with some hope for automatic interpretation. In order to be able to do this, we must consider the way in which human beings work. To make this assumption more precise, let us consider the following two points.

First, only specialists can make an interpretation. Specialist is a person who has a lot of knowledge about the field - he may be a geologist, chemist, physician, etc. Moreover, he has extensive experience in interpretation; the learning period for a specialist can take several years.

Second, during the process of interpretation, the specialist takes into account the context of the interpretation. For instance, a geologist interpreting well-oil measurements knows the location of the drill and the neighboring drill interpretations. This contextual knowledge is not always quantifiable; it has to be expressed by high-level concepts. Therefore, there exist some data which must be taken into account during the interpretation process and which are not included in the numerical set of data given by physical sensors.

Thus, a system which does not contain expert knowledge and which cannot deal with symbolic data might not make a correct interpretation. The integration of symbolic data with the analysis of large amounts of numerical data is not an easy task. Our main purpose in this chapter is to discuss this problem, and to show how expert systems may be used in order to solve it. Moreover, to make our assumptions more concrete, we shall exemplify them by presenting the LITHO project [Bonnet, et al, 1982] which achieved such an integration.

3. PRESENTATION OF THE LITHO PROJECT

A crucial problem in petroleum geology is the interpretation of subterranean rock based on physical property measurements such as density, electrical resistivity, sound transmission, radioactivity, etc. These measurements are represented by curves (called logs) which reflect the physical properties of the geological formation penetrated by the drill at each depth. Hydrocarbons are produced by the decomposition of organic matter contained in a detrital deposit, so the detection of hydrocarbons requires historical knowledge about the rock's deposition, maturation, and migration processes. All of this information is encoded in the geological facies or description of the petrophysical, petrographical, and genetic aspects of the rocks. In order to facilitate our understanding, we review below the definition of the necessary geological terms.

The *lithofacies* is the sum of the petrophysical and petrographical aspects of rock. The porosity, permeability, chemical and mineral composition of rock, the arrangement of the different grains and particles (texture), the type of layering, the presence of lenses, pebbles, laminations, holes, cracks, fissures (structure) define the lithofacies.

The *facies* is the lithofacies plus the genetic aspects of a rock (e.g. the sandstone deposited in tidal channels of a delta).

The *electrofacies* is the image of the lithofacies seen through the logs.

The goal of the interpretation process is to obtain a description of the rocks penetrated by the drill in terms of facies. Unfortunately the information contained in logs allows us to get only electrofacies. Obtaining facies requires additional knowledge concerning geography, description of the cuttings detected in the drilling mud, paleontology (i.e. knowledge about the wildlife and the flora in the geological age), etc. Indeed, the electrofacies of several lithofacies usually overlap and the facies are obtained by observing sequences of lithofacies. The LITHO project is intended to interpret logs in terms of lithofacies taking into account the external data (i.e. data which are not contained in logs). In order to achieve this task, three techniques have been merged: The expert system technique (production rules) which lends itself to symbolic reasoning; the pattern recognition technique (mainly the split and merge algorithm) which analyses the morphology of the logs; and the clustering techniques.

The overall LITHO system is shown in Figure 1.

The data are obtained from the logs, and from external data. External data are of the eight types:

Geography: geological province, basin, fields.

Tectonic activities: folds, faulting.

Stratigraphy: geological eras, epochs, periods, subperiods etc.

Paleontology: fossils.

Mineralogy: calcite, clays, quartz etc.

Petrography: limestone, shale, sand etc.

Sedimentology: reefs, tidal channels etc.

Petrophysics: porosity, permeability etc.

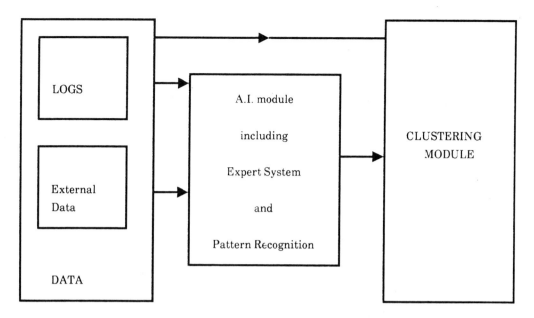

Figure 1 Block-structure of the LITHO system

Some of these data, such as paleontological, are not always available and others, such as the location of the bearing, are always known.

The well is divided into several gross zones, each gross zone corresponding to a homogeneous response from the logs. The A.I. module has to describe each gross zone in geological terms, such as the main lithological type or the paleoenvironment etc. These descriptions are used to adjust the parameters of the clustering module and to name each cloud of points by a lithofacies appellation. Thus the clustering module is able to affect one such appellation to each depthpoint of the drilling.

The next major section provides a description of the A.I. module which merges the expert system and the pattern-recognition techniques. However, before presenting it we want to show how this methodology may be generalized in a framework usable in any domain where numerical data must be merged with symbolic data in order to be interpreted.

4. GENERAL FRAMEWORK

Our thesis is that expert systems may be used in signal processing because they allow introducing the experience of specialists into the automatic data interpretation. Expert systems are particularly well-suited for the following reasons:

(A) They allow symbolic inferencing. The use of symbolic reasoning is one of the most original accomplishments in data processing. It makes reasoning possible in terms understandable by specialists, and going beyond the mere computation of numerical data.

(B) The discrimination between the knowledge base and the control structure makes the modification of pieces of knowledge easier, especially for a specialist who is not a computer expert.

(C) The modularity of the knowledge base makes local and partial correction possible.

(D) Explanation facilities are useful during the adjustment of the knowledge base. Moreover they allow the establishment of some kind of consensus among the interpretation experts. This consensus must validate the performances of the system.

Taking into account all of these arguments, we may design a general framework for data processing whereby an expert system may play the main role during the qualitative and quantitative data integration. But, we must add some components in order to integrate the expert system into data processing. The following three points are in order:

(1) Expert systems deal only with qualitative data. Thus, if we want to take into account some global characteristic of numerical data during the merging process, we have to express these characteristics by symbolic data. To make our point more precise let us consider the LITHO Project. The log-analyst, who has to interpret logs, makes two kinds of observations before interpreting. The first one concerns the morphology of the curves, detecting regularities such as ramps and plateaus which give him some indications about the deposition mechanism. The second one concerns the global characteristics of the most frequent points on the logs. This analysis gives him some indication about the main lithology of the gross zone under study. In petroleum jargon this operation is called a cross-plot. As we shall see in the section 5 these two kinds of conversion are done in LITHO. In order to reproduce them, we need the use of a module whose role is to transform the numerical data into a symbolic set of data usable by the expert system.

(2) The output of the expert system must support decisions made by the clustering module. However, the expert system responses, particularly in

cases where certainty factors are used, are often unclear and imprecise. Moreover, there are some cases where data are incomplete or erroneous. We must therefore add to the expert system a module which refines the diagnosis and detects the cases where data are so disparate that even a human expert cannot come to a reasonable conclusion.

(3) Finally, the output of the expert system needs to be interfaced with the clustering module, which requires the use of an interface module.

The following section gives an overview of the organization of the modules mentioned above.

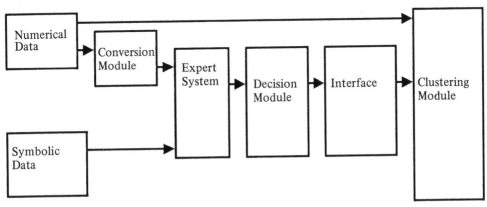

Figure 2 Block diagram of the organization between the different modules.

5. CONVERSION OF NUMERICAL DATA INTO SYMBOLIC DATA

The first step consists of a rough interpretation of numerical data. In order to do that, traditional tools such as statistical analysis or pattern recognition may be used. The main objective in this step is to isolate a set of characteristic features used by the expert system during the design of the system. To do so we have to observe activities of a specialist in the process of interpretation. But this is difficult because an expert usually makes rough and fine analysis simultaneously. Therefore, we have to isolate key features from the expert description of data. We must also make sure that all symbolic features identified can be easily detected by the automatic processes.

In the LITHO project the symbolic features extracted from the logs are related to the morphology of the curves and the cross-ploting operation.

171

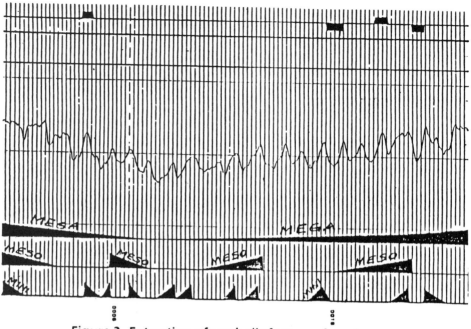

Figure 3 Extraction of symbolic features from logs.

The morphology of the curves is expressed in terms of ramps and plateaus where a ramp is a progressive increase or decrease on the logs and a plateau is a constant line on the logs over a certain interval. Other key points of these features are their size and frequency. Features are clustered into classes according to their form and size (e.g. a megaramp is a progressive increase or decrease upwards on the logs over more than 25 meters). The automatic detection of ramps and plateaus is produced by a two-step algorithm: The first step gives a polygonal approximation of the curve by a split and merge algorithm, and the second step parses the approximated logs according to a grammar that detects occurences of desired features, for example the extraction of characteristic features in a piece of logs. (For more details see [Bonnet and Dahan, 1983]).

The cross-plotting operation consists of the localization of the depth points in the logs' space : if we consider two or more logs corresponding to the recording of different measurement devices, then each point of the space generated by these logs corresponds to several lithofacies. The ambiguity is due partly to the overlapping, and partly to the oil and gas effect. Nevertheless, in a first approximation the location of the most frequent points of a gross zone in the logs' space gives a rough characterization of the lithology such as "sand," "shale," or "salt." This operation currently practised by log-analysts is modeled by LITHO.

172

The result is a histogram that describes the percentage of each of fifteen rough electrofacies in a gross zone. These fifteen electrofacies correspond to the fifteen following lithofacies : "dolo-compact," "dolo-uncompact," "limy-compact," "limy-uncompact," "salt," "FePO$_4$," "conglomerate," "sand," "gypsum," "anhydrite," "coal," "gas," "shale," "limonite," and "quartzite."

6. THE EXPERT SYSTEM

The expert system plays the main role in the qualitative and quantitative data merging process. It is intended to characterize the context in order to facilitate the treatment of numerical data. Therefore, initially we have to isolate points belonging to the same context, i.e., roughly segment the signals before processing. But this it is not always required, and it is not always possible. It is crucial to determine whether a rough segmentation is feasible and determine the properties of the isolated contexts. In cases where it is feasible and where contexts do not influence each other, we can use an inference engine, comparable to EMYCIN, wherein each context is separately analyzed. The inference rules are comparable to propositional logic, simplifying the design of the expert system considerably. The main disadvantage of this solution is that we cannot construct inference rules while taking into account two or more different contexts. In cases where a rough segmentation is not feasible, i.e. each context influences the others, we need to use an expert system with variables such as in SNARK [Lauriere, 1982] or OPS [Forgy and McDermott, 1977]. Then the inference rules become more general and they may be compared to first-order predicate logic. Although there is no limit to their expressive power, we face the risk of combinatorical explosion. Such expert system requires complex control strategies.

Due to the ease of isolating contexts in the logs, the LITHO system uses an expert system without variables, built with the EMYCIN structure. A well considered for analysis is divided into gross zones, each corresponding to a homogeneous response on the logs. Thereafter, each gross zone is analyzed by the LITHO expert system. The input to this expert system consists of the characteristic features of the logs' morphology and of the histogram of electrofacies which are the output from the conversion module, and of the external data.

Within LITHO the events are represented by 4-plets of the type:

(PARAMETER CONTEXT VALUE CF)

173

The CONTEXT is instantiated by the name of a zone. Each PARAMETER corresponds to an attribute of this zone and the VALUE qualifies the attribute. Finally, the certainty factor (CF) defines the plausibility of the event. The plausibility is a number in the [-1, +1] range (where -1 means false, +1 means true) and where all the possibilities between the absolutely true and the absolutely false are represented by numbers between -1 and +1.

Example: (MEGARAMP-RAMP ZONE-1 YES +1.) signifies that there exists in the context ZONE-1 an increasing upward megaramp (i.e. a progressive increasing value of the log over an interval larger than 25 meters) on the resistivity log. (CLAY-TYPE ZONE-1 LAMINATED -.5) signifies that it is not probable that the clay type of the zone ZONE-1 is laminated.

Inference rules are defined as situation-action pairs [Davis and King, 1977]. The left member (i.e. the situation) describes a constraint on each of the certainty factors associated with several events. When the constraint is satisfied then the right member (i.e. the action) of the rule is triggered. This "action" modifies the certainty factor associated with all the events belonging to the right member of the rule following the certainty factor combination law.

Example: For instance consider LITHO rule 008:
If:
   1) there exists plateaus on the GR log, and
   2) the radioactivity of the zone is lower than 40 A.P.I.
Then:
   There is suggestive evidence (+0.8) that the zone is a cleanzone.

This rule is triggered on the zone ZONE-1 if the two following conditions are satisfied:
1) The certainty factor associated with the event (PLATEAU-GR ZONE-1 YES) is greater than +0.2 and,
2) The value associated with the parameter radioactivity is lower than 40 A.P.I. in ZONE-1.

The activation of the rule 008 modifies the certainty factor associated with the event (CLEANZONE ZONE-1 YES) by combining it with +0.8. The combination law for certainty factors possesses some mathematical properties:

First it is associative and commutative, so the result does not depend on the order of the triggering rules. Moreover, the combination law is monotonic except for the -1 and +1 values, and the combination of a certainty factor $-w$ with a certainty factor $+w$ is equal to 0. For more details about certainty factors see [Duda et al, 1978], [Shortliffe, 1976], and [Hàjek, 1982].

The output of the LITHO expert system is a characterization of each gross zone in terms of its main lithological type, paleoenvironment and plausible lithofacies.

The main lithological type is the most common lithology to be encountered within a certain zone (e.g. carbonates, silicates, salts, or granites). More precisely it corresponds to a certain deposit genesis. The parameter MAIN-LITHO which describes the main lithological type may be qualified by one of the four following values: BIOLOGICAL, DETRITAL, EVAPORITIC, and PLUTONIC. BIOLOGICAL means "mainly due to the action of life," DETRITAL means "mainly siliceous sediments carried by winds, glaciers, or water," EVAPORITIC means "mainly due to chemical precipitations," and PLUTONIC corresponds to "an up motion of igneous or metamorphized rocks through the Earth's crust."

The paleoenvironment contains all the climatic and geographical conditions that lead to a certain environmental context of deposition (e.g. reefal, deltaic, arid, fluvial, and glacial).

As we have previously seen (Section 2) the lithofacies is the sum of the petrophysical and petrographical aspects of rocks. Every rock has been classified by 90 lithofacies. LITHO is intended to select the 20 - 30 lithofacies which are more likely to be present in a zone. This section must "disambiguate" the affectation process: Each electrofacies (see Section 3) does not correspond to more than one lithofacies. The determination of the main lithological type and the paleoenvironment is used both to determine the plausible lithofacies, and to adjust the parameters of the clustering module.

The LITHO expert system contains 98 parameters and the geological knowledge is encoded within 500 production rules. It happens that the data do not directly match the rules because there is a hierarchical relationship between the data and the rules. Such hierarchies have been added to the system in order to "recognize" the too-particular data as instances of the rules. The first LITHO system results are reasonably good but, as we shall see in the next section, they are too ambiguous and imprecise to be used directly by the clustering process.

7. DECISION MODULE

There are different classes of expert systems, each of them implementing various strategies. Some expert systems such as SNARK [Lauriere, 1982] or MECHO [Bundy, 1979] are for problem-solving. Once a solution to a problem has been found, the problem is considered to have been resolved even though a more "sophisticated" or "natural" solution may exist.

Example: Let us consider a system intended to do formal integration. As soon as a solution to a given problem is found, this solution is regarded as valid. However, the way in which integration is obtained may be complicated, making it difficult to check its validity.

Other expert systems, such as MYCIN [Shortliffe, 1976] and its sub-products EMYCIN [Van Melle, 1980], CLOT [Bennett and Goldman, 1980] etc. are designed as diagnostic aids. Such systems help user to define a problem by asking relevant questions, and then provide him with a diagnosis. This diagnosis does not constitute necessarily a correct solution for the given problem; it only is an advice. In other words, diagnostic systems are characterized by the fact that there is no proof procedures for checking the validity of the proposed solutions. In many disciplines dealing with experimental fields such as geology, medicine, or chemistry, solutions are induced by inexact reasoning. A diagnosis is generally hypothesized by the presence or absence of symptoms. Expert systems with plausibilities are well-suited for solving such problems.

In this chapter our main subject of interest is merging the qualitative and the quantitative processing. This problem is central in experimental fields where a great amount of numerical data have to be interpreted. In such cases we can enhance data processing by introducing symbolic reasoning. These data lead to a partial interpretation, but since we are dealing with an experimental field, complete proof procedures which check the validity of this interpretation often do not exist. Thus, the expert system achieving this interpretation is a diagnostic system, producing hypotheses, rather being a problem-solver. Thus we shall restrict our discussion to diagnostic systems.

Since a complete proof procedure does not exist, the results tend to be imprecise or erroneous. Errors may be caused either by mistakes in the knowledge base, or by contradictions in the data set. Now let us examine these two possibilities.

1. In designing an expert system the problem of knowledge acquisition is regarded central. Correcting a knowledge base is a hard task requiring many testing sessions. No characterization of mistakes exists in the knowledge base; the only usable indication is that some pieces of knowledge belonging to the knowledge base lead to a faulty result. Nevertheless, we may detect irregularities such as circularities, incompatibilities, or redundancies, between rules. Each piece of knowledge taken independently may seem to be correct, yet the global behavior of the system is erroneous. It is therefore useful to characterize dependence between rules, and to define procedures capable of detecting errors. In order to achieve this, such tools as metarules or inference schemas can be used. The TEREISIAS system [Davis, 1979] is an example of such a system. Every rule and every parameter submitted to the expert system is matched with general schemas. In case of failure, the system asks the expert some relevant questions about the knowledge base consistency.

2. Now let us suppose the expert system is free of mistakes. Results might still be erroneous or imprecise because of contradictions in the data. For instance, let us examine an expert system in medicine. If the result of laboratory analysis is erroneous, then the diagnosis may be completely wrong. Moreover, in some disciplines such as in log interpretation, contradictions in the data are not only due to human mistakes, but are inherent in the data-collection methodology. For example, the caving phenomena in a drilling cavity may cause a "mélange" in the data; some coming from the caving, and some coming from the rock drill. Therefore, it is important to detect cases wherein the data are so disparate that even a human expert cannot form a valid conclusion. That is why we have to add a decision module whose role is to examine the results of an expert system and say "I cannot conclude" in cases where no conclusion is possible, and to specify conclusions whenever possible. To make our ideas more clear, let us use an example.

Example: The assigned values to the parameter MAIN-LITHO during a LITHO expert system session can be:

$$\text{DETRITAL } +0.835$$
$$\text{BIOLOGICAL } +0.785$$

The difference between the certainty factors associated with the values DETRITAL and BIOLOGICAL is too low to be able to discriminate between them. Our ultimate aim in this case is to solve the following problem: Is the main lithological type "detrital," "biological," is it a mixture of "detrital and biological," or is this result derived from an inconsistency in the data? MIRLITHO, which is the decision module of LITHO, is intended to detect and to solve problems of this type.

There are three possible kinds of reasons for the data inconsistency:

(A)   Due to erroneous data, as we have previously seen.

(B)   Due to a lack of data.

(C)   Due to a bad rough segmentation (Section 6), in which case contexts are not homogeneous, and cannot be qualified by the 3-plets

(PARAMETER CONTEXT VALUE).

The purpose of the decision module is to detect the inconsistency between the data and its cause and, in cases where data are consistent, to refine the result. In building LITHO it appeared necessary to introduce a decision module. MIRLITHO which stands for Module for Interpreting the Results of LITHO, has been designed to play this role. For more details about MIRLITHO see [Ganascia, 1983].

Finally, the organization that we propose here requires some interface between the output of the decision module and the input of the numerical data process. However this interface is so dependent on the type of numerical process used that it is not useful to describe it here. Now we shall present an example of the LITHO performance.

8. PRESENTATION OF THE LITHO RESULTS

Using the methodology presented in this chapter, the LITHO system is intended to integrate qualitative data into the interpretation of quantitative data. Figure 4 shows (right column) the manual interpretation of logs, and (left column) the automatic interpretation of the same logs.

It appears that the fine segmentation made by the numerical process of LITHO is almost the same as the manual one. Identifications of each zone corresponding to the lithofacies are also very similar in the manual and automatic interpretations.

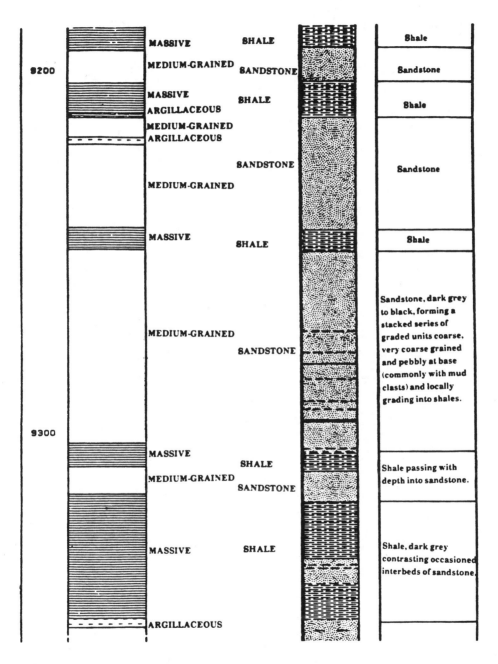

Figure 4 Interpretation of logs:

(left) automatic interpretation, (right) manual interpretation.

9. CONCLUSION

This chapter illustrates how the methodology of expert systems can be integrated with numerical data processing, and what are the limits of this approach. In the cases where rough segmentation in contexts is possible, and where the contexts do not influence each other, the proposed methodology is effective. In other cases, we hope that continuously improving expert systems techniques will help. The most original contribution described in this chapter is the use of a decision module which interprets the results of an expert system. It would be preferable to include this module in the expert system itself but this has not been attempted.

Our main conclusion is that knowledge-based systems for numerical data interpretation are possible.

They help experts to see the key role that their activity plays in the process of interpretation, and the power of their techniques. They allow justification of the adjustment of parameters in data analysis processes.

They also help specialists who are not computer experts to control easier numerical computing processes. Finally, the results obtained during the LITHO design and use indicate that numerical analysis can be combined with AI techniques to provide sophisticated hybrid systems capable of matching human expertise is restricted domains.

10. ACKNOWLEDGEMENT

I am indebted to A. Bonnet, C. Dahan, E. Feigenbaum, J. Harry, Y. Kodratoff, and P. Nii for many stimulating discussions.

LITHO [Bonnet et al, 1982] was sponsored by the Schlumberger firm. The Expert System is the result of a collaboration between two geologists J. Harry and O. Serrat, and many computer scientists: A. Bonnet, E. Feigenbaum, Y. Kodratoff, P. Nii, and myself. The pattern recognition technique was introduced by C. Dahan [Bonnet and Dahan, 1983].

REFERENCES:

Bennett, J. and D. Goldman, "CLOT, a Knowledge-based Consultant for Bleeding Disorders," Computer Science Department, Stanford University, Memo HPP-80-7, 1980.

Bonnet, A., J. Harry, and J. G. Ganascia "Un Système Expert Inférant la Gèologie du Sous-sol," Techniques et Sciences Informatiques, Vol. 1, No. 5, pp. 393 - 402, 1982.

Bonnet, A., C. Dahan, "Oil-well Data Interpretation Using Expert System and Pattern Recognition Technique," 9th IJCAI, 1983, Karlsruhe, proc. pp. 185 - 189.

Bundy, A., "Solving Mechanics Problems Using Meta-level Inferences." 6th IJCAI, 1979, Tokio, proc. pp. 1017 - 1027.

Bundy, A., "MECHO: A Program to Solve Mechanics Problems," Working Paper 50, Dept. of Artificial Intelligence, Edinburgh, 1979.

Davis, R. and J. King, "An Overview of Production Systems," Mach. Int. 8 (1977), 3000-332.

Davis, R., "Interactive Transfer of Expertise: Acquisition of New Inference Rules," Artificial Intelligence 12, 1979, pp. 121-157

Duda, R., P. Hart, P. Barrett, J. Gaschnig, K. Konolige, R. Reboh, and J. Slocum, "Development of the Prospector Consultation System for Mineral Exploration," SRI International Technical Report, October, 1978.

Forgy, C. L., and J. Mc Dermott, "OPS, a Domain-dependent Production System Language," IJCAI 5, pp. 933 - 939.

Ganascia, J. G., "MIRLITHO: Dètection des Contradictions et Validation des Rèsultats Dans les Systèmes Experts de Diagnostic, Thèse de Docteur-ingènieur," Univ. Paris Sud L.R.I. Bat. 490, F-91405 Orsay, 1983.

Hajek, P., "Combining Functions for Certainty Factors in Consulting Systems," Artificial Intelligence and information-control systems of robots, 1982, Smolenice, proc. pp. 107 - 110.

Lauriere, J. L., "La Programmation Sans Instructions: L'approche des Systèmes Experts," AFCET, Nancy, 1982a.

Lauriere, J. L., "Rèprèsentation et utilisation des connaissances," TSI, volume 1, 1982b, No. l, pp. 25 - 42, No. 2, pp. 109 - 133.

Mc Dermott, J., "Rl: a Rule-Based Configurer of Computer Systems," Report CMU-CS-80-119, Department of Computer Science, Stanford University, Stanford, 1980.

Shortliffe, E. H., "Computer-based Medical Consultations: MYCIN," American Elsevier, 1976.

Van Melle, W., "A Domain-independant Production Rrule System for Consultation Programs," PhD Thesis, computer science department, Stanford University, June, 1980.

5

KNOWLEDGE BASED SYSTEMS
FOR
COMPUTATIONAL AERODYNAMICS
AND FLUID DYNAMICS*

UNMEEL MEHTA
COMPUTATIONAL FLUID DYNAMICS BRANCH
NASA AMES RESEARCH CENTER

6.1 INTRODUCTION

The knowledge base of aerodynamics has experienced tremendous growth during this century. Before World War I, the foundations of aerodynamics were established. During the years between the beginning of World War I and the end of World War II, there was a surge in the establishment of low-speed aerodynamic knowledge. Following World War II, there was a great increase in high-speed aerodynamic knowledge. At present, we are at the threshold of acquiring new aerodynamic knowledge primarily through computational aerodynamics. This new knowledge is sought in a number of complex aeronautical problems, such as the understanding of helicopter flows, drag-reduction devices, high-lift devices, turbulence-control mechanisms, vortex flows and flows with separation, and highly maneuverable aircraft. During the next few decades, there will be a surge in vortex aerodynamic knowledge and in unsteady aerodynamic knowledge.

Another area in which computational aerodynamics will play a major role is aerodynamic design. Currently, computations based on the linearized inviscid and linearized inviscid plus boundary-layer approximations are routinely used in the design process, and those based on nonlinear inviscid and nonlinear inviscid plus boundary-layer approximations are in limited use. One can safely predict that before the end of this century, numerical solutions of the Reynolds-averaged Navier-Stokes equations will be routinely applied to solve aeronautical flow problems.

---

*The ideas and conclusions expressed in this chapter are not necessarily those of the National Aeronautics and Space Administration.

The extent to which computational aerodynamics can provide new knowledge depends on computational efficiency, manageability of computational complexity, and improvement of turbulence models. These factors are pacing the advances in computational aerodynamics. Computational efficiency includes both computer speed and memory and the speed of numerical algorithms. Manageability of computational complexity includes grid generation, body definition, data-base and programming logic management, data analysis, and computational method formulation. On the other hand, how effective computational aerodynamics is likely to be in applying knowledge to the aerodynamic design process depends on the speed at which a design process can be completed with the use of computational aerodynamics, and on the degree of confidence designers have in computational aerodynamics relative to their confidence in experimentation and analytical methods. These are the factors pacing the acceptance of computational aerodynamics by management. Artificial intelligence (AI) will play a useful role in all of the above factors (Figs. 6.1 and 6.2), because the software necessary to utilize future supercomputers efficiently and optimally will require some of the AI ideas and capabilities.

There are two possible applications of AI ideas and capabilities to computational aerodynamics. First, in the process of acquiring new knowledge, it can make some of the complex research problems manageable by efficiently using available knowledge. Second, in the process of applying available knowledge to tractable aeronautical design and development problems, it can reduce the time required for their numerical solutions. With ever-increasing knowledge, the limitations to progress is timely access to and ease of use of what is known rather than knowledge itself.

This chapter discusses the above applications of AI in computational aerodynamics. A brief discussion of automated-reasoning systems is first presented. After discussing how AI is likely to influence computational aerodynamics, the anatomy of an idealized knowledge computational system called AERODYNAMICIST is described. Then suggestions are presented on the probable use of knowledge-based systems in computational fluid dynamics (CFD) and of expert systems in the aerodynamic design and development process. In this chapter, the emphasis is on aerodynamics rather than on fluid dynamics. This emphasis is based on the observation made by Birkhoff [1983] that it was the development of aerodynamics that gave fluid mechanics its current, more technical and empirical orientation, and on the expectation that this trend will continue.

6.2 AUTOMATED-REASONING SYSTEMS

In 1844, Augusta Ada Byron, Countess of Lovelace, possibly the first computer programmer, recognized that the dichotomy between the programmer and the computer was false and that the computer is a symbol processor (Pavelle et al. [1981]). Further, computers can be programmed for reasoning, since

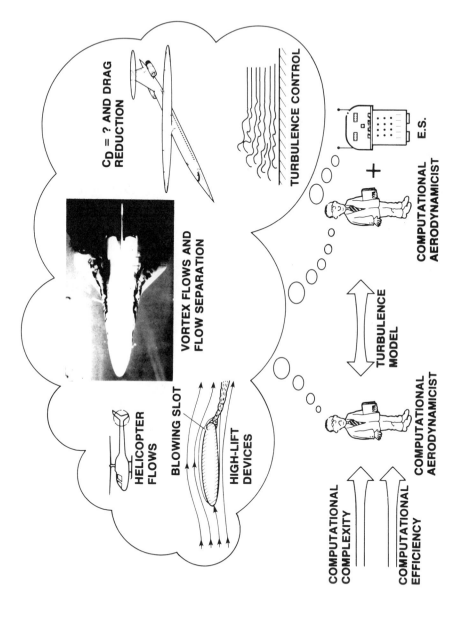

Figure 6.1 - Computational aerodynamics is assisted by AI in the acquisition of new knowledge.

185

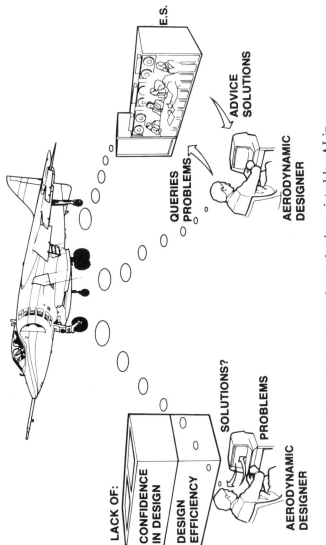

Figure 6.2 - Computational aerodynamics is assisted by AI in aerodynamic design and development process.

they are capable of manipulating any sort of symbol. Today, a computational aerodynamicist primarily selects among difficult choices by symbolic manipulations, inferential procedures, and by drawing upon working rules of thumb or heuristics based on experiential knowledge, and manipulates algebraic symbols, leading to the development of a computer program. On the other hand, a computer is principally confined to arithmetic calculations or computation. This division of labor between the computational aerodynamicist and the computer is neither necessary nor appropriate. Unlike computation aerodynamicists, applied mathematicians and physicists extensively use computers for symbolic manipulations.

If a comparison were made between current intelligent machines and intelligent humans, it would be observed that both the computer system and the human brain would have certain limitations. The computer system does not have all five sophisticated human senses (sight, hearing, smell, taste, and touch), although some computer systems do have sight and hearing capabilities. The computer system generally lacks common-sense reasoning. It does not usually have an instantaneous flash of recognition or intuition. On the other hand, the conscious state of a human brain has a short attention span. It is not capable of entertaining more than a few, say three or four, hypotheses simultaneously; and it is limited in speed. Minsky [1982] has observed that the difference between future intelligent machines and intelligent humans, at present, is unknown because of insufficient information.

Automated-reasoning systems are computer programs that can reason (logically and heuristically), make judgments, and draw conclusions in a specific domain by drawing on encoded factual and heuristic knowledge, problem-solving methods, inference procedures, and by generally drawing on search techniques. These systems are either weak or strong depending on how good the problem formulation and knowledge base are. If knowledge is the gist of an automated reasoning system, then it is known as a knowledge-based system. Knowledge is usually inexact, incomplete, and ill-defined. Just as amateurs become experts incrementally, amateur knowledge-based systems can be caused to evolve into expert knowledge-based systems. Therefore, those knowledge-based systems are known as expert systems.

An expert system performs a specialized, usually difficult and complex, professional task at the level of (or sometimes beyond the level of) a human expert. It produces high-quality results in a minimal amount of time.. The minimum accepted range of behaviors associated with the nature of expertise in expert systems consists of knowledge, public and private, about a narrow specialized domain, and skill at solving some of the domain problems. MACSYMA [1983] and DENDRAL (Lindsay et al. [1980]) are examples of such systems. Some expert systems have begun to explain results, for example, PUFF (Kunz et al. [1978]), and to learn, for example, EURISKO (Lenat [1982]). Davis [1982] reports that in addition to these capabilities, systems capable of exhibiting the other behavioral characteristics associated with the word "expertise" were

187

nonexistent as of 1981. These are abilities of reorganizing knowledge, breaking rules by understanding not only the letter of the rule but the spirit as well, knowing when a problem is outside the sphere of expertise, and of gradually decreasing expertise as the boundaries of expertise are approached. Further, expert performance means, for example, the level of performance of expert aerodynamicists doing research, design, or development in aerodynamics, or of very experienced people doing scientific, technical, or managerial tasks. The power of an expert system lies in the knowledge it possesses rather than in a collection of domain-independent solution methods.

In domains that are well bounded, expert systems work the best. An expert system is characterized by the generic task that the system is constructed to perform. Most of these tasks are control, design, diagnosis, debugging, instruction, interpretation, monitoring, planning, prediction, and repair (Hayes-Roth et al. [1983]).

There are generally seven stages of development of an expert system – conception, feasibility demonstration, prototype construction, extended use in a prototype environment. acceptance of the performance of the prototype system, commercial system construction, and commercial system release. Very few existing systems have gone through all of these stages. The unfavorable characteristics of the domain for building an expert system may terminate the expert system project in its initial stages of development. Another factor which may limit the development of the expert system is the lack of knowledge-engineering tools.

The discipline of knowledge engineering is the most crucial in the development of knowledge-based systems. It involves knowledge representation, knowledge acquisition, knowledge refinement, knowledge system architecture, and knowledge system performance. Knowledge engineering is the pacing item for advances in expert system technology because, at present, knowledge engineering has four significant shortcomings (Fig. 6.3). First, there is a scarcity of knowledge engineers. Second, there is a lack of knowledge-engineering tools. Existing tools for knowledge-representation and problem-solving structures are not always amenable to new applications. Often, laboratory tools must be modified or new tools must be constructed. Third, knowledge engineering is still in a research stage. Although there are ways machines can learn, knowledge is often handcrafted because human-like knowledge-acquisition modes are not yet thoroughly understood. Fourth, there is a knowledge-representation mismatch between the way a human expert normally states knowledge and the manner in which it must be represented in a knowledge-based system. Therefore, the expertise of a knowledge engineer in programming the expertise of a human expert is extremely crucial in building knowledge-based systems.

An expert must be acknowledged to perform the problem-solving task well in the domain of interest. He or she must be to able to articulate expertise, which comprises: (1) factual and heuristic knowledge; (2) inferential, judgmen-

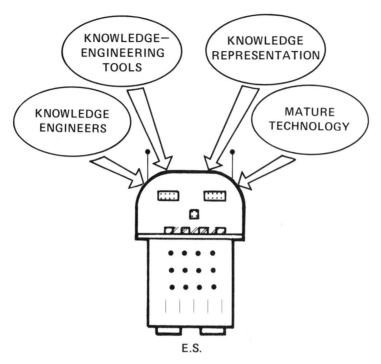

Figure 6.3 - Pacing items for knowledge engineering.

tal, and experiential procedures; and (3) problem-solving methods. Further, he or she must be available for constructing a knowledge-based system. If there are a number of experts that meet these requirements, they may have differing and conflicting views. In such cases, one of them is appointed as knowledge czar, and the knowledge-based system is built based on that person's views.

The basic concepts of AI and the characteristics of conventional programs result in a number of differences between automated-reasoning programs and current computational aerodynamic programs. These are listed in Table 6.1 for different features of these programs. Because of some of the features, namely programming style, program architecture, types of data, and programming tools that are used in developing automated-reasoning programs, these programs grow incrementally, and they are usually easy to modify. On the other hand, because of the same features, the conventional programs for computational aerodynamics grow by revision, and they are difficult to modify.

Another way of comparing the above two types of programs is to consider the hierarchy of solution methods, as shown in Fig. 6.4. Algorithmic (logical) programs for narrow domains, for example conventional computational aerody-namic programs, are usually powerful but not general or domain-independent. On the other hand, programs that are domain-independent are not that depend-able. In between these two we have automated-reasoning programs. Those

189

FEATURE	AUTOMATED-REASONING PROGRAMS	COMPUTATIONAL AERODYNAMIC PROGRAMS
EMPHASIS	WHAT IS TO BE DONE	HOW IT IS TO BE DONE
SOLUTION METHOD	INFERENCE RULES AND HEURISTIC SEARCH	ALGORITHMIC
PROGRAM ARCHITECTURE	CONTROL STRUCTURE SEPARATE FROM DOMAIN KNOWLEDGE	DATA AND CONTROL INTEGRATED
DATA BASE	PRIMARILY SYMBOLIC	PRIMARILY NUMERIC
TYPES OF DATA	IDEAS, KNOWLEDGE, NUMBERS, AND PROGRAMS	NUMBERS
DATA RELATIONSHIPS	COMPLEX	SIMPLE
PROGRAMMING STYLES	FUNCTIONAL, OR LOGICAL, OR OBJECT-ORIENTED, OR COMBINATIONS OF THESE	VON NEUMANN STYLE
PRIMARY LANGUAGES	LISP, PROLOG, SMALLTALK, AND VARIANTS OF THESE	FORTRAN
PROGRAM GROWTH	INCREMENTAL GROWTH	GROWTH BY REVISION
PROGRAMMING TOOLS	AVAILABLE	BECOMING TOOL CONSCIOUS
MODIFICATIONS	USUALLY EASY TO MODIFY	DIFFICULT TO MODIFY

Table 6.1 Comparison of automated-reasoning programs and computational aerodynamic programs for various programming features

automated-reasoning programs that mainly contain heuristics, are more general but less powerful than comparable programs using only algorithms. However, automated-reasoning programs that contain both algorithms and non-algorithmic procedures are both powerful and more general than comparable conventional programs. Note that almost all automated-reasoning programs for computational aerodynamics and fluid dynamics will be of this type.

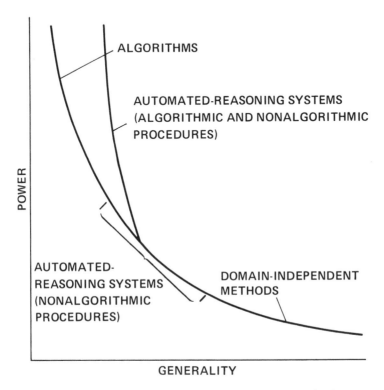

Figure 6.4 - Hierarchy of solution methods.

6.3 EFFECTS OF ARTIFICIAL INTELLIGENCE ON COMPUTATIONAL AERODYNAMICS

Computational efficiency, computational complexity, and modeling of turbulence determine the extent to which computational aerodynamics is likely to be effective in aeronautics. Computational aerodynamics is now being applied to increasingly time-consuming and complex problems, and to problems in which the nature of turbulence is poorly understood. Available computer power and programming languages are limiting the size and complexity of problems that can be addressed. Just as mathematics is applied in computational aerodynamics, the science of AI can be used in computational aerodynamics. Artificial intelligence will help improve computational efficiency. It is also the contention here that automated-reasoning systems will assist in managing computational complexity. Further, automated reasoning will aid in the development of turbulence models. In this section, we discuss how AI is likely to assist computational aerodynamics (Fig. 6.5).

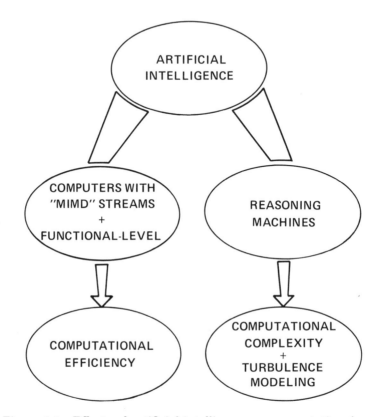

Figure 6.5 - Effects of artificial intelligence on computational aerodynamics.

Computer hardware has advanced tremendously, from the vacuum tubes of early computers (circa 1954) to very-large-scale integrated (VLSI) circuits of current computers (circa 1983), producing a net improvement in computation cost effectiveness of 10^3 (National Research Council [1983]). In the same period, both the architecture of computers and the programming languages used to control them have remained substantially the same. This has limited the full exploitation of VLSI circuit technology. Although there are vast differences in hardware and performance of the first four generations of computers, they are all based on a single basic design – the von Neumann processor. The von Neumann architecture causes a traffic jam, the von Neumann bottleneck, between the processor and memory, limiting the speeds existing computers can attain. Even array processors that have single-instruction, multiple-data (SIMD) path architectures use sequential instruction-stream, von Neumann programming methods. Buzbee and Sharp [1985] report that single-processor computers appear to be close to the maximum performance feasible. Therefore, demands for significantly increased computer performance can only be met by a totally different computer architecture.

Since conventional programming languages, such as FORTRAN, are modeled on the von Neumann processor, programs are complex, concerned with the smallest data entities, and rarely reusable in constructing new programs. Consequently, the writing and improving of software are becoming more expensive every year. Software is the limiting factor in putting computer power to its maximum use. In other words, the von Neumann programming-language barrier limits the potential usefulness of the advances in microelectronic circuit technology for computing. In order to efficiently and optimally make use of potential computer capabilities and to maximize the productivity of users, a dramatically different computer architecture along with the AI ideas and capabilities are needed.

The potential applications of knowledge-based systems are enormous in many human endeavors dealing with problems of a scientific, technical, and commercial nature. As Feigenbaum and McCorduck [1983] have observed, knowledge is the new wealth of nations. Realizing this, a number of nations have embarked on plans to develop the next generation of computers for knowledge-based systems. These systems require high-performance inference machines that utilize multiple processors.

Demands for superfast and easy to use computational processors and for knowledge processors are leading to the development of the next generation of computers. However, Wallich [1983] reports that it is AI that is generally believed to be the cornerstone of next-generation computer technology. Advances in knowledge processors are likely to assist advances in computational processors. This will definitely be advantageous to computational aerodynamics.

In the view of many researchers in the field of computer architecture, the fifth-generation computers will use multiple-instruction, multiple-data (MIMD) streams and many processors (Lerner [1984]). This will make a break with the von Neumann architectures and programming languages. Two of the probable language types to emerge as predominant languages on the fifth-generation computers are the functional-level programming (Backus [1977] and [1982]) and a combination of LISP and PROLOG. In the functional-level programming, programs are put together with so-called program-forming operations to build new programs. These in turn can be used to construct even larger ones. This approach allows parallel or concurrent operations to be expressed easily. LISP is an example of functional programming style, but it retains some features of von Neumann programming. The functional-level of programming will greatly reduce the complexity of FORTRAN-like computer codes, and consequently, the software cost.

193

The most fundamental task of a computational aerodynamicist is to interact with computers through programming. The AI capabilities and ideas will remarkably improve his or her current programming environment. These will provide knowledge-based programming environments and automated-programming systems that will simplify and accelerate the interaction with computers (Lerner [1982], Balzer et al. [1983], and Barstow [1984]). Consequently, programming productivity will substantially increase. Beginning efforts toward programming automation for computational fluid dynamics are reported by Engquist and Smedsaas [1980], Cook [1982], Roache and Steinberg [1983], Engquist [1983], and Steinberg and Roache [1985], who have generated FORTRAN codes using symbolic manipulations.

There are two related aspects of computational aerodynamics (Fig. 6.6): *reasoning* and *calculating*. Reasoning is based on factual and heuristic knowledge of both computational procedures and aerodynamics, and it is carried out by symbolic manipulation and inferential procedures. Calculating is based on reasoning. It is impossible to calculate without doing some reasoning. Although limitations in computational speed are considered to be a pacing item of the advances in computational aerodynamics, the mere existence of a piece of hardware that can execute instructions rapidly does not, by itself, guarantee that a particular problem can be solved quickly. Again, it is reasoning that is going to extract high performance out of a computing machine. The science of AI offers the opportunity of using computers as reasoning machines to set the stage for efficient computations.

It behooves the computational fluid dynamicist to exploit the expertise of systems like MACSYMA for reasoning before computation. There are at least two advantages of algebraic programs over purely numerical ones. First, a result in algebraic form is more valuable than one in numerical form. Second, simplifying an expression algebraically before evaluating it numerically reduces the computation time. Furthermore, there are at least four advantages of automatic algebraic computations. First, months or years of work with pencil and paper can be done in a few minutes. Second, a human being is more prone to make a mistake than is a computer system. Third, a general mathematical expression stating a scientific theory can be easily simplified under certain assumptions by algebraic manipulations which may be very difficult for the human being. Fourth, a human being is freed from usually tedious algebraic manipulations to pursue more stimulating and interesting scientific activities.

The domains of computation and aerodynamics are complex and difficult. Obviously, the domain of computational aerodynamics is then complex and difficult. Automated-reasoning systems in these domains will be a great benefit to the computational aerodynamics community as discussed in some of the following sections. These systems will become "intelligent" assistants to a computational aerodynamicist. They will accelerate the advances in computational aerodynamics, and they will speed design and development processes. These achievements are possible simply because these assistants are the reservoirs of

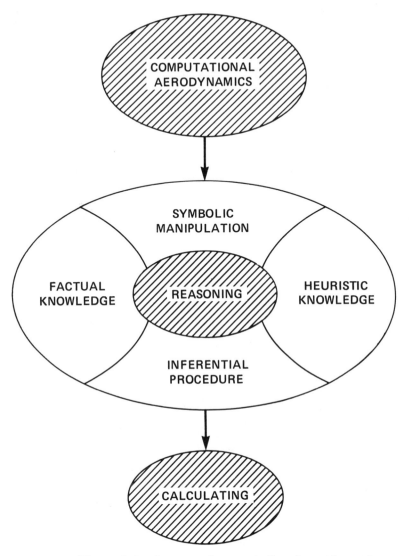

Figure 6.6 - Aspects of computational aerodynamics.

knowledge, and because they are capable of making manageable the complexity associated with difficult computational problems. In addition, the expertise in continuously updated software of an automated-reasoning system remains an asset forever. Unlike its human counterpart it never dies, moves on, performs inconsistently, or contains obsolete knowledge.

An automated-reasoning system can be of tremendous utility in the analysis of experimental data. For example, a laser Doppler system produces a huge amount of data. These data can be statistically processed; they can be used for developing theories of turbulence. The automated-reasoning system can seek orderly patterns in irregular data and thereby hit on predictable laws of turbulence. This is not far-fetched; already, a system called BACON simulates some of the important processes of scientific discovery. It has independently rediscovered laws of planetary motion, electrical resistance, and Black's law of temperature equilibrium, as well as concepts of atomic weight and specific heat from physical data (Bradshaw et al. [1983]). Another example is EURISKO, which develops its own theories and ideas once it is given the principles of a discipline. A third example is LOGIC THEORIST, which follows rigid rules and logic to find alternative proofs of theorems in *Principia Mathematica* (Whitehead and Russell [1925-27]). And the fourth example is the development of elaborate mathematical theories from a few simple axioms of set theory (Lenat [1977]).

6.4 ANATOMY OF A KNOWLEDGE COMPUTATIONAL SYSTEM: AERODYNAMICIST

Figure 6.7 shows the *idealized* anatomy of a knowledge computational system called AERODYNAMICIST. It consists of two intertwined systems: a knowledge-based system for symbolic manipulations, and a computational system for numerical computations. It could be used in various subdomains of computational aerodynamics and CFD. An expert system with such an anatomy could also be used in the domain of computational aerodynamic design and development. None of the existing knowledge-based systems has the anatomy of this idealized system, although some parts of it are contained in every existing system. The idealized system is based on requirements of the above domains. It is constructed considering what is technologically feasible and is likely to be feasible. It would be incrementally designed and built, and continuously updated. The architecture of this system would be such that it could grow and contain various capabilities. It would, therefore, avoid the limitations of the first generation of expert systems.

AERODYNAMICIST can be used in four modes: the assistant mode, the expert mode, the learning mode, and the teaching mode. The aerodynamicist employs the system as an assistant or an expert. The knowledge engineer communicates with the system to build its knowledge base and its inference system. The student learns how to use the system.

AERODYNAMICIST contains the following subsystems: (1) a language processor or an input/output system, (2) a system manager, (3) a knowledge base comprising factual and heuristic knowledge, (4) an inference system containing methods of reasoning and of solving problems, (5) a knowledge and inference acquisition system, (6) an expertise controller, (7) a status recorder, (8) an explanation system, and (9) a computational processor. Each component of this system is described briefly below.

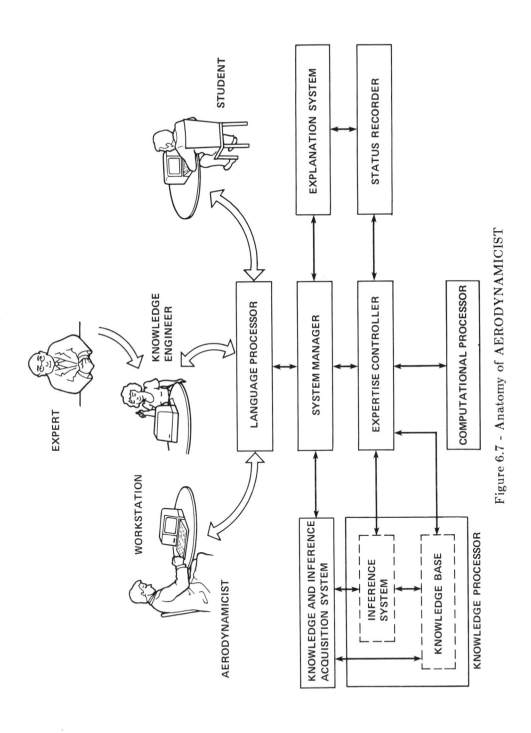

Figure 6.7 - Anatomy of AERODYNAMICIST

A workstation is the principal user interface to AERODYNAMICIST. It includes keyboard, pop-up menu, mouse, voice, window, video, cameras (still and movie), and printed output subsystems for human-machine dialog. It has significant symbolic processing, floating point processing, and high-resolution, dynamic, color graphic capabilities. Further, it supports network interface capabilities for communicating with other local or remote computing systems. An aerodynamicist or a student communicates with the knowledge computational system using the workstation in domain-oriented language, which is generally some limited variant of English, or by means of a graphics editor. In addition to these modes of communication, a knowledge engineer may use a structure editor for knowledge and inference acquisition.

The language processor acts as an intermediary between any one of the above users and the rest of the knowledge computational system, and also transforms natural language or graphics communication of the user into a language that can be understood by the system manager. This processor also transmits to the user the response of the system to the user directives.

The system manager directly or indirectly controls the other subsystems of AERODYNAMICIST. It sends directives to and receives responses from the knowledge and inference acquisition system, expertise controller, and the explanation system. It receives commands from and sends its response back to the language processor. It monitors the errors and interrupts of systems that are under its control.

Knowledge-based systems are problem-solving systems. These usually have three main components, a data base, a set of operators, and a control strategy. The data base is the knowledge base associated with the current task-domain and the desired goal. Operators, such as rules of inference, help achieve the goal by manipulating the data base. A control strategy is used for deciding what operator to apply and where to apply it. A method of search for an appropriate operator sequence for achieving the goal is an example of a control strategy. A problem-solving method is formulated as a search procedure in many knowledge-based systems.

The most important part of the anatomy of any knowledge-based system is the knowledge base, because the performance of a knowledge-based system depends on the knowledge it has. In the domain of utility, the knowledge-based system contains the following different types of knowledge that would make it behave knowledgeably: facts about objects; actions and events; the time-history of a sequence of events; cause-and-effect relations; performance knowledge, that is, knowledge about how to do things; meta-knowledge, that is, knowledge about what is known; the theory of the domain; and heuristic knowledge, that is, experiential and judgmental knowledge and rules of good guessing. Some domains may not contain all of these types of knowledge.

In knowledge-based systems, knowledge is most likely to be represented by the propositional doctrine (Nilsson [1983]), by procedures (Barr and Feigenbaum [1981]), and by scripts (Gevarter [1985]). The propositional doctrine utilizes a declarative knowledge base plus an inference mechanism. In declarative representations, the static aspects of knowledge, such as facts about objects, events, and their relations, are stressed. Knowledge is represented declaratively by methods based on mathematical logic, such as first-order predicate calculus which allows manipulation of knowledge by logical operations and rules of inference. Production systems are equivalent to expressions of first-order predicate calculus. The basic concept of these systems is that the knowledge base consists of production rules in the form of condition-action pairs, that is, IF-THEN expressions. In this, the action part of the rule pair is executed only if the condition side is invoked for a piece of knowledge or in the reverse manner when substantiating hypotheses. On the other hand, procedural representations of knowledge stress how to use knowledge in well-specified situations. Knowledge is contained in procedures that know how to do specific things, how to find relevant facts and make inferences. Furthermore, scripts are framelike structures for representing stereotype objects, events, or situations.

The next most important part of any knowledge-based system is the inference system. It contains inference procedures and problem-solving methods, which reason by manipulating and acting upon the combination of knowledge contained in the knowledge-based system and the problem submitted by the user. The inference system may contain different kinds of reasoning. Formal reasoning based on mathematical logic deduces new data structures from given data structures by syntactic manipulation of given data. Procedural reasoning involves simulating, answering questions, and solving problems as, for example, computations done in computational aerodynamics. Meta-level reasoning deals with meta-knowledge, that is, knowledge about what is known. Nonmonotonic reasoning withdraws a previously deduced conclusion in response to learning some new fact. Various combinations of these four kinds of reasoning are contained in existing knowledge-based systems. Reasoning by divide-and-conquer, reasoning by analogy, reasoning through generalization, and other abstract reasoning approaches are just beginning to be implemented in knowledge-based systems. Common-sense reasoning is difficult at present to implement.

Knowledge and inference acquisition are a form of machine learning. When AERODYNAMICIST is being used in the learning mode or when it needs to capture its own experience, the knowledge and inference acquisition system is used. The knowledge engineer encodes the knowledge of the expert and inference rules utilizing this acquisition system as an aid. There are three other ways of acquiring knowledge: (1) The expert can interact directly with this acquisition system using an "intelligent editing program" (Hayes-Roth et al. [1983]); (2) induction programs may generate knowledge based on experience, obtained from the expert and from textbook cases (Boose [1984]); and (3) knowledge may be acquired directly from textbooks using text-understanding programs. The last one is not yet demonstrated. The knowledge and inference acquisition system decides how knowledge and inference shall be organized, controlled, propagated, and updated. It handles the difficult task of managing the knowledge base. It determines how the inference system will use knowledge. An example of an acquisition system is TEIRESIAS (Davis [1977]). It assists the expert in acquiring, correcting, and using new inference rules without calling on a knowledge engineer.

The expertise controller actually controls the solution process for solving the problem submitted by the aerodynamicist or the student. It performs three functions: scheduling, interpreting, and enforcing consistency (Hayes-Roth et al. [1983]). It solves the problem by using the knowledge system, the inference system, and the computational processor. It formulates a list of things to do, controls that agenda, and determines what action should be executed next. It interprets the inference procedures and applies them to the knowledge base and problem data. It ensures that plausible solutions or conclusions are arrived at, and that inconsistent ones are rejected.

Search is generally unavoidable, but unlike the knowledge base it is not imperative in knowledge-based systems. The expertise controller may contain different search techniques: (1) the data-directed or forward-chaining strategy, which starts from known conditions and proceeds toward the goal; (2) the goal-directed or backward-chaining method, which begins from the goal to be achieved and progresses toward facts; (3) the generate and test search technique; (4) the difference reduction or mean-ends analysis, which tries to reduce the difference between the current and the goal state; (5) the blackboard model, which mixes forward- and backward-chaining strategies, and in which multiple sources of knowledge check the status of the emerging solution on the blackboard in order to decide what these sources can contribute; and (6) the bidirectional search, which involves searching from both ends of a search space. The data-directed, goal-directed, and bidirectional search strategies could involve blind search strategies, which are not practical for large problems. Heuristic search techniques reduce the amount of computation by using heuristic knowledge about the problem.

The status recorder records all the activities of the expertise controller. Particularly, the status recorder has the following information: (1) status of three types of actions taken by the expertise controller; (2) record of the strategy embarked upon in order to solve the problem; (3) agenda of potential actions awaiting execution; (4) record of the intermediate hypotheses, decisions, and successful solutions, and their dependencies; and (5) list of failures during the problem-solving process. In addition to this record-keeping activity, it provides information to the explanation system.

The explanation system explains the actions of the expertise controller either to the aerodynamicist or the student user by tapping the information generated in the status recorder. The explanation system answers questions about how the solution of the problem was determined, why the knowledge computational system failed to provide the answer, why some decision, conclusion, or hypothesis was reached while some other was rejected. The explanation system assists the user in evaluating AERODYNAMICIST, deciding whether to use the built-in expertise, and in debugging, modifying, and expanding the built-in expertise. This is particularly important for building confidence of designers of aerodynamic vehicles in computational aerodynamics.

The knowledge processor primarily computes by reasoning. On the other hand, the computational processor primarily computes by "number-crunching." The knowledge processor helps to make efficient and optimal use of the computational processor. The knowledge processor and the computational processor are either a part of a single computer system or two different computer systems.

6.5 KNOWLEDGE-BASED SYSTEMS IN COMPUTATIONAL FLUID DYNAMICS

Computational fluid dynamics involves the synthesis of many facets: physical problem formulation, grid generation, software method formulation, programming, validation, data processing, and utilization. By and large, a computation fluid dynamicist attempts to carry out this synthesis alone. However, each of the above facets requires decisions by one or some of the following experts: the fluid dynamicist, grid generator, numerical analyst, software designer, graphic display engineer, or applications engineer. Knowledge-based systems can assist the computational fluid dynamicist by taking over some responsibilities.

It is conceivable that a knowledge-based system could be designed that would act as a synthesizer of the above facets; that is, act on all of these facets for a computation. However, it would be appropriate to begin with construction of knowledge-based systems in each facet separately. Major characteristics and capabilities of knowledge-based systems are briefly described in the following areas encompassing most of the above facets: definition of the flow problem, grid generation, construction and analysis of numerical schemes, flow-solver selection and use, and data reduction, analysis, and display (Fig. 6.8). These are a few of the potential applications of knowledge-based systems in CFD.

Before a computational fluid dynamicist begins constructing a computer program to solve a flow problem, he or she has to completely define the problem based on the physical aspects of it, for example, as discussed by Mehta [1984] for viscous flows. This process could be performed by a knowledge-based system with extensive fluid dynamic knowledge encompassing flow regimes, local flow characteristics, acceptable assumptions and their shortcomings, governing equations, turbulence models, physical boundary and initial conditions, and identification of possible solution methods. The knowledge-based system in essence could develop a blueprint for tackling the flow problem. Such a system could be used by a computational fluid dynamicist or an aerodynamic designer. It could be used for education; and it could also be used by a person not familiar

FLOW-PROBLEM DEFINITION

- PHYSICAL ASPECTS OF FLOW
  SPEED REGIME
  TURBULENCE
  BOUNDARY LAYERS
  DISCONTINUITIES
  ETC.

- SURFACE AND FIELD VARIABLES

- BOUNDARY AND INITIAL
  CONDITIONS

- SOLUTION METHODOLOGY

CONSTRUCTION AND ANALYSIS OF NUMERICAL METHODS

$$\frac{\partial U}{\partial t} = \frac{\partial^2 U}{\partial x^2}$$

$$\frac{U_i^{n+1} - U_i^n}{\Delta t} = \frac{U_{i+1}^{n+1} - 2U_i^{n+1} + U_{i-1}^{n+1}}{\Delta x^2}$$

- DEVELOPMENT OF SCHEMES
  WITH SPECIFIC PROPERTIES

- STABILITY ANALYSIS

- ACCURACY ANALYSIS

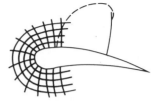

GRID GENERATION

- CONCEPTUAL OR TOPOLOGICAL
  DISCRETIZATION

- DEFINITION AND APPLICATION
  OF GRID-GENERATION PROCEDURE

- GRID-QUALITY ANALYSIS

- GRID-POINT LOCATION ADJUST-
  MENTS

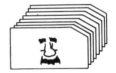

FLOW SOLVERS

- NAVIER-STOKES SOLVER

- PNS SOLVER

- BOUNDARY LAYER SOLVER

- INVISCID SOLVER

DATA REDUCTION (ANALYSIS AND DISPLAY)

- ENGINEERING QUANTITIES

- FLOW VISUALIZATION

- ERROR ANALYSIS

Figure 6.8 - Knowledge-based systems in CFD (Mehta and Kutler [1984]).

with fluid dynamics.

One of the most important steps required to accurately solve a three-dimensional CFD problem using finite-difference or finite-element procedures involves the proper location of the nodal points in the flow region to be resolved. There are basically two grid-generation stages and a grid-adaptation stage involved in the discretization process (Mehta and Lomax [1982]). The two grid-generation stages involve (1) the grid topology, and (2) the grid-generation scheme; the grid-adaptation stage involves an analysis and modification of the grid. Grid generation and appropriate grid-point distribution are intrinsically complex, difficult, and largely heuristic reasoning processes. This is a combinatorial problem because the degrees of freedom in distributing grid-points are directly proportional to the number of grid-points. There is no theory that would indicate what is the appropriate grid system; and it is highly improbable that one would be developed. What is considered to be an acceptable grid system is primarily based on heuristic reasoning. Therefore, a knowledge-based system, called SPIDER, can greatly reduce the complexity associated with the creation of acceptable grid networks.

Once SPIDER is supplied with the physical problem to be solved in mathematical terms (that is, the governing equations, boundary and initial conditions, domain of computation, flow parameters, and computational parameters, such number of grid-points and desired level of accuracy), it would appropriately segment the computational domain, determine grid topology, and choose a grid-generation method based on factual and heuristic knowledge consisting of good practice and judgement for constructing an acceptable grid system. SPIDER would dynamically adapt the grid system in the course of computing a numerical solution to concentrate grid-points in regions of strong variation of one or more appropriate flow quantities based on the grid metrics, the flow-solver algorithm that is being used, and the flow-solution generated. The selection of what flow quantities are to be monitored and how to distribute grid-points require judgement. A more detailed description of SPIDER is given by Mehta and Kutler [1984].[†]

A knowledge-based system can be constructed for building and analyzing numerical methods. Such a system could develop a numerical method that has specified properties and capabilities. It could perform a stability analysis, and determine phase and amplitude errors of any numerical method. It could be made to compute test problems and present sample results. It could summarize all the characteristics of the numerical method. It could check for and construct compatible numerical schemes that might be used in different parts of the flow field. Sometimes it is difficult to perform a stability analysis; for example, it is generally difficult to perform a stability analysis with nonperiodic boundary conditions. For such situations, the knowledge-based system could be advantageous. Engquist and Smedsaas [1980], and Engquist [1983] have reported some

---

[†]A similar description is presented by Kutler, et al. [1984].

efforts toward achieving these objectives.

Just as MACSYMA solves ordinary differential equations, a knowledge computational system could be developed to solve the partial differential equations governing fluid flows. This system would contain knowledge of existing flow solvers. It would determine the type of the partial differential equations –elliptic, hyperbolic, parabolic, or mixed. It would solve the equations analytically, if this is feasible; otherwise, numerically. It would analyze the problem structure as a basis for choosing and developing an algorithm. It would automatically select the solution method and generate the corresponding code for a specific problem. Based on a dynamic analysis of an ongoing solution, it could change the solution method. That is, it would tailor a computation to a particular problem using adaptive methods. It would identify discontinuities and singularities, and treat them appropriately. In addition, the system would assist in determining a correct solution by checking whether the problem is well-posed. This system would be widely used by aerodynamicists in aerodynamic research, design, and development. It would not be necessary that the user have any knowledge of the solution procedures used by this system. Note that a feasibility study of the construction of an expert system for solving partial differential equations in various physical domains has been recently reported by Technology Development of California [1984]. A partial demonstration of such a system with limited capabilities had been reported earlier by Engquist [1983].

The usefulness of any applied computational approach clearly depends on the availability of various graphical displays that provide insights into the physics. Three-dimensional CFD solutions generate vast amounts of data. The processing of these data for analysis and display is somewhat analogous to signal interpretation in space and military applications. It is highly conceivable that a knowledge-based system could be constructed to make decisions, and to process and display useful data in an appropriate form. This system would use color to draw attention to gross structures. It would draw contours to emphasize details and to give a better feeling for gradients. It would decide what part of the flow field to analyze, what analysis to perform, and what to display. It would choose how to display the data in order to enhance the perceptibility of essential details. It would track some flow quantity as a function of time. It would have an ability to make spatial and temporal correlations and compute moments of flow quantities. It could also summarize the significant physical, analytical, computational, and design aspects of the computed results.

6.6 EXPERT SYSTEMS FOR AERODYNAMIC DESIGN AND DEVELOPMENT

Flight vehicle designers need sophisticated computational aerodynamic tools to simulate the flow field about complicated three-dimensional flight configurations. They would prefer to have expert simulation tools at their disposal in a relatively short time. They would also like to use these tools without the need to know exactly how they work. Furthermore, they would like these tools to be easy to use, versatile, reliable (thus improving productivity), robust, and accurate (so that the design and development of more efficient configurations would be feasible). The development of sophisticated computational aerodynamic tools requires vast expertise and enormous resources in terms of both manpower and computer capacity (i.e., speed and storage). The creation of these simulation tools requires knowledge, for example, in the disciplines of aerodynamics, structural dynamics, propulsion, design methods, fluid dynamics, numerical analysis, and computer science. Such tools demand an inordinate amount of development time. To provide simulation programs that are easy to use, reliable, and versatile, and to alleviate a long development process, expert systems can be employed. These systems offer a way around spiraling design and development costs. Further, these systems would help keep the productivity of designers in pace with the demands of increasing complexity of designs.

There are at least nine areas in which expert systems can be developed. These areas are potential flow, Euler equations, thin-shear layer (boundary-layer) equations, Reynolds-averaged Navier-Stokes equations, parabolized Navier-Stokes equations, computational design, aerodynamics, structural dynamics, and aerodynamic design.

Abundant knowledge is available for determining the potential flow around aerodynamic vehicles. The numerical procedures and techniques are well understood. For transonic flows, the aircraft industry is routinely using potential-flow codes, such as the series of FLO codes (Nixon [1982]). The strengths and weaknesses of small-disturbance and full-potential methods are well known. The characteristics and capabilities of various numerical methods are also well known. For incompressible flows, the panel method and the Douglas-Neumann code exist. In short, the numerical determination of potential flow is no longer a basic research topic. It is just a matter of proper and timely utilization of the available knowledge. All this knowledge can be codified into an expert knowledge computational system that would automatically generate the grid system using SPIDER and solve for the potential flow around any vehicle. The expert system could make all the relevant decisions based on the requirements specified by the user, and then it would direct a supercomputer designed for number processing to perform the calculations. Upon receiving the computed data, it would analyze the data and report the significant results. A similar case, based on availability of enormous knowledge, can be made for developing an expert system for automatically and expertly computing thin-shear layers.

During the last 5 years, there has been significant progress in computing solutions of the Euler equations. Although there is still a lot to learn about solution procedures for these equations, it makes more sense to begin building an expert knowledge computational system now than developing a portfolio of codes for each application that arises. The expert Euler equation system could be continuously updated, and thus its capability would incrementally grow. Conventional programming techniques generally produce codes that need to be redesigned when their requirements are modified. An expert system that is incrementally developed, on the other hand, would result in a code that would remain operational with changing requirements within the same domain. A similar case can be made for developing an expert system that would solve Reynolds-averaged Navier-Stokes equations and the parabolized Navier-Stokes equations.

Aerodynamic design methods are classified as either inverse-solution methods or numerical-optimization methods. Inverse methods determine the aerodynamic body surface that produces the desired pressure distribution. These methods, at present, are best suited for initial design because it is difficult even for an experienced designer to specify the pressure distribution that would achieve the design objective and because structural constraints are difficult to impose (Lores and Hinson [1982]). But an expert system can search through a knowledge base containing various pressure distributions associated with the shapes of the bodies and their design characteristics, and it can construct the possible pressure distribution that would satisfy the design conditions. This pressure distribution can then be used for the inverse problem.

On the other hand, numerical-optimization methods couple flow solvers with numerical-minimization schemes to produce designs that achieve user-specified design objectives. In these methods, the designer specifies an initial aerodynamic body, design objectives, design constraints, and design conditions. The effect on the design objectives and constraints is determined by computing the flow field. A search direction is established that minimizes one of the design objectives while satisfying the constraints. In this fashion the design variables are perturbed independently, and the design objective and constraints are again evaluated. When the objective can no longer be reduced in the current direction, a new search direction is chosen, and the process is repeated. The number of design points that can be considered by numerical optimization is theoretically unlimited; however, computer capacity limits the number of these points (Hicks and Vanderplaats [1977]). In such instances, an expert system with heuristic search procedures utilizing a knowledge base of previous designs and experience related to the optimum way to perturb the variables could benefit the optimization process. Tong [1985] has recently demonstrated that the essence of this idea is feasible.

Figure 6.9 shows relevant parts of an expert knowledge computational system called OPTIMIZER along with some of the possible contents of these parts. At the workstation, the user provides the design objectives, design constraints, and design conditions. The initial configuration is either provided by the user or generated by OPTIMIZER. The expertise controller directs the computational processor to use either the potential flow solver or the minimization procedure based on the reasoning carried out by the inference system using the knowledge base. If the expertise controller finds that the user requirements are satisfied by the actions of the computational processor, it transfers the optimized design and its characteristic to the user via the workstation. If this is not the case, then the expertise controller calls upon the inference system and knowledge base to provide a perturbation in the previous configuration and initial variables that would accelerate the analysis to be performed by the computational processor.

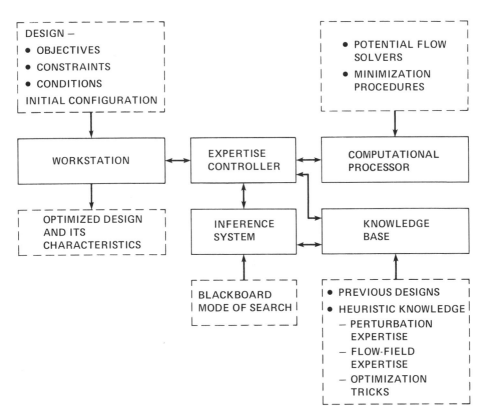

Figure 6.9. - OPTIMIZER, an expert system
for aerodynamic design optimization.

Knowledge of aerodynamics, structural mechanics, and mechanical design pertinent to the design and development process of an aerodynamic configuration in knowledge-based systems could be a great asset to designers and developers. For example, substantial heuristic and experiential knowledge is used in the design and development of aircraft operating in the transonic regime.

The above potential expert systems would be particularly powerful because expert performance is based largely on compiled experience. They can have substantial economic value. They can also alter the perception of management concerning realities. These benefits are achievable because they fulfil one or more of the following objectives[‡]: (1) sustaining growth through duplication

---

[‡]Feigenbaum and McCorduck [1983] have identified most of these objectives.

207

of expertise, (2) capturing and distributing expertise for new ventures, (3) combining the expertise of many experts, (4) solving intrinsically complex problems that resist solution by other means, (5) managing knowledge, (6) providing a competitive advantage, (7) preserving perishable expertise, and (8) improving skills of low-skill workers. The net effect of meeting any one of these objectives is to increase the level of available expertise (Fig. 6.10).

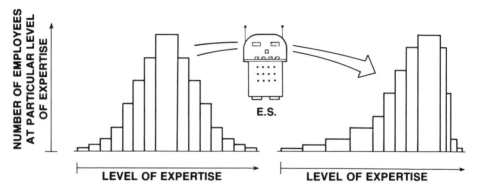

Figure 6.10. - Expert system increases the availability of expertise.

6.7 CONCLUDING REMARKS

There are two ways the science of artificial intelligence will benefit computational aerodynamics. Directly, it will greatly influence the reasoning aspect of computational aerodynamics based on available knowledge and expertise. It offers the opportunity of using computers as reasoning machines to set the stage for efficient numerical calculating. This will be accomplished through the use of automated-reasoning systems. Artificial intelligence will make knowledge easily available and usable. It will make computational complexity manageable. It will provide designers of aerodynamic vehicles with reliable, easy to use, and versatile expert computational aerodynamic tools, as well as related design tools. Indirectly, a major worldwide interest in knowledge-based systems will lead the development of the next generation of computers and the higher-level programming languages based on functional programming style that will replace von Neumann computers and von Neumann programming languages such as FORTRAN. This will result in faster computers and in greater simplicity in programming, both of which will be advantageous to computational aerodynamics.

Knowledge computational systems will be a new asset of institutions involved in aeronautics, particularly for various aspects and tasks of computational aerodynamics. Knowledge-based systems will introduce a new way of preserving knowledge, and, consequently, they will change the way knowledge is passed from one generation to the next. They will liberate people from concentrating on narrow domains of knowledge and allow them to entertain broad-range problems. On the other hand, the widespread use of only one or a few knowledge-based systems may lead to uniformity; and overdependence on knowledge-based systems may limit individual creativity and innovation.

There are three major stages of the computational aerodynamic development cycle: (1) research, (2) technology transfer, and (3) design and development. The first stage, research, is the stage in which a computational procedure is conceptualized, algorithms are developed, and pioneering applications are performed. After the feasibility of the computational tool has been demonstrated, technology transfer or dissemination from the research mode to the design and development mode occurs. In this stage, the engineering user requirements are considered and different technology components are assembled for engineering applications. When this is completed, the design and development stage begins, in which the developed technology from the research stage is utilized in the design process, as well as in creative and innovative developments. These three stages will be greatly accelerated by the use of AI concepts (Fig. 6.11).

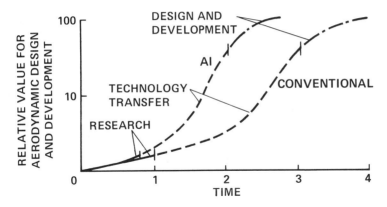

Figure 6.11. - Artificial intelligence accelerates research, technology transfer, and design and development stages of computational aerodynamics development.

Predicting the future is a difficult and hazardous business. Nonetheless, we have ventured into the unknown future world of computational aerodynamics and fluid dynamics by suggesting or rather inventing the role that artificial intelligence will play in computational aerodynamics. The ultimate goal is to bring automated-reasoning systems to bear on the present and future complex computational tasks of the aerodynamic designer and fluid dynamicist. Further, we have assumed that challenges facing the applied science of artificial intelligence (Nilsson [1983]), particularly in the field of knowledge engineering, will be successfully resolved by those engaged in applied AI research.

6.8 BIBLIOGRAPHY

BACKUS, J., "Can Programming be Liberated from the von Neumann Style? A Functional Style and its Algebra of Programs," 1977 ACM Turing Award Lecture, *Communications of the Association for Computing Machinery*, 21, (1978), 613-41.

BACKUS, J., "Functional-Level Computing," *IEEE Spectrum*, Aug. 1982, 22-27.

BALZER, R., T. E. CHEATHAM, Jr., and C. GREEN, "Software Technology in the 1990's – Using a New Paradigm," *Computer*, Nov. 1983, 39-45.

BARR, A., and E. A. FEIGENBAUM, eds., *The Handbook of Artificial Intelligence*, Vol. 1. Los Altos, Ca.: William Kaufmann, Inc., 1981.

BARSTOW, D., "A Perspective on Automatic Programming," *The AI Magazine*, Spring 1984, 5-27.

BIRKOFF, G., "Numerical Fluid Dynamics," *SIAM Rev.*, 25, (1983), 1-34.

BOOSE, J. H., "Personal Construct Theory and the Transfer of Human Expertise," in *Proceedings of the National Conference on Artificial Intelligence*, University of Texas, Austin, Tex, Aug. 1984.

BRADSHAW, G. F., P. W. LANGELY, and H. A. SIMON, "Studying Scientific Discovery by Computer Simulation," *Science*, 222, (1983), 971-75.

BUZBEE, B. L., and D. H. SHARP, "Perspectives on Supercomputing," *Science*, 227, (1985), 591-97.

COOK, G., "Development of a Magnetohydrodynamic Code for Axisymmetric, High-Beta Plasmas with Complex Magnetic Fields," Ph.D. Thesis, LLNL Report UCRL-53324, Dec. 1982.

DAVIS, R., "Interactive Transfer of Expertise – Acquisition of New Inference Rules," *International Joint Conference Artificial Intelligence*, 5, (1977), 321-28.

DAVIS, R., "Expert Systems – Where Are We? And Where Do We Go from Here?," *The AI Magazine*, Spring 1982, 3-22.

ENGQUIST, B., "Some Techniques for General Software for Partial Differential Equations," presented at the Conference on Large Scale Scientific Computation, University of Wisconsin, Madison, Wis., May 1983.

ENGQUIST, B., and T. SMEDSAAS, "Automatic Computer Code Generation for Hyperbolic and Parabolic Differential Equations," *SIAM J. Sci. Stat. Comput.*, 1, (1980), 249-59.

FEIGENBAUM, E. A., and P. McCORDUCK, *The Fifth Generation*. Reading, Mass.: Addison-Wesley Publishing Company, 1983.

GEVARTER, W. B., *Intelligent Machines: An Introductory Perspective of Artificial Intelligence and Robotics*. Englewood Cliffs, N. J.: Prentice-Hall, Inc.,

1985.

Hayes-Roth, F., D. A. Waterman, and D. B. Lenat, eds., *Building Expert Systems*, Teknowledge Series in Knowledge Engineering, Vol. 1. Reading, Mass.: Addison-Wesley Publishing Co., Inc., 1983.

Hicks, R. M., and G. N. Vanderplaats, "Application of Numerical Optimization to the Design of Supercritical Airfoils without Drag-Creep," SAE Paper 770440, 1977.

Kunz, J. C., R. J. Fallat, D. H. McClung, J. J. Osborn, R. A. Votteri, H. P. Nii, J. S. Aikins, L. M. Fagan, and E. A. Feigenbaum, "A Physiological Rule-Based System for Interpreting Pulmonary Function Test Results," Report HPP-78-19, Heuristic Programming Project, Computer Science Department, Standford University, Stanford. Calif., 1978.

Kutler, P., U. B. Mehta, and A. Andrews, "Potential Application of Artificial Intelligence Concepts to Numerical Aerodynamic Simulation," NASA TM-85976, June 1984. (Also in Proceedings of Ninth International Conference on Numerical Methods in Fluid Dynamics, *Lecture Notes in Physics*, Vol. 218. Berlin, West Germany: Springer-Verlag, 1985.)

Lenat, D. B., "Automated Theory Formulation in Mathematics," *International Joint Conference Artificial Intelligence*, 5, (1977), 833-42.

Lenat, D. B., "The Nature of Heuristics," *Artificial Intelligence*, 19, (1982), 189-249.

Lerner, E. J., "Automating Programming," *IEEE Spectrum*, Aug. 1982, 28-33.

Lerner, E. J., "Data-Flow Architecture," *IEEE Spectrum*, Apr. 1984, 57-62.

Lindsay, R. K., E. A. Buchanan, E. A. Feigenbaum, and J. Lederberg, *Applications of Artificial Intelligence for Organic Chemistry – The DENDRAL Project*. New York, N. Y.: McGraw-Hill, 1980.

Lores, M. E., and B. L. Hinson, "Transonic Computational Design," in *Transonic Aerodynamics*, D. Nixon, ed., Progress in Astronautics an Aeronautics, Vol. 81, pp. 377-402. New York, N. Y.: American Institute of Aeronautics and Astronautics, 1982.

MACSYMA Reference Manual, version 10. (Mathlab Group, Laboratory for Computer Science, Massachusetts Institute of Technology, Cambridge, Mass., 1983.)

Mehta, U., "Physical Aspects of Computing the Flow of a Viscous Fluid," NASA TM-85893, 1984.

Mehta, U., and P. Kutler, "Computational Aerodynamics and Artificial Intelligence," NASA TM-85994, June 1984. (Also AIAA Paper 84-1531, AIAA 17th Fluid Dynamics, Plasma Dynamics, and Lasers Conference, Snowmass, Colo., 1984.)

MEHTA, U., and H. LOMAX, "Reynolds Averaged Navier-Stokes Computations of Transonic Flows – The State-of-the-Art," in *Transonic Aerodynamics*, D. Nixon, ed., Progress in Astronautics and Aeronautics, Vol. 81, pp. 297-375. New York, N. Y.: American Institute of Aeronautics and Astronautics, 1982.

MINSKY, M., "Why People Think Computers Can't," *The AI Magazine*, Fall 1982, 3-15.

NATIONAL RESEARCH COUNCIL, "The Influence of Computational Fluid Dynamics on Experimental Aerospace Facilities, A Fifteen Year Projection," Prepared by the Committee on Computational Aerodynamics Simulation Technology Developments, Aeronautical and Space Engineering Board, Commission on Engineering and Technical Systems, NRC. Washington, D. C.: National Academy Press, 1983.

NILSSON, N. J., "Artificial Intelligence Prepares for 2001," *The AI Magazine*, Winter 1983, 7-14.

Nixon, D., ed., *Transonic Aerodynamics*, Progress in Astronautics an Aeronautics, Vol. 81. New York, N. Y.: American Institute of Aeronautics and Astronautics, 1982.

PAVELLE, R., M. ROTHSTEIN, and J. FITCH, "Computer Algebra," *Scientific American*, 245, (1981), 136-52.

ROACHE, P. J., and S. STEINBERG, "Symbolic Manipulation and Computational Fluid Dynamics," AIAA Paper 83-1952, AIAA Computational Fluid Dynamics Conference, Danvers, Mass., 1983.

STEINBERG, S., and P. J. ROACHE, "Symbolic Manipulation and Computational Fluid Dynamics," *J. of Comp. Physics*, 57, (1985), 251-84.

TECHNOLOGY DEVELOPMENT OF CALIFORNIA, "Expert Partial Differential Equation Solver," TDC, Inc., Santa Clara, Ca., 1984.

TONG, S. S., "Design of Aerodynamic Bodies Using Artificial Intelligence/ Expert System Technique," AIAA Paper 85-0112, AIAA 23rd Aerospace Sciences Meeting, Reno, Nev., Jan. 1985.

WALLICH, P., "Designing the Next Generation," *IEEE Spectrum*, Nov. 1983, 73-77.

WHITEHEAD, A., and B. RUSSELL, *Principia Mathematica* (2nd ed.). Cambridge, U. K.: Cambridge University Press, 1925-27.

6

KNOWLEDGE ENGINEERING OF THE
AIRCRAFT DESIGN PROCESS

ANTONIO L. ELIAS
FLIGHT TRANSPORTATION LABORATORY
MASSACHUSETTS INSTITUTE OF TECHNOLOGY

1 INTRODUCTION

Donald A. Hall, designer of the *Spirit of St. Louis*, estimated that the effort required to design that historical aircraft totaled 775 labor-hours[1][1]. By comparison, it is estimated that the C5A aircraft required some 49 *million* engineering labor-hours -- not counting flight tests [2], and this figure may be dwarfed by the complex airborne and space systems under consideration today. This trend towards greater and greater expenses in the design of aerospace systems seems to be made up of two components:

1. The natural increase in the complexity of the vehicles designed; although the historical relevance of Lindbergh's flight may surpass that of the first wide-body transport jet aircraft, the fact remains that the C5A is structurally, aerodynamically, and electronically a much more complex system that the *Spirit of St. Louis*.

2. As the complexity, therefore the required design effort, increases, there is the tendency to parallel the effort to reduce or at least keep constant the required elapsed time; observations from the well-documented world of software engineering have lead to the postulation of a "one-third power"

---

[1]The actual design and engineering effort was reported to be 850. Of these, 775 were spent by Hall himself - over a period of 74 days, a remarkable performance by itself - in "design, weight and balance analysis, stress analysis, drawings, inspection, performance analysis, and flight test engineering," and the rest by the company's purchasing agent, who helped Hall in the weight and balance, and the factory manager, who helped lay out the fuel and oil systems.

law, which states that the cost of partitioning a design effort in n parallel tasks increases the size of the effort by a factor of $n^{1/3}$ [3], so had the *Spirit of St. Louis* been designed by four engineers, it may have required 775 x $4^{1/3}$ or about 1230 labor hours. This ignores, of course, the problem of finding three more engineers of the caliber of Donald A. Hall.

Concern with the increase in design complexity and partition of design tasks is not merely one of cost, but also of quality; the holistic nature of the individual design effort - or that of a close-knit small team - is lost earlier in the design process of larger systems, thus leading to poor integrated performance and the intrusion of political and personality factors in the design process: the dreaded *design-by-committee* and *not-invented-here* syndromes. Therefore, the availability of computer-aided design and engineering tools could not merely reduce the cost of designing complex aerospace systems, but perhaps enable the realization of otherwise hopelessly complex systems. Finally, increasing the productivity of outstanding individuals in an essentially creative role seems to be a better solution than a brute force increase in the number of individuals involved, not all of whom have the same creative talents.

While these considerations apply all along the designing and engineering process, from the conceptual or preliminary stages, through analysis and development, into detailed and final design, it is in these latter stages that most efforts in Computer-Aided Design (CAD) and Computer-Aided Engineering (CAE) have been concentrated. CAD systems began as sophisticated electronic drafting systems but are continually growing both in the upwards direction, with capabilities to perform geometry-oriented analysis such as moments of inertia and weight calculations, as well as towards the manufacturing side, with electronic alternatives to blueprintes - Computer-Aided Manufacturing.

In contrast, little has been achieved in the area of *generic* tools for the preliminary design stages; there are reasons for this:

- The operations involved in detailed design are simpler to model numerically than those involved in the preliminary stages. Computers being traditionally number-crunching machines, it was easier to visualize their application at the drafting stage than at the conceptual stage.

- There are clear short-term payoffs in increasing the productivity of drafting and detailed-design personnel, whose numbers are very large and whose turnover rate is high enough to allow retraining and experimentation with alternative methods.

Recent advances in Computer Science, particularly as a result of research in Artificial Intelligence, have resulted in the development of alternatives to the classical numerical view of computation which may very well constitute the *enabling technology* that will make generic *Preliminary Design Tools (PDT's)* possible [4]. Also, there is a new consciousness of the economic impact of the quality of preliminary design work, harder to quantify than the number of drafting labor hours but with much higher potential payoffs than automating the drafting loft, considering the resource invested. The rest of this chapter develops a possible paradigm for the preliminary design process; a number of abstractions are proposed and their implementation on "Paper Airplanes," a prototype PDT core, is shown. Paper Airplane was developed at the Flight Transportation Laboratory of the Massachusetts Institute of Technology as a test bench for experiments with design abstractions and symbolic PDT's[2]. Problems and issues that arose out of this implementation are discussed; finally, a number of ideas and suggestions for future research are proposed.

2. CHARACTERIZING THE DESIGN PROCESS

Attempts at characterizing the design process have usually been of one of two types: tutorial or analytical. Tutorial characterizations have as their objective to introduce the reader to the process of designing a specific system, such as a subsonic transport aircraft; such descriptions are usually found in books on aircraft (or spacecraft) design, of which [5] is an outstanding example. The intended audience are individuals familiar with each discipline involved in the design of the vehicle or system in question, but not with the tradeoffs resulting from the integration of these disciplines. Thus the description results necessarily centered around that specific vehicle or system.

Analytical descriptions are usually derived from observation of an actual design experience and usually are large in scope, very detailed, and specific to a particular organization. Their intended use is to a large extent diagnostic, either to identify bottlenecks or opportunities for improvements in the process, or as a

---

[2]A "symbolic PDT" is a design tool that manipulates design abstractions, rather than specific parameters or models for a particular vehicle.

baseline to design management support systems, data base systems, and the like [6]. They usually encompass the entire design cycle, up to the manufacturing interface (and beyond, to engineering testing of the product), and stress the *form* of the process as much as its substance.

Neither type of description claims to create *abstract* models of the design process, that is, independent of either the vehicle or the organizational structure performing the design. In contrast, the model we need is functional, rather than formal; for example, a formal model would begin by describing the *specification* of the product by the client. This is the *form* the design process takes in our contemporary industrial environment because of the customer-supplier relationship that has evolved over the past 50 years or so[3], and our neglect of the form of the design process does not imply denial of its importance, but simply a limitation on the scope of this work.

Our paradigm for the design process consists of a number of basic abstractions and a functional model. We will underline the first appearance of a keyword used to denote an element of these abstractions or basic concept of the functional model.

2.1 A Preliminary Design Requires a Set of Variables and a Set of Constraining Functions

We begin by assuming that at the preliminary stage of design, the vehicle or system we are designing can be completely specified by the values of a set of variables which we will call underline design variables. These variables may be of different types, some of which are:

1. Actual dimensions or characteristics of the vehicle, such as wing area, propeller diameter, or seating arrangement. The values of these variables are *unquestionably* under direct control of the designer's whim - or skill - subject to the constraints implied by the "design functions" defined below.

2. Measures of performance of the design, such as direct operating cost or cost

---

[3]Consider, for example, that the only specification laid upon Hall by Lindbergh for the *Spirit* was the use of a Wright Whirlwind engine; not even the number of engines was specified, although a single engine aircraft was always in Lindbergh's mind, since the company he selected to build the *Spirit* only produced small, single-engine aircraft. This was actually a form of *meta-design* - which will be discussed shortly - on the part of Lindbergh.

per seat-mile; they are less under direct control of the designer than the previous variables in that:

> (a) They are traditionally regarded as a "consequence" of the other parameters, rather than as something that can be arbitrarily specified.
>
> (b) Minimum values are usually stated in design specifications.
>
> (c) There is one clear "desirability direction": reduce landing distance, increase range, reduce weight; any increment in the "undesirable" direction is made to improve another performance (i.e., a tradeoff).

3. Indices of the performance of a certain technology, such as structural weight parameters, engine thrust-to-weight ratios, and the like. The designer may have indirect control over their values, e.g., by changing engine types, construction technology, etc., but is not at liberty to arbitrarily alter their values.

4. Environment variables which, although literally not under the control of the designer, represent parameters whose variation may give insight on the design process, such as the assumed en route winds or FAR-required design load factors.

Design variables cannot assume arbitrary values; they are constrained by a number of relationships, usually equality relationships. For example, dynamic pressure $\bar{q}$ is equal to $\frac{1}{2}\rho V^2$, aspect ratio is b^2/S and so on. These relationships, which we will call <u>design functions</u> actually represent a number of different types of constraints:

1. Definitions, such as those of dynamic pressure and aspect ratio. Being definitions, these models are "perfectly accurate."

2. Models of the physical world, such as the relationship between air density and altitude, or $\mathbf{F} = m\mathbf{a}$. The accuracy of these models may be debatable, but their applicability - hence the "firmness" of the constraint they represent - is beyond debate.

3. Models of the performance of the object being designed or its constituent elements, such as the Bréguet range equation or an actuator-disk model of the thrust-power relationship of a propeller.

4. Models of the performance of the design or fabrication process, such as a statistical model for the fabricated weight of a wing assembly given a number of shape and load parameters, or of a standard operational

procedure, such as the balanced-field length which assumes a certain sequence of acceleration and deceleration, pilot reaction time, etc.

Note that these constraints are of a different nature from the inequality constraints that are sometimes referred to as *design boundaries* and which we normally associate with design specifications, such as "the balanced field lengths shall not be greater than 5,000 ft." The difference between these two kinds of constraints is whether there is any design value to *bargaining* the value of the constraint: we assume that there is no advantage, from the design point of view, in violating a design function, either because they represent a definition or physical constraint or because they represent an agreed upon level of model detail or accuracy; on the other hand, there may be a design advantage in bargaining the later type of constraints, as where a slight violation of one of them may significantly improve one of the performance measures of the design. For example, a 500-ft relaxation of the balanced field length may result in a 20% increase in loitering time for an Anti-Submarine Warfare aircraft due to a combination of increased wing loading and reduced engine size.

We will call a <u>design set</u> the combination of a set of design variables related by a set of design functions. To give some body to an otherwise too abstract discussion, we will be carrying a "running example" of a very simplistic design problem. Since we cannot afford to use an entire aircraft, let us consider a specific *aspect* of an aircraft's design: the tradeoff between takeoff and range performance. Nineteen design variables are sufficient to represent this aspect of aircraft design; these variables are summarized in Table 1, which includes their classical mathematical symbol, a brief description, and the name that will be used for that variable in the discussion of the Paper-Airplane implementation. Constraining these nineteen variables, our running example includes six design functions which we will label **f1** through **f6**. The definitions of these six functions are:

f1 calculates the takeoff velocity as a function of the gross take-off weight, the takeoff altitude (via the air density function $\rho(h_{to})$), the take off lift coefficient, and the wing area, and works by simple equating lift and weight at takeoff, with a 20% margin added in for good measure:

$$V_{to} = 1.2 \frac{2W_g}{\rho(h_{to})C_{L_{max}}S}$$

Symbol	Paper-Airplane name	Description
C_{D_0}	cd0	Zero-lift drag term of the drag polar.
$C_{D_{C_L^2}}$	cdcl2	Lift-square coefficient of the drag polar.
$C_{L_{cr}}$	cruise-cl	Lift coefficient in cruise flight conditions.
$C_{L_{max}}$	clmax	Lift coefficient at takeoff.
h_{cr}	cruise-altitude	Cruise altitude.
h_{to}	takeoff-altitude	Altitude at which the aircraft is assumed to take off (i.e. the density altitude).
M_{cr}	cruise-mach	Cruise Mach number.
sfc	sfc	(Thrust-) specific fuel consumption.
S	wing-area	Reference wing area.
(T/W)	t-over-w	Aircraft's thrust-to-weight ratio at takeoff conditions.
$(T/W)_e$	thrust-to-engine-weight	Engines' weight per unit of thrust.
W_g	gtow	Gross take-off weight.
W_p	payload	Weight of the payload.
(W/S)	wing-loading	Aircraft's (gross take-off) weight per unit of wing area.
V_{to}	vto	Takeoff velocity.
x_{cr}	cruise-range	Cruising range.
x_{to}	takeoff-distance	Takeoff distance (ground run).
δ_f	cruise-fuel-fraction	Fuel used during cruise, as a fraction of the gross take-off weight.
δ_s	structural-fraction	Empty airframe weight (engines excluded) as a fraction of the gross take-off weight.

Table 1: Running example design variables

f2 is a simplified formula for the take-off distance, which assumes a constant acceleration determined by the thrust-to-weight ratio, up to the takeoff velocity:

$$x_{to} = \frac{V_{to}^2}{2g_0(T/W)}$$

f3 is the definition of wing loading:

$$(W/S) = \frac{W_g}{S}$$

f4 is another "lift equals weight" relationship but particularized at cruise conditions and manipulated to express lift coefficient as a function of gross take-off weight, altitude (via both density and speed of sound), wing area, and cruise Mach number:

$$C_{L_{cr}} = \frac{2W_g}{\rho(h_{cr})S(M_{cr}a(h_{cr}))^2}$$

f5 is the Bréguet range equation for constant lift-to-drag and constant velocity, manipulated to express the cruising range as a function of the specific fuel consumption, the lift-to-drag ratio computed from the cruise lift coefficient and the two drag polar coefficients, the cruise Mach number, altitude (via speed of sound a), and the fuel fraction. The coefficient 0.592483 is the conversion factor between feet per second (supposedly used for a) and Knots; sfc also must have specific dimensions, namely hours[-1], to have the result come up in nautical miles, making this a very unit-dependent relationship:

$$x_{cr} = 0.592483 \left(\frac{1}{\text{sfc}}\right) \frac{C_{L_{cr}}}{C_{D_0} + C_{D_{\sigma_L^2}} C_{L_{cr}}^2} M_{cr}a(h_{cr}) \log\left(\frac{1}{1-\delta_f}\right)$$

f6 is the weight equation, using fractions for fuel, structure and engine weights, and dimensional quantities for the gross takeoff weight and the payload weight; also, since δ_f represents the *cruise* fuel, it is multiplied by 1.25:

$$W_g = \frac{W_p}{1 - \delta_s - 1.25\delta_f - \frac{(T/W)}{(T/W)_s}}$$

In this example, **f3** is a definition type of design function, while **f4** is a form of a physical law. **f5** and **f2** are classical performance functions, while **f1** and **f6** are actually a mixture of one of these types and the fourth type of design function: a standard assumption about how something is designed. In the case of **f1**, a physical law is modified by the standard assumption that takeoff velocity should be 1.2 times the stall speed; in the case of **f6**, the definition of the various weight fractions is modified by the assumption that the cruise fuel is 80% of the total fuel. A more indepth discussion of these functions, and the variables involved, can be found in any textbook of aeronautical design, such as [7].

2.2 The Preliminary Design Process has a Meta-Design Phase and a Sizing Phase

The classical view of computer-aided preliminary design focuses almost exclusively on the problem of determining the values of selected ("output") design values so that the value of a, possibly complex, performance function is extremized [8]. Although the methodology used to determine these values is an essential part of the preliminary design process, it is by no means the only or even the most important part. In addition to the problems encountered when attempting to capture the entire vector of design quality measures with a simple scalar, there are other problems:

- The selections of which variables to use actually constitutes the first design decision.
- It is not clear which variables should be given input values and which should be computed.
- It is not clear that every design aspect can be captured as the value of a variable.

Consider, for example, the configuration of an aircraft as a monoplane or biplane. Can this decision be solely represented by the value of a variable such as number-of-wings? Is the decision *not* to include this variable completely equivalent to making its value equal to 1? Similarly, there is a design decision implicit in the selection of a given design function. Consider, for example, the selection of a certain model for wing weight; if this model assumes traditional aluminum design and construction practices, as opposed to, say, composite materials, this is a design decision. Moreover, the weight model, which we consider "un-bargainable," now can be violated, not in its numerical value, but in that it can be replaced by a graphite-composite model yielding lower wing weights.

At the end of the preliminary design stage, all design variables must have values which do not violate any of the chosen design functions. In the process of

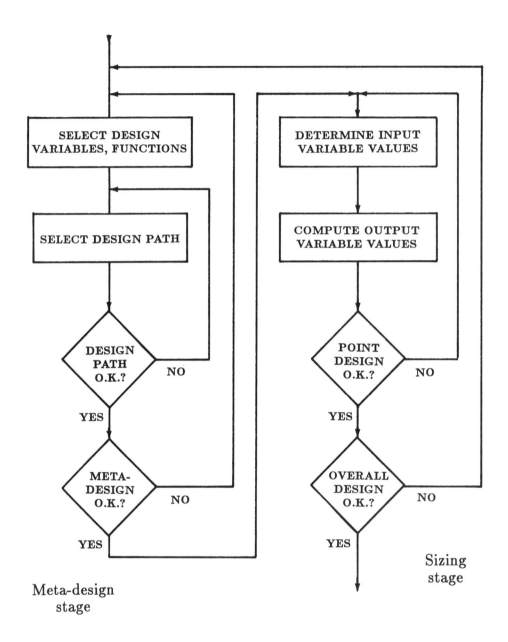

Figure 1: A functional model of the preliminary design process

arriving at these values, the designer must choose which of the design variables will receive values - either by hand or as a result of some formal mathematical procedure - and which will have their values computed by means of design functions (so as to satisfy these functions). We will call the latter the output design variable set, or simply <u>output variables</u>, and the former the input design variable set, or <u>input variables</u>. The sequence of design functions invoked to compute the values of the output variables from the values of the input variables will be called the <u>computational path</u>; included in the computational path is the direction in which the design functions are used, that is, which of the design variables involved in a particular function is the one whose value is being computed. The input variables set, output variables set, and, implicitly, the resulting computational path constitute what we will call the <u>design path</u>.

Using these definitions, we will model the entire preliminary design process as an iterative process made up of three inner iterations:

1. A set of design variables and design functions, i.e., the design set, is chosen.
2. A design path is determined among the chosen variables and functions.
3. The resulting design path is - somehow - evaluated. If found satisfactory, we proceed; if not, we return to step 2.
4. The resulting design process - variables, functions, and path - is evaluated. If found satisfactory, we proceed; if now, we return to step 1 (we have exhausted the possibilities of manipulating the design path, so we must change variables, functions, or both).
5. Values are given to the input design variables, and values for the output variables are computed.
6. The results are evaluated; if found satisfactory, we proceed; if now, we return to step 5.
7. The resulting preliminary design is evaluated. If found satisfactory, we are done; if not, we must return to step 2, or possibly step 1.

The entire process is shown pictorially in Figure 1. We will use the term <u>meta-design</u> to indicate the first two stages, that is, selection of the design variables and functions and selection of the design path, and the classical term <u>sizing</u> to indicate the iterations around numerical values of the design variables. The set of values of all the design variables at any point in the sizing stage is called the <u>design point</u>.

Significant work has already been performed on the problem of assigning numerical values to input variables to achieve specific performance objectives [9], but we are barely beginning to analyze the process of constructing and selecting design sets. The present work focuses on the intermediate step, that is, the construction, selection, and implementation of the design path.

2.3 The Perceived Use of Design Variables Determines the Design Path

While we may not know enough about the process by which the design set is constructed to build a model for it, we can identify some of the logic behind the selection of the input and output variable sets, the first stage in defining the design path. Let us consider how we would rationalize the selection of an input set for our example design set and then try to draw some general conclusions from that experience.

Traditionally, there has been a strong interaction between input set selection and computational path construction; in particular, the explicit directionality of classical computer procedures prevented any of the procedures' input variables from being part of the output set and any of the procedures' outputs to be part of the input set. We deliberately "wish away" the problem of inverting explicit functions (that is, compute one of its input variables given the values of the output variable and the other inputs) and assume that all design functions are reversible, and thus do not force design variables out of either the input or output sets.

In our running example, there are a number of variables, specifically C_{D_0}, $C_{D_{C_L^2}}$, $C_{L_{max}}$, sfc, $(T/W)_{\bullet}$ and $\delta_{\bullet}$, that can be considered "technology parameters" and thus may be given appropriate *fixed* values. By this we mean that there is little utility, from a design point of view, in computing their values, i.e., assigning them to the output set[4]. Similarly, there is normally little value in computing the takeoff altitude h_{to} (an "environment parameter"), unless one wishes to find

---

[4]It may be useful, however, to do so in order to answer questions of the style "what maximum lift coefficient would be required to satisfy this set of performance requirements" - which is a *technology assessment* question rather than a design question

out the maximum density altitude at which the aircraft will take off. Since it is reasonable to assume that these seven variables should not be in the output set, we assign them to the input set.

At this point, in order to select which of the other 19 - 7 = 12 design variables to designate as inputs, we must consider what kind of aircraft we are designing: if it is a subsonic jet transport, long experience has shown that cruise conditions around 33,000-ft altitude and Mach number 0.8 are a clear optimum in the tradeoff between productivity and direct operating costs. Our design set does not include any variable or function relating to productivity or costs, but we may nevertheless use this knowledge both to include h_{cr} and M_{cr} in the design set, and later, in the sizing stage, to use these numbers as tentative initial values for these variables[5]. In the same vein, since most successful transport aircraft have takeoff thrust to weight ratios of around 0.3, we also may want to include (T/W) in our input set.

Since we have specified values for 10 variables, and we have six design functions, we still must specify the values of three more design variables out of the 9 remaining to make the design set "perfectly constrained," at lease as far as nominal degrees of freedom are concerned (but see section 4.2). In this admittedly contrived example, it is clear which three variables should complete the design set: payload weight W_p, cruise range x_{cr}, and takeoff distance x_{to}, since these variables are clear indices of the performance of the aircraft and are likely to be part of the performance specifications for the design. It is here where we exercise our assumption of separation between the design path and the computational path; traditionally, these three variables would be outputs of design functions and therefore could not be included in the input set, but we would construct a sizing iteration loop to iterate over values of the available input set until the values of these variables were found to be satisfactory. This is merely a mathematical solution to a mathematical problem, rather than an essential part of the design process itself.

Although we have now perfectly constrained our design set, we can still identify alternative arguments that could have been used to include or exclude a

---

[5]This does not preclude us, of course, from altering these values during the sizing step, e.g , to determine the effect of cruise altitude and Mach on performance measures that *are* included in the design set.

design variable from the input set. Weight, in all its manifestations, is clearly the main enemy target in aerospace engineering; we would like to minimize both the gross take-off weight W_g and the fuel fraction δ_f. It is therefore illogical to include them in the input set. Similarly, V_{to} is not a significant design variable in the limited context of our example (it could be if, for instance, we were also looking at approach speed constraints); indeed, the only reason for the inclusion of V_{to} in the design set is. as a tie-in between design functions f1 and f2[6]; therefore, it is not reasonable to include it in the input set.

After having walked through this example, let us try to rationalize and classify the various arguments used to place into or exclude variables from either the input or the output set:

1. Variables over which the designer has little effective control, given the design set, as for example C_{D_0}, should not be in the output set. These are "technology parameter" kinds of variables (see footnote on page 7). If our design set had included a *model* for C_{D_0}, e.g., a wetted area model driven by fuselage size and wing thickness, then C_{D_0} could be assigned to the output set.

2. Variables for which specific values are clearly design goals, such as the payload or cruising range - as opposed to "open-ended" goals, such as reducing the gross weight. These variables therefore belong in the input set.

3. Variables which should not be in the input set by virtue of their irrelevance or transitory nature (such as V_{to} in our example) or a clear desire for extremization (such as the various weights).

4. Variables over which the designer has effective control but there are *external arguments* for giving them a specified value, as was the case with the cruise conditions. It is not as imperative that these variables be part of the input set; they are, to a certain extent, "wildcards" that could be pulled in and out of the input set as required to increase or decrease the number of constraints on the design set.

---

[6]In other words, we could eliminate that variable completely by combining these two functions into a single function.

3. DETERMINATION OF THE COMPUTATIONAL PATH

In traditional "hard-wired" preliminary design computer programs, such as [10], the computational path is fixed, since the design path is also fixed[7]. In addition, the computational logic of such programs:

- Is constrained by the directionality of the design functions used.
- Assumes that the problem is "perfectly constrained," i.e., will not accept under- or over-constrained specifications.
- Iteration around the input and output sets, as when a guess value is given to gross weight and the computed gross weight is fed back to "refine" the guess, is done only as a "last resort" when there is no way of otherwise exercising the available design functions (see example in section 4.3).

The problem of determining the computational path - assuming its independence from the input set selection process - is currently being addressed as a means for integrating large existing disciplinary codes, i.e., existing programs which address a specific disciplinary design problem, such as airbreathing propulsion or aerodynamic performance[8]. These "smart executives" should be able to negotiate with the designer both what constitutes an acceptable input set - given the directionality constraints of the disciplinary codes - and what the sequence of invocation should be. In addition, these executives should be able to identify under- and over-constrained design paths and take intelligent action as a result[9].

In our generic computational path abstraction we have two additional problems, both caused by our assumption that design functions are reversible: an increase in the freedom to choose the design path - hence an increase in the dimensionality of the solution space for the computational path problem - and the

---

[7]Sometimes a limited number of alternative input sets are made available, with suitable modifications in the computational path by means of flags indicating which design path had been chosen by the user.

[8]It is worth noting that these disciplinary codes embody, for a specific discipline, an entire design set, design path, and computational path. A fascinating alternative to integrating these large codes would be break them into their constituent design variables and functions, and integrate the resulting "primordial soup." This is one of the goals of the "Long Term Memory" concept suggested in section 5.1.

[9]What constitutes "intelligent" action remains to be seen; at this point, we mean something more sophisticated than a mere informational message to the user.

"minor" problem of actually obtaining an inverse solution from an arbitrary design function.

3.1 Determining The Computational Path Requires Translation of Declarative Knowledge into Imperative Forms

We usually describe mathematical knowledge in a *declarative* form [11], since when we make a statement like "$x = 2y + 3z$" we merely declare the existence of a relationship between x, y and z, without describing either how to compute any of these variables as a function of the other two, or, for that matter, which of the three is to be computed! On the other hand, effective computer procedures require an *imperative* description of the knowledge, as in "X = 2 * Y + 3 * Z," or maybe "Y = 0.5 * (X - 3 * Z)," or even "Z = (X - 2 * Y) / 3." Indeed, as required by a present-day computer, there are three possible (imperative) meanings for the apparently univocal declarative form "$x = 2y + 3z$."

Unfortunately, transformation of declarative knowledge into an imperative form is not as simple as specifying which variable is to be the "output" and then performing a little bit of algebraic manipulation:

- The function may not be capable of being analytically inverted, as would be the case with a numerical integration or a stochastic function.
- Some additional knowledge (e.g., about the variables themselves) may be required to uniquely identify the correct imperative form.

Consider, for example, the classical expression for the thrust required to fly (subsonically) at a given velocity V, which states that the thrust equals the sum of the form drag and the lift-induced drag:

$$T = (\frac{1}{2}\rho S C_{D_0}) V^2 + (\frac{2W^2}{\rho S} C_{D_{\sigma_L^2}}) \frac{1}{V^2}$$

If the design path requires the velocity as a function of thrust, an imperative description of the form $V = f(T)$ must be sought. But since $T = f(V)$ is a fourth-order relation, there are actually four values of V which satisfy the original, declarative form! Selecting which of the four possible values of V should be used requires two rather different forms of knowledge.

1. Since the original equation depends only on V^2, it is possible to substitute -V for V without modifying the result; in other words two of the four solutions are mathematically trivial. Thus, some *mathematical* or analytical knowledge is requires.

2. There are indeed two steady-state velocities at which an aircraft requires the same amount of thrust to maintain equilibrium flight. Realizing this fact requires some *aeronautical*, or engineering, knowledge; realizing which of the two velocities is desired requires knowledge about the *design problem* in progress: are we looking at a cruise velocity, in which case the higher value is probably the desired one? Are we looking at an approach case, in which case we probably want the lowest one? Are we constraining ourselves to flying on the front side of the L/D curve, in which case we may *always* want to use the highest value?

In order to automate the process of determining and implementing the computational path, we must store our design functions in declarative form and then transform them to the appropriate imperative form that will result in an effective computational path capable of being executed in the sizing step. Artificial Intelligence researchers have spent significant effort on the generic problem of transforming declarative knowledge into imperative knowledge, leading to approaches such as Logic Programming [12] and Automatic Programming [13]. The kind of transformation required in the computational path problem is much more restricted, and two approaches seem to have been actually implemented: Constraint Propagation and Fixed Point.

The Constraint Propagation model is actually a complete paradigm for a computing device [14]; in it, *elementary* operations are implemented by means of non-directional "contract boxes" connected by means of "signal paths." Each contract box has a number of ports, each of which can be viewed as an input or an output, and a functional relationship between the values appearing at each port, or "contract." This contract is triggered when all but one of the ports presents a value to the box, at which time the remaining port is forced to acquire the precise value that will satisfy the contract.

Several such boxes can be interconnected to form an entire "program" which itself can be viewed as a large contract box with many ports; Figure 2 shows the interconnection of two simple kinds of contract boxes ($a = kb$ and $a = b+c$) to mechanize the system of linear algebraic equations;

$$x = 2y + 3z$$
$$x = y + z$$

This approach to transforming a declarative form of a functional relation to the imperative form appropriate for a given input set has a number of advantages:

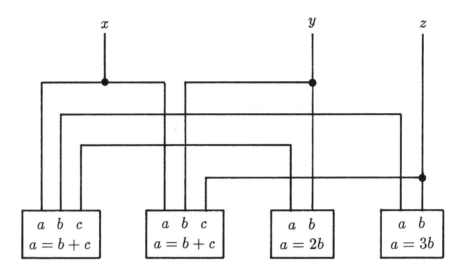

Figure 2: A system of algebraic equations programmed in the Constraint Propagation mode

- The construction and connection of these "contract boxes" amounts to precompilation of the descriptive form, so that evaluation of the appropriate imperative form once the inputs are selected is efficient and almost automatic.
- This transformation is based uniquely on the mathematical (i.e., functional) structure of the design function, and does not require any further information or knowledge about the function, the design path, or about any of the design variables involved in that function.

At the same time, this approach has a number of disadvantages:

- Only analytical functions, capable of being decomposed into individual operations, can be handled. There are many important design functions which cannot be decomposed in this way, such as numerical integrations.
- Multiple-valued functions, such as the square and trigonometric functions, present a problem unless a global convention is adopted, e.g., always

taking the positive branch of a square root or the principal value of an inverse trigonometric function. Such global conventions often do not yield the correct value.

- There is no clear *internal* mechanism for detecting the need for iteration, and, once detected, implementing it.

Because of these problems, the Fixed Point scheme of producing an imperative form of the design functions has been developed. This scheme is based on two assumptions:

1. The unit of functional definition is an entire design function, rather than atomic operations, and the entire function is, if needed, inverted numerically.

2. There is some knowledge about either the specific design function or the design variables involved; this is used both to decide which solution to select in the case of a multiple-valued design function and to assign at least a *guess* value to every design variable.

In this approach, a network of functional relationships such as the one shown in Figure 3 is constructed, which may involve inverting individual design functions, as well as assigning guess values to all uncomputed output variables, then repeating the problem using the computed values as the new guesses until it converges to a "fixed point" with respect to these iteration variables (hence the name)[10]. The Fixed-Point approach is briefly described in section 4.4.

3.2 The Introduction of Digital Computers Reverses the Relative Cost of the Meta-design and Sizing Phases

Before modern electronic computers, design functions took the form of tables, graphs, and simple mathematical formulas or procedures. Since these functions were to be used for manual calculations, they were stored in a form readily understood by technical support personnel, possibly less declarative than a designer would choose for his or her own manipulation, but certainly not as imperative as a computer program would require. For example, since graphs and tables are essentially reversible relations, it was easy to reverse their computational direction, and simple written descriptions of the sequence of

---

[10]The fixed point of a function $f(x)$ is that value of x for which $f(x) = x$.

231

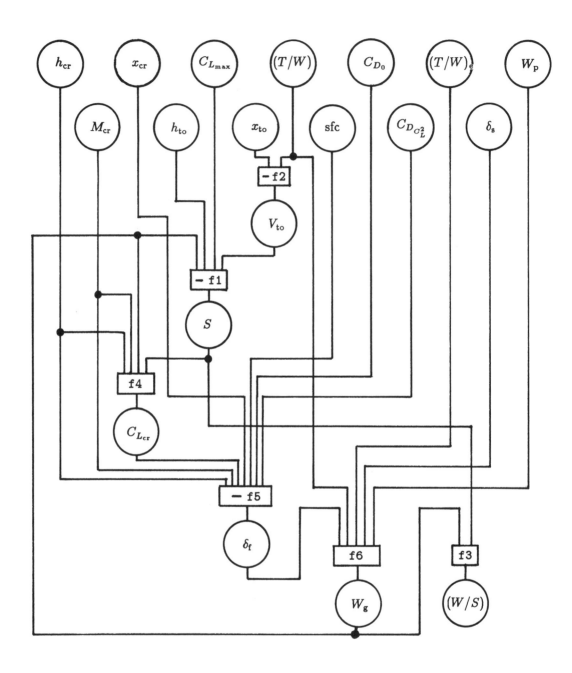

Figure 3: Functional Network representation of the Computational Path

functions involved were all that the individuals performing the actual computations required. By comparison, the process of manually performing the required numerical operations was long, tedious, and comparatively expensive; while the chief designer could change his mind about the design path in a matter of minutes, it sometimes took several weeks for the ensuing computations to be carried out, by scores of clerical personnel.

With the advent of electronic digital computers, the situation is precisely reversed: design functions must be specified in a very imperative form, while the numerical computations themselves become ridiculously inexpensive. While this computational abundance improved the design process by making sizing iterations more affordable, an incentive was also created to immortalize design sets and design paths that had been "cast in concrete" in the form of a successful preliminary design computer program[11]. If we believe that sizing is the essence of preliminary design, this would not be a totally unsatisfactory situation; on the other hand, if we believe on the importance of the Meta-design stage, we see that the cost of converting declarative knowledge to computer-suitable imperative form is an obstacle to the design process.

4. AN EXPERIMENTAL IMPLEMENTATION

Work on knowledge representation of the design process began at the Flight Transportation Laboratory of the Massachusetts Institute of Technology in early 1982. The initial motivation for this work was the recognition of the reversal of the costs of the Meta-design and Sizing phases brought about by the introduction of the computer in the design process. In particular, two questions were asked:

1. Since computers can manipulate abstract symbolic objects as well as numbers, can we build a system that would perform the declarative-to-imperative transformations required to implement the computational path resulting from a given design path?
2. How would lowering the cost of modifying the design path affect the designer's behavior?

---

[11]It is the author's experience that the degree of permanence of these programs is inversely proportional to the number of individuals in the organization that understand how it operates internally.

Initially, the problem of stringing a set of independent mathematical functions so as to achieve an independently prescribed computational objective looked very much like an Automatic Programming (AP) problem. Actually, this problem is different from the generalized AP problem in several respects: on the one hand, the system is allowed to have specific knowledge about the computational domain being manipulated, which simplifies the problem; on the other hand, it must be able to cope intelligently with both under-constrained and over-constrained situations (as a human programmer could), and with *any* form of design function, which complicates the problem.

This research is centered around a prototype symbolic Preliminary Design tool dubbed *Paper-Airplane*. Originally developed on a MIT "CDR" Lisp Machine, the project then shifted to the Maclisp dialect of Lisp on a DEC PDP-20 machine running under the TOPS-20 operating system, and finally to the NIL (New Implementation of Lisp) language system for the DEC VAX family of processors, under the VMS operating system. The NIL system [15] essentially simulates the language system of a Lisp Machine on a VAX processor, albeit at a reduced speed, and allows the development of Lisp Machine compatible code on the VAX.

4.1 Paper-Airplane Deduces the Design Path from the User's Inputs

Paper-Airplane was designed with the following operating scenario in mind:

1. The user would supply a design set, that is, design variables and design functions.
2. Paper-Airplane would present to the user Tableaux showing the design variables and their current values.
3. The user would then modify the value of any design variable, and Paper-Airplane would invoke the appropriate design functions (in the correct order and in the correct direction) to compute the values of all the unspecified design variables. In other words, Paper-Airplane would determine the computational path by observing which design variables were in the input set.

In this sense, Paper-Airplane's user interface was intended to look very similar to a spreadsheet program, with the notable exceptions that the variables need not be topologically related to the rows and columns of matrix and that the relationships between the variables do not force the computational path, as is the case with a spreadsheet. This is also the goal of the commercial microcomputer program TK!Solver[12][16], which appeared later in the same year. The fundamental differences between TK!Solver and Paper-Airplane are worth noting:

- TK!Solver is based on the Constraint Propagation model of computation described in section 3.1. By comparison the Paper-Airplane Fixed Point approach treats each design function as an atomic constraint and has the additional problem of often having to invert them.

- TK!Solver does not require any domain-specific knowledge about the variables and functions it manipulates; that is, it only looks at their mathematical form. As a consequence, it cannot determine, for instance, which branch of a square root should be taken to arrive at the correct value of a variable. By comparison, Paper-Airplane requires the user to provide some limited information about each design variable and will attempt to use this information to resolve uncertainties caused by multiple-valued functions such as the square root.

- TK!Solver is, as a consequence of its Constraint Propagation foundation, oriented towards perfectly constrained systems, that is, design sets with exactly as many unspecified variables as design functions and with no topologically disjoint design functions. Only as many variables as can be functionally derived from the input set are computed, and no attempt is made to guess or iterate on the values of the unspecified design variables.

4.2 Paper-Airplane Communicates with the User by Means of Tableaux

Figures 4 and 5 show typical Paper-Airplane *Tableaux*. These are active displays that allow the user to examine and modify the value or the intended use (state) of each design variable. In this case, Paper-Airplane was loaded with our running example design set; the 19 variables are shown in two tableaux, labeled TAKEOFF and CRUISE[13]. Each design variable is identified by the computer

---

[12]TK!Solver is a Registered Trademark of Software Arts, Inc.

[13]In a typical Paper-Airplane application, which may include 100 to 200 design variables, individual tableaux are typically defined so as to focus on a specific aspect of the vehicle, such as takeoff, performance, costs, weights, fuselage, etc. A design variable may appear on more than one tableau; indeed, frequently referenced variables, such as gross takeoff weight, often end up in every tableau.

name listed in Table 1. The *state* of each design variable is then shown by means of a single letter. Each design variable may be in one of three states:

I   initial state; this indicates that this particular variable has been given a hard value by the user, and this value is not to change.

G guess state; this indicates that the variable has an approximate or trial value which may be changed in order to satisfy a constraint.

C computed state; this indicates that the variable had originally a guess value, which had to be changed (computed) in order to satisfy a constraint.

Initially, that is, before a Paper-Airplane computational pass, all variables are in either the I or the G states. After a pass, some (or all) of the G-state variables have computed values which are guaranteed to satisfy the design functions in that design set, to a specified error tolerance. The I-state variables retain, of course, their initial values. Since no computational passes have been performed, all variables in Figures 4 and 5 are in the guess state.

TAKEOFF

```
-->GTOW                   G  100000.0000 lb
   WING-AREA              G    1614.0000 ft 2
   WING-LOADING           G     100.0000 psf
   T-OVER-W               G       0.3000
   CLMAX                  G       2.2000
   TAKEOFF-ALTITUDE       G       0.0100 ft
   VTO                    G     125.0000 Kt
   TAKEOFF-DISTANCE       G    6561.6798 ft
   STRUCTURAL-FRACTION    G       0.4500
   THRUST-TO-ENGINE-WEIGHT G      5.0000
```

Figure 4: TAKEOFF Initial Paper-Airplane Tableau

```
                              CRUISE

-->GTOW                     G 100000.0000 lb
   WING-LOADING             G    100.0000 psf
   CRUISE-MACH              G      0.8000
   CRUISE-ALTITUDE          G  33000.0000 ft
   CRUISE-CL                G      0.5000
   CRUISE-RANGE             G   1125.8099 nm
   CRUISE-FUEL-FRACTION     G      0.2500
   CDO                      G      0.0180
   CDCL2                    G      0.0468
   SFC                      G      0.6500 hr -1
   PAYLOAD                  G  44092.4524 lb
   TAKEOFF-DISTANCE         G   6561.6798 ft
```

Figure 5: CRUISE Initial Paper-Airplane Tableau

After the state, the tableau shows the current value of each design variable. Paper-Airplane assumes for guess values *the last known value of a variable - be it computed, entered by the user, or previously guessed.* However, this rule does not cover the very first display of the tableau (before there was a "previous value" of each variable). In this case the order of magnitude of the variable (see section 4.5) is used for a guess value. Finally, the units *in which the tableau reads and displays* each design variable are shown. The user may dynamically change these units, with Paper-Airplane taking the responsibility of checking for correct dimensionality of the requested units, converting from the internal system of units to the display units and vice versa, etc. [17].

The input set is determined by designating each input variable, which in the present mechanization is done either by explicitly "pointing" at the variable or implicitly by assigning a value to it[14]. Figure 6 shows the CRUISE tableau after a number of variables have been given initial values; the input set selected is exactly the set described in section 2.1. Note that the state of these variables has changed from G to I. A single keystroke command is available which tallies the number of specified and free variables, and informs the user whether the system is under, over, or perfectly constrained. Invoking that command in this case would result in the message: "Design D1[15] has 6 free variables, 13 initialized variables, and 6 functions. The design is perfectly constrained[16]."

CRUISE

```
-->GTOW                    G 100000.0000 lb
   WING-LOADING            G    100.0000 psf
   CRUISE-MACH             I      0.8000
   CRUISE-ALTITUDE         I  33000.0000 ft
   CRUISE-CL               G      0.5000
   CRUISE-RANGE            I   2000.0000 sm
   CRUISE-FUEL-FRACTION    G      0.2500
   CDO                     I      0.0180
   CDCL2                   I      0.0468
   SFC                     I      0.6500 hr -1
   PAYLOAD                 I  20000.0000 kg
   TAKEOFF-DISTANCE        I   6000.0000 ft
```

Figure 6: The CRUISE Tableau after variable initialization

---

[14]The current user interface with Paper-Airplane is designed to be usable at low communications speed (1200 baud) and with conventional ANSI terminals such as DEC's, VT220, in order to allow remote demonstrations of the system; thus, it does not take advantage of the latest developments in operator interfaces available on Lisp Machines.

[15]Paper-Airplane allows the user to have multiple design sets active simultaneously, thus requiring a label such as D1 for each design set.

[16]Actually, this is a white lie; it is possible for a design with as many free variables as functions to be partially under-constrained and partially over-constrained.

At this point, the user has only to press a function key in the terminal to activate the numeric computation process. If successful, the result will be new values for the non-initialized variables - now sporting the C state - which will satisfy all the design functions, as shown in Figure 7. The 1983 version of Paper-Airplane, developed using M.I.T. "CDR" Lisp Machines, attempted to perform a numerical calculation pass every time the value of any variable was changed. This gave the illusion of instantaneous changes in the state of the design in response to user changes in the values of input variables. The slower Lisp execution speeds of the current host machines made this approach impractical in the current implementation.

CRUISE

```
-->GTOW                    C 138767.5339 lb
    WING-LOADING           C    210.3704 psf      above suggested upper-value
    CRUISE-MACH            I      0.8000
    CRUISE-ALTITUDE       I 33000.0000 ft
    CRUISE-CL              C      0.8568
    CRUISE-RANGE          I  2000.0000 sm
    CRUISE-FUEL-FRACTION   C      0.1378
    CDO                    I      0.0180
    CDCL2                  I      0.0468
    SFC                    I      0.6500 hr -1
    PAYLOAD               I 20000.0000 kg
    TAKEOFF-DISTANCE      I  6000.0000 ft
```

Figure 7: The CRUISE Tableau after a computational pass

TAKEOFF

```
-->GTOW                      C 138767.5339 lb
    WING-AREA                C    659.6343 ft 2    below suggested lower value
    WING-LOADING             C    210.3704 psf     above suggested upper-value
    T-OVER-W                 I      0.3000
    CLMAX                    I      2.2000
    TAKEOFF-ALTITUDE         I      0.0000 ft
    VTO                      C    201.7232 Kt
    TAKEOFF-DISTANCE        I   6000.0000 ft
    STRUCTURAL-FRACTION      I      0.4500
    THRUST-TO-ENGINE-WEIGHT  I      5.0000
```

Figure 8: The TAKEOFF Tableau after the first computation pass

239

To the right of the value for WING-LOADING the message "above suggested upper-value" is shown. At the present time, this is produced by simply comparing the value of each variable with a "suggested lower value" and a "suggested upper value" that are part of a design variable's attributes. These values were included for use by the computational path logic to estimate the degree of variability of each design variable; however, since that knowledge about each design variable was available, it was very simple to also use it to flag abnormal values (at least with respect to that criterion).

Indeed, as any aeronautical designer would immediately recognize, 210 psf is a higher wing loading that even a mid-60's jet fighter[17]. Why is that value so high? Well, let us consider for a moment how the diverse value were computed; we can find out by asking Paper-Airplane to display the computational path:

```
VARIABLE            COMPUTED BY
-----------------------------

VTO                    -F2
GTOW                    F6
WING-AREA              -F1
WING-LOADING            F3
CRUISE-CL               F4
CRUISE-FUEL-FRACTI     -F5
```

This Paper-Airplane display shows the sequence in which design functions were invoked, the design variable whose value was computed, and whether the function had to be inverted to compute this value (minus sign in front of the function name). We see that wing loading was computed using f3, which is simply W_g/S. Therefore, either the gross weight was unrealistically high or the wing area unrealistically low or both. A quick check of the TAKEOFF tableau (Figure 8) shows that wing-area is indeed too low. Looking again at the computational path, we see that wing area was reverse-computed by f1, which was the takeoff velocity function, used in this case to compute S, since V_{to} was

---

[17]That was the era of the "fast and dumb" approach to fighter design; since then, the requirement for high-g maneuvering has lowered the average wing loading of modern fighters.

previously computed (again, in reverse) by **f2**, which uses takeoff distance x_{to}, its normal output, as an input.

CRUISE

```
-->GTOW                   C 135561.8837 lb
   WING-LOADING           C    140.2568 psf
   CRUISE-MACH            I      0.8000
   CRUISE-ALTITUDE        I 33000.0000 ft
   CRUISE-CL              C      0.5712
   CRUISE-RANGE           I   2000.0000 sm
   CRUISE-FUEL-FRACTION   C      0.1318
   CDO                    I      0.0180
   CDCL2                  I      0.0468
   SFC                    I      0.6500 hr -1
   PAYLOAD                I  20000.0000 kg
   TAKEOFF-DISTANCE       I   4000.0000 ft
```

Figure 9: The CRUISE Tableau after the second computational pass

TAKEOFF

```
-->GTOW                     C 135561.8837 lb
   WING-AREA                C    966.5949 ft 2
   WING-LOADING             C    140.2468 psf
   T-OVER-W                 I      0.3000
   CLMAX                    I      2.2000
   TAKEOFF-ALTITUDE         I      0.0000 ft
   VTO                      C    164.7062 Kt
   TAKEOFF-DISTANCE         I   4000.0000 ft
   STRUCTURAL-FRACTION      I      0.4500
   THRUST-TO-ENGINE-WEIGHT  I      5.0000
```

Figure 10: The TAKEOFF Tableau after the second computation pass

241

So one possible explanation for the high wing loading is a low wing area caused by a high takeoff velocity caused by a long takeoff run. Indeed, if we reduce the value of takeoff run from 6000 ft to 4000 ft, we get the results shown in figures 9 and 10. By establishing a form of cause-effect relationship, displays of the computational path actually aid the mental design process, even if they change with the design path, and work has begun on converting this simple list representation into a graphical, multiple-tree form on which the entire "pedigree" of a variable's value can be shown.

4.3 Guess Values are Necessary to Uncouple the Design Path from the Computational Path

The current approach used in Paper-Airplane to determine and execute the computational path is described in section 4.4. In order to justify and rationalize that approach, we will now briefly describe an earlier version of this process and the problems associated with it.

The original computational path logic of Paper-Airplane would only compute as many output design variables as could be perfectly deduced from the input variables, i.e., there were no "guesses" (indeed, the state of the uncomputed output variables was labeled F, for free, rather than the current G). The logic for determining the sequence of design functions to invoke was this:

1. Find a design function with all of its input variables defined (i.e., in either the I or C states) and its output variable undefined (i.e., in the F state).

2. If such a design function can be found, compute the value of its output variable and, since there is now one more design variable defined, search again (step 1). If no more design functions satisfying the requirements of step 1 can be found, this *forward computational pass* is terminated, and we proceed to step 3.

3. Find a design function with its output variable and *all but one* of its input variables defined, and *reverse-compute* the remaining undefined input variable using this function. Since we have a new variable in the C state, there is a chance that a previously unused design function may be usable in the forward direction, so we immediately terminate this *backwards computational pass* and go to step 1 again.

4. The process terminates when there is a failure of step 3 immediately after a failure of step 1, that is, there is no chance for either a forward or a

backwards pass. Any variables remaining in the F state are considered "unreachable" by the computational process.

It is important to realize that this unreachability could happen even if the design set was nominally perfectly constrained. For example, if we had selected the input set specified in our running example, the only design function meeting any of the criteria would have been **f2**, which we could have used to reverse-compute V_{to}. After this single reverse pass, no other design function can be found with only one free variable, and the computational process would have terminated. An alternative design path (that is, re-selection of the input variable set) would have been required to achieve a usable computational path.

By comparison, a human designer would attempt to compute *all* the output variables by assuming guess values for as many of the output variables as are necessary to "bootstrap" the computational path; since these values will be computed eventually - it is, after all, a perfectly constrained design set - the process must be repeated until we converge to what in effect is a fixed point of these iteration variables[18]. How many output variables must be turned into iteration variables depends, of course, on the design path; since there is a statistical majority of design functions that depend on the gross weight (both in our running example and in most real-life aircraft design situations), it is a sure bet that W_g should be an iteration variable. Indeed, if we were to design the computational path by hand, assuming a guess value for W_g, we could come up with the following path:

Variable	Computed by
V_{to}	-f2
S	-f1
$C_{L_{cr}}$	f4
δ_f	-f5
(W/S)	f3
W_g	f6

---

[18]To be precise, the values of the iteration variables are the simultaneous fixed points of the design functions used to compute these variables.

after which we could use the computed value of W_g to iterate again until the magnitude of the change in value is satisfyingly small. Other design paths may require fewer and more iteration variables.

4.4 The Fixed-Point Approach Modifies Guess Values to Satisfy Design Functions

The Fixed-Point approach developed to overcome this difficulty attempts to construct a network of functional dependences between design variables - linked by design functions - similar to the one shown in Figure 3. Central to this approach are the assumptions that every output design variable has a tentative guess value and that every design function can be inverted, although it is sufficient that this inversion be numerical.

Numerical inversion of an individual design function is accomplished in Paper-Airplane by the following means. Assume the design function to be inverted is <u>naturally defined</u>[19] as:

$$y = f(x_1, x_2, \ldots, x_n)$$

and we know the value of y and all the x's but one, say x_j. We begin by examining the order of magnitude, upper and lower typical values, and previous values of x_j to prepare a list of <u>smart initial guesses</u> of x_j. The resulting values of y are computed by using the function in its natural direction, and the value closest in absolute magnitude to the given value of y is chosen as the initial guess in a Newton-Ralphson iteration:

$$x_j^{i+1} = x_j^i - \frac{y^i}{(\partial y / \partial x_j)^i}$$

The necessary value of $\partial y/\partial x_j$ is obtained by a dithering process, that is, observing the variation of y resulting from a small change in x_j. Again, knowledge of the order of magnitude and typical variation of the x_j design variable is used, this time to select a magnitude of the dithering increment, resulting in a more robust numerical estimation of $\partial y/\partial x_j$ than would be possible with a fixed dithering increment. Indeed, although there is no mathematical proof that this process will always converge to the correct value of x_j, this

---

[19]That is, the way the function body is explicitly specified in the knowledge base; see section 4.5

numerical inversion approach has proven extremely successful for a very wide range of design functions; it obviously fails when there is a stationary point, that is, $\partial y / \partial x_j = 0$, but that is a generic problem of the Fixed Point approach itself.

The functional network which embodies the computational path is constructed by iterative applications of the following heuristic:

1. Identify the eligible design functions; these are the functions that have not yet been used in this computational pass[20] and that have at least one variable - be it the natural output variable or one of the natural input variables - in the "guessed" state (that is, it has neither been given an initial value nor been computed so far).

2. Select the eligible design function with the fewest number of remaining guess-state variables, that is, the *most constrained* one.

3. If there is a tie, select the function whose guess-state variables appear the most often in the remaining unused design function.

4. If the selected design function has more than one design variable in the guess-state, select as the output of the computation of this function the variable which appears the *least often* in the remaining eligible design function. If there is a tie among these variables, select the one with the *least* typical variability, as determined by the variable's typical low and high values (see section 4.5).

5. Use the design function to compute the value of the selected guess variable; tag that variable as "computed" and that function as "used."

The process ends when there are no more eligible design functions, either because they have all been used or because none remain with at least one guess variable. In addition to stationary points, the Fixed Point approach also suffers from the problems of non-existing solutions to design functions and global divergence of the iteration process, and research is being vigorously carried out to improve the performance of the approach in these two areas [18].

On the other hand, there is no need, with this approach, to explicitly identify the iteration variables and place their computation at the tail end of the computational sequence, as is normally done by hand. Also, this approach allows for *underconstrained* design sets; in the extreme case, *all* the design variables can be declared output variables, in which case the Fixed Point method will

---

20All design functions are tagged as "unused" at the beginning of the pass.

modify as many guess values as necessary to satisfy the design functions; unfortunately, there is no control over which design variables are modified and which retain their guess values.

There is also the possibility of an *overconstrained* design set; in this case, Paper-Airplane used as many design functions as are needed to determine the values of all the guess variables. The "leftover" design functions are then exercised in their natural directions and the output variable's value checked against the previously computed value. If the values differ significantly (again, using the order of magnitude as a guide), all the I-state variables involved in that design function are tagged as having one (1) <u>degree of incompatibility</u>. The total number of incompatibilities assessed against each input variable is shown on any tableau displaying that variable[21]. This information may help the user decide which variables to remove from the input set in order to reduce the degree of overconstraint of the system.

4.5 Paper-Airplane Abstracts Design Variables and Design Functions by Means of Lisp Structures

The abstractions used in Paper-Airplane to represent design variables and functions, as seen from the user's viewpoint, as shown in figures 11 and 12. Figure 11 is a portion of the Paper-Airplane <u>source file</u>, containing the definitions of the design variables for the running example used in this chapter. These definitions take the form of a Lisp function, **pa-intern**, whose first argument is the symbol that will be used to identify that design variable in Paper-Airplane. The rest of the parameters to **pa-intern** are *keyword* parameters, allowing them to be specified in any order.

The information required with each design variable includes:

1. The *order of magnitude* of that variable; this knowledge is used by the numerical function inverted to initialize the Newton-Ralphson iteration, to terminate the iteration, and to choose among multiple values; by the global computation process to detect convergence; and as a "default" initial guess before the first computation process.

---

[21]Ideally, the "blame" for incompatibility should be transmitted via the C-state variables in that design function to the I variables that contributed to determine the value of that C variable.

```
(pa-intern payload
        :order-of-magnitude 20000.0        :TeX-name "$W_{\rm p}"
        :upper-value 40000.0               :lower-value 10000.0
        :dimensions "m"                    :default-units "Kg")

(pa-intern takeoff-altitude
        :order-of-magnitude 0.01           :TeX-name "h_{\rm to}"
        :upper-value 3000.0                :lower-value -1000.0
        :dimensions "1"                    :default-units "ft")

(pa-intern clmax
        :order-of-magnitude 2.2            :TeX-name "C_{L_{\rm max}}"
        :upper-value 4.0                   :lower-value 0.8
        :dimensions "")
```

Figure 11: Typical Paper-Airplane design variable definitions

2. The TeX-name is a string used by Paper-Airplane to prepare tables and reports involving the design variables by means of the TeX mathematical typesetting system.

3. The *upper* and *lower* values are used by the computational path logic to determine the variability of each design variable, which is used to break ties between otherwise equally desirable candidate design function.

4. The *dimensions* of the variable are specified in the so-called Paper-Airplane Dimensions and Units Package (PDUP), a system for the representation and manipulation of dimensions and units. Dimension information is used to check the validity of the units information used in the definitions of variables, functions, and tableaux. An empty string is used to indicate a dimensionless variable, as for example clmax in Figure 11.

5. The *default-units* are simply the units in which that design variable is assumed to be measured - both in functions and in tableaux - in the absence of an explicit declaration.

```
(pa-defun f2
        :computed-variable (takeoff-distance "ft")
        :input-variables    ((vto "ft s-1") t-over-w)
        :function-body      (/ (* vto vto)
                               (* 2.0 *g0* t-over-w))
        :source "Constant acceleration assumption")

(pa-defun f3
        :computed-variable (wing-loading "lbf ft-2")
        :input-variables    ((gtow "lb") (wing-area "ft2"))
        :function-body      (/ gtow wing-area)
        :source "Definition of wing loading")
```

Figure 12: Typical Paper-Airplane design function definitions

Figure 12 shows the structure used to represent knowledge about the design functions, again from the user's standpoint, i.e., not including all the control structures used by Paper-Airplane internally to mechanize the computational path logic of section 4.4 and many other research features of the system[22]. The first two data items are the list of design variables which are the natural input to the function, as defined below, and the naturally computed variable. Included with each design variable name are the *units that the function body assumes are used for that variable.* Again, Paper-Airplane's PDUP package takes care of checking for dimensionality and of performing the necessary value conversions to and from the "internal unit system," as it did on the tableaux.

The next attribute is the function body; in the present Paper-Airplane implementation, this must be a Lisp function; the system invokes the compiler automatically upon reading a **pa-defun** expression in order to produce a compiled code version of this body. Both the symbolic (source) and compiled versions are kept internally, with the symbolic form used to display the design

---

[22]Such as an individual function exerciser tableau which allows the user to test an individual design function or step through its code.

248

function definition, drive the single stepper, etc., and the compiled version used in the Fixed-Point computational procedure for efficiency.

It would be a simple matter to include a standard VMS object code in this attribute slot, thus allowing the design functions to be coded in any language available under VMS (FORTRAN, Pascal, PL/1, etc.). However, this is not considered to be a significant research issue [23]. Finally, an information field is included in the set of attributes to indicate the source of the design function. At the present time this field is used for identification only, but it is expected that this will become the anchor of a more complex knowledge structure that will allow manipulation of the design set itself.

5. DIRECTIONS OF FUTURE RESEARCH

So far, research performed at M.I.T. with the help of Paper-Airplane has focused on the development of the generic abstractions mentioned in section 2 and testing of the automatic computational path mechanisms described in section 3. Current efforts are aimed at improving the performance of the Fixed Point and Numerical Inversion processes, including their extension to discrete-valued design variables and functions[24]. During the course of this effort, a number of high-potential concepts have been identified and are expected to direct the priorities of future research for the next few years. These concepts cover the areas of design set determination and numerical sizing methodology that have not been addressed in this chapter. Some of these ideas are related to the real-life problem of communicating and exchanging design ideas and decisions. Thus, Paper-Airplane has been linked to the TeX text composing system in order to produce tables that can be merged into a TeX text source. Similarly, work is underway to produce an automatic graphing system that would create graphs of sensitivities of specific design variables with respect to one another around the current design point. The rest of these section describes some of the more substantial ideas for further research.

---

[23]It would be if we wanted to re-use large amounts of existing code for the design functions.

[24]An example of a discrete-valued design variable would be "engine model," with discrete values such as "IO-360K" "O-520" etc. A related discrete-valued design function would produce the horsepower associated with each discrete model.

5.1 A Long-Term Memory of Design Variables and Functions Requires a Unification Process

The actual knowledge stored in a system such as Paper-Airplane is in the definitions of design variables and design functions. In the present system, the user is required to create and enter these definitions; the logical next step is to have a large, organized collection of design variables and functions, covering both a wide range of disciplines and a wide range of levels of detail. Such a library would necessarily be the result of contributions from a number of different individuals, groups, and organizations, perhaps over a long span of time; hence the name <u>long-term memory</u>. The principal feature of this long-term memory, or LTM, is the storage of all design functions and associated design variables by means of a uniform set of abstractions. As a consequence, all of them could be uniformly accessed by symbolic tools such as Paper-Airplane. These abstractions could take care of the same trivial programming details that the current Paper-Airplane abstractions take care of: dimensionality of the variables, differences in systems of units, etc.

A possible scenario for the use of an LTM in the selection and construction of a design set could run like this:

1. The user begins by selecting an initial set of design variables that capturers the principal goals of his design; for example, if an Anti-Submarine Warfare (AWS) aircraft is being considered, range, payload, and loiter endurance would certainly be a part of this initial set[25].

2. The user next selects a number of design functions that *involve* the variables in the initial set (traditionally, we would have said that these functions are chosen because they *compute* these variables, but we now know better than that).

3. These selected design functions will involve other design variables, which are therefore included automatically in the design set; now, it is up to the

---

[25]This association of vehicle type with an initial set of design variables appears to be an ideal application for a classical "expert system"; however, it is debatable whether there are sufficient economic or design quality factors to justify coding that kind of knowledge.

user to decide whether to include additional design functions to handle these new design variables - which in turn may or may not require more variables - or to accept the new expanded design set as it is.

As an example of this *interactive meta-design* process, consider the design of an ASW aircraft; as mentioned before, loitering endurance is a key performance measure for such a vehicle and thus is included in the initial design set. The user then could ask the LTM the question, "What is loitering endurance related to?" (through design functions, that is.) The interactive LTM should answer by displaying the various choices of design functions and related new design variables that relate to loitering endurance. Typically, such a function will involve aerodynamic parameters, such as lift to drag ratio (L/D); it is now the choice of the designer to either stop here and use (L/D as a simple design variable, or inquire about models involving (L/D), perhaps relating it to more detailed design variables such as aspect ratio and wing profile.

Before such a repository of design functions and variables can be compiled, the *names* and the *precise meaning* of each design variable used in the LTM must somehow be <u>unified</u>[26].

The naming problem results from either using the same symbol to denote clearly different variables[27] or using different variables to denote the same design variable concept[28]. This problem could be tackled in a way similar to that of natural language differences: by means of a two-way *symbolic dictionary* which would convert the Long-Term Memory's internal symbols into the symbols preferred by each individual or organization accessing or contributing to the LTM. In this case, the LTM's internal symbols could be rather arbitrary (indeed, there would be significant political advantages in having these symbols be otherwise meaningless, e.g., randomly generated names).

The second problem is significantly more subtle and difficult to handle: that of minor differences in the *definition* of a design variable. For example, different

---

[26]This terminology is borrowed from Logic Programming and Automatic Theorem Proving, where differences in the bindings of symbols pose a similar, but much better defined problem.

[27]The canonical example is the use of the symbol q to denote dynamic pressure in aerodynamics, heat flow in thermodynamics, and pitch rate in flight mechanics.

[28]e.g., Reference Area is variably denoted with the symbols S and A sporting a wide range of subscripts.

authors include different airframe components in the apparently well-defined term "usable empty weight." Resolution of subtle differences in the definitions of design variables may require inclusion of information about these assumptions in the data abstraction for that variable, information which could then be used both to access and select the design variables desired to construct a design set and to insure that indeed two arbitrary design functions can be linked through a common design variable.

5.2 Hierarchical Design Functions Require Design Set Management

Were a Long-Term Memory available, the user would be likely to have available various design functions, all relating the same - or similar - design variables, but differing in level of detail, accuracy, etc. The simplistic approach taken in the Paper-Airplane experimental PDT is to allow a single design function relating the same set of variables in a design set, but an intriguing possibility would be to simultaneously process "redundant" design functions of different levels of detail; for example, structural fraction may be related simply to design load factor, to load factor and wing geometry, etc.

A possible use of this layering of design functions would be as a cross-check of the particular value selected by the function inversion mechanism among multiple possible values. Indeed, something very similar is already used in Paper-Airplane in the form of the **order-of-magnitude** attribute of design variables. This attribute can be construed as a very simple design function and is used to steer the Newton-Ralphson algorithm towards an initial condition that will result in the correct inverse solution.

Another possible use of redundant design functions would be to speed up the computational part of the design process; simple, approximate design functions could be used to determine an initial set of numerical values for the input variables, after which a smaller number of more expensive iterations would be required using the more accurate, detailed functions.

Eventually, the Long-Term Memory access system should be responsible for retrieving not a single design function, but a hierarchy of design functions relating the design variables that the designer wishes to constrain.

It should be mentioned here that the use of orders of magnitude, upper, and lower limits in Paper-Airplane is quite passive: the user enters this data, and it is accepted at face value by the system. On the other hand, the system has all the information necessary to check the *consistency* of these values with respect to the design functions, and this could be another function in support of Long-Term Memory building.

5.3 With Interactive Optimization the User Manipulates Goals, Not Values

The sizing process currently supported by Paper-Airplane is quite simplistic: values in, values out. An interesting possibility would be to combine into Paper-Airplane the functions of a classical multivariate optimization procedure which, when presented with a user-constructed performance function, will manipulate the values of the input variables so as to minimize the performance function. Of course, since the variables available for manipulation depend critically on the design path, this algorithm would have to be implemented in a symbolic fashion - even if it eventually executes numerical operations - in order to have it "connect" automatically with whatever design set and design path is entered into Paper-Airplane.

With such an algorithm in place, the user could manipulate the coefficients of the performance function interactively, by means of tableaux; Figure 13 shows

			CRUISE		J=550247.5348
-->GTOW	0	135561.8837	lb	4.000
WING-LOADING	C	140.2568	psf	
CRUISE-MACH	I	0.8000		
CRUISE-ALTITUDE	I	33000.0000	ft	
CRUISE-CL	C	0.5712		
CRUISE-RANGE	0	2000.0000	sm	-2.000
CRUISE-FUEL-FRACTION	C	0.1318		
CDO	I	0.0180		
CDCL2	I	0.0468		
SFC	I	0.6500	hr -1	
PAYLOAD	0	20000.0000	kg	-1.000
TAKEOFF-DISTANCE	0	4000.0000	ft	8.000

Figure 13: Hypothetical Interactive Optimization Paper-Airplane Tableau

253

what such a tableau would look like. At the right of each design variable, the user may specify a coefficient or weight which would determine this variable's contribution to the performance function; the current value of the performance function is indicated at the top of the tableau, after the tableau name (in the example of Figure 13, a linear performance function has been assumed, but other types, such as quadratic, could be used). When the user requests a computational pass, the multivariate optimization procedure is invoked, rather than the simple computational process. Note that the variables whose values affect the performance function are not inputs, but rather output, or objective, variables (state "O"), and they replace the guess variables of the present Paper-Airplane tableaux. The resulting sets of values (both C's and O's) would then be evaluated by the designer; however, instead of manipulating the values of the input variables, as would be the case with Paper-Airplane today, the designer would manipulate the *weights* and let the optimizer find out the values that minimize the performance function. For example, if in the example of Figure 13 the optimized design would have ended up with too low a range but more than sufficient payload, the designer would probably increase the weight of the former and reduce that of the latter.

6. ACKNOWLEDGMENTS

The work described in this chapter was made possible in part by a major equipment grant from the Digital Equipment Corporation. The author is also indebted to the scores of students in the senior aircraft design course at M.I.T. who have been his guinea pigs for the past two years, whose constructive criticism and suggestions have proven invaluable, and who were able to produce outstanding aircraft designs in spite of a constantly changing Paper-Airplane program.

REFERENCES

[1] Hall, Donald A., "Technical Preparation for the Airplane *Spirit of St. Louis*," N.A.C.A. Technical Note No. 257, Washington, D.C., July 1927.

[2] Large, Joseph P., Harry G. Campbell, and David Cates, "Parametric Equations for Estimating Aircraft Airframe Costs," Technical Report R-1693-1-PA&E, The Rand Corporation, Santa Monica, CA, February 1976.

[3] Elias, Antonio L., "On the Cost of Paralleling Design Efforts," Memo No. 85-4, Flight Transportation Laboratory, Massachusetts Institute of Technology, May 1985.

[4] Elias, Antonio L., "Computer-Aided Engineering: The A.I. Connection," *Astronautics and Aeronautics*, July 1983, pp. 48-54.

[5] Torenbeek, Egbert, *Synthesis of Subsonic Airplane Design*, Delft: Delft University Press, 1982.

[6] Meyer, Donald D., "Development of Integrated Programs for Aerospace-Vehicle Design (IPAD) - Reference Design Process," NASA CR-2981, December 1979.

[7] Hale, Francis J., *Aircraft Performance, Design and Selection*, New York: John Wiley & Sons, 1984.

[8] Jensen, S. C., I. H. Rettie, and Edward A. Barber, "A Role of Figures of Merit in Design Optimization and Technology Assessment," *Journal of Aircraft*, Vol. 17, No. 6, pp. 429 - 433, June 1980.

[9] Dixit, C. S., and T. S. Patil, "Multivariate Optimum Design of a Subsonic Jet Passenger Airplane," *Journal of Aircraft*, Vol. 17, No. 6, pp. 429 - 432, June 1980.

[10]   Lancaster, J. W., and D. B. Bailey, "Naval Airship Program for Sizing and

Performance (NAPSAP)," Journal of Aircraft, Vol. 18, No. 8, pp. 677 - 682, August 1981.

√[11]   Abelson, Harold, and Gerald Jay Sussman, *Structure and Interpretation of Computer Programs*, Cambridge, MA: The M.I.T. Press, 1985.

√[12]   Kowalski, Robert, *Logic for Problem Solving*, New York: North-Holland, 1979.

[13]   Barr, Avrom, and Edward A. Feigenbaum, Eds. *Handbook of Artificial Intelligence*, Vol. II, pp. 297 - 305, Los Altos, CA: William Kaufmann, Inc., 1982.

[14]   Steele, Jr., Guy L., "The Definition and Implementation of a Computer Programming Language based on Constraints," Ph.D. Thesis, Department of Electrical Engineering and Computer Science, Massachusetts Institute of technology, July 1980.

[15]   Burke, Glenn S., George J. Carrette, and Christopher R. Eliot, "NIL Reference Manual," Report No. TR-311, Laboratory for Computer Science, Massachusetts Institute of Technology, January 1984.

[16]   Software Arts Inc., Wellesley, MA, *TK!Solver Program Instruction Manual*, 1982.

[17]   Elias, Antonio L., "Paper-Airplane Dimensions and Units Package (PDUP)," Memo No. 85-3, Flight Transportation Laboratory, Massachusetts Institute of Technology, May 1985.

[18]   Kolb, Mark A., "Problems in Numerical Solution of Simultaneous Non-linear Equations in Computer-Aided Design," Memo No. 85-1, Flight Transportation Laboratory, Massachusetts Institute of Technology, May 1985.

7

A MACHINABILITY KNOWLEDGE BASED SYSTEM

T. J. JARDINE
BOEING ARTIFICIAL INTELLIGENCE CENTER
BOEING COMPUTER SERVICES

1. INTRODUCTION

In this chapter we present a distillation of the results of an experiment. This experiment involved the construction of a knowledge based system linked to an analytical software model performing machinability computations. We first outline the nature of the manufacturing problem, focusing on sufficient information to provide a context for the machinability computation task. Following this we describe the experiment by discussing the specific problem to be addressed, our approach to solving this problem, the design of the knowledge based system, and an analysis of the results of the experiment to date.

The work we describe was jointly sponsored by the Manufacturing Research and Development organization of the Boeing Aerospace Company, and the Boeing Artificial Intelligence Center.

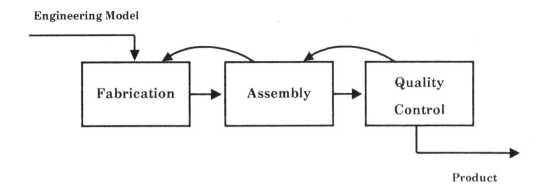

Figure 7-1: High-Level Description of Manufacturing

2. SUMMARY OF THE METAL MANUFACTURING TASK

In one sense manufacturing may be thought of as the task of transforming a description of a product into the product itself. At this level of abstraction a considerable amount of detail and activity is not visible. Figure 7-1 shows the description of a product as an engineering model. Three high-level functions are performed: fabrication, assembly, and quality control. The feedback shown provides for the assembly of fabricated parts that then require further fabrication operations, or the reassembly and/or refabrication of parts not satisfying quality control requirements.

Operations performed during fabrication may include:

Boring	-	enlarging previously drilled holes to a specified diameter.
Cutting	-	sizing material using a saw, shears, laser, or similar device.
Drilling	-	creation of cylindrical holes of specified diameter and depth.
Grinding	-	material removal by abrasion.
Milling	-	material removal "a chip at a time."
Tapping	-	converting drilled/bored holes to threaded ones.
Turning	-	material removal using a lathe.
Welding	-	joining material, especially metal or plastic, using heat and/or pressure.

Machine tools have been created that will perform each of these operations. Some will perform any selected one of several of these operations; e.g., the same machine tool may be capable of milling, drilling, boring, or tapping, depending on the tool used. Some machine tools are designed to perform a series of related operations with the partially manufactured product moving automatically from one type of operation to the next. With respect to metal materials, the tools used to perform milling or boring operations are collectively referred to as cutters. There are literally hundreds, perhaps thousands, of different types of cutters, particularly for milling since many different shapes and curvatures are required for the complex products being manufactured today.

The concept of having a computer control the operation of a machine tool is not new. Such machine tools have existed for nearly thirty years. Since the "computers" of the earlier period were very limited in capability, paper tapes were punched with holes. These holes represented the numbers corresponding to the operations to be performed in controlling the machine tool. These "computer programs" became known therefore as Numerical Control (NC) programs. Machine tools of today are controlled by more sophisticated computers that do not use punched holes to represent their programs, but the term Numerical Control programming has been retained to describe the similar task of creating programs to control machine tools.

Manufacturers of machine tools furnish information, such as handbooks and slide calculators, presenting recommendations about:

- The general considerations for optimum results.

- The recommended feeds, speeds, and cutter material to be used.

This information is intended to serve as a general guide or starting point only and is expected to be amended to fit specific conditions. These conditions might include interrupted cuts, thin sections, workpiece hardness variations, and workpiece surface condition variations. It takes years of actual NC machining experience to successfully apply the varied criteria to the industry recommendations. Indeed, the complexity of modern manufacturing requires considerable effort be applied to correctly plan the operations needed to create a product or part.

Numerical Control planning starts with an engineering model and proceeds through some thirty-nine tasks to a manufactured part (Squier [1984]). These tasks include decomposing the geometry of the desired part, producing a manufacturing plan, selecting numerical control strategies and tactics, selecting raw materials and tools, executing the created plan, and quality control of the manufactured product.

One of these tasks is the application of machining techniques. It is in the execution of this task that the machinability model is used. Figure 7-2 shows the types of information used by the machinability model and its primary computational results. The model incorporated as part of this experiment was designed to support the manufacture of metal parts made from aluminum, steel, or titanium using operations such as milling, drilling, boring, and tapping. The description of the cutting tool is entered either by means of a stock number reference, or by describing appropriate features of the cutter such as number of flutes, flute length, flute diameter, and cutter material. The type of machine tool to be used is normally specified using a designator called a factory work code. The pertinent parameters here include the maximum horsepower of the machine tool, its spindle load limit, and its spindle speed limit. The cut description includes the size of the cut in the direction of the axis of the cutting tool and in a direction perpendicular to the axis, as well as the shaping technique to be used, the type of cut being made (e.g., face, slot, slab, peripheral), and whether a cutting fluid is to be used.

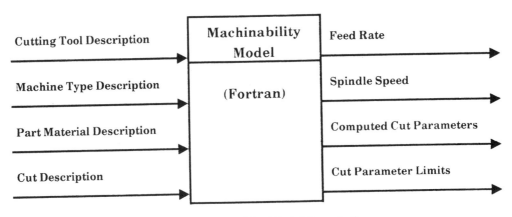

Figure 7-2: Machinability Model Description

The machinability model computations produce the types of results shown in Figure 7-2. Of primary concern to the NC programmer are the feed rate and spindle speed values. Other cut parameters which are frequently useful include the tool deflection force, the metal removal rate, the required horsepower, and the feed rate per cutter flute. Limit determinations include an indication of the source limiting the force applied during cutting, i.e., is the strength of the cutter shank the limiting factor? As indicated earlier, these computations use general information about the machine tool and the cutter to be employed. As a result, there is specific information affecting the cutting operation that is not considered, and hence the feed rate and spindle speed values frequently require modification prior to completion of the NC program incorporating them.

3. PROBLEM DEFINITION

The problem for investigation using knowledge based techniques has two parts:

1) Input to the machinability model requires the application of considerable knowledge and experience in order to avoid numerous repetitions before obtaining usable results.

2) The creation of usable results requires the modification of model output to account for factors not embedded in the model's computations.

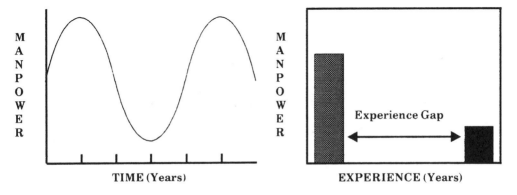

Figure 7-3: Aerospace Industry Cycle   Figure 7-4: Experience Distribution

A factor involved in both parts of the problem is the retention of critical skills and knowledge that are provided by the human experts in a manufacturing organization. The problem of skill retention is not unique to but is exemplified by the aerospace industry. Historically, the aerospace industry cycles, or "bottoms-out," every three to five years, as illustrated in Figure 7-3. Data collected pertaining to the experience base during these time spans and graphically represented would appear as shown in Figure 7-4. During periods of low activity the numbers of the younger, less experienced NC programmers are reduced, creating noticeable gaps in the continuity of NC machining knowledge. The majority of the early pioneers of NC programming have retired, and the remainder will soon follow. The extremely valuable knowledge base of actual NC machining conditions they possess needs to be captured and made available to those who follow them. Even though methods and technology may change, this knowledge will continue to have value.

4. PROBLEM APPROACH

The approach to solving this problem needs to account for both the application of knowledge to the use of the machinability model and the acquisition, retention, and application of machining expertise. The knowledge based system constructed has the structure shown in Figure 7-5 and provides two types of interface that:

1) Permit the specification of input parameters to the machinability model by NC programmers with a wider range of experience than is presently the case.

2) Permit NC and machining experts to validate and modify the machinability model output and to specify rules and other knowledge to the system that will permit it to transform model output to specifications that require minimum, if any, subsequent modification.

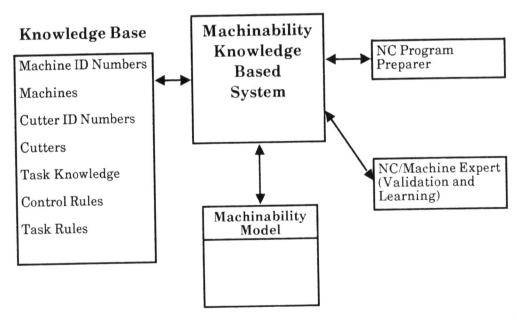

Figure 7-5: Machinability Model Knowledge Based System Structure

Depending on the experience level of the NC program preparer, the contents of the knowledge base either guide the specification of input parameters or permit such specification. The approach to acquiring the knowledge needed for validation and modification of model output is to use case histories of NC programs actually used in the factory. These case histories are matched against the NC program preparer's current case and modifications made to the machinability model's feed and speed values in accordance with the case history which has the best fit to the current case. The best fit determination is represented as a confidence factor, providing a measure of the closeness of the case history to the current case.

5. DESIGN CONSIDERATIONS

In the initial design of the machinability knowledge based system we needed to consider:

- The selection of an inference engine and development environment.

- The means of interfacing to the two classes of user.

- The means of interfacing to the machinability model.

- The means of acquiring and representing the case history knowledge.

As is normally the case, these design decisions were not disjoint. We began by selecting a DEC* VAX-11/780* running Ultrix*, a Unix** based system. Primarily this was done to permit the retention of the machinability model algorithm, which was written in VMS* Fortran in as near its original state as possible. Secondarily, we had just acquired the Metalogical Representation System (MRS) for use as a research tool from Stanford University (see Genesereth [1980], Genesereth [1981], Genesereth [1982], and Genesereth [1983]) and were interested in applying it to this problem.

---

*   DEC, VAX, VMS, and Ultrix are trademarks of Digital Equipment Corp.
**   Unix is a trademark of AT&T

We decided to develop a set of rules and related knowledge that would permit a menu interaction method to be used with both classes of user. Figure 7-6 describes the generic menu processing tasks, some of which use terminology that is rather closely linked to MRS. The activation or deactivation of knowledge components are tasks that use an MRS capability to activate or deactivate theories (a name for components of a knowledge base that can be manipulated as a unit). Considering the characteristics of a menu interface, the remaining tasks shown are appropriate to almost any situation.

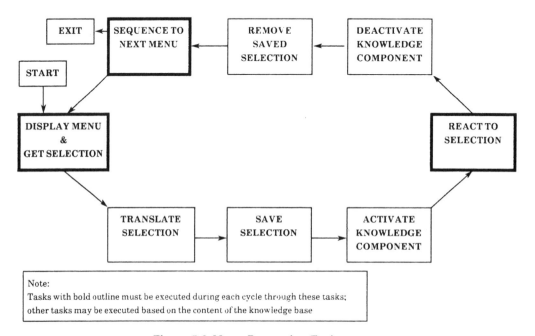

Figure 7-6: Menu Processing Tasks

The interface to the Fortran subroutine containing the machinability algorithm was also done by specifying the knowledge of the subroutine interface to MRS and using its capabilities to initialize input variables, construct and execute the subroutine call, and return the subroutine output to the knowledge base. MRS provides the ability to execute a task that constitutes a sequence of actions. Among these actions may be the execution of a Lisp procedure. The initialization of input variables, execution of the subroutine call, and the return of output variable values to the knowledge base were each performed within Lisp procedures that depended heavily on the ability to retrieve information from the knowledge base and store relations into the knowledge base using MRS commands. The machinability model Fortran source code was modified so that all subroutine input values were obtained from the calling sequence, and all results were returned via the same path.

The task of acquiring, representing, and manipulating the case history knowledge was to be illustrative only, so a very simple mechanism was chosen. A set of case history data was obtained by selecting existing NC programs that had been processed through the machinability model and executed to produce manufactured parts. The case histories consisted of:

- Input values to the machinability model (e.g., part material, surface finish, cut type, cutter description, cut shape, axial and radial depth of cut, Brinell hardness of part material, and maximum machine horsepower and rpm).

- Output values from the machinability model (e.g., cutting horsepower, volume removal rate, cutter deflection, surface removal rate, source of limit on force used, chip load, source of limit on chip load, feed rate, and spindle speed).

- Validated feed rate and spindle speed values.

These case histories were entered into the knowledge base as sets of relations. The NC program preparer would provide a current case to the knowledge based system by supplying its input values. After execution of the machinability model to obtain the current case's output values, a pattern match would be performed between the current case and the set of case histories. The objective of the pattern match was a closeness of fit, represented as a confidence factor. Adjusted feed rate and spindle speed values were then determined using the best fit case history as a model.

6. ANALYSIS OF DESIGN IMPLEMENTATION

As a result of using MRS for this experiment and other similar tasks it is apparent that MRS provides a powerful set of capabilities. Indeed the MRS Dictionary (Genesereth [1980]) is a forty-seven page document defining the functions available in MRS. We used a substantial subset of these functions, but felt that we used only a small fraction of the power available.

We chose to use assert, an MRS command, to do forward chaining in implementing the rules for the menu tasks. The final action of each task is an assertion of a form that triggers the rule governing the next action to be taken. In the initial stages of development, where we were executing at most a few cycles through the menu processing tasks, no problem was visible. However, once we had grown the system to a more sophisticated stage of development, we were presented with the evidence that the mechanism we had chosen consumed more space than was available. Rather than completing the task of triggering a rule and executing its prescribed actions, we had merely stacked the next rule and its actions on top of the remains of the previous rule. A study of MRS showed a way to solve this problem, with only a small amount of "fiddling" with global MRS variables.

A significant portion of the activities of the machinability knowledge based system involves the search for information in the knowledge base. This was done using the backward chaining facilities of MRS. Pattern searching involved exact matches (usually to confirm that something was in the knowledge base) as well as searches for relations where at most ten percent of the pattern was known a priori. Of particular value both in backward chaining searches and in the execution of forward chaining rules was the ability MRS provided to manipulate components of the knowledge base referred to as theories.

Partitioning the knowledge base using theories permitted knowledge regarding operations that were not applicable to be hidden. When such operations became applicable a simple activation of the appropriate theory had the desired affect. In addition to activation and deactivation of theories, MRS provides a means of structuring a hierarchy of theories so that activation or deactivation of a theory at a particular node in the hierarchy tree would serve as an activation of all the theories attached to this node.

MRS nominally operates in an interpreted mode. Using the version of MRS on the VAX, which is based on Franz Lisp (Foderaro [1983]), we were able to obtain noticeable performance improvement by compiling the source code for our experimental system. Further careful analysis by Steve White of the Boeing Artificial Intelligence Center unveiled a method of restructuring the system to obtain more than an order of magnitude improvement in speed. One of the tasks, that of formatting the machinability model output and corresponding adjusted values for display to the user, had taken more than six minutes, even with compiled code. With the restructured system this task consumed at most fourteen seconds (no other changes were made except the restructuring).

Frame representation languages provide default value specification capability. In the nature of a side issue to our main experiment we were able to replicate the desired behavior using the facilities of MRS and a very small auxiliary Lisp function. While it is certainly not surprising that this was possible, the reduction in the size of the knowledge base was significant.

A singular temptation that repeatedly arose during the development of this experiment was to solve a problem by encoding its solution as a procedure. It is not our intention to continue the procedural vs. declarative knowledge argument. We have, however, observed that declarative knowledge presents its content explicitly and hence requires minimal background knowledge for correct interpretation. This is not true of procedural knowledge, since its understanding normally requires a sizable amount of knowledge regarding the programming language(s) involved in its construction. We found during this experiment that the control that seemed to be lacking in the declarative representation could be provided by the use of inferencing coupled with appropriate ancillary declarative knowledge. Not only could we represent the desired knowledge explicitly, but once done, we were able to apply the inherent ability of the inference engine to reason about this form of the knowledge. The mechanism for doing this with the procedural form is as yet not apparent.

One of the issues that we have encountered repeatedly in the development of knowledge based systems is the apparent lack of support provided by traditional software development methodologies, particularly those using the label top-down. Not as an original idea, we believe that the cause of this lack of support is the fundamental difference in the development process. Traditional software development methodologies assume a linear development process with perfect knowledge flowing down from the top. The user's requirements must be completely specified prior to design, otherwise the design will be incomplete or prone to error. This continues through the life-cycle of the software system. Knowledge based systems are developed using an iterative refinement mechanism which expects that all the answers will not be known, and perhaps many of the questions as well. Knowledge engineers produce a prototype and "try it for size," observing the results in an experimental fashion. A fuller discussion of this subject requires another time and place, but we believe that as knowledge based systems become available for distillation of their attributes a methodology will emerge that will support knowledge based system development and will subsume traditional software development methods.

7. ACKNOWLEDGEMENTS

I would like to thank Miroslav Benda, John Boose, Steve Elwell, Cathy Kitto, Steve White, Bruce Wilson, and Guy Younie for their assistance in the implementation of the ideas discussed in this chapter.

8. REFERENCES

Foderaro, J. K., Sklower, K. L., Layer, K., *The Franz Lisp Manual*, University of California, Berkeley, 1983.

Genesereth, M. R., Greiner, R., Grinburg, M. R., Smith, D. E., *The MRS Dictionary*, Stanford Heuristic Programming Project, Report No. HPP-80-24, December 1980 (revised January 1984).

Genesereth, M. R., Smith, D. E., *Meta-Level Architecture*, Stanford Heuristic Programming Project, Report No. HPP-81-6, May 1981 (revised December 1982).

Stanford Heuristic Programming Project, Report No. HPP-82-27, October 1982 (revised January 1984).

Genesereth, M. R., *The MRS Casebook*, Stanford Heuristic Programming Project, Report No. HPP-83-26, May 1983.

Squier, Bailey, "The Automated NC Processor Is On The Way," *Modern Machine Shop*, January, 1984.

8

LEARNING IN SECOND GENERATION EXPERT SYSTEMS

LUC STEELS AND WALTER VAN DE VELDE
ARTIFICIAL INTELLIGENCE LABORATORY
VRIJE UNIVERSITEIT BRUSSELS

1. INTRODUCTION

Second generation expert systems offer a substantial leap forward in current expert system technology. Steels [1985] introduces this development and sketches the advances for each of the components of an expert system. This chapter focuses on learning techniques for second generation expert systems.

The first section briefly introduces the notion of a second generation expert system. Then an example application is introduced. This is followed by a section that develops various components of a second generation expert system and a section which describes the proposed learning mechanism. The fifth section contains an implemented example of learning.

The chapter concludes with a comparison to other work and directions for future research.

2. WHAT ARE SECOND GENERATION EXPERT SYSTEMS?

Whereas first generation systems rely purely on heuristic knowledge in the form of rules, second generation systems have an additional component in the form of a deeper model which gives them an understanding of the complete search space over which the heuristics operate. This makes two kinds of reasoning possible: (1) the application of heuristic rules in a style similar to the classical expert systems; (2) the generation and examination of a deeper search space following classical search techniques, beyond the range of heuristics.

The introduction of a deeper model solves a number of fundamental problems of current expert systems.

First generation expert systems are brittle, in the sense that as soon as situations occur which fall outside the scope of the heuristic rules, they are unable to function at all. In such a situation, second generation systems fall back on search which is not knowledge-driven and therefore potentially very inefficient. However, because these traditional search techniques can theoretically solve a wider class of problems, there is a graceful degradation of performance instead of an abrupt failure.

First generation systems base their explanations purely on a backtrace of the heuristic rules that were needed to find a solution. It is well known, however, that the path followed to find a solution usually differs from a convincing rational argument why the solution is valuable, particularly if a considerable amount of heuristic knowledge entered into the reasoning process. Because second generation systems have access to a deeper understanding of the search space, they are capable to formulate a deeper and more convincing explanation which goes beyond the mere recall of the rules that fired.

The most important advantage lies in knowledge acquisition. Finding heuristic rules has turned out to be extremely difficult. Experts typically take a long time to come up with solid rules. The rule-set never seems complete and is continuously changing, showing inconsistencies across experts (and even for the same expert).

These inconsistencies are apparently due to different experiences which are the source of heuristic rule discovery. Second generation expert systems constitute major progress in current technology because they exhibit learning behavior in the sense that they are capable of acquiring new heuristic rules. It is this learning capability which is the subject of the chapter.

3. INTRODUCTION TO THE EXAMPLE APPLICATION

Because second generation expert systems require a deep model, they can only be applied to domains where such a model is available. A typical example (which is the one we are using in our own experiments) is reasoning about technical systems like vehicles, electronic devices, computer programs, or power plants. Many tasks supportable by expert systems could be envisioned for this domain: discovery of design failures, diagnosing faulty components, designing variants, monitoring, etc. We will be interested here in diagnosis for proper servicing and repair.

3.1 Models

Various models can be used to describe and reason about a technical system. For example, one could develop an anatomical model which focuses on the various components and their part-whole relations. One could develop a geometrical

271

model which focuses on the general layout of the geometrical relations between components.

One could also construct a functional model which is capable of predicting the behavior of the device based on the functioning of its components. A functional model typically assumes that the components of a device are functioning correctly and that the external controls are the way they should be. For example, if the ignition key of a car is turned, a functional model predicts that the engine will start, assuming that gas is present, the battery is working, the car is in parking mode (if it is an automatic), etc.

A functional model may be represented in the form of rules, constraint systems where the constraints represent functional descriptions of each component (Steele and Sussman [1979]), or complex programs which simulate the device in great detail. Functional models have been an active research topic in AI for some time (see e.g., Bobrow and Hayes [1984]).

Yet another way to look at a technical system is through a causal model. A causal model knows about the causal connections between various properties of the components but does not know how each of the components actually works. A causal model represents an alternative, more abstract, view of a device which is particularly effective for diagnosis in cooperation with a functional model.

We will be interested in developing an expert in diagnosis of technical systems based on causal models. The functional model is assumed to be represented by a human technician interacting with the expert system and available to the system only through questioning.

3.2 Causal Models

A causal model consists of a set of properties of components (e.g., wheel is turning, lamp is on, switch is closed) which are causally related in the sense that the value of one property is determined by the values of one or more other properties. Some of these properties are observable, most of them are not or only with difficulty. Causal relations can easily be represented in a network where the nodes represent the properties of the components.

Figure 1 shows a simple circuit consisting of a relay with two contacts and a lamp connected to each of them. The two lamps will be burning when there is power, the ground is okay, and the switch is closed.

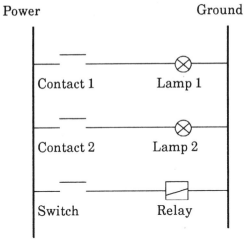

Power   Ground

Contact 1   Lamp 1

Contact 2   Lamp 2

Switch   Relay

Figure 1

Figure 2 shows a simple causal model for this circuit. It consists of a number of properties (Lamp 1 = On, Contact 1 = Powered, Switch = Closed, etc.) and causal relations between them.

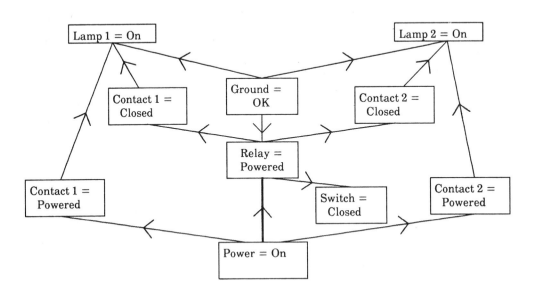

Figure 2

3.3 The Task

We assume a user who is capable of predicting the value of certain properties based on a (mental) functional model, and of comparing his predictions with their corresponding properties in an actual device. Thus a user of capable of predicting that the engine of a car will start when you turn the ignition key and of observing whether the engine has actually started.

We say that there is an anomaly when there is a mismatch between an observed and a predicted value. For example, a car may not start after the ignition key is turned on.

Such an anomaly may be due to three factors:

1. Wrong functional model: The functional model does not correspond to the actual functioning of the device. This situation is ignored here, because we are interested in an expert system for causal models, not functional models.

2. Improper servicing: External switches or other controls were incorrectly set. A causal expert should be able to identify these controls and propose an action to change them.

3. Malfunctioning: Some components are no longer functioning properly. A causal expert should be able to identify the components and propose a correction (e.g., replacement).

Take for example the circuit of Figure 1. If power is on, ground is okay, the switch and the contacts are closed, but one lamp is not on, then there are three possible diagnoses: The lamp may be broken, the corresponding contact may be malfunctioning and thus not letting through power, or the contact may get no power in the first place. All other explanations for the anomaly (namely that the lamp is not on as expected) would cause the other lamp to be out too and should therefore be eliminated.

Or assume that the switch is open, the contacts closed, and power and ground okay. Suppose also that a user of the device (erroneously) expects the lamp to be on. The diagnosis should then say that the open switch is the cause of the anomaly and therefore the expectation can be satisfied by closing the switch. The problem here was to discover which assumptions of the user about the state of the device were erroneous and to correct these assumptions.

The task that will be taken as example application in this paper can now be summarized:

Given a technical device described as a network of causal relations between properties of components, given a state of the device and an anomalous property, i.e., a property whose observed value differs from the expected value, find an explanation either in terms of malfunctioning components or in terms of external controls that need to be changed.

3.4 Example Device

Trouble-shooting an ordinary car (more specifically a Dyane-6) will be used as a source for concrete examples in the rest of this text. The heuristic rules are based on rules supplied by the manufacturer for diagnosing and repairing minor car problems (Olyslager, [1979]). The causal models are based on a technical description of the car. Traces of the reasoning and learning processes have been taken from an actual implementation.

4. COMPONENTS

Rule learning is the main subject of this chapter. But before this can be discussed in any detail we have to establish a format of the rules (the target of learning) and a method for deep causal reasoning (the source of learning). Our goal for the initial experimentation was to find simple rule formats and simple deep reasoning methods, so that a learning process could be elucidated. Work is now in progress to investigate learning for more complex rule systems and more complex deep reasoning schemata.

4.1 Tools

Second generation expert systems require more sophisticated knowledge representation tools than the ones common for first generation expert systems such as Emycin (Van Melle [1980]) or OPS5 (Forgy [1981]). First of all a variety of formalisms is needed: frame-structured representation to represent the models, rule formalisms to represent the heuristic knowledge, constraints to drive deep reasoning, etc. Moreover it must be possible to represent knowledge about each of these items, requiring the capacity for meta-representation and meta-reasoning. For example, it must not only be possible to represent and use heuristic rules, but also to represent facts or rules about the rules and reason explicitly about their structure. Similarly, it must be possible to represent and reason explicitly about deductions that have been made, new concepts that have been introduced, questions that have been asked, etc. We use the knowledge representation system KRS (Steels [1984]) which contains tools supporting these functions, as well as extensive graphical interfacing. The details of this system or its specific use in the construction of expert systems will not be elaborated upon in this paper.

4.2 Heuristic Rules

We use the simplest rule-formalisms we could think of that are still effective in solving problems in the task domain. Properties of components are modeled as simple propositions. Some examples are: Gas = Present, Coil = Weak, Starter = Faulty, Pump-pressure = High, Plugs = Worn. Conditions or conclusions may take the form of logical combinations of propositions.

Clancey [1983], Breuker and Wielinga [1985], and others have argued convincingly that a richer structure is needed for a rule to better support knowledge acquisition with a human expert. Thus a diagnostic rule will not only consist of an IF-part grouping all conditions, but of preconditions, necessary symptoms, possible symptoms, plausible symptoms, etc. Although each of these plays logically the role of a condition, they have different functions in the reasoning process and aid the human expert in structuring his experience. As we will see, this richer structure is also crucial for learning, in the sense that the richer a rule, the more that can be learned. To illustrate this, the rules we will use are also internally structured. Specifically, the following types of rules are used: focus-rules, inspection-rules, and solution-rules.

Focus-Rules

Rules are grouped in rule-sets which are associated with contexts. For example, all rules about a certain component or a certain function are put together. The purpose of a focus-rule is to focus the reasoning process on one set of rules. A focus-rule relates a number of symptoms with a new context. The rule fires if all symptoms are present. Here are two examples:

Rule for start-problem
    A focus-rule
        Symptom: Not Car = Starts
        New-focus: Start-Function
Rule for ignition-problem
    A focus-rule
        Symptom: Starter = Turning

Not All-plugs = Sparking

New-focus: Ignition-Function

The first rule states that if the car does not start, reasoning should focus on the start-function of the car. The second rule states that if the starter is turning but not all plugs are sparking, the ignition-function should be examined. Start-function and ignition-function have associated rule-sets which are activated when these contexts become active.

Inspection-Rules

Inspection-rules establish an interface between heuristic rules and deep reasoning. They associate a number of symptoms with a causal network. Moreover they indicate for which property the network should be investigated (more about this in the next section). This property is called the trigger. The rule fires if all symptoms are present.

Thus, suppose there is a causal network called start-circuit; then the following rule suggests to inspect this network for the property of a turning starter.

Rule for start-motor does not turn

An inspection-rule

Symptom:	Lights = Can-burn
	Not Sound-of-starter = Humming
Network:	Start-circuit
Trigger:	Starter = Turning

Solution-Rules

The solution-rules associate symptoms directly with solutions. A distinction is made between primary and secondary symptoms. A primary symptom can be viewed as the key property that a rule tries to deal with. The anomaly to be explained needs to be a primary symptom of a solution-rule before the rule is considered at all. Secondary symptoms delineate additional constraints on the situation for which the rule is relevant.

The solution is in the form of a number of properties which have to become normal. They are called corrected-properties.

The following rule says that if the lights cannot burn, the solution is to charge the battery.

<u>Rule for battery is flat</u>

    A solution-rule

        Primary-symptoms: Not Lights = Can-burn

        Secondary-symptoms: -

        Corrected-properties: Battery = Charged

We assume a forward reasoning control structure. Based on initial observations, focus rules will fire to pinpoint the problem in specific areas. If there are solution rules they provide immediate solutions. Otherwise deep reasoning is performed, triggered by inspection-rules. The user is asked questions if the status of an observation is unknown and if this is required by a rule or by the deep reasoning system.

4.3 Deep Reasoning

The goal of deep reasoning is to find explanations for an anomaly using the causal network. Backward reasoning is applied, based on the following principles:

1. If the effect of a property is normal, then there is reason to believe that the property itself is normal.

2. If the effect of a property is anomalous, the property may be anomalous too.

Thus if the engine is not starting and one of its causes is the presence of gas, then this property becomes suspect.

The deep reasoning algorithm starts from an anomalous property (e.g., a lamp is supposed to be on and it is not). Then the causes of this property are investigated, and so on until observable properties are arrived at. The user is queried about these properties, and if they are anomalous (i.e., different from the expectation of the functional model) an explanation has been found. If they are normal (i.e., matching with the expectation) then the explanation for the original anomaly lies elsewhere.

When none of the observed properties which ultimately caused the anomalous property were anomalous, the cause of the anomaly must lie somewhere in the causal network. In other words, one of the internal components must be faulty.

The number of faulty components can often be reduced if there are other observables which also were caused by the same properties. Consider, for example, the following network which depicts the causes emanating from X and Y.

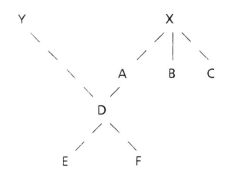

X is anomalous and needs to be explained. E, F, B, and C are observable properties and they are all normal. So the fact that X is anomalous must be due to either A or D, because there is a faulty component between them. But if Y is also normal, it can be deduced that its cause, namely D, must also be normal, and therefore the only possible explanation for the anomaly of X is that A is anomalous, i.e. the component of which A is a property must be malfunctioning.

4.4 An Example

Figure 3 shows a causal net which represents part of the causal chains leading to the starting of the engine. There are three requirements before the engine will start: the starter must turn the engine, the two sparkplugs must fire, and the starter-transmission must be okay. The starter can only turn if it is powered. This requires that the battery is charged and the contact is on.

The plugs fire if their cables are okay and if the ignition coil delivers power. Other requirements for an engine start, like the presence of gas, are already taken care of by the heuristic rules. Note that the causal net is not limited to electrical properties. Causal reasoning is applicable to any system which can be described in terms of cause-effect relations.

The causal net is used after the following rule fires.

Rule for starter does not turn

An inspection-rule

Symptoms: Lights = Can-burn

Not Starter = Turning

Network: Start-circuit

Trigger: Starter = Turning

However, deep reasoning may start from other properties in the net as well. For example, the following rule would use the same net if Plug-1 is not firing:

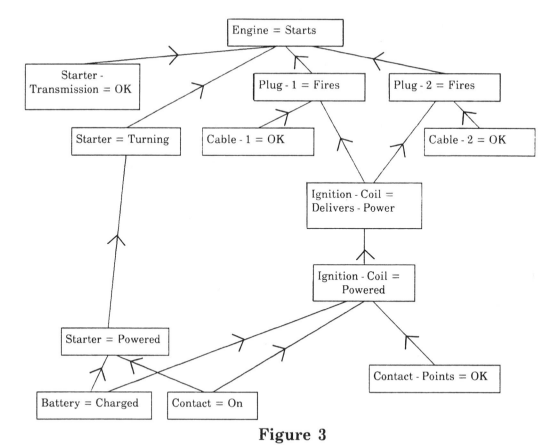

Figure 3

<u>Rule for Plug-1 does not fire</u>

An inspection-rule

    Symptoms: Not Plug-1 = Fires

    Network: Start-Circuit

    Trigger: Plug-1 = Fires

Let us consider an example where the network is examined because the starter is not turning. The other relevant properties have the following status.

    Starter = Turning is Anomalous

    Battery = Charged is Normal

    Contact = On is Anomalous

When we say that X is normal we mean that what was expected is equal to what was observed. For example, Contact = On is normal because it is expected to be true, and it is observed to be true. Conversely, when we say that x is

280

anomalous, we mean that what was expected is different from what was observed. For example, Starter = Turning is anomalous because the property was expected to be true, but the starter is not turning. (The trigger of an inspection - rule is always assumed to be anomalous.)

Note that a decision on whether an expectation equals an observation is up to the user. His functional model will predict the expectation and his senses or measurement tools will perform the observation. The functional model could of course also be a computer model, in which case the user only has to do the observation. The observations could in some cases also be made automatically, which would make the complete system computer-based.

Deep reasoning starts from the triggering symptom, in this case Starter = Turning. Backward examination of its causes leads to Starter = Powered. This is not observable so the reasoner descends further in the network. The causes of Starter = Powered are Battery = Charged and Contact = On. Battery = Charged is normal, so that cannot provide the explanation for the original anomaly. On the other hand, Contact = On is anomalous; therefore an explanation has been found.

4.5 Differences Between Heuristic Rules and Deep Reasoning

Based on the above discussion, the differences between heuristic and deep causal reasoning become clearer. Thus, there could be a heuristic rule that says "when the headlights are not on, check whether they have been turned on." A deep reasoning system would follow the causal connections starting from the headlights and would eventually arrive at the switch to turn them on, but it would possibly check many other things on the way or start wandering around in the causal network in directions that have little to do with the initial problem.

So we see the following differences:

Heuristic rules make shortcuts: Intermediate steps are skipped because those steps are unlikely to lead to a quick solution of the problem.

Heuristic reasoning does not refer to the working of the internals of the system but associates a number of easy to make external observations with a plausible conclusion. A deeper causal model will be able to come to the same conclusion, but would in general also examine many other things, some of which might not be easy to explain without extra testing devices.

Our objective is to combine two models, i.e., to use heuristic rules when they are available but to fall back on deep reasoning when the rules are inadequate.

Moreover, after a deep reasoning sequence a new rule should be extracted in case the same or similar situations occur again. The following section describes a learning mechanism that performs this function. We will focus on the learning of solution-rules to simplify the exposition.

5. LEARNING BY PROGRESSIVE REFINEMENT

A deep reasoning sequence potentially investigates many causal connections and queries the user about many observations. To be worthwhile, heuristic rules must do the opposite: They should be as simple as possible, leaving out all the details and all the observations that did not directly contribute to a solution of the problem. (For real systems, the causal connections investigated by a deep reasoner increase quickly to thousands, so the savings are potentially enormous.) The main problem, of course, is that it is not immediately clear what is essential in any given situation. One approach is to view learning as a search process. A hypothesis is made and backtracking is performed when this hypothesis is invalidated by new examples.

We propose an alternative: rule-learning by progressive refinement, which does not involve backtracking. Initially a new rule implies as much abstraction as possible using circumscriptive reasoning (McCarthy [1983]): everything which is not mentioned in a rule is supposed to be irrelevant or normal. Later the conditions of a rule are progressively refined to discriminate between the rules whose conditions overlap but whose conclusions are different. Interestingly enough, the proposed method is monotonic. A learned rule never becomes invalid, although its applicability may become restricted.

5.1 Initial Rule Formulation

A rule is initially constructed from a deep reasoning sequence as follows:

1. The primary-symptom of the rule is equal to the anomalous property that triggered the deep reasoning sequence.

2. The corrected-properties are equal to the conclusions of the deep reasoning sequence, i.e., the list of properties which deep reasoning deemed ultimately responsible for the anomaly. It is assumed that a change of these properties either directly or indirectly causes the anomaly to disappear and that the user has verified that this is indeed the case.

3. The secondary-symptoms are initially void.

For example, if the car did not start, and deep reasoning determined that this was due to the car not being in parking mode, then the initial rule extracted from this situation looks as follows:

Rule for not in parking

    A solution-rule

        Primary-symptoms: Not Car = Starts

        Secondary-symptoms: -

        Corrected-properties: Mode = Parking

Clearly this is an extreme form of abstraction. It assumes that the encountered situation is the only situation that can ever go wrong! The triggering symptom is therefore linked directly with the corrections that worked. Such a rule should be interpreted under the circumscriptive condition that what is not mentioned has nothing to do with the primary symptom or was normal.

If this was the only rule so far in the rule-set, then nothing more is done to it. Otherwise the rule is integrated with the other existing rules to see whether refinements are needed, either of the new rule, or of already existing rules. The integration procedure is described in the next section.

5.2 Rule Integration

The objective of rule integration is to add a new rule to the set of remaining rules in such a way that they remain mutually exclusive. No two rules should fire and propose a different solution for the same primary symptom.

Rule-integration is trivial if the rules are orthogonal, which is the case if their primary symptoms are different. The new rule can simply be added to the rest of the rule-set.

If two rules have the same primary symptoms, then the following procedure is used:

1. The corrected-properties of the new rule are added as secondary-symptoms of the old rule, unless the property is one of the corrected-properties of the old rule.

2. The negation of the corrected-properties of the new rule is added as a secondary-symptom of the new rule, unless the property is one of the corrected-properties of the old rule.

For example, suppose we had already the first rule:

Rule for not in parking

    A solution-rule

Primary-symptoms: Not Car = Starts
Secondary-symptoms: -
Corrected-properties: Mode = Parking

and now add:

Rule for no gas

A solution-rule

Primary-symptoms: Not Car = Starts
Secondary-symptoms: -
Corrected-properties: Gas = Present

Then the new rule-set looks as follows:

Rule for not in parking

A solution-rule

Primary-symptoms: Not Car = Starts
Secondary-symptoms: Gas = Present
Corrected-properties: Mode = Parking

Rule for no gas

A solution-rule

Primary-symptoms: Not Car = Starts
Secondary-symptoms: Not Gas = Present
Corrected-properties: Gas = Present

The rules now say: If the car does not start and there is gas present, put the car in parking mode. If the car does not start and there is no gas present, make gas be present.

The intuition behind this integration procedure is that symptoms are added to make sure that the rules remain mutually exclusive. This is done by adding a property as symptom of one rule and the negation of it as symptom of the other rule. But not every property can be used to do this. Suppose we have two rules, Rule-1 and Rule-2, with the same primary symptoms (in this case Not Car = Starts). The negation of a corrected property Rule-1 may always be added to its symptoms. Because it occurs as corrected-property, we know it influences the primary symptoms. Therefore, because of the way rules are abstracted, it was normal in the situation from which Rule-2 was abstracted if and only if it is not a corrected property of Rule-2.

Note that the refinement process so far is still monotonic. A learned rule never becomes invalid but its applicability gets restricted. Note also that there can be rule chaining, in the sense that if there is no gas present and the car is not in parking mode, the second rule will first correct the gas problem and then the first rule can fire to correct the parking mode problem.

Suppose there is now a third rule:

Rule for empty battery

A solution-rule

Primary-symptoms: Not Car = Starts

Secondary-symptom:

Corrected-properties: Battery = Working

Then the new rule-set after integration looks as follows:

Rule for not in parking

A solution-rule

Primary-symptoms: Not Car = Starts

Secondary-symptoms: Gas = Present

Battery = Working

Corrected-properties: Mode = Parking

Rule for no gas

A solution-rule

Primary-symptoms: Not Car = Starts

Secondary-symptoms: Not Gas = Present

Battery = Working

Corrected-properties: Gas = Present

Rule for battery empty

A solution-rule

Primary-symptoms: Not Car = Starts

Secondary-symptoms: Not Battery = Working

Corrected-properties: Battery = Working

5.3 Rule Failure

If a new problem is presented to the system, the rules constructed following the above procedure are tried before any deep reasoning is done. If a rule fires because the primary-symptom and the secondary-symptoms have been observed, then the corrected-properties are tested out. If they resolve the initial anomaly, then the rule is confirmed and no changes need to be made. If not, there are two cases:

1. Some correction cannot be carried out because the property to be corrected had already the correct value (e.g., a rule proposes to turn on a switch but the switch was already turned on). This is an indication that the rule was based on the circumscriptive assumption that a certain property was irrelevant, and indeed it was irrelevant in the case which formed the basis of the rule. But now there is a case where the property IS relevant, so it should be added to the conditions of the existing rule and a new rule should be constructed which has its negation as one of the conditions.

2. The proposed corrections do not resolve the problem (e.g., a rule proposes to turn on a switch but after the switch has been turned on the anomaly remains present). Again this shows that something was erroneously assumed to be irrelevant.

In both cases deep reasoning is started again to perform a more thorough diagnosis. From the result a new rule can then be extracted and incorporated. This incorporation process follows the same procedure.

5.4 Learning Through Rule Combination

Although the rule-set obtained through the above construction process will progressively solve an increasing number of problems, it is far from efficient. Rules that partially overlap remain independent, and the same conditions can be checked many times over.

An optimization method which can improve this situation involves a combination of rules which have corrected-properties in common but have different conditions. Here is such a combination rule (an example will follow):

Combination-Rule - 1

If two rules, Rule-1 and Rule-2, have the same set of corrected-properties, than a new rule may be generated whose :

1. Primary-symptoms are equal to the union of the primary-symptoms of Rule-1 and Rule-2.

2. Secondary-symptoms are equal to the intersection of the secondary-symptoms of Rule-1 and Rule-2.

3. Corrected-properties are equal to the corrected-properties of Rule-1 and Rule-2.

Note that both rules Rule-1 and Rule-2 can only be formed due to the restrictions on rule firing, i.e., the anomaly to be explained must be one of the primary-symptoms. Without this restriction, Rule-2 would never have been generated in the first place. This demonstrates the earlier remark that a richer structure for rules to ease knowledge acquisition through human experts is also of great importance for learning.

5.5 A Note on Convergence

The rule-set will continue to grow as long as there are anomalies that are not explained with the existing rule-set. The rule-set will shrink through the combination of rules. This combination occurs specifically if two rules have equal or similar corrected-properties. Therefore the set of rules remains small if the problems with the device being modeled are always caused by similar failures.

In the worst case a rule will be generated for every possible combination of observations of the device. But this method has been designed for a system that learns rules for a device operating in the real world. It is essential that learning is driven by situations that occur in practice. The rules will then embody relevant experience with the device over a period of time.

5.6 Examples of Learning

This section illustrates the learning procedures for the car example. Recall the causal network representing the Start-Circuit.

A. Initial Rule Formulation

The first example of learning takes place after the deep reasoning sequence explained earlier on. Because Starter = Turning was the triggering symptom, it becomes the primary symptom of the rule. Because Contact = On was the explanation, it is the corrected-property. The rule therefore looks as follows:

Rule-1 for contact not on
  A solution-rule
    Primary-symptoms: Not Starter = Turning
    Secondary-symptoms: -
    Corrected-properties: Contact = On

B. Orthogonal Rules

Consider now another situation which also leads the system to examine the circuit using deep reasoning triggered by the fact that Plug-1 does not fire. The following observations are assumed:

287

Plug-1 = Fires is Anomalous
Battery = Charged is Normal
Contact = On is Normal
Contact - Points = OK is Normal
Cable-1 = OK is Anomalous
Engine = Starts is Anomalous

Backward reasoning starts from Plug-1 = Fires. There are two causes: Cable-1 must be okay and the Ignition-coil must deliver power. The first cause is already anomalous, so that is a sufficient explanation for the original anomaly. In any case the three causes of Ignition-coil = Powered are all normal, so no explanation could come from that causal path.

Based on this reasoning sequence the following new rule can be extracted:

Rule-2 for Cable-1

   A solution-rule

      Primary-symptoms: Not Plug-1 = Fires
      Secondary-symptoms: -
      Corrected-properties: Cable-1 = OK

Because the rule is about different primary-symptoms and has different corrected-properties, it is completely orthogonal with the previous one and therefore no further changes need to be made.

C. Rule Integration

Rule integration becomes more interesting if two rules are learned about the same primary-symptoms. Consider now a reasoning sequence over the same network, again triggered by the anomaly for Plug-1 = Fires. The following observations are assumed:

Battery = Charged is Normal
Contact = On is Normal
Contact - Points = OK is Anomalous
Starter = Turning is Normal
Cable-1 = OK is Normal
Plug-1 = Fires is Anomalous
Engine = Starts is Anomalous
Starter - Transmission = OK is Normal

Deep reasoning proceeds backward from Plug-1 = Fires looking for an explanation. Since Cable-1 is now normal the anomaly must come from

Ignition - coil = Delivers - Power. Descending the causal chain further from there, the anomalous cause is detected: the contact points are not working properly.

From this the following rule is extracted:

Rule-3 for contact - points defective

A solution-rule

Primary-symptoms: Not Plug-1 = Fires

Secondary-symptoms: -

Corrected-properties: Contact - Points = OK

The Overlapping rules Rule-2 and Rule-3 have to be adapted to make them exclusive. The extra corrected-properties of the new rule are only Contact-Points = OK. As described before, this property is used to discriminate between the two possible solutions. The refined rules are:

Rule-2 for Cable-1

A solution-rule

Primary-symptoms: Not Plug-1 = Fires

Secondary-symptoms: Contact - Points = OK

Corrected-properties: Cable - 1 = OK

Rule-3 for contact - points defecive

A solution-rule

Primary-symptoms: Not Plug-1 = Fires

Secondary-symptoms: Not Contact - Points = OK

Corrected-properties: Contact - Points = OK

Note that by chaining these rules the correct solution will be generated if Cable-1, the contact-points, or both are the cause. This way the power of the rules is fully exploited.

D. Rule Combination

Rule combination takes place as soon as two rules are learned with the same corrected-properties. Suppose the same net is used but now Plug - 2 = Fires is the triggering property. The following observations are assumed:

Battery = Charged is Normal

Contact = On is Normal

Contact - Points = OK is Anomalous

Starter = Turning is Normal

Cable-1 = OK is Normal

Cable - 2 = OK is Normal

Plug - 2 = Fires is Anomalous

Engine = Starts is Anomalous

Starter - Transmission = OK is Normal

This situation is identical to the previous one except that the network is examined to explain the anomaly with another plug. Note that the symptoms of Rule-3 are all true, and its conclusion is indeed correct. However, since Plug - 2 = Fires is not in the primary symptoms of that rule, it will not fire. Deep reasoning is done, starting from Plug - 2 = Fires. With a similar line of reasoning as in the previous case the cause of the anomaly is found, namely that the Contact-points are not working properly.

The newly generated rule is:

Rule-4 for contact - points defective

A solution-rule

Primary-symptoms: Not Plug-2 = Fires

Secondary-symptoms: -

Corrected-properties: Contact - Points = OK

As to the symptoms, this rule is completely orthogonal to the others. Its actions however are the same as in Rule-3. It was thus found that defective Contact-points cause an anomaly with both Plug-1 and Plug-2. The occurrence of both anomalies together can be interpreted as strong evidence that the cause is to be found in the Contact - points (as far as experience can tell). Therefore the following rule is justified:

Rule-5 for contact - points defective

A solution-rule

Primary-symptoms: Not Plug-1 = Fires

Not Plug-2 = Fires

Secondary-symptoms: -

Corrected-properties: Contact - Points = OK

Rule-3 and Rule-4 have become obsolete after this rule is added. They are removed from the set of learned rules.

The rules that were learned after four cases are:

Rule-1 for contact not on

A solution-rule

Primary-symptoms: Not Starter = Turning

Secondary-symptoms: -

Corrected-properties: Contact = On

<u>Rule-2 for Cable-1</u>

A solution-rule

Primary-symptoms: Not Plug - 1 = Fires

Secondary-symptoms: Contact - Points = OK

Corrected-properties: Cable - 1 = OK

<u>Rule-5 for contact - points defective</u>

A solution-rule

Primary-symptoms: Not Plug-1 = Fires

Not Plug-2 = Fires

Secondary-symptoms: -

Corrected-properties: Contact - Points = OK

E. Fault Analysis

The previous anomalies were all explained by anomalous external observations. Now follows an example where the deep reasoner detects that the anomaly is due to a malfunctioning of an internal component. This situation occurs if all observations are normal, but the engine does not start. The following observations are assumed:

Battery = Charged is Normal

Contact = On is Normal

Contact - Points = OK is Normal

Starter = Turning is Normal

Cable - 1 = OK is Normal

Cable - 2 = OK is Normal

Plug - 2 = Fires is Normal

Engine = Starts is Anomalous

Starter - Transmission = OK is Normal

Deep reasoning starts from Engine = Starts. Descending down along the causes, no anomaly is detected for the various observations, therefore the cause of the anomaly must be caused by an internal component, more specifically a component on the path which leads from Engine = Starts via Plug - 1 = Fires (which is assumed to be not observable), Ignition - Coil = Delivers - Power, and Ignition - Coil = Powered to Battery = Charged, Contact = On, and Contact - Points = OK. However, because Plug - 2 = Fires which is another effect of Ignition - Coil = Delivers - Power is normal, the anomaly cannot be due to the Ignition - Coil = Delivers - Power and therefore not to Ignition - Coil = Powered. So the only explanation remaining is Plug - 1 = Fires. Therefore the sparkplug must be faulty.

5.7 Other Forms of Learning

There are many other forms of learning which can take place once the initial rule-sets have been formed. We mention below some examples that were also implemented in our initial experiments, but they will not be developed further in this chapter.

Learning Through Generalization

Deep reasoning typically applies to a small part of a complex system. Often there are other portions of the same device (or different devices) which have the same causal structure. By making abstraction of the specific area for which it was discovered, rules get a wider applicability. If the causal structures are not equal but similar, then further learning through adaptation can refine the rule-set acquired elsewhere.

Learning New Concepts

A subset of the necessary symptoms may be common to many rules. In such cases it is possible to introduce a new concept which can be used to formulate an intermediate conclusion in reasoning. It will be more efficient to first establish this intermediate conclusion, instead of reconsidering all of its components. This also opens perspectives for learning in richer causal models.

Learning Through Rule-Ordering

The rule-set needs to be restructured so that rules are ordered. This leads to greater efficiency because symptoms present in more than one rule are not investigated more than once. The ordering itself again depends on experience, so that rules covering situations which are more frequent get priority.

Learning For Other Types of Rules

Learning techniques described so far are mainly concerned with solution rules. Other techniques must be used for focus and inspection rules.

For example, the division of rules in smaller sets and the learning of rules that lead from one set to another is the goal of learning focus rules. This division can often be based on the underlying model. Rules which relate to one component may be grouped in one set. Focusing during reasoning may then take place along the part-whole relation: first rules for the device as a whole are considered; some of these rules will partition the problem to one of the parts. Then rules for a part are considered which may further point to smaller subparts.

6 CONCLUSIONS

The chapter discusses learning mechanisms for second generation expert systems. A second generation expert system not only uses heuristic rules, but has also a model of the domain so that deeper reasoning is possible if the rules are inadequate. A learning component looks at the result of deep reasoning and abstracts new rules out of it. A method called rule-learning by progressive refinement was introduced and illustrated with concrete implemented examples.

Our approach to learning differs substantially from inductive learning over a (possibly large) set of examples (Langley [1981], Michalski [1983], Michie [1983]). Inductive systems have no deep model which is the source of learning; instead operators are proposed to gradually abstract features away to arrive at the essential properties of a concept or a rule. No such operators are used here.

On the other hand, there are closer relations to other work on learning. For example, the LEX-system by Mitchell [1983] tries also "to improve its problem-solving expertise through experience, by generating selected problems in the domain, solving them, and learning by analyzing their solutions." However, the method he uses is very different, based on version spaces to represent the plausible range of a heuristic and using induction (generalization and refinement) to obtain or shrink the version space.

Other related work is the proposal by Anderson [1984]. His ACT system combines deep models (in this case declarative representation of geometrical knowledge) with heuristic rules (called procedural knowledge). His discrimination and composition operators are similar but not identical to the integration and combination rules used in our experiments.

There has been a substantial amount of work recently in causal reasoning about technical systems (see e.g., Bobrow and Hayes, [1984]), although most of it is concerned with functional models. A discussion of the advantages and limitations of causal reasoning as used here would be interesting in itself but falls outside the scope of this chapter.

Our current research is concentrating on the further development of the various learning techniques operating over the rules and on an investigation of their properties. At the same time we are looking at the effect of more complex rule formats and more complex or other forms of deep reasoning related to the learning strategies proposed here.

7 ACKNOWLEDGMENT

Several people at the Free University of Brussels AI Laboratory have in many ways contributed to the ideas presented in this paper or to their implementation. The KRS-system is a team effort with Peter Van Damme and Kris Van Marcke as prime implementers of the LISP-machine version used for the experiments reported here. Leo De Wael and Patrick Backx are other members of the team involved in technical expert systems. They have been instrumental in the development of models for deep and heuristic reasoning in this domain. This research has been partially sponsored by the Belgian Ministry of Scientific Planning.

REFERENCES

Anderson, J. R. [1984] "Acquisition of Proof Skills in Geometry." In Michalski, R., J. Carbonell and T. Mitchell (eds.). *Machine Learning. An Artificial Intelligence Approach*. Springer-Verlag. Berlin.

R Bobrow, D. and Hayes, P. [1984] "Special Issue on Qualitative Reasoning." In *Artificial Intelligence Journal*. North Holland Pub. Amsterdam.

? Breuker, B. J. and Wielinga, J. A. [1985] "KADS: Structured Knowledge Acquisition for Expert Systems." In *Second International Workshop on Expert Systems*. Avignon.

√Clancey, W. J. [1983] "The Epistemology of a Rule-Based Expert System-A Framework for Explanation." In *Artificial Intelligence Journal*. North Holland Pub. Amsterdam.

Forgy, G. [1981] *The OPS-5 manual*. Technical Report. Carnegie Mellon University.

Langley, P. [1981] "Data-Driven Discovery of Physical Laws." *In Cognitive Science*. Ablex Publishing Corporation. Norwood, New Jersey.

McCarthy, J. [1983] "Circumscription - A Form of Non-Monotonic Reasoning." In *Artificial Intelligence Journal*. North Holland Pub. Amsterdam.

√Michalski, R. [1983] "A Theory and Methodology of Inductive Learning." In *Artificial Intelligence Journal*. North Holland Pub. Amsterdam.

Michie, D. [1983] "Towards a Knowledge Accelerator." In *Proceedings of IMPACT-84*, SPL-Insight. Abingdon, Oxfordshire, UK.

√Mitchell, T. M. [1983] "Learning and Problem Solving." Computers and Thoughts Lecture. In A. Bundy (Ed.). *Proceedings of IJCAI-1983*. William Kaufmann, Inc.

Olyslager, P. [1979] *Vraagbaak voor Citroen Dyane6*. Kluwer. Deventer.

Steels, L. [1984] "The Object-Oriented Knowledge Representation System KRS." in T. O'Shea (ed.). *Proceedings of ECAI-84*. North-Holland Pub. Amsterdam.

√Steels L. [1985] "Second Generation Expert Systems." To appear in *Future Generation Computer Systems*, North-Holland Pub. Amsterdam.

Steele, G. and Sussman, G. [1979] *Constraints*. AI Memo No. 502. Massachusetts Institute of Technology. A.I. Lab.

√ Van de Velde, W. [1985] "Naive Causal Reasoning For Diagnosis." In *Fifth International Workshop on Expert Systems*. Avignon, France.

? Van Melle, W. [1980] *A Domain-Independent System that Aids in Constructing Knowledge Based Consultation Programs*. Rep. No. 820, Computer Science Dept., Stanford.

9

ARTIFICIAL INTELLIGENCE IN TRANSITION

PETER E. HART
SYNTELLIGENCE
SUNNYVALE, CALIFORNIA

1. INTRODUCTION

The field of Artificial Intelligence is in the midst of a deep and irreversible structural change. The older research institutions that were almost alone on the AI landscape (at least in North America) in the late 60's and early 70's have been joined by a host of newer ones; new products based on the fruits of AI research have began to appear; and the public at large is beginning to believe that "intelligence" can be put in machines.

These changes raise many issues for the AI leadership, and indeed for all who have an interest in the field. New choices must now be made regarding research, development, educational, and business goals. New problems have arisen in communicating both the premise and the present limitations of AI to a wider audience. New institutional problems and opportunities have arisen.

In this chapter, I will first describe some of the dimensions of the AI transition and then use these to suggest a number of issues that deserve close considerations. No panaceas are offered - each individual and each institution will ultimately resolve these issues in their own way - but perhaps enough controversial views will be put forth to stimulate a healthy discussion.

In undertaking a review of these issues, I have been struck by their number and the consequent need for selection. The selection made in an attempt to reflect the diversity of questions and choices facing the field as a whole. The reader will

This chapter combines the articles "Artificial Intelligence in Transition," which originally appeared in *The AI Magazine*, Volume 5, Number 3, 1984 (reprinted with permission from the American Association for Artificial Intelligence), and "Direction for AI in the Eighties," which first appeared in *SIGART Newsletter* 79, 1982 (reprinted with permission from SIGART).

have little trouble identifying topics that are of no direct concern and can pass rapidly to the second part of the chapter that may be of greater interest.

In the second part I consider technical issues, in particular those broad classes of problems that seem important for AI to address. These may be characterized as three types of complexity to be dealt with: conceptual complexity, computational complexity, and developmental complexity. Most of my attention will be spent on the first of these, the other two receiving only cursory consideration.

2. AI IN TRANSITION

We can get a nice feel for the nature of the AI transition by considering in turn the projects, the institutions, and the people that have comprised the field over the past fifteen years.

Projects. First, then, let us recall some typical projects of three different eras: the late sixties, the mid-seventies, and today.

The AI projects of the late sixties were for the most part pure research; i.e., they were "guaranteed useless" in immediate practical terms, though their intellectual contributions were of great importance. As typical examples of that era we might select the celebrated General Problem Solver developed at Carnegie-Mellon University by Newell and Simon, the SHAKEY robot developed at Stanford Research Institute by Rosen, Nilsson and others, and the blocks world and shape-from-shading vision research pioneered at MIT by Horn and his colleagues.

By the mid-seventies, a new class of applied research projects took its place along side of the continuing stream of basic research projects. Good representatives of this class would be the influential MYCIN medical diagnosis system developed at Stanford by Shortliffe, and the LADDER system for English-language access to distributed databases developed at SRI by Hendrix and others. In addition, a group of "industrial vision" projects were exploring the applicability of earlier vision research to problems of inspection and part manipulation. The hallmark of these projects was their focus on problems of practical significance, though few in this class were brought to the marketplace.

Today, with both basic and applied research flourishing, a new class of commercial products has begun to appear. Examples of these are software products like Intellect, an English-language front end supplied by Artificial Intelligence Corporation, and KEE, a knowledge engineering tool offered by IntelliCorp. Examples of hardware products are the various Lisp workstations offered by Symbolics, Xerox, and others. In addition, a large number of visual inspection systems are being sold by a variety of vendors. In a sense, the emergence of products like these completes the conventional progression of basic research, applied research, and product development.

Institutions. As before, let us recall the institutional landscape of AI in the late sixties, mid-seventies, and today.

In the late sixties, at least in North America, the most prominent AI institutions were a small number of universities and contract R&D organizations; MIT, Stanford, Carnegie-Mellon, and SRI are prime examples. A notable exception to this rule was Xerox, which alone among large corporations (in the U.S.) established a significant AI group at this time.

By the mid-seventies, the traditionally strong AI universities and R&D organizations has been joined by a few more, but there was still very little activity in the private sector.

Today, of course, private sector interest in AI is growing explosively. Within the past few years, any number of major corporations have started significant individual efforts; Schlumberger and Digital Equipment Corporation are good examples. Multi-company consortia have been started in Japan, the U.S., and Europe, of which the Fifth Generation Project has attracted the most attention. In addition, many new companies have been formed to pursue opportunities in expert systems, natural language, and image understanding. Clearly, the big institutional changes of late have been in the private sector.

People. It is a bit harder to document the change in the population of "AI people" than it is for AI projects and institutions, but we can get some perspective by considering the influx of people from other disciplines. One measure of this is the attendance at AAAI and IJCAI tutorials, since these tutorials are typically attended by technologists and managers with little formal training or experience in AI.

The first tutorials, held at the 1980 AAAI meeting at Stanford, were attended by about 300 people. Starting from this base, attendance doubled in 1981 to 600, tripled in 1982 to 900, and in 1983 went up by a factor of six to some 1800 people. Evidently, someone out there is interested in learning more about artificial intelligence.

A Parallel: Genetic Engineering. We are told that those ignorant of the past are doomed to repeat it. With this admonition in mind, it is interesting to review developments in genetic engineering, a field whose recent history offers a striking resemblance to our own. Consider some of the parallels:

1. There is a general perception that a genuine revolution is at hand; extraordinary high payoffs are in the offing that go well beyond the normal evolution of a technology. (This perception apparently feeds on the fact that few understand in any detail what the revolution is about.)

2. At the outset of the perceived revolution virtually all the expertise is housed at universities or quasi-university research organizations. For practical purposes, no significant expertise exists in the private sector.

3. Next comes the race to exploit the revolutionary technology. New companies are formed, and large companies establish internal groups. Well over a hundred molecular genetic companies have been started in the past several years. For comparison, it is said that vision companies were being formed at the rate of one a week during 1982. As we have seen, many large companies are now building AI capabilities of some kind. For comparison, today every major drug house world-wide has a gene-manipulation activity of some sort.

4. Finally, philosophical or societal issues are raised concerning the moral or physical hazards associated with the revolution.

I would estimate that the field of genetic engineering is about three years ahead of AI in its evolution. We would do well to watch its development carefully, learn from its successes, and try to avoid its mistakes. (See Dickson [1985]).

Some Issues. All of these changes present many challenges for those who guide, or who participate in the development of, the field of AI. Since limitations of space force a selection, it seems to me most worth focusing on issues connected with the most radical changes in the field, *viz.*, the explosive growth in the private sector. Accordingly, I will consider problems associated with the development of AI products, with interactions between product development activities and research and educational activities, and with allied problems of communication with the vast majority of people who are not AI cognoscenti.

Issues for AI Development Activities. Many of the problems associated with the development of AI products are not unique to our field; similar generic problems exist in the development of virtually all software and hardware. However, the field of AI as a whole has thus far had little experience with these problems, and in any case there is value in recalling from time to time a few things that "everybody knows."

A first basic fact is that products based on AI technology compete in the marketplace with substitute products - i.e., with products based on different technologies that functionally substitute for the AI product. One example of this is the extent to which user-friendly front ends have substituted for natural-language (whether typed or spoken) front ends. Of course, a user-friendly system based, say, on menu selection may be less flexible than a large natural-language system. Further, one could always claim that future natural language front ends will ultimately be the preferred choice. Nonetheless, it is certainly true today that user-friendly systems, arguably based on a non-AI technology, have functionally substituted for AI products in many applications.

Other examples of substitute products can be found in virtually all areas of AI. In manufacturing automation, any problems of orienting and feeding parts can be done more easily by an old device called a bowl feeder than by a vision-based manipulator. Many kinds of classification problems can be solved by conventional statistical techniques more accurately than by a knowledge-based system. Naturally, all approaches have their limitations, and the extreme are usually obvious. (A large robot manipulator can handle parts upwards of a hundred pounds; a bowl feeder for parts that big would be the size of a large building.) Good judgment is required for dealing with the great majority of problems that fall between obvious extremes.

A second point is that AI products frequently do not stand alone. They are used with, or must be incorporated within, other systems in a larger context. For example, an organization interested in providing natural language front ends to databases might in short order discover that it was in the database business as much as it was in the natural language business. Similarly, a group involved with smart manipulators might discover that many of its problems involved visual or tactile sensing. This point and the preceding one suggest that breadth of technical view will be more important for successful applications than for successful research.

A third point is that we frequently underrate the value of simplicity. Many successful AI applications are based on old technology that is considered elementary at the time of its application. For example, many of today's commercial vision systems use approaches that were pioneered a decade ago. Some of the most valuable experience accumulated during that decade led to an understanding of which specific techniques could be applied to which specific tasks. Put differently, we learned what does not work, a lesson as valuable as learning what does work.

Notice, incidentally, that while I have used commercial applications as examples, these observations about AI development activities apply equally well in principle to defense applications.

Educational Issues. The AI transition places new stress and demands on the educational system. A full exposition of these issues would properly be a subject for a separate discussion; however, as before, we can gain some perspective by recalling past experience.

The late sixties were the era of what might be called the Universal AI Researcher. So little had been done that a researcher could attack problems in what today are rather separate sub-disciplines. Moreover, virtually everyone in the field at that time was a migrant from some other discipline: to some extent, AI education at that time consisted of finding such migrants and teaching them Lisp.

By the mid-seventies, the educational system was considerably more mature. Interest in applied AI research - together with the emergence of rather clear distinctions between sub-disciplines such as vision and natural language - had an effect on shaping AI education.

Today, as development activities become more prominent, it will be important for the educational system to recognize new needs. Specifically, we can anticipate that AI education will become more like conventional computer science or electrical engineering education, with different curricula and degrees for research, teaching, and development careers.

R and D Interactions - The Innovation Trajectory. For at least the past four decades, high technology products have been the end result of what has been called a trajectory of innovation. As the figure suggests, the early part of the trajectory is the basic research phase. Most research is funded by the public sector, with relatively low accountability for results, and is performed in university or quasi-university environments. As time progresses and ideas are refined, projects move through an applied research phase toward the product development phase. Private funding becomes far more significant and greater emphasis is placed on achieving workable solutions.

It is interesting to note that this general trajectory has to some extent not been followed by AI in recent years. Some of the most widely cited applied developments have come from universities, while some very significant basic research results have been obtained in privately funded industrial laboratories. This compression, and even inversion, of the conventional innovation trajectory is one sign of the AI transition. It is not clear that it is a healthy sign, but in any event it is likely to be an anomaly that will disappear in a short time.

It does, however, suggest that more attention be paid to the continuing question of what the appropriate mix is of basic research, applied research, and development projects. The answers will of course be very different for various types of institutions, but one can argue on general grounds that a thoughtful policy has a better chance of being right than a non-policy that exists only by default.

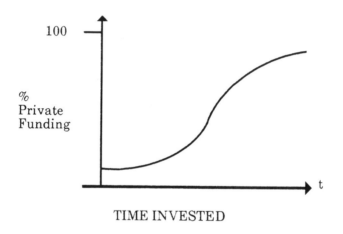

TIME INVESTED

The Innovation Trajectory

Figure 1.

Communications. Communications problems have increased in AI as the number of interested constituencies has grown. Again, a backward look gives some perspective on current problems.

Some fifteen years ago, there were two principal constituencies: those who performed AI research and those who funded it. The funders were public sector agencies such as the Defense Advanced Research Projects Agency, the National Science Foundation, and the Office of Naval Research. These agencies - without which the field of AI would not exist in anything like its present form - often had great technical sophistication, and in fact were staffed in part with people from the field. The relative homogeneity of these constituencies made communication between them easy. (Of course, understanding the other person doesn't necessarily mean you agree with him!)

Today there are many other interested constituencies, and the great variability in their backgrounds and motivations have made communications for more difficult. The performers of AI now include a full range of research, applied research, and development people housed in a variety of organizations. Funders of AI have broadened to include less sophisticated public agencies as well as representatives of the private sector. Moreover, there are now user populations (there was very little to use 15 years ago) who need to be educated and supported. Finally, the public at large has been made aware of AI and the Fifth Generation, and has (for the moment at least) great interest in the problems and opportunities.

One consequence of the proliferation of constituencies is that communication has become, to some degree, stenographic. Indeed, there are--unfortunately-- many instances where content has collapsed to form. For example, a senior executive in a large high technology company may decide to develop "an expert system to do X," where X might be so unfortunate a choice as "design a major new computer system." From the executive's point of view there are (human) experts who do X, and since expert systems evidently duplicate human expertise very little further discussion is needed.

As this example illustrates, a particularly delicate communications problem exists at the interface between senior AI technologists and senior operating officials of either public or private organizations. Opportunities for misunderstanding abound, and managing the communication channel is itself a substantial challenge.

A broader challenge centers on how we communicate with the public at large. With the current intense interest in our field, we all need to be aware of our responsibility to communicate honestly and accurately the accomplishments, the potential, and the present limitations of AI. The media will be happy to oblige us if we adopt a policy of "better infamous than anonymous."

3. TECHNICAL ISSUES

The range of opinion about the most important questions facing AI is at least as diverse as the current crop of research proposals. Rather than attempt to list or prioritize issues in a fine-grained way, I would like to consider three broad classes of problems that seem important for AI to address. These may be characterized as three types of complexity to be dealt with: conceptual complexity, computational complexity, and developmental complexity. Most of my attention will be spent on the first of these, the other two receiving only cursory consideration.

Conceptual Complexity. All of us understand at an intuitive level that some systems are more complex conceptually than others, although we have no crisp definition or quantitative measure for this notion. Notwithstanding this lack, it seems to me useful to consider systems at two different levels of complexity and to introduce the metaphor of surface systems versus deep systems.

By surface systems I mean those having no underlying representation of such fundamental concepts as causality, intent, or basic physical principles; deep systems, by contrast, attempt to represent concepts at this level. At the extremes, a surface system directly associates input states with actions, whereas a deep system makes deductions from a compact collection of fundamental principles.

The metaphor is made clearer by considering some examples.

Example 1. The HARPY and HEARSAY II system are both speech understanding systems (Lowerre and Reddy [1980], Reddy et al. [1976]). HARPY compiles all knowledge of speech and language into a graph that is then searched to find a legal utterance, whereas HEARSAY II has explicit representations for knowledge at phonetic, syntactic, semantic, and other levels. I would characterize HARPY as a surface system and HEARSAY II as a deep system.

Example 2. MYCIN and CASNET (Shortliffe [1976], Weiss et al. [1978]) are both systems for diagnosing medical problems. MYCIN works on backtracking on a set of production rules that link observation and conclusion, while CASNET attempts to model the causal relations among the detailed disease states of a family of diseases (glaucomas). The first system is a surface system, the second a deep system.

Example 3. Rl and QUAL (McDermott [1980], de Kleer [1979]), are both systems dealing with engineering tasks. Rl analyzes VAX configurations by chaining through a set of production rules, while QUAL attempts to represent the causal and teleological relations associated with electrical networks. Again, the first is a surface system, the second a deep system.

Deep and surface systems have different properties, as illustrated in Figure 2 (which was originally suggested by Gary Hendrix in a more limited context). A task of modest difficulty can be performed at a cost of lower complexity by a surface system than by a deep system. As the task difficulty increases (or as we increase our aspirations for the system), the complexity of the surface system grows as new features are added and patches are made. Ultimately, a barrier is reached at a point where the underlying representations used by the surface system are simply inadequate.

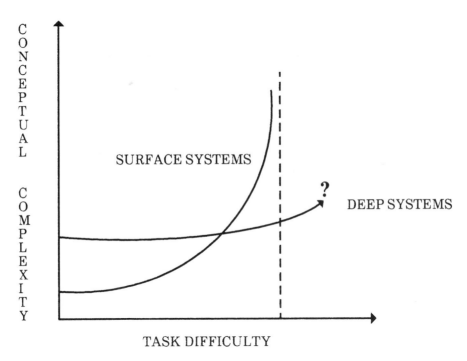

Figure 2. Deep vs. surface systems.

By contrast, deep systems have a higher startup cost for tasks of modest difficulty; the hope, of course, is that they are ultimately able to do tasks of greater difficulty.

Put differently, surface systems are the ones that currently "work." Most practical applications systems, or impressive demonstrations that appear to be close to applications, are likely to be surface systems. Deep systems tend to be the research vehicles of the field; they may be nameless, slow, and are likely to deal with very restricted problem domains.

It is worth noting that we do not understand the properties of surface and deep systems very well. Most obviously, what are the performance limitations of surface systems? Although we cannot answer that question in a satisfying way, we do know that the performance of the current generation of surface systems is substantially greater than many knowledgeable workers would have anticipated in the mid-70's.

Symmetrically, what is the minimum knowledge base needed for deep systems to "work"? It may be that there is a critical mass point beyond which the performance of deep systems can be improved with relative ease. (This is the premise behind the KLAUS project (Haas and Hendrix [1980]).

Finally, there is the interesting possibility of combining deep and surface systems into a multi-level system that offers some of the best features of both. This possibility is sufficiently engaging that I would like, by means of an example, to explore it next.

Multi-Level Systems. Well-codified scientific and engineering disciplines offer perhaps the best domains in which to explore multi-level systems. In such fields, it is common to have models which purport to represent "reality" at varying levels of fidelity. For example, electrical engineers are comfortable with the general distinction between linear, lumped-parameter systems and non-linear, distributed systems. As a specific example, I will select a problem from the field of petroleum engineering that illustrates many of the basic issues.

A central notion in petroleum engineering is a petroleum reservoir, a body of different types of rock containing crude oil, gas, and water in its pores. A central problem is to understand the reservoir in sufficient detail to allow an efficient recovery scheme to be planned. (There is a large economic incentive to do this well, since it is usually economic to extract only about a third of the oil in a given reservoir.) When examined in detail, the simple notion of a body of porous rock containing three types of fluids expands into an enormously complex physical object. For example, even though - roughly speaking - gas floats on top of oil, which floats on top of water, in reality physical effects result in each pore containing varying "saturations" of the three fluid types. The movement of the fluids through the rock, which of course occurs during oil production, is governed by such things as the permeability of the rock and the viscosity of the fluids. The compressibility of the rock, as well as the temperatures and pressures through the rock, all play an important role.

To represent this complexity, petroleum engineers have developed models at several levels of detail. I will describe two existing models, after first suggesting a purely hypothetical model that could have been invented in the course of an AI project aimed at creating an expert system for petroleum engineering. Here, then are three levels of models ranging from surface to deep, for this domain (no puns intended).

Surface Level Model. We can imagine a rule-based system for guiding a petroleum engineer in his work. A single rule from this imaginary system might look something like this:

IF:

The reservoir is volumetric

AND:

There is no gas cap

THEN:

Pressure is less than the bubble point.

While a rule of this type may contain information important to the user, it does not represent notions like physical causality in any obvious way.

Second Level Model. A simple quantitative model of a petroleum reservoir is called a tank model. It represents the reservoir as a sealed tank, with all movement of fluids out of the tank occurring only via an oil well. Algebraically, the model balances the volume of fluid removed with an expansion of the rock and fluid remaining ("nature abhors vacuum"). As the remaining rock and fluid expands, the pressure in the reservoir must drop.

This model can be thought of as a form of lumped parameter model; there is no consideration of how fluids move through the reservoir. The model does, however, in some sense capture gross notions of physical causality ("remove some fluid $=>$ remaining matter expands $=>$ pressure drops"). In terms of complexity, the tank model leads to back-of-the-envelope types of computations; nevertheless, it is useful to make rough estimates, and to check on the validity of other, more detailed, calculations.

Deep Model. The most detailed representation available to model a reservoir consists of a set of partial differential equations. Physically, these equations embody some appealingly intuitive ideas. For example, one component of the model is Darcy's Law, which simply states that the movement of fluid is driven by the pressure gradient and opposed by the "resistance" (literally, the permeability) of the rock. Another component of the model is the continuity equation, which effectively states "everything has to be someplace."

Although the intuitive notions are easy to grasp, the mathematical details are formidable. The equations cannot be solved analytically and are simulated computationally as a set of difference equations instead. The simulator itself is a large piece of code representing a large investment in software. (The cost of acquiring the source code of a commercial simulator can amount to several hundred thousand dollars.) Reservoir simulators are limited not only by computational costs, but by the need to provide them with a very large number of parameters ahead of time; these parameters are not readily available in typical situations. These difficulties notwithstanding, simulators embody the deepest "physical" representation of the complex phenomenon of a petroleum reservoir.

Issues for Multi-Level Systems. The foregoing example illustrates how several levels of models provide different perspectives on the same underlying "reality." In principle, it should be possible to use these levels for purposes of validation, explanation, and control. The details of how this can be done, of course, are far from obvious. Some specific issues that need to be addressed are:

For a given problem domain, important levels of representation have to be identified. It may turn out that these levels do not arrange themselves in a strictly hierarchical way. For example, the law of conservation of energy, though simply stated, is not normally thought of as an approximation to some more complex and more accurate statement.

A second issue is the selection of representational formalisms for each level of model. Specifically, the issue of communication among levels will be important.

A third issue is the identification of formal relations that may - or should - exist between levels. In physics, for example, the Correspondence Principle states that the formulas of quantum mechanics simplify to the formulas of Newtonian mechanics when evaluated for "ordinary" values of energy and velocity. Should this be a general principle for multi-level systems?

Finally, there is the issue of how multiple levels of representation can be exploited. Can surface models guide the application of deep models effectively? How can a system recognize the limits of its own applicability in non-trivial ways? When can a "back-of-the-envelope" model be used to check the plausibility of an answer derived at a different level? More interestingly, can a surface model be "compiled" from a deep model to generate a faster system? Artificial intelligence as a field has little experience with these issues, although some precedents exist (e.g., Sacerdoti [1977], Patil et al. [1981]).

Computational and Developmental Complexity. Along with the general problem of conceptual complexity, we face the problem that our programs have apparently unbounded appetites for cycles and memory. The computational demands made by AI programs make it natural to consider whether VLSI-based architectures can be developed for "AI-style" computation. Of specific interest would be architectures that provide high levels of concurrency. Today, we know in principle how to achieve this for very regular computations, such as those associated with early vision processing. Much less is known about how to achieve high levels of concurrency for less regular computations, although some serious suggestions have been put forth (Hewitt [1980], Fahlman [1980]).

An opposing point of view is that striving for concurrency is likely to be unproductive, because it pits at best a constant speed-up factor against exponential computations. It seems to me that this argument, while asymptotically valid, misses the point that finite-factor speed-ups can lead to significant improvements in performance in non-asymptotic situations. (This may be one of the lessons to be learned from work in chess-playing systems.)

While AI is likely to reap large benefits from advances in VLSI technology, it is symmetrically the case that VLSI can benefit from work at AI. Designing and testing VLSI systems has reached the point where complexity itself has become the major issue. AI techniques for representation, problem solving, and convenient interaction with machines should all help in easing these problems. Further, the possibility of realizing AI functions in VLSI opens the way to new applications of silicon technology. (See, for example, Sussman et al. [1981]).

The cost of designing and implementing AI programs - and the knowledge bases they may require - represents another very real obstacle to progress on both research and applications fronts. It is not unusual for large AI systems efforts to absorb 10 - 25 man-years of effort, which represents a substantial commitment of resources. Accordingly, although almost any field can be subject to a Parkinsonian charge of being overly preoccupied with tool-building, I think that we must as a field continue to press for better programming environments, better knowledge-acquisition tools, and computational resources that adequately support scarce and costly human resources.

REFERENCES

deKleer, J., *Causal and Teleological Reasoning in Circuit Recognition*, MIT AI Laboratory Report AI-TR-529, September 1979.

Dickson, E. M., "Comparing Artificial Intelligence and Genetic Engineering: Commercialization Lesson," *AI Magazine*, Vol. 5, No. 4, Winter 1985.

Fahlman, S., "Design Sketch for a Million-Element NETL Machine," *Proc. First Annual National Conference on Artificial Intelligence*, pp. 249 - 252, 1980.

Haas, N., and G. G. Hendrix, "An Approach to Acquiring and Applying Knowledge," *Proc. First Annual National Conference on Artificial Intelligence*, Stanford University, pp. 235 - 239, August 18 - 21, 1980.

Hewitt, C., "The Apiary Network Architecture for Knowledgeable Systems," *Proc. LISP Conference*, Stanford, California, pp. 107 - 118, August 1980.

Lowerre, B. and R. Reedy, "The HARPY Speech Understanding System," in *Trends in Speech Recognition*, W. Lea (ed.), Prentice-Hall, Englewood Cliffs, N. J., 1980.

McDermott, J., "RI An Expert in the Computer Systems Domain," *Proc. First Annual National Conference on Artificial Intelligence*, Stanford University, August 18 - 21, 1981.

Patil, R. S., P. Szolovits, and W. B. Schwartz, "Causal Understanding of Patient Illness in Medical Diagnosis," *Proc. Seventh International Joint Conference on Artificial Intelligence*, pp. 893 - 899, Vancouver, B. C., Canada, August 24 - 28, 1981.

Reddy, R., L. Erman, R. Fennell, and R. Neely, "The HEARSAY Speech Understanding System: An Example of the Recognition Process," *IEEE Transactions on Computers C-25*, pp. 427 - 431, 1976.

Sacerdoti, E., *A Structure for Plans and Behavior*, American Elsevier, New York, 1977.

√ Shortliffe, E. H., *Computer-Based Medical Consultations: MYCIN*, American Elsevier, New York, 1976.

Sussman, G. J., J. Holloway, G. L. Steele, and A. Bell, "Scheme-79-LISP on a Chip," *Computer*, Vol. 14, No., 7, pp. 10 - 21, July 1981.

Weiss, S., C. Kulikowski, and A. Safir, "Glaucoma Consultation by Computer," in *Computers in Biology and Medicine*, Vol. 8, pp. 25 - 40, 1978.

10

THE INDUSTRIALIZATION
OF ARTIFICIAL INTELLIGENCE

S. JERROLD KAPLAN
TEKNOWLEDGE, INC.
PALO ALTO, CALIFORNIA

Over the past few years, the character of the AI community has changed. AI researchers used to be able to go about their work in peace, while the rest of the world ignored them. As the promise of practical applications of AI has slowly become reality, new players have entered the field, changing its nature forever. The quiet, intellectual community of AI researchers has been augmented by a hoard of other interested parties, including the press, the financial community, and the technology entrepreneurs.

Since we cannot go back and hide in the ivory tower, we may as well take the time to explore our new environment. I invite you to join me in a guided tour of the new AI community. Let's begin by analyzing the basic motivation for the commercial interest in AI.

THE "VALUE-ADDED" OF ARTIFICIAL INTELLIGENCE

Artificial intelligence is not in itself a commercial field, but a science and a technology. As an academic discipline, it is a collection of concepts and ideas which are appropriate for research, but which cannot be marketed. However, artificial intelligence is the scientific foundation for several growing commercial technologies. The three most important are robotics and vision (which for simplicity's sake I will consider as one field), natural language processing, and knowledge engineering. Supporting markets are forming which will provide hardware and software tools for use in these three areas.

Reprinted with permission from *The AI Magazine*, Vol. 5, No. 2, 1984, published by the American Association for Artificial Intelligence

ARTIFICIAL INTELLIGENCE VS. NATURAL INTELLIGENCE

The potential value of Artificial Intelligence can be better understood by contrasting it with natural intelligence. Artificial intelligence has several important commercial advantages:

- AI has *permanence*. Natural intelligence is perishable from a commercial standpoint in that employees can change their place of employment or forget information and techniques. Artificial Intelligence, however, is as permanent as computer systems and programs.

- AI offers *ease of duplication*. Transferring a body of knowledge from one person to another usually requires a lengthy process of apprenticeship: even so, expertise can never be naturally duplicated. However, when knowledge is embodied in a computer system it can be copied and easily moved to another location.

- AI can be *less expensive* than natural intelligence. There are many circumstances in which buying a small or even a large computer costs less than having corresponding human power carry out those same tasks.

- AI - being a computer technology - *is consistent and thorough*. Natural intelligence is erratic because people are erratic; they don't perform consistently.

- AI is *documentable*. Decisions made by a computer can be documented by tracing the activities of the system. Natural intelligence is difficult to reproduce in the sense that a person may reach a conclusion, but at some later date be unable to recreate the reasoning process that led to it or even to recall the assumptions that were a part of it.

Let me stress that I am in no way suggesting that artificial intelligence is generally superior to natural intelligence - simply that it is different. To present a balanced picture, let's take a brief look at some advantages of natural intelligence:

- Natural intelligence is creative, whereas artificial intelligence is rather uninspired. The ability to acquire knowledge is inherent in human beings, but with artificial intelligence, tailored knowledge must be built into a carefully constructed system.

- Natural intelligence enables people to benefit by and use sensory experience directly, whereas artificial intelligence systems must work with symbolic input.

- Perhaps most important of all, human beings in their reasoning processes are able to make use at all times of a very wide context of experience and bring that to bear on each individual problem, whereas artificial intelligence systems typically gain their power by having a very narrow focus.

A look, however, at the previously mentioned advantages of AI over natural intelligence - permanence, ease of duplication, cost effectiveness, consistency and thoroughness, and documentability - reveals that the list really describes the advantages of computer systems in general, not just AI systems. This seems to suggest that the commercial advantages of AI are derived from the nature of computational systems themselves, not from symbolic processing techniques. I'd like to explore further this intriguing hypothesis by contrasting two fields which I see as structurally related: data processing and knowledge engineering.

Knowledge engineering is the representation and use of symbolic knowledge in electronic form to solve problems that normally require human intelligence or attention. The primary difference between data processing and knowledge engineering is that data processing deals with the representation and use of data, whereas knowledge engineering deals with the representation and use of knowledge. Data processing is concerned with algorithmic, repetitive processes: knowledge engineering is concerned with judgmental and inferential processes. Data processing is focused on the efficient handling of large data bases and large numbers of transactions, but knowledge engineering is concerned with the effective handling of knowledge bases and decisions. Despite the difference, there is a clear correspondence between the goals of these two fields.

In short, a hard look in a broader context reveals that AI simply extends the current commercial advantages of computer systems - their speed, accuracy, consistency, availability, and affordability - from clerical to intellectual applications.

One final thought on this subject: This extension of the role of computer systems is likely to go essentially unnoticed by the end-users of these systems. Most people interact with computers in limited ways - they do not have the same sense of the boundaries of computer technology that a computer scientist develops. To most people, computers are tools that help them solve certain specific problems - word processing, filing, billing, budget planning, etc. Each year, new and more useful applications are added. AI-based systems will simply expand the range of new applications most people experience - its business as usual. Indeed, good evidence for this is that most companies incorporating AI end-user systems into their products (as opposed to selling tools to the AI community) rarely mention AI in their promotional material.

THE DEVELOPMENT OF COMMERCIAL MARKETS

I am often asked by people investigating the field what industries AI will benefit. Where will it be used - oil, medicine, manufacturing, consumer goods, etc.? The problem with this question is that it is a little like asking where computers can be used. The benefits do not fall along normal industry lines, but rather along certain classes of use.

Nonetheless, our experience at Teknowledge to date does suggest that there are three basic segments to the commercial market for knowledge systems (the end-product of knowledge engineering projects). These are the industrial segment, the service segment, and the management segment.

Some typical industrial applications are in scheduling, production planning, maintenance, process control, and quality assurance. Many of the systems you are likely to have heard about, in the oil industry, mining, manufacturing, etc. are likely to fall into this category.

In the service sector, some typical applications are in automation of routine advice, standardization of service, quality control, worker productivity, advice on accessing and using computer systems, and training. Perhaps the most interesting of these applications are the first two, automation of routine advice and standardization of service. Knowledge based systems can handle relatively routine questions that require a minimum of intelligence. For example, a person opening a bank account usually needs advice on what type of account is most appropriate, given his or her particular mix of financial characteristics. Given the changing character of the banking industry, systems providing routine advice that accurately reflects the particular services of that bank would have a tremendous impact on, and value to, that organization. Second, in terms of standardizing service, it is very difficult for banks to ensure that their personnel are trained in the same ways, give the same advice, and provide the same level of service. Using a knowledge-based system would ensure that the level of service that is provided to each customer is constant, controlled, and monitored. These same advantages accrue to a wide variety of service industries that are concerned with the dissemination of accurate and timely knowledge, such as travel planning, real estate, accounting, medicine, and sales consulting.

Surprisingly, the third segment of the market for knowledge systems is the management area. One important problem, in fact the single most critical problem for today's large corporations, is the syndication of "corporate culture." Each corporation has its own view of what it is, how it does business, how it is positioned. It is extremely difficult to inculcate an entire organization - which may encompass thousands of people - with the corporate culture. A system which distributes the corporate culture by providing advice and guidance to people faced with business decisions could help to focus and align the efforts of the organization. Knowledge systems could also be built to aid in strategic planning and fusing information from many diverse sources (where managers may not have the time or inclination to cull out what they really need).

A structure is emerging for the insertion of knowledge-based technology into the industrial, service, and management market segments. Figure 1 is a graph of the development of knowledge engineering technology over time versus the payoff or perceived impact of the systems.

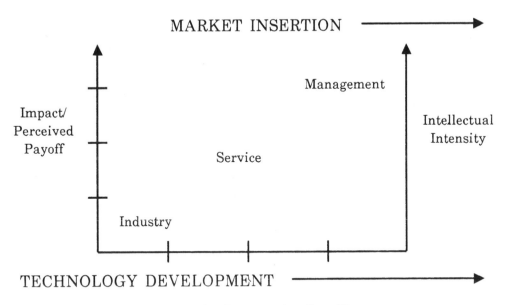

Knowledge Engineering Over Time
Figure 1.

For a variety of reasons, principally social, the insertion of knowledge engineering technology into the commercial sector appears to be moving from industrial, to service, and finally to management applications.

Industrial applications have been the first major area of impact, primarily because these potential applications are the most visible and most accessible to knowledge engineers. Now, we are seeing increased activity in the service sector, as people in that sector - less accustomed to seeking out technological innovations - begin to recognize the potential value of knowledge engineering to their businesses. Finally, as central corporate staffs become aware of the technology, they are considering applications to the management of organizations. There has been little actual work and even less publicity about this last area, but it is growing.

The expected value of knowledge systems increases in proportion to the "intellectual intensity" of the applications. As indicated in Figure 1, management applications tend to be more intellectual than service applications, which in turn tend to be more intellectual than industrial applications. Thus, the payoffs of operational systems will escalate as the focus shifts from industry to service to management.

In a sense, all commercial problems are really management problems: they result from failure to plan and apply resources effectively, misunderstanding of markets, and inability to recognize and exploit organizational strengths to achieve tactical advantages. We may eventually find that the highest payoffs will be derived from applications in the management area. Improving the productivity of a manufacturing facility is important, but not as important as correctly determining whether the plant should be operated in the first place.

Turning to the other various commercial technologies within AI, we note that each major area - robotics and vision, natural language, and knowledge engineering - has a natural market segment which it addresses. Figure 2 points out that robotics and vision mainly have applications in the industrial segment, natural language mostly deals with the service and management segments, and knowledge engineering can be applied to all three.

THE BARRIERS TO COMMERCIALIZATION

Although the press glorifies the promise of AI, there are some significant barriers to the commercialization of AI technologies.

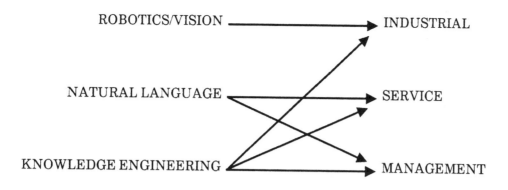

Applictions of Artificial Intelligence.
Figure 2.

The first and biggest barrier is the abstract quality of artificial intelligence. This makes AI difficult for customers to comprehend and distinguish from other technologies. Many people who perceive a great value in artificial intelligence do not know how to apply it. In fact, there is a growing subindustry of people who help organizations decide where to apply artificial intelligence. Artificial intelligence could be described as a solution in search of problem.

A second barrier to commercialization is unrealistic expectations about the actual capabilities of the technology and the length of its gestation period. When people don't see results occur as soon as they expect, they may be disappointed.

There are three basic sources of unrealistic expectations in today's arena. The first is the amount of media attention given in the field. There are a great many articles published about artificial intelligence; a kind of "AI fever" is sweeping the press. Unfortunately, if the media don't see results that they can say something interesting about within the next year, they may swing the other way.

The second source is charlatanism, most of which is unintentional. Just about everybody is climbing on the AI bandwagon. Many companies are falsely claiming that their products "contain AI," as though this were an ingredient they recently added.

A major source of unrealistic expectations is being created by excessive government funding commitments combined with a shortage of qualified AI researchers. In the next few years, the government will probably submit hundreds of millions of dollars' worth of requests for proposals involving AI research. If there are not enough researchers to carry out these projects, government funding for AI may be cut later on.

Another barrier to the commercialization of artificial intelligence is the slow growth of the technical prerequisites and development of expertise. While there is a distinct shortage of experienced personnel who have a background in artificial intelligence, the people who do have the experience often do not have an understanding of real business problems. Many of the new AI companies must reeducate their academically oriented technicians to understand what value the clients will receive from the systems that the company develops.

Besides a shortage of human expertise, there is also a shortage of reliable, supported tools for performing AI activities. Many companies, including Teknowledge, are working to make the technology more accessible by supplying more sophisticated commercial tools.

Curiously, a significant barrier to commercialization can be traced directly to the terms "artificial intelligence" and "expert systems" themselves, with their cognitive connotations. If we think of artificial intelligence as simply imitating natural intelligence, we will miss its real commercial value. This "machine replaces human" orientation obscures the true potential of the field - extending the use of the computer as a commercial tool. Accepting and understanding the technology would be much easier if the field were called something like "symbolic processing" - arguably a much more descriptive name. To compound this problem, the term "artificial intelligence" has a rather bad reputation in some circles - it is identified with large, slow, impractical systems.

The term "expert systems" is equally problematic. It suggests that the role of the technology is to replace experts. In fact, knowledge engineering is a means to capture, reason about, distribute, and use symbolic knowledge in an organization. This knowledge doesn't necessarily have to come from experts; in fact, for practical reasons it is greatly preferable if it doesn't. It may come from manuals, documents, databases, procedures, schedules, or other passive sources, but it becomes much more useful when represented and distributed electronically in a symbolic form. At Teknowledge, when we are asked to identify high-value applications, we seek out "knowledge bottlenecks," where knowledge is poorly distributed, rapidly changing, or too voluminous to handle conveniently on a routine basis. Most often this does not involve an "expert."

Finally, utilizing AI technology within a commercial organization requires imagination and creativity. AI systems may change the structure of the business, rather than augment or replace existing systems. The application of AI will create novel opportunities, but actually identifying these opportunities might require some creative thinking.

THE IMPACT OF COMMERCIALIZATION ON AI RESEARCHERS

Until recently, AI researchers have worked mostly in the academic community. As they have ventured out into the commercial sector, they have discovered that the rules of the game are different. Techniques useful for success in academic institutions do not transfer well to business organizations.

For instance, consider the problem of selecting an appropriate domain of application for a system. In the academic community, research must lead to publishable papers. Therefore, selected applications should be interesting to peers and resistant to criticism ("That's an easy problem"). It is often helpful to select a problem requiring collaboration with professors in other departments - they may prove valuable allies when applying for grants or being considered for tenure. Consequently, the classic academic applications have been extremely sophisticated problems, such as medical diagnosis and scientific discovery. By picking difficult problems, the research has contributed tremendously to our understanding of the field.

In a commercial environment, it is best to select easier problems. These may be less interesting, but they usually have payoffs comparable to those of hard problems and lower technical risk. Applications are selected to improve productivity, enhance products and services, and increase profits.

Most academic researchers develop only prototype systems. However, selecting a problem and implementing a prototype are only a very small portion of the overall effort required to field and maintain an operational system. A commercial AI company must be able to handle documentation, training, and quality assurance; analyze the requirements for a final, fielded system; and integrate, operate, and maintain that system. Figure 3 shows that these activities absorb most of a company's time and resources.

Finally, artificial intelligence researchers must undergo an unusual psychological transition when they move from the academic to the business community. In the academic world, researchers compete internally with their colleagues for resources, students, and tenure slots. However, they tend to cooperate externally, in part, because funding agencies favor inter-institution or inter-disciplinary proposals. In a business environment, researchers cooperate internally to achieve results, but compete externally with other companies for a share of the market and for commercial and technical advantage.

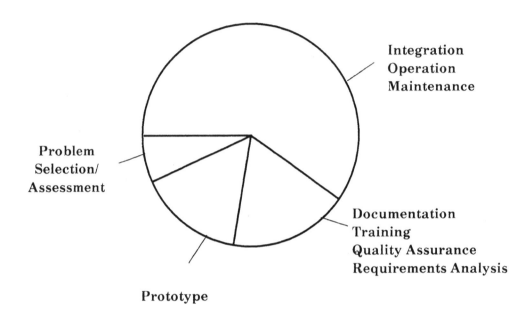

The Organizational/Operational Environment.
Figure 3.

A LOOK TO THE FUTURE

Venturing into the dangerous province of the futurist, let me make some modest predictions on the development of the field for the next few years, followed by some wild speculation on where we might be after the next few decades.

One question is whether artificial intelligence will remain a distinct discipline, carried out by identifiable and separate groups, or whether it will be subsumed into the larger mass of data processing and computer technology in general. It now seems clear that separate artificial intelligence groups will perform artificial intelligence work. For example, many large corporations, probably 40 or 50 in the U.S. alone, have formed knowledge engineering departments and are providing their staffs with equipment separate from the company's data processing equipment. This implies that, in the short run at least, artificial intelligence will remain a distinct technology.

A second question is how the market for artificial intelligence products will be structured. The market now forming can be described as three hierarchical levels. At the bottom are AI tool suppliers, who supply hardware and software to development groups. These groups - the next hierarchical level - use these tools to build systems for specific applications, so-called "vertical systems." The top level are the purchasers of these problem-solving systems. As discussed earlier, the fact that they are buying artificial intelligence systems may be invisible to this market.

Let's look in more detail at the suppliers of AI tools. There are two types of tools - hardware tools and software tools. On the hardware side, virtually every major computer manufacturing is watching the market closely. Since the barriers to entering the hardware tools market are relatively low, in the next couple of years there will probably be heavy competition in the manufacturing of work stations for symbolic processing.

Similarly, there is likely to be a flood of software tools entering the market. For a period of time, these tools will be nearly indistinguishable, as similar claims will be made for the best and the worst of them. Unlike the benchmarks for hardware, however, there is no easy way to compare the power and quality of software tools. Compounding this problem, most first-time tool purchasers don't know how to use the tools, and, therefore, can't easily determine if one is more appropriate for their problem than another. Over time, however, the market will shake out. Software tool suppliers that can exploit practical experience to design useful tools, help train their customers to select problems, and provide applications consulting will dominate in this market.

Vertical systems will probably be built by two different types of organizations. The first type consists of internal departments of major corporations that for all practical purposes function as specialized, captive companies. These will use AI tools to enhance and deliver the products and services of their parent organization.

The second type consists of specialized companies which usually attack some particular vertical market segment. These organizations are not "selling AI"; rather, they are selling a product or service which incorporates AI to some other market. For example, an AI company that builds expert systems for financial

321

institutions is in the financial consulting business and uses AI as a means to deliver their service. In short, the organizations that build vertical systems are quite distinct from the organizations that supply them with the tools they need.

Looking into the crystal ball, it is interesting to speculate on where we might find things in the more distant future. I will discuss the three major commercial AI technologies separately.

The development of robotics and vision systems will probably lead to the creation of much more generalized machines. Today, a wide variety of machines provides specific solutions to specific kinds of problems. In the future, there will be more general machines, which will provide a cost-effective replacement for a number of more specialized machines. As with general computing machines, volume production will offset the individual inefficiency of applying these machines to individual tasks for which they may be less than optimal.

To bring this point down to earth, imagine the effect on the typical household of a robot that could perform general chores. If this device were to exist, it would provide an inexhaustible pool of cheap domestic labor, and the economic structure for building special-purpose machines would disappear. Dishes could be washed by hand (so to speak), as could clothes, eliminating the dishwasher, washer, and dryer. Cans would be opened "manually". Vacuums, mops, carpet sweepers, brooms, and other labor-saving cleaning aids would be unnecessary, since surfaces could simply be scrubbed or brushed when required. In this vision, homes in the next century would look more than those in the last century than those of today - simpler, more comprehensible, less technological.

Natural language will eventually provide the means for people to interface effectively with the remaining simplified technology, and to increase its accessibility and utilization. Today, most people are somewhat alienated from the technology around them. With the development of robotics and natural language, people will feel much more integrated; they will have a greater sense of control over their environment.

Eventually, knowledge engineering systems will perform simple, day-to-day cognitive tasks, such as giving directions, planning, aiding human memory, directing traffic, scanning the news to select information of interest, helping to select merchandise and vendors. More important, knowledge engineering will revolutionize the way knowledge is captured and distributed. Today, there are two ways to capture and distribute knowledge - through teaching and through books, films, and other media. However, these methods and the knowledge they transmit are rarely as accessible or useful as a knowledge system could be.

One interesting effect will be to improve communication and flow of information in our society. Since markets (such as stock exchanges) thrive on the differential distribution of information, we can expect these functions to abate, or disappear altogether. There is no reason to advertise or promote if every potential customer has access to perfect information about the suitability of a given product or service for their specific needs. In this case, nearly everything would become a commodity.

Besides improving the overall quality of our lives, these changes are likely to alter many people's perception that they are drowning in masses of useless information. Knowledge will be available where and when it is needed, in a useful, integrated form. Rather than being inundated with radio, television, magazines, junk mail, and advertising, life should seem simpler and quieter.

CONCLUSION

As AI technologies have begun to fulfill their commercial promise, new constituencies have appeared with vested interests in developing and applying artificial intelligence outside of the research environment. These newcomers have created some concern or discomfort in the academic community: How will this expanded interest affect AI researchers and their institutions? Will it disrupt the flow students, faculty, and funding? Will the AAAI annual meetings turn into massive trade-show extravaganzas?

The first step to answering these questions lies in recognizing that these changes in the AI community are both natural and inevitable. Just as the emergence of commercial computer technology ultimately enhanced the quality and quantity of computer science education and research, this new interest in applied artificial intelligence will in the long run attract more students, faculty, and funding into basic AI research.

In the short run, however, there will be a brief period of instability, when commercial and academic segments appear to compete for resources and dominance. Once the commercial segment has matured, it will have the resources and motivation to support and enhance basic research in the field, just as in any other science associated with commercial uses.

I believe it is in the best long-term interests of the AI community to facilitate and plan for this transformation. Fundamental to this process is to accept two principles: that the interests of the new constituency are legitimate and that the commercial segment will ultimately come to be viewed by the public as dominant.

What we are experiencing is a natural growth of artificial intelligence from its academic roots to productive application within society. On balance, the effects of this growth can only prove positive to the AI community and society at large. As scientists, we must be prepared to face the new responsibilities and challenges that this transition brings.

INDEX

INDEX

Buchanan, B. G., 2, 31, 69, 98, 104
Building Expert Systems (BES) (Hayes-Roth), 28
Bundy, A., 176
Burton, R. R., 31
Buzbee, B. L., 193

CAD (computer-aided design), 214
CADUCEUS, 47, 48
Case-specific model, 47-48
CASNET, 43-45, 48, 304
Causal models, for second generation expert systems, 272
Causal-process classification, 39, 42-43
Causal relations, heuristic classification and, 25-26
CENTAUR, 55
Certainty factors:
  in Expertise Transfer System (ETS), 81-84
  in LITHO, 174-75
Chandrasekaran, B., 55, 58
Chi, M.T.H., 56
Clancey, W. J., 1, 39, 40, 51, 106
Classes, attributes as relation among, 17
Classification:
  causal-process, 39, 42-43
  definition of, 4-5
  heuristic (*See* Heuristic classification)
  problems of, 27
  simple, 22, 27
CLOT, 176
Cohen, B., 14, 57
Commercialization of artificial intelligence, 311-23
  advantages of AI and, 312-13
  barriers to, 316-19
  development of markets and, 314-16
  future of, 320-23
  impact on AI researchers, 319-20
Computational aerodynamics (*See* Aerodynamics, computational)
Computational complexity of AI programs, 309

Computational Fluid Dynamics (CFD), 184, 201-4
Computational path, in aircraft design, 227-33
Concepts:
  new, learning, 292
  research on nature and formation of, 56-58
Conceptual graphs:
  inference structure and, 21-23
  relating heuristics to, 18-21
  schemas in, 14-18
Conclusion rules, 81-84
Configuration, planning distinguished from, in heuristic classification, 32-36
Constraint Propagation model, 229, 235
Constrictor, 39
Construction cycle, in expert systems, 36
Construction of solutions, constructing implication paths vs., 48
Constructive problem solving, 49-54
Construct management system, 109
Constructs, 71 (*See also* Personal construct theory)
  implications between, 72-74
Context of analogical statements, 137-45
Cook, G., 194
Cox, D. J., 35
CRYSALIS, 55

Dahan, C., 172
DART, 50-51
Data abstraction, in heuristic classification, 5-6, 22
Davis, R., 3, 98, 104, 174, 177, 187
DEBUGGY, 31
Decision module, in LITHO, 176-78
Decision tables, Expertise Transfer System (ETS) and, 101
Deep reasoning (*See also* Deep systems; Second generation expert systems)
  differences between heuristic rules and, 281-82

Roache, P. J., 194
Robotics, 37, 322
Robson, D., 34
Rocky's Boots (game), 35
Rosch, E., 56, 57
Rubin, A. D., 39
Rumelhart, D. E., 56
Russell, B., 196

Sacerdoti, E., 309
SACON, 9, 27, 37, 56
Sattath, S., 108
Schank, R. C., 12, 56, 57
Schemas:
  alternative encodings of, 15-18
  definitions vs., 14-15
  research on, 56
Schemata, 14
Schmolze, J. G., 12, 52, 55
Screening clauses, in OPS5, 93
Search control (*See* Inference control)
Search techniques, 200
Second generation expert systems, 270-93
  causal net in, 279-81
  compared to first generation expert
    systems, 270-71
  deep reasoning in, 278-79
  example application of, 271-75
    causal models, 272-73
    models that can be used, 271-72
    task used in, 274-75
  heuristic rules of, 276-78
  knowledge representation tools used in,
    275-76
  learning by, 282-93
    combination of rules, learning
      through, 286-87, 289-91
    concepts, learning new, 292
    examples of learning, 287-92
    fault analysis, 291-92
    focus and inspection rules, 292-93
    generalization, learning through, 292
    initial rule formulation, 282-83, 287
    orthogonal rules, 287-88

other work on, 293
  rule failure, 285-86
  rule integration, 283-85, 288-89
  rule-ordering, learning through, 292
Semantic networks, 100
Sense-test, for analogy-like statements,
  157
Sequential heuristic classification, 37
Service sector, applications of AI in, 314,
  316
Sharp, D. H., 193
Shaw, M.L.G., 70, 73, 74, 78, 81, 103,
  104
Shortliffe, E. H., 2, 175, 176, 304
SHRINK, 52
Similes, analogical statements
  distinguished from, 162
Simon, H. A., 34, 36, 48, 49, 51, 57
Slater, P., 73, 103, 108
Smedsaas, T., 194, 203-4
Smith, S. F., 33
SNARK, 173, 176
Solution-rules, in second generation
  expert systems, 277-78
SOPHIE, 12, 13, 37, 43, 47, 48
Sowa, J. F., 12, 14, 15, 22, 27, 34,
  58-59
SPIDER, 203
Spirit of St. Louis, 213-14
Squier, B., 259
Status recorder, 200
Steele, G., 272
Steels, L., 270, 276
Stefik, M., 33, 50, 53
Steinberg, S., 194
Stepp, R. E., 58
Stevens, A., 38
Structuralism, 38
Surface systems, in multi-level systems,
  306-9
Sussman, G. J., 53, 272, 309
Swartout, W. R., 1, 26-
System, definition of, 29
System-oriented approach to problem
  categorization, 29-32
Szolovits, P., 39, 43